Why Tillich?

Why Now?

MERCER *Tillich* SERIES

MERCER UNIVERSITY PRESS

Endowed by

TOM WATSON BROWN
and
THE WATSON-BROWN FOUNDATION, INC.

Why Tillich?

Why Now?

Thomas G. Bandy, Editor

MERCER UNIVERSITY PRESS
Macon, Georgia

MUP/ P635

Published by Mercer University Press
1501 Mercer University Drive
Macon, Georgia 31207

25 24 23 22 21   5 4 3 2 1

Books published by Mercer University Press are printed on acid-free paper that meets the requirements of the American National Standard for Information Sciences—Permanence of Paper for Printed Library Materials.

Printed and bound in the United States.

This book is set in Adobe Caslon Pro.

Cover/jacket design by Burt&Burt.

ISBN 978-0-88146-810-6

Cataloging-in-Publication Data is available from the Library of Congress

CONTENTS

Preface

Paul Tillich continues to be relevant as the twenty-first century unfolds. The idea for this book originated from conversations among members of the North American Paul Tillich Society in the tumultuous times following the sixtieth anniversary of Tillich's death in 2015.

Although Tillich has often been described as a *systematic* theologian, I think he is better understood as a *philosophical* theologian, or better yet as a *religious philosopher*. He organized a set of ideas that do not necessarily have to be taken as a closed system and are not limited to Christian theology. Any single idea can be incredibly compelling for any given intellectual pursuit or professional discipline. His methodology has the power to engage other philosophies of life, religious traditions and personal spiritualities, scientific research, political structures, moral quandaries, social changes, culture shifts, and lifestyle diversity critically and appreciatively.

In short, Tillich provides the means for people in all walks of life to "go deeper" and "go further" than they ever imagined. This is why he has appealed to academics and pragmatists, professionals and amateurs, older and younger generations alike. He crosses boundaries between the academy and the community. One moment his language can be so dense and abstract that it requires an advanced degree to interpret it, and the next moment his insights can be so pithy and concrete that it only requires an inquiring mind to grasp it.

Yet if these insights are taken together, they can also provide a foundation for a philosophy of life. Tillich takes us deeper. His critique of the "herd" and "consumer" mentalities that have pervaded modern society is often described as "prophetic." This is not in the sense that he predicted the future of technology, economy, or diversity, but rather in the sense that he perceived ultimate meaning behind cultural phenomena and moral consequences resulting from human behavior. He challenged a society that is obsessed with material things while ignoring significant events, preoccupied with appearance and popularity while ignoring relational sensitivity and self-awareness, passionate about competition and personal success while indifferent to community health and peaceful coexistence. These are not just the failings of *some* people, in *some* contexts, but represent temptations to which *all* people are vulnerable and which globalization seems to have made habit-forming.

If Tillich is right it is because he has synthesized the insights of philosophers, theologians, and cultural observers from the past and across cultural contexts. If he is wrong it is because his analysis has missed a vital component within, or emerging from, another culture, race, gender, sexual orientation, or generation. His greatest strength, however, is not whether he is right or wrong, but that he provides a method to discern which is which and act courageously on the decision.

I think what is most compelling about Tillich is that he continues to give hope for the first half of the twenty-first century as he did for the second half of the twentieth century. The past generation of students recognized his promise for the *courage to be*, and a new generation of students recognizes his promise for the *courage to become*.

—Tom Bandy

WHY HAS TILLICH ENDURED?

Needing Tillich Now More than Ever Before

Adam Pryor

Shared at the *North American Paul Tillich Society* Banquet, San Diego, November 2019

Every scholar studying Paul Tillich has a story about how they became engrossed with his thought. It is no different for me. I encountered Tillich's writings for the first time in a small, liberal arts college course on Christian theology. At the time, I spent most of my days as a typical, modern college student. I read a little of what I was supposed to read, did countless extracurricular activities, and partied a lot. (When I get frustrated with my undergraduates today who only read a third of whatever I assign, I remind myself that I was certainly not the model of an industrious scholar at twenty years old either.) Despite my haphazard undergraduate reading, whenever Søren Kierkegaard or Paul Tillich appeared on a reading list I read every word. Understanding myself to be a good Lutheran, there was something inherently appealing about the idea that these two thinkers were part of the same tradition in which I had grown up. Kierkegaard's anguish over the existential authenticity of the single individual spoke to my own sense of coming-of-age angst. But Tillich was something different altogether. His work did not sound like the things I had heard about theology or church while growing up in an ELCA congregation in the Deep South.

However, Tillich was, surprisingly, what I was hearing at home. My grandfather was a Lutheran pastor. After he died, I read through many of his sermons and realized that he was steeped in Tillichian themes. So it shouldn't have been too surprising when I was in college that he sent me a copy of *Biblical Religion and the Search for Ultimate Reality.* I sat down to read a chapter after opening the package in the mailroom. I got up five hours later bewildered, not sure I had actually understood what I just read. But, I was hooked.

Something about this person's writing helped me better understand the way I looked at the world. His account of personalism spoke to a tension I really felt. What was my personal responsibility for the world I was living in? And, how could I make sense of my participation in wider communities that seemed to dwarf my ability to act as an individual in any meaningful way?

For me, Tillich gave a contemporary framework to what Martin Luther said in 1520: "A Christian is a perfectly free lord of all, subject to none. A

Christian is a perfectly dutiful servant of all, subject to all."[1] Five hundred years later, this idea seems more important than ever. In turn, Tillich's exploration of the depths of this tension between personal responsibility and freedom through his accounts of the ontological polarities—individualization and participation, dynamics and form, and freedom and destiny—continue to plumb the depths of existential questions that each of us must ask ourselves over and over in our lifetimes. What I found in Tillich during college was an intellectual companion to carefully explore fundamental questions of human meaning, a Christian thinker unafraid to explore those questions even if they might be in tension with 'traditional' accounts of that faith tradition.

In seminary and graduate school the opportunities to keep reading Tillich persisted (despite whispered warnings during my interview at Princeton Theological Seminary that "we study a lot of Barth here.") In particular, though, it was in a doctoral seminar taught in part by Robert Russell—my eventual dissertation advisor—that I was first pushed to not only understand what Tillich was saying but find ways to critique his thought and build upon it. I was encouraged to be my own theologian alongside Tillich, not a simple devotee to a master that had already asked all the pertinent existential questions and given all the relevant theological answers. After all, as Russell pointed out to me repeatedly, this is precisely what existential theology encourages us to do: rework, rephrase, and reconstruct meaningful answers to the changing nature of our existential questions.

I eventually presented a modified version of the work from that seminar to the North American Paul Tillich Society as a critique of Tillich's account of symbols in light of Karl Rahner's work. It was intimidating to critique Tillich in front of a society dedicated to studying his thought. I was terrified. Everyone's first academic presentation includes some bumps along the way. Mine was no exception. (I referred to a scholar in the room in the past tense, and he assured me during the question and answer time that he was very much alive).

I survived the gaffe and found this society to be welcoming and encouraging to a new scholar. This was a group that took my work seriously. Rob James even convinced me to give that first paper to the North American Paul Tillich Society Bulletin, although even as that Bulletin was circulated to the membership, I was sure it was not really sufficient. What amazed me most was that my experience with Tillich scholars was not unique. Paper after paper, year after year, a pattern emerged. This was not a group dedicated to

---

[1] Martin Luther, "Freedom of a Christian," in *Career of the Reformer I*, ed. Helmut T. Lehmann, Luther's Works: American Edition, vol. 31 (Philadelphia: Fortress Press, 1955).

holding up Paul Tillich with the hagiographical reverence of a feted theological patron saint. This was a group where anyone was welcome because they took Tillich's idea of the 'method of correlation' so seriously.

Perhaps what anyone beginning to study Paul Tillich learns first is his 'method of correlation.' Simply put, for Tillich, the process of theological reflection is one that correlates existential questions with theological answers. Subsequent scholars of correlational theology would nuance the strict methodological movement Tillich establishes, but Tillich's approach validated the fundamental importance of articulating and understanding the questions that animate our sense of self. Without understanding these existential questions, our theology risks becoming "tone-deaf". It risks becoming mere doctrinaire commitment to meaningless dogmatic principles that no longer speak to the real needs and longings of human beings in the contemporary world.[2]

When one takes existential questioning seriously, no idea or principle is too sacred as to be beyond critique. Every religious symbol must be interpreted generation after generation so it continues to speak to our deepest concerns. Moreover, when it no longer can speak to us in this way, we must recognize that this symbol has died and look for new symbols—for new expressions of our human anxieties. Tillich took this process of existential questioning so seriously that he famously asserted, days before his death, that in light of what he had learned about other world religions, he would need to rewrite what some consider his magnum opus: the three volumes of his *Systematic Theology*.[3] What I have found as a Tillich scholar, and sense in other contemporary Tillich scholars around me, is that commitment to correlational theology is simultaneously a commitment to intellectual wondering. Existential questioning is no longer merely confined to the personal but reflects deep concern for the ways social embeddedness (in all the senses that might take) is inextricable from existential questioning. For Tillich, this is the greater challenge to life.

The continuing theological significance of Tillich's work may not be easy to imagine at first, but it can be traced in a wide variety of theological conversations today. My own research is a testament to just one facet of Tillich's continuing import for theological thinking today. His work has been, and continues to be, a critical source for all of my major research projects, often

---

[2] See, for instance, Paul Tillich, *Systematic Theology*, vol. 1 (Chicago: University of Chicago Press, 1951), 59-66; and Paul Tillich, "Religious Symbols and Our Knowledge of God," *The Christian Scholar* 38, no. 3 (September 1955), 193.

[3] Paul Tillich, "The Significance of the History of Religions for the Systematic Theologian," in *The Future of Religions*, ed. Jerald C. Brauer (New York: Harper & Row, 1966), 80–94.

forming a foundation upon which I can build. Whether discussing the doctrine of God, Christology, Spiritual Presence, or even space exploration, Tillich's reflections generate a history of existential questions and theological answers that forms the basis for my own constructive theological research as it presses toward *new* existential questions or modifications of questions asked by previous generations. While Tillich seriously considered phenomenological approaches to categorizing religious experience, he did so without limiting the capacity or surrendering the importance of making normative claims from within a single theological tradition. Anyone who continues to do theology with a deep respect for phenomenology and various existentialist philosophies has to wrestle with the historical significance of his work within a "genealogy" of correlational theologies. Tillich treats correlational theology as a set of discursive techniques that may not be linearly mapped by a genealogy per se but can be organized around the ongoing correlation of critical ideas to changes in the constitutive settings in which the term is used.

Yet, perhaps even this is too narrow for illustrating the ongoing significance of Tillich's thought for today. Tillich's "Belief-ful" Realism, along with Niebuhr's Christian Realism, represents an approach to public theological thinking that makes formulating responses to human anxiety in the context of love, power, and justice central to the task of any Christian thinker. Each may have framed the quality of our existential anxieties too narrowly by any current standard, but the structure of Tillich's work—particularly his account of *kairoi* and attention to justice serving as a means of creatively actualizing the drive to unity in love—provide sorely needed categories for facilitating deliberation across ideological, theological, and political differences.[4]

Certainly, we can critique how critical biases remain in the way that either Tillich or Niebuhr frame our existential anxieties too narrowly by any current standard taking seriously the systemic sins of racism, sexism, and classism. Various liberationist and prophetic critiques of Tillich and Niebuhr do this quite well.[5] However, I would argue that in the case of Tillich, these critiques are not so much about his accounts of *kairoi* or justice specifically, but they are about how the principles he outlines are applied, while the principles themselves remain helpful and valid. For instance, in his short work *Love, Power, and Justice*, Tillich identifies four principles that comprise his

[4] Adam Pryor, "Tillich and Niebuhr," in *The Oxford Handbook of Reinhold Niebuhr*, eds. Robin W. Lovin and Joshua Mauldin (Oxford: Oxford University Press, forthcoming).

[5] See, for instance, James H. Cone, *The Cross and the Lynching Tree*, Reprint edition (Maryknoll: Orbis Books, 2013), chap. 2; and Robin W. Lovin, *Christian Realism and the New Realities* (New York: Cambridge University Press, 2008).

vision of justice: adequacy, equality, personality, and liberty. He is quick to admit that there is no way of mechanically prescribing principles that will guarantee justice in all situations; however, he suggests his principles should apply in all situations that seek the reunion of the separated.[6]

Adequacy refers to the correlation of form and content: the way in which justice is pursued cannot violate the justice it intends to promote. In terms of the language of the holy, the adequacy principle suggests justice must be pursued in a form that never inhibits the actualization of the holy. Tillich identifies that adequacy is most often violated when laws outlive their usefulness (i.e. when laws inadvertently create systems of injustice because, while adequate in the past, they no longer promote justice in the present). The final three principles are all strongly interrelated. Equality is the dignity due any person as one who, admittedly partially, actualizes the power of being. Personality refers to the need for justice to treat people as ends and not means. It is to respect and support the power of any person to pursue a sense of ultimate concern. Finally, liberty is the principle referring to the preservation of freedom and self-determination that is fundamental to enacting personality. I would relate these four principles by suggesting that no form of justice can be deemed adequate where the forms of that justice do not minimally promote equality, personality, and liberty.[7]

I would suggest that by Tillich's account, we might use these four principles to guide our interpretation of both what and how holy or existential concerns might justly claim to symbolically manifest ultimacy. Such concerns would be those that develop the unity of wholeness between self and world (a unity that avoids any totalizing collapse that eliminates distinction between these poles) while promoting a sense of justice characterized by adequacy, equality, personality, and liberty. That these principles of justice are oriented toward actualizing unity in love means that they are only effective insofar as they help us reach across ideological, theological, and political differences.

The importance of this aspect of Tillich's work has been borne out for me not only in my *research* but also in my *teaching*. First, as I teach in an interdisciplinary context that includes significant co-teaching with faculty from other departments, Tillich's theological language has created a bridge that helps my more secular colleagues feel comfortable teaching with a theologian. Concepts such as ultimate concern, the relationship of love to power and justice, and his consideration of courage and anxiety invite religiously skeptical

---

[6] See Paul Tillich, *Love, Power, and Justice* (New York: Oxford University Press, 1974), 55-56.

[7] Tillich, 57-62.

colleagues into a dialogue that they perhaps did not anticipate in an interdisciplinary classroom. His framework invites conversation from across the liberal arts and sciences.

Second, my students seem to resonate with Tillich's approach. This is especially true for my increasing number of students with no religious affiliation. I find this really remarkable. There are not many other texts from the 1950s and 1960s that they find so compelling, and particularly his language for ultimate concern, faith, anxiety, courage, and love. While Tillich's ontological approach can be frustrating and confusing at first glance, it is also deeply personal and remarkably relatable. Once students move past the abstract concepts Tillich uses, they can find their own experiences narrated in his account.

Surely, I am not alone in watching this experience unfold for students. Nor am I alone in the experience of introducing Tillich to a colleague, who then opens up to your research in ways that suddenly make you a more acceptable professional. In a time when deliberate and constructive dialogue is made increasingly difficult by bitter partisan rhetoric, Tillich's language can bring people around a common table of discussion. In short, Tillich's ideas could address the dogmatic and ideological polarization of our times and encourage reconciliation.

For instance, consider the four principles of justice outlined previously. These concepts are broad enough to be applicable in a variety of sociopolitical communities and can easily be agreed upon by diverse sets of persons as a set of goods we should pursue in a common society or institution. Yet, the content of each term, what constitutes adequate equality, personality, or liberty requires deep interpretation. Not everyone who agrees we should pursue these principles will agree upon what they *exactly* mean. When we have the courage to listen to one another in community and have empathy for the ways in which our colleagues, neighbors, or other community members are anxious over the ways in which these principles of justice are being violated in their own experience, then Tillich's model of justice can serve as a means for diffusing partisan rhetoric. That is a power I hope will be wielded more widely today to facilitate conversations across disciplinary boundaries in highly relevant ways to situations Tillich could not have possibly imagined in his wildest dreams.

Perhaps, then, the future of Tillich scholarship may not be found solely in religious studies or theological research. Rather, the future of Tillich scholarship will possibly be found in integrating theological reflection with other disciplines. This should not be too surprising given Tillich's concern for explicating the significance of God language in terms of the "unconditional element in the structure of reason and reality."[8] When praising great thinkers of the Western intellectual tradition, Tillich specifically highlights Kant and Augustine, who both attempted to explicate how God's presence as the unconditioned permeates all forms of knowing and ethical action. Ultimately, Tillich critiques these intellectual heavyweights for seeking to transform the unconditional into something existent, but the course of Tillich's argument makes clear how human being, acting, and knowing are "indelibly linked" to the divine.[9] Within any other academic field of study, by Tillich's account, we should expect to find a kernel of the divine that can be subjected to theological analysis.

We might go one step further than Tillich at this point. If Tillich's search for the unconditional as the indelible link between humanity and God led him back to prospects of a deepened theological analysis, it might also lead us forward to a means of addressing the ideological polarization we face today. These elements of the unconditioned that permeate our being, acting, and knowing provide a common ground that animates the courage to listen to one another in pursuit of justice as described above. Intellectual study and ethical deliberation, by Tillich's account, allows this permeating element of the unconditional to grasp us and drive us beyond ourselves such that we might discover the presence of the unconditional in other fields of study, in communities of which we are not a part, or in the actions of my neighbor with whom I may not agree. Paradoxically, we might say that discovering this element of the unconditioned helps us imagine ways that we might bridge the unbridgeable chasm that separates myself from that which is Other. In the wider context of education, this is highly significant. I would suggest Tillich's model is one that advocates for the wide study often identified with the liberal arts in higher education today: that the well-rounded formation of good citizens through education creates a common ground promoting civic dialogue.

Tillich's concept of Spiritual Presence and latent Spiritual Communities are especially significant for this way of interpreting Tillich's continued significance. These concepts provide a foundation upon which we can envision building a series of interdisciplinary collaborations in scholarship across all public sectors (religious, social service, health care, environment, business, education, media, politics, and more.) Certainly this would entail a radical extension of what Tillich intended regarding identifying a religious or spiritual

[8] Tillich, *Systematic Theology*, vol. 1, 208

[9] See also Duane Olson, *The Depths of Life: Paul Tillich's Understanding of God* (Macon: Mercer University Press, 2019), 81.

community. Nonetheless, his account lays the groundwork for envisioning interdisciplinary collaboration as a form of Spiritual Community building.

Notably, Tillich identifies Spiritual Presence with an ecstatic experience that unifies the power of being and the meaning of being. In the midst of our finitude this experience of Spiritual Presence is always fragmentary and partial; the power and meaning of being are not eternally set into a proper relation of harmonious unity, and we continually return to the everyday experience of living in the polar tensions Tillich identifies as fundamental to human experience. Yet, these experiential moments of Spiritual Presence are never ambiguous. It is not as though the polar tensions themselves collapse or become unclear. In these experiential moments, for Tillich, we still feel the tensions of individualization and participation, dynamics and form, and freedom and destiny that describe our existence. However, the discord, opposition, and friction that characterize the struggle between these polar terms in our everydayness falls away. In moments of felt Spiritual Presence, unambiguous life comes into focus—the polar tensions of existence really are, if only fleetingly, harmoniously experienced in a transcendent union.[10] Among skeptical students and religious "nones," it is Tillich's *pneumatology* in the third volume of his Systematic Theology that will be most relevant. Tillich casts a larger and far more inclusive vision for the Realm of God than institutional churches imagine.

Tillich offers a rich phenomenological description of faith and love as ways to describe how actual being ecstatically becomes the true expression of potential being.[11] These are descriptions he associates with the church as the manifest Spiritual Community. But, Tillich's notion of latent Spiritual Communities, *kairoi*, and phenomenological descriptions of secular (or nonreligious) ecstatic experiences of the Spirit sprinkled throughout this same section all indicate just how broadly Spiritual Presence is being construed. In short, faith and love as experiences of Spiritual Presence are not confined to manifest Spiritual Community, they also occur in latent Spiritual Communities with no less force. The experience of Spiritual Presence is always unambiguous whether occurring in a manifest or latent Spiritual Community. The continuation of that experience of Spiritual Presence (just how partial and fragmentary or long-lasting the experience is) might be different in manifest and latent Spiritual Communities, but the quality of the experience of Spiritual Presence is fundamentally similar.

[10] Paul Tillich, *Systematic Theology*, vol. 3 (Chicago: University of Chicago Press, 1963), 111-19

[11] Tillich, 129-60

What these references make clear is that analyzing Spiritual Presence is not a task for theologians alone, nor is the experience of Spiritual Presence the province of Christian churches alone. Instances of Spiritual Presence can emerge across traditionally conceived disciplines as issues related to the power and meaning of being arise. Navigating the tensions of our existence and prolonging moments of felt Spiritual Presence is no easy task even if these experiences might occur anywhere or at any moment in our lives. Equipping students of various disciplines to more deeply understand how these moments of felt Spiritual Presence are transformative within their own fields of study is a crucial next step for research that extends Tillich's work. It is only in working across disciplinary boundaries to better characterize the phenomenological experiences of those that experience Spiritual Presence in latent Spiritual Communities that we can gain a richer sense of the many ways that the intersection of the power and meaning of being can come to be expressed.

Elsewhere, I have described this widely abounding sense of Spiritual Presence as a kairotic liminality—building on Tillich's use of *kairos*, *eschatos*, and *chronos*. Liminality, here, implies a threshold experience that eludes our usual means of classifying our experience. It refers to places, concepts, or things that are betwixt and between. In short, Tillich's use of a *kairos* moment has this liminal quality. A *kairos* moment is one where the co-presence of the eschatological is available to our awareness. It makes new understandings of the dynamic force of God's presence to history possible. Herein the dynamic co-presence of the *eschatos* entangles with our present experience, which then conditions what we experience as the future possibilities of *chronos* time. In such an understanding, the *kairos* event is an experience of liminality. It is a moment where the entangled co-presence of the divine as *eschatos* reveals itself through the betweenness of a liminal event. Liminal "betweenness" reveals a divine hope for realizing our fundamental relationality that is so often hidden in our everyday experiences. This kairotic break of the liminal into the structure of *chronos* then draws us toward a transformed future.[12]

Could the future of Tillich research be in interdisciplinary studies? Perhaps the new task for theologians will be to participate with other research teams to name and find ways to facilitate the emergence of Spiritual Presence or meaningful being in kairotic moments experienced as divine in-breaking or liminal "betweenness." Perhaps, or perhaps the future of Tillich research will look completely different.

[12] Adam Pryor, "The Liminal as Kairos: A Cyborg Example for Theology and Science," in *The Many Voices of Liminality*, ed. Timothy Carson (Cambridge: Lutterworth Press, 2019), 141–52.

In any case, I believe we need Tillich's work now more than ever. Certainly, his work provides critical resources for correlational theologies and continues to speak to new situations that Tillich never would have imagined possible. But, it does something more as well. I hope that we push a bit further, that we use not only the method but also his insights integrating the power and meaning of being as broad categories for engaging in interdisciplinary research that builds on a Tillichian inspired appreciation of the depth of being. This is a call to move away from our feelings of fear, anxiety, and despair toward a shared sense of Spiritual Presence that takes seriously the *breadth* of existential questions offered by diverse persons. It is a call to empathize with the fears and anxieties of our neighbors, which might not be one's own, in order to facilitate deliberation across difference. In a time of increasingly factional rancor, Tillich's work calls us back to the meaning of being found by participating in authentic spiritual community.

Is Tillich's Thought Still Relevant in Today's Undergraduate Classroom?

Frederick J. Parrella

A brief glance at the Pew Research Center on Religion and Public Life, which examines the religious life and church attendance of college and graduate students, reveals a picture that should deeply concern both the holy fathers and holy rollers of the American religious establishment.[1] Less than forty percent of high school, college, and graduate school graduates attend church or synagogue on a regular basis. The term "Nones," created by Barry A. Kosmin, a research professor at Trinity College in Hartford, Connecticut, serves as a shortened form of "None of the Above" in religious questionnaires.

This essay will explore the value and relevance of the thought of German and American professor, Paul Tillich (1886-1965), to young people of college age two decades into the twenty-first century. It will consider three issues: first, his method of correlation and its attractiveness to young people; second, his theology of culture, especially Tillich's unique connection between religion and culture (special attention will be given to the problem of "Nones" in our college and university classrooms);[2] and, third, his treatment of the Protestant Principle and Catholic Substance, where Tillich offers both content and substance to young minds and hearts in a world where many college students make faith individualistic but ultimately find it empty and unfulfilling. Each of these areas applies to issues that millennials and post-millennials continue to confront and question. Can Tillich's writings help today's college students and young adults find a solution to both their spoken and unspoken questions? Can someone like Tillich who, in terms of age, is radically out of touch with

---

[1] "In US, Decline of Christianity Continues at Rapid Pace," Pew Research Center, October 17, 2019, https://www.pewforum.org/2019/10/17/in-u-s-decline-of-christianity-continues-at-rapid-pace/.

[2] An outstanding treatment of "Nones" in our culture can be found in my colleague Elizabeth Drescher's book, *Choosing Our Religion: The Spiritual Lives of America's Nones* (New York: Oxford University Press, 2016).

the millennials, the post-millennials, and future generations still have an answer to their quest for something beyond their own individual growth personally, psychologically, and financially?[3]

Tillich's Theological Method

We begin by exploring the relevance and the vitality of Tillich's theological method, what he called the method of correlation. An interesting comment by the British author, teacher, and noted proponent of agnostic or secular Buddhism, Stephen Batchelor, might shed some light on Tillich's own approach; Batchelor claims to write books in order to answer this singular question: "What does it mean to practice the dharma of the Buddha in the context of modernity?"[4] These words are remarkably similar to those of Paul Tillich, who writes, "Can the Christian message be adapted to the modern mind without losing its essential and unique character?"[5] Even more significant are Tillich's words in an interview just before his death in 1965: "My work is for those who ask questions, and for them I am here."[6]

Perhaps some personal autobiographical information will help the reader here understand Tillich's method of correlation. In a theology course today, one popular with many students, I usually assign one book written in the 1920s and another in the 1960s.[7] One college senior inquired whether the books were too old-fashioned and irrelevant in the postmodern world. My response was simple: we are still reading the works of Plato, Aristotle, Dante, Shakespeare, Dickens, and Dickenson. We are still listening to Bach, Mozart, and Brahms. Are all of these gifted thinkers, poets, and composers irrelevant?

At the same time, no great work can completely transcend its historical time and its cultural place, and this is certainly as true of Paul Tillich writings

---

[3] Generation Z is a matter of debate. For some clarification, see WJSchroer, the social marketing firm, "Generations X,Y,Z and the Others," accessed March 23, 2018, http://socialmarketing.org/archives/generations-xy-z-and-the-others/. This means that the majority of students reading Tillich's writings in a college classroom today would be from Generation Z, with some holdouts from Generation Y, Echo Boomers, or Millenniums.

[4] See, for example, Stephen Batchelor, *The Faith to Doubt: Glimpses of Buddhist Uncertainty* (Berkeley: Parallax Press, 1990); *Alone with Others: An Existential Approach to Buddhism* (New York: Grove Press, 1994); *The Awakening of the West: The Encounter of Buddhism and Western Culture* (Brattleboro: Echo Point Books & Media, 2011).

[5] Paul Tillich, *Systematic Theology*, vol. 2 (Chicago: The University of Chicago Press, 1957), 7.

[6] Paul Tillich, interview by Kenneth Bagnell, "Paul Tillich: An Interview," *The United Church Observer* 27, no. 15 (November 1965), 24.

[7] The classic works of Martin Buber, *I and Thou*, and Rollo May, *Love and Will.*

as anyone else's. Is Tillich's thought, with its roots in the nineteenth century and its full flowering in the first six decades of the twentieth century, still relevant more than a half century later? And if so, how much is relevant, and what may be dated? More specifically, what in Tillich's corpus is worth reading and rereading? Will the postmillennial generations, those of college age now (including mature high school students, recent college graduates, and young people in the work force) still be moved by Tillich?

In much the same way a half century ago, I was as a senior in college when the professor, a Catholic priest from the Archdiocese of New York, assigned Tillich's first volume of sermons, *The Shaking of the Foundations*.[8] It was a moment that, quite simply, changed my life. Three years later I was in a doctoral seminar with Professor Tom Driver, a recent student of Tillich's and, for many years, the Paul Tillich Professor of Theology and Culture at Union Theological Seminary in New York City. Tom Driver became the intellectual midwife of Tillich in my own life, opening up works such as the *Systematic Theology*, *The Protestant Era*, and *The Courage to Be*, among many others. He was an exceptional teacher, with an unmatched lucidity and a remarkable depth of insight. Have I, and will younger teachers and scholars of Tillich, unlock today's college students' minds and hearts to Tillich in the same way my mind was so transformed a half century ago?

My enthusiastic answer, of course, is yes. Tillich's method is essential in the college classroom today; for Tillich, the work of theology is mediation "between the eternal criterion of truth as it is manifest in the picture of Jesus as the Christ, and the changing experience of individuals and groups, their varying questions and their categories of experiencing reality."[9] In so far as many young people today, even if they have left religion behind, are still asking questions, those deep down questions about their lives and human existence, then Tillich's words will resonate in their minds and hearts. No more important period than the college years exists in young people's lives for wrestling with the meaning and purpose of their existence. For this reason, I believe that few theologians of modern times are more relevant in the college classroom than Tillich. For if Tillich were still with us today, he would surely have been aware that first he had to understand the questions of the millennials and

---

[8] Paul Tillich, *The Shaking of the Foundations* (New York: Charles Scribner's Sons, 1948).

[9] Paul Tillich, *The Protestant Era*, trans. with a concluding essay by James Luther Adams (Chicago: University of Chicago Press, 1948), ix.

postmillennial students before he could make theology relevant and meaningful to them.[10]

Tillich's theological method of correlation avoids a constant danger in all theology—its abstract nature makes it seem aloof from the practice of daily living. (In short, the days of the medieval *Summas* are behind us.) Good theology, in contrast, must link the ontological with the existential and the experiential; theological answers created by the Church must correlate with human existential questions. In Tillich's method, theology seeks, first, to answer the specific human questions that are expressed in philosophical terms and, second, to answer them in the form in which the questions are posed.[11] The genius of the method lies in the absolute balance between two poles of question and answer. In Tillich's *Systematic Theology*, God is the answer to the question of being, Jesus the Christ to the question of existence, and the divine Spirit answers the question of life. As Tillich says, "whenever an idea of God is enunciated, it is always in correlation with an interpretation of man, and vice versa."[12]

Although the method of correlation is not unique to Tillich, it was Tillich who brought it to the attention of theology in the clash between nineteenth century liberal theology and twentieth century neoorthodoxy. It is not a new method. Tillich suggests that Jesus himself may have used it. Rather, it is implied whenever theology successfully articulated divine truth to the limited and doubtful human mind. The method attempts to answer the lasting question in apologetic theology: "Can the Christian message be adapted to the modern mind without losing its essential and unique character?"[13]

On the one hand, theologians who emphasize the unique and exclusive character of Christianity often isolate and elevate the message from the human situation, so that the truth of faith is *deduced* from God's revelation in Scripture and Church tradition. Tillich associated this tendency with neoorthodoxy. Tillich's method of correlation works to overcome the isolation and elevation of the message from the human situation, such as he believed the kerygmatic theology of Karl Barth tended to do. Tillich complained that in Barth's theology the message, in Tillich's well-known phrase, was "thrown

[10] While I have often wondered with some amusement what Tillich would have made of today's world of social media and a generation hooked on cell phones, I am certain he would have understood and supported our present technology.

[11] Paul Tillich, *Systematic Theology*, vol. 1 (Chicago, University of Chicago Press, 1951), 59-66.

[12] Paul Tillich, *The Rediscovery of the Prophetic Tradition of the Reformation* (Washington, D.C.: Henderson Services, 1950), 11.

[13] Tillich, *Systematic Theology*, vol. 2, 7.

like a stone" to those in the concreteness of the human situation. Tillich argued that "even charismatic theology must use the conceptual tools of its period. It cannot simply repeat biblical passages. Even when it does it cannot escape the conceptual situation of the different biblical writers."[14] (This is certainly what the "religious right" has done in America in our own days during the campaign and subsequent presidency of Donald Trump.)

On the other hand, theologians who begin with human experience and the needs of modern and postmodern consciousness often avoid the transcendental dimension in the Christian tradition. They lose the sense of the "numinous," as Rudolf Otto described it, surrendering the *Mysterium tremendum et fascinans,* the mighty vertical presence of the divine, to the simple horizontal movement of life.[15] According to Tillich, at the end of the nineteenth century and the beginning of the twentieth, this was the fate of liberal Protestantism, liberal Judaism, and Catholic modernism.[16] Theology is thus reduced to what is primarily politics, psychology, ethics, aesthetics, popular morality, or self-help programs. This is what the pastor of the Rutgers Presbyterian Church in New York City said recently about his church's foundation: "sharing a belief in God, any God, isn't necessary."[17] In this situation, one attends church not to worship a God who is both transcendent and immanent, but to come away with good feelings about oneself. This is what Philip Rieff, the sociologist of Freud, described a half century ago as the triumph of the therapeutic culture.[18]

Thus, while the "deductionists" seek security, regardless of the lessons of modern experience, the "reductionists," in Lutheran sociologist Peter Berger's phrase, inevitably "bargain with modernity," so that meaning survives, often in watered down form, at the expense of the prophetic challenge of the Gospel

---

[14] Tillich, *Systematic Theology*, vol. 1, 7.

[15] Rudolph Otto, *The Idea of the Holy: An Inquiry into the non-rational factor in the idea of the divine and its relation to the rational*, trans. John W. Harvey (New York: Oxford University Press, 1958); First published as *Das Heilige - Über das Irrationale in der Idee des Göttlichen und sein Verhältnis zum Rationalen* in 1917.

[16] Paul Tillich, *The Religious Situation,* trans. H. Richard Niebuhr (New York: H. Holt, 1932; reprinted by Cleveland and New York: Meridian Books, 1956, 1962), 159; originally published in German as *Die religiöse Lage der Gegenwart* (Berlin: Ullstein, 1926). Page references are to the Meridian edition.

[17] Rick Rojas, "United By Cause If Not By Faith," *The New York Times*, September 8, 2019.

[18] See Philip Rieff. *The Triumph of the Therapeutic: Uses of Faith After Freud*, 2nd ed. (New York: Harper Torchbooks, 1987).

message.[19] On the one hand, Tillich sought to avoid *transcendentalizing* the Christian message, where the Word of God becomes words spoken from on high,[20] and on the other, to prevent the dissolution of the message into the human situation, an *immanentizing* of the Gospel truths into categories convenient to the listener. As Gustave Weigel, one of Tillich's earliest Catholic commentators and critics, shrewdly saw, "the method of correlation is not a plea for relativism, but rather an effort to overcome it."[21] Even though Tillich lived a century earlier, I know my college students and young people of the twenty-first century, even though Tillich lived a century earlier, intuitively understand the relevance of Tillich's method and his deep commitment to their needs.

Tillich's practical, concrete, and correlational understanding of theology is a direct result of his experience as a chaplain in the German army in World War I. His ministry to the wounded, maimed, disconsolate, and those between life and death profoundly changed his inner life, his idea of God, his theological method, and his relationship to the church. According to his definitive biography, the four years of the war (1914-18) represent "the turning point in Tillich's life—the first, last, and only one."[22] The war was the defining boundary of his life, and living "on the boundary," his permanent home.[23] The reality of death and dying at a massive wartime level changed his politics, his understanding of history, and the importance of culture for religion.

Some years ago, I was asked to give two talks on the theology death and afterlife to two very different audiences. One was a group of high school seniors, the second comprised of nuns in a rest home for the aged in their community. The content of both presentations was the same—the meaning of dying in Christ for the Christian and the symbols of the classic "four last things" (add a fifth, purgatory, if you are Roman Catholic!). Yet, addressing a

---

[19] "Deductionism" and "reductionism" are terms of Peter Berger in his *The Heretical Imperative: Contemporary Possibilities of Religious Affirmation* (New York: Doubleday Anchor, 1980), chaps. 3 and 4.

[20] Paul Tillich, "A Theology of Education," in *Theology of Culture*, ed. Robert Kimball (New York: Oxford University Press, 1959), 154.

[21] Gustave Weigel, "Recent Protestant Theology," *Theological Studies* 14 (1953): 578.

[22] Wilhelm Pauck and Marion Hausner Pauck, *Paul Tillich: His Life and Thought*, vol. 1, *Life* (New York: Harper & Row, 1976), 41; reissued, with a new preface by Marion Hausner Pauck (Eugene: Wipf and Stock, 2015). Page references are to the Harper & Row edition.

[23] See Tillich's autobiographical reflections: *On the Boundary: Autobiographical Reflections* (New York: Charles Scribner's Sons, 1966); reprint by (Eugene: Wipf and Stock, 2012).

group of young people who are beginning their lives and questioning their faith, or whatever faith they may have had and speaking to a group of devout religious women near life's end required very different presentations. I was challenged to anticipate the questions each audience was asking about its concrete existence and experience of life; I was compelled, first, to attempt to answer their very different set of questions, and, second, to answer them in the diverse forms in which the different questions were expressed.[24]

What is essential in employing the method of correlation is not only the proper use of the method itself objectively, as Tillich himself has described it and used it, but also the correct application of the method itself subjectively, that is, by the individual college professor employing the method. The individual professor today can only use Tillich's questions in the broadest existential sense as questions about estrangement, the distortions in human existence, and the ambiguities of life.[25] The contemporary professor must understand his/her students subjectively, reconnoiter or explore into their minds and hearts to discover their specific questions about life, about meaning and purpose, and about their specific goals. After decades of teaching, I ask myself, "What are the students I face today thinking and what questions are they asking?" This is what professors, both young and old, must ask themselves before they enter a classroom, and this, I must add, is true of all professors whether they teach English, chemistry, or theology and religious studies. Ironically, in many cases, professors, like myself, old enough to be their students' grandfathers/grandmothers, are sometimes more likely to understand the questions than younger professors who might be their students' older brothers and sisters. Of course, one of the overwhelming differences in classrooms in recent decades has been the emergence of technology—the computer, web, the smart phone, et al. Our smart-phone-world has changed the questions dramatically. Technology has not only changed and expanded the content of learning, but it has also changed the very texture of learning itself. "The younger one is, the more one knows technologically" is an embarrassing truism to many still teaching at a college level who were themselves educated, at least in part, in a pre-technological world. One can safely presume this pace of technological

[24] In this way, good theology is like good preaching. Too many Catholic priests make an intellectual exercise of preaching by demonstrating how the three readings of the Sunday or feast are connected in theme. Forced to sit through this boring intellectual exercise, no wonder many Catholics are no longer attending Sunday Mass.

[25] This, of course, summarizes volumes 2 and 3 of the *Systematic Theology*.

change will continue, compelling people teaching religion to continue to grow in technological knowledge as well as theological wisdom.[26]

Tillich's Theology of Culture

In surveys of religious attitudes among young people, one still hears the common phrase, "I'm probably not very religious, but I consider myself a deeply spiritual person."[27] Many young people believe that spirituality is a good thing and religion, at least in its structured and institutional state, a bad thing—or, at least, an unnecessary thing in the complex pattern of their high tech lives. Of course, if we consider Paul Tillich's ideas, the dichotomy between religion and spirituality quickly disappears. Here is precisely Tillich's important contribution to college age students and young people. As the state of ultimate concern, religion is a quest for an unconditional meaning in life that embraces and transcends all other meanings that we hold significant. Ultimate concern is the silent presupposition of meaning in every finite meaning we accept. If ultimate concern promises ultimate fulfillment, it also demands ultimate surrender of the individual.[28] The source of our ultimate concern is the infinite inside us to which we belong but from which we have become separated and alienated. Theologically, we are ultimately concerned because we are made in God's image and likeness. That is, we reflect in our limited beings the ultimate and infinite being of God, but through sin we have fallen from grace and from the perfection of this image within us. Of course, anyone who denies his or her ultimate concern proves, by this very fact, that he or she is ultimately concerned—because he or she is ultimately concerned about denying any ultimate concern. One can deny the infinite only be affirming it at the same time.

---

[26] See Tillich's writings on science and technology, including *The System of the Sciences According to Objects and Methods*, trans. with an introduction by Paul Weibe (Lewisburg: Bucknell University Press, 1981), published in German in 1923; an excellent compilation from his German years to the year of his death, *The Spiritual Situation in Our Technical Society*, ed. J. Mark Thomas (Macon: Mercer University Press, 1988). Some chapters were published previously, and others appeared for the first time from the Paul Tillich Archives at Harvard University. It contains one of his last articles: "How Has Science in the Last Century Changed Man's View of Himself?," first appearing in *The Current* 6, no. 1-2 (1965): 85-89.

[27] See, for example, Meredith B. McGuire, "Mapping Contemporary American Spirituality: A Sociological Perspective," *Christian Spirituality Bulletin* 5, no. 1 (1997): 1c.

[28] See Paul Tillich, *The Dynamics of Faith* (New York: Harper and Brothers, 1956); reprint, with a new introduction to the Perennial Classics Edition by Marion Hausner Pauck (New York: HarperCollins, 2001), chapter 1.

Therefore, for Tillich, ultimate concern, faith, and religion are universal and fundamentally all three terms mean the same thing. Too often, both in church teachings and individual Christian minds, spirituality has been mistaken for a personal and individual reality, while religion appears objective and institutional. Yet, if spirituality and religion both involve a quest for the ultimate in being and meaning, as Tillich teaches, spirituality is as much communal and social as religion is, and religion is as personal and as interior as spirituality.[29] The real issue is to link the inner and outer realities, the frenetic, fast-paced high tech world in which we all live and the inner life of the mind, heart, and soul. Too many people, especially young people, are trapped in the visible world, the world of external accomplishments, of exterior temptations, of a fulfillment that ultimately leaves one hollow inside. David Brooks, a columnist for the *New York Times*, recently described our cultural situation well: "American life is so raucous and dynamic because people are inflamed by visions of creating a heaven on earth. As George Santayana put it, Americans often don't make a distinction between the sacred and the profane. In building material wealth, they see themselves creating a country that will redeem humanity, that will become the last best hope of earth."[30]

Tillich's theology of culture and the broad inclusive understanding he has of religion itself and its relationship to culture, is appealing to many college age students. In a recent class on relationships and marriage, I asked if smart phones were a positive or negative factor in the creation and maintenance of significant relationships. I was utterly shocked to see that three quarters of the class held a negative view! In his most famous statement on this subject, Tillich says that "Religion is the depth of culture and culture is the form of religion."[31] Thus, any cultural form, when it manifests genuine depth, can be considered religious, whether it is explicitly religious or not—and in

---

[29] See Owen C. Thomas, "A Tillichian Critique of Contemporary Spirituality," in *Religion for the New Millennium: Theology in the Spirit of Paul Tillich*, eds. Frederick J. Parrella and Raymond F. Bulman (Macon: Mercer University Press, 2001): 221–34. See also Frederick J. Parrella, "Tillich and Contemporary Spirituality," in *Religion for the New Millennium: Theology in the Spirit of Paul Tillich*, eds. Frederick J. Parrella and Raymond F. Bulman (Macon: Mercer University Press, 2001): 241–67.

[30] A comment by the columnist, David Brooks, in his op-ed. piece, "Donald Trump Hates America," *The New York Times*, July 19, 2019.

[31] In *Systematic Theology* vol. 3, Tillich describes the "essential belongingness of religion and culture to each other." He says, "I have expressed this principle frequently in the statement that religion is the substance of culture and culture the form of religion." Paul Tillich, *Systematic Theology*, vol. 3 (Chicago: University of Chicago Press, 1963), 248.

most cases is not. For Tillich, a painting by Picasso such as the famous *Guernica* (Tillich publicly proclaimed his belief on more than one occasion that *Guernica* was the most Protestant religious painting of the twentieth century[32]), a poem by Rilke such as one of the *Duino Elegies*, or a piece of music by Mozart such as his Divertimento, K 136 could be authentically religious. In contrast, a Renaissance portrait of the Resurrection or of the Madonna could be secular because of its superficiality and lack of depth. For Tillich, any cultural expression is religious in so far as it reveals the depth of things. Thus, one does not have to leave the secular to discover the religious; one merely has to enter the depth of the secular to find what transcends the secular, the religious expressed as ultimate concern. In Tillich's simple phrase that "religion is the depth of culture and culture the form of religion," Tillich makes religion an inescapable reality for all people. An important consequence of Tillich's existential concept of religion, as he says, "is the disappearance of the gap between the sacred and the secular realm. If religion is the state of being grasped by an ultimate concern this state cannot be restricted to a special realm."[33] As he states: "Christianity is not a set of doctrinal or ritual or moral laws, but is rather the good news of the conquest of the law by the appearance of a new healing reality. They must feel that the Christian symbols are not absurdities, unacceptable for the questioning mind but that they point to that which alone is of ultimate concern, the ground and meaning of our existence and of existence generally."[34]

A significant number of college age students are demographically described as "Nones."[35] Another common name for Nones, often used before Nones became popular, is "unchurched." Data from the spring of 2019 suggests that the percentage of the population of Nones—at about twenty-three percent—is now equal to those who are evangelical or Catholic.[36] This is a remarkable statistic that should be a major concern for campus ministers and

---

[32] Paul Tillich, "Theology and Architecture," in *On Art and Architecture*, eds. John and Jane Dillenberger (New York: Crossroad, 1987), 191–92.

[33] Paul Tillich, *Theology of Culture* (New York: Oxford University Press, 1959), 41.

[34] Tillich, 50.

[35] While our concern is with American Christians of college age, see the definitive report on worldwide religious affiliation: Pew Research Center, "The Future of World Religions: Populations, Growth Projections, 2010-2050," April 2, 2015, https://assets.pewresearch.org/wp-content/uploads/sites/11/2015/03/PF_15.04.02_ProjectionsFullReport.pdf.

[36] Jack Jenkins, "'Nones' now as big as evangelicals, Catholics in the US," Religion News Service, March 21, 2019, https://religionnews.com/2019/03/21/nones-now-as-big-as-evangelicals-catholics-in-the-us/.

professors of religion and theology today. For it seems to be much easier to teach college students about a different religious tradition from the one in which they were raised than to teach a religious tradition to those students who have no background whatsoever. These Nones do not understand the categories of faith and belief, of ritual and doctrine, and the religious foundations of moral truths. In the same way, one can dialogue about spirituality with someone of a different faith more easily than someone who professes no faith tradition at all.

Pedagogy with so-called "Nones" is difficult for the very reason that they lack the categories and framework of religious and theological understanding and interpretation; put differently, they lack access to the vertical dimension of life and live only in a horizontal world.[37] At the same time, it would be a mistake to understand the Nones in a too homogeneous manner. In her book on the Nones, Elizabeth Drescher points out that there is "hardly an archetype for the wide array of Americans who select 'none of the above' on surveys of religious affiliation." In contrast, she notes "the tremendous diversity of self-identification of American Nones." This, she says, "is among the most difficult things for commentators to grasp about a demographic category that does not, in fact, describe a distinct social group."[38] According to Drescher, Nones can be found in every part of the United States, are present in every denomination of Protestantism, and exist in approximately a quarter of those from the Roman Catholic tradition in America. Nones are present in both genders and in every age group.[39]

The Nones in our culture, from early in high school, through their college years, and through the years immediately following college, often reject the visible facade of religion, expressed in superficial or vapid form in many of our churches. Today's culture is witness to a great conflict between secular and religious consciousness, between different answers to the essential human questions: what do I take with unconditional seriousness and without reservation? Is the ultimate meaning of life to be found within the finite passage of time or in an absolute or infinite Otherness that is, at the same time, intimate, indeed, identical with the deepest self?

Many people, in sociologist Peter Berger's phrase more than a half century ago, which is just as apropos for the Nones of our own time, are living in

---

[37] Paul Tillich, "Vertical and Horizontal Thinking," *The American Scholar* 15, no. 1 (Winter 1945-1946), 102-5, https://www.jstor.org/stable/41204765.

[38] Drescher, *Choosing Our Religion*, 5.

[39] See Drescher's extensive and detailed Appendices A and B, 252-73. "Nones" are slightly more visible among men than women and much more likely to be people in the first half of their lives.

a "world without windows."[40] At the same time, many Nones pause in the rapid horizontal movement of life and look for something that endures, something that lasts, a breakthrough of the vertical dimension, or, if you will, a breath of the eternal. Although young people are leaving religion in its organized forms, they are certainly not abandoning some form of spirituality. The Nones are not a lost generation as long as they are asking questions, searching for meaning, seeking something beyond their own individual successful and pleasurable lives, and, most important, as long as they see that what they have is lessened by those who do not have. Tillich's gift is that his theology offers the Nones in our time an alternative to the often-sectarian denominational approaches found in many churches and church-related organizations, and regrettably in many undergraduate programs in religious studies and theology.

Tillich is of enduring value to people before, during, and immediately after college age. Many begin by reading his sermons—perhaps, "You Are Accepted," from *The Shaking of the Foundations*,[41] "The Meaning of Joy," from *The New Being*,[42] or "The Riddle of Inequality," from *The Eternal Now*.[43] These sermons, written more than a half century ago, are as engaging, relevant, and filled with wisdom today as they were when they were first delivered at the Chapel at Union Theological Seminary in New York City or at the Chapel at Harvard Divinity School. In a course I have taught for more than three decades, The Theology of Marriage, I have assigned the sermon, "Loneliness and Solitude,"[44] with the proviso that they should never enter marriage out of loneliness but only when they have reached a state of genuine solitude where they are able to be alone but want to share their life with another because of precisely who the other person is. Many Nones (as well as church goers for that matter) tell me it was their favorite reading in the course and want to read more Tillich after having read one of his well-known sermons. Likewise, in a graduate counseling psychology course at my university, a colleague always invites me in to teach his long graduate class on existential psychotherapy. The book? *The Courage to Be.* The students, many of whom are

[40] Peter Berger, "For a World with Windows," in *Against the World and For the World: The Hartford Appeal and the Future of American Religion,* eds. Peter Berger and Richard John Neuhaus (New York: Seabury, 1976), 8-19.

[41] Paul Tillich, "You Are Accepted," in *The Shaking of the Foundations* (New York: Charles Scribner's Sons, 1948), 153-63.

[42] Paul Tillich, "The Meaning of Joy," in *The New Being* (New York: Charles Scribner's Sons, 1957), 141-51.

[43] Paul Tillich, "The Riddle of Inequality," in *The Eternal Now* (New York: Charles Scribner's Sons, 1963), 36-46.

[44] Paul Tillich, "Loneliness and Solitude," in *The Eternal Now*, (New York: Charles Scribner's Sons, 1963), 15-25.

just out of college or recently employed in a counseling situation, wrestle with Tillich's complex ideas on anxiety in their ontic, moral, and spiritual forms. Some of the students in the class are part of the community of Nones but are usually deeply committed to make the world a little better place in their own way.

To place the Nones in a broader cultural and historical perspective, the Nones are classic examples of western European and American culture. One could characterize the world today as the encounter of these Western cultures, primarily through global politics, commerce, and science and technology, with other great worlds—Islamic, Chinese, Japanese, Latino, African, etc. In Samuel Huntington's phrase, it has become "the West against the rest."[45] In this struggle, non-Western cultures have inevitably become, for good or ill, more and more westernized. This holds true, first, in Asian culture, and then Latino culture, and even in the more liberal pockets of Islamic culture. Members of these cultures no longer define their lives in and through their familial and community traditions as was always the case; even more so, and perhaps sadly, they often have little awareness of what these traditions taught and required. Young people of all cultures today have grandparents who are still devoted to the tradition; their parents' generation often dismissed the inherited faith as no longer relevant in the modern secular order; their children are our Nones, often caught and confused between their grandparents and parents.

With the absolute and inclusive power of the familial faith tradition broken, faith ceases to be unquestionable; it is one choice among others and can be conveniently postponed to another time. With a mixture of traditions, now relativized and competing with one another, it is just as easy for today's college aged individual to choose "none." Most still search for an ultimate meaning to their lives but, with little or no guidance from the religious sphere, all they have to aid them is secular culture—in all of its wrongheadedness, superficiality, and demonic potential. Today's young practice their religion on their smart phones and laptops, aided by the doctrines of Google, Facebook, and the myriad of programs that keep them "linked in" and connected to one another. Their culture, their reality, is now "virtual," but sadly rarely flesh and blood. College students have told me (and I could never fabricate this story) that they sometimes even break off a serious relationship by texting rather than a personal conversation!

---

[45] Samuel P. Huntington, "The Clash of Civilizations?" *Foreign Affairs Quarterly* 72, no. 3 (1993): 22-49. His ideas are more developed in his book, *The Clash of Civilizations and the Remaking of World Order* (New York: Simon and Schuster, 1996). This book and its ideas received much attention after the disaster of September 11, 2001.

Tillich's Protestant Principle and Catholic Substance

Paul Tillich said many times, undoubtedly with a twinkle in his eye, "I am more Catholic than the Catholics, and more Protestant than the Protestants."[46] In Tillich's words, Protestant Principle and Catholic Substance is "one of the main problems of my theology."[47] While Tillich was quintessentially a Protestant theologian and a great proponent of the Protestant Principle, he was also more than aware that Protestantism needed "earthen vessels," concrete symbols in words, actions, and ritual, for the reception of its message of grace. In its struggle with Catholicism, Protestantism rejected many of the older forms of grace that had become demonic because of their idolatrous nature before the Reformation. However, Protestantism would have destroyed itself as a movement if it did not adopt new forms that had arisen within Catholicism itself. It had to select "from the wealth of material in Catholicism what was suited for the purpose of transmitting prophetic criticism and the scriptural message of grace to the individual."[48] Grace could not be purely invisible but needed a *Gestalt*, an historical form.[49] A sacrament is present in what Tillich calls a "Gestalt of grace," a grace that is "actual in objects, not as an object but as the transcendent meaning of an object."[50] These forms of grace "are finite forms pointing beyond themselves. They are forms that, so to speak, are selected by grace, that it may appear through them."[51] The history of Protestantism is the quest for form and the simultaneous negation of it. As Tillich states, "the inner dilemma of Protestantism lies in this, that it must protest against every religious or cultural realization which seeks to be intrinsically valid, but that it needs such realization if it is to be able to make its protest in any meaningful way."[52] Tillich calls this the "inner contradiction" of Protestantism that constitutes at the same time "its

---

[46] Relayed to the author in a conversation with Marion Hausner Pauck, October 16, 2019. Frau Pauck with her husband, Wilhelm Pauck, one of Tillich's closest friends, published what, up till now, has been Tillich's definitive biography. See note 33 above.

[47] Paul Tillich, "Aspects of a Religious Analysis of Culture," *World Christian Education* 11, no. 2 (1956): 41-43; reprinted in *Theology of Culture*, 169.

[48] Paul Tillich, "Protestantism as a Critical and Creative Principle," in *Political Expectation*, ed. James L. Adams (New York: Harper & Row, 1971), 30-31, 34. Tillich wrote this article in German in 1929.

[49] Tillich, 30-31, 34.

[50] Tillich, 25.

[51] Paul Tillich, *The Protestant Era* (Chicago: The University of Chicago Press, 1957), 212.

[52] Tillich, *The Religious Situation*, 192-93.

greatness and tragedy."[53] He is seeking another alternative to the objectified forms of Roman Catholicism on one side and to an unstructured (Gestaltless) Protestantism on the other.[54]

Although college age students live in a world questioning the reality given to them in both their popular and academic cultures, and although many of them reject the universes of meaning given to them, today's junior in high school, sophomore in college, or first year graduate student are not without the need of a Gestalt of meaning, meaning expressed in some form beyond their individual conscious imagination. The fact that Western culture has placed undue emphasis upon the individuality of every young person does not lessen the universal need for community, to be part of something greater than oneself. The primary reason for the growth of enduring friendships among young people is their desire, indeed their need, to share meaning. Sometimes young people embark on romantic relationships too early in the need for validation by someone they know and respect. When wrong people are chosen for such validation, enduring harm can take place to a young person's life and future. Parents must nourish and allow their children's growth and freedom, but they must also protect their children by offering them a Gestalt of meaning (which theologically is also a Gestalt of grace). When young people share a common religious tradition, this tradition often serves as a pathway to a lifetime of meaning. Of course, such pathways can easily and tragically become demonic and destructive if finite teachings take on infinite power. Even the Nones need some Gestalt of meaning and often seek other Nones to help create and validate the structures of meaning that make sense to them beyond their own individual, and sometimes timid and frightened, consciousness.

In the twenty-first century, young people will still be, in Tillich's phrase, "searching for guiding stars."[55] Put differently, they will be searching for what he called Catholic substance, and in spite of the superficiality and shallowness of so many communal cultural expressions of young peoples' objects of faith and commitment today, they will continue to look for that transcendental di-

---

[53] Tillich, 192-93. See also, Tillich, *The Protestant Era*, 206.

[54] Tillich, *The Protestant Era*, 210.

[55] Paul Tillich, *My Search for Absolutes* (New York: Simon and Schuster, 1967), 103-4.

mension, that vertical reality, even in the midst of their rapidly moving horizontal world.[56] For Tillich, the vertical reality is the breakthrough of the eternal into the dusty roads of the temporal.[57] Tillich's entire system of thought, from his three volumes of sermons to his three volumes of the Systematic Theology, appeals to a wider group of people than professional theologians and others confined within the sometimes narrow and unimaginative boundaries of the church. He also touches not only the minds but also the hearts and the souls of those seeking the infinite, the absolute, that which is ultimately important and life-transforming. In spite of his essentialist framework in all of his philosophical theology, Tillich was also an existentialist to his very core.[58] To young people confused about the role of the Bible, especially ones exposed to fundamentalist ideas, *Biblical Religion and the Search for Ultimate Reality* is often an extraordinarily helpful work.[59] To other young people searching for answers to fundamental moral and ethical questions, *Love, Power, and Justice: Ontological Analyses and Ethical Applications*[60] and *Morality and Beyond* are salutary.[61] To young persons, in college or the workforce, desperate for meaning or struggling with anxiety or depression, *The Courage to Be* offers authentic self-affirmation and an unconditional source of hope. To those adrift and without belief, *The Dynamics of Faith* presents a surprisingly fresh interpretation of faith in the context of their particular tradition.

My young students are particularly taken with the third chapter of *Dynamics*, where the class explores the meaning of symbols, myths, breaking the myth, and natural and reactive literalism. Since everyone in the class, even students with a Muslim or Buddhist background, have been introduced to the Santa Claus story, it is the perfect example of a myth. Whether this story, or

---

[56] See Tillich's article on this topic in the publication of Phi Beta Kappa: "Vertical and Horizontal Thinking." *The American Scholar* 15, no. 1 (1945–46): 102–5, 110–12.

[57] Tillich treats of this breakthrough in one of his most brilliant sermons "The Riddle of Inequality," in *The Eternal Now*, his third volume of sermons, 15-35.

[58] See, for example, Paul Tillich, "Psychoanalysis, Existentialism, and Theology (1958)" and "Existentialism and Psychotherapy (1960)," in *The Meaning of Health: Essays in Existentialism, Psychoanalysis, and Religion*, ed. Perry LeFevre (Chicago: Exploration Press, 1984). (A collection essays and articles published from 1944 through 1972.)

[59] Chicago: University of Chicago Press, 1955.

[60] Ed. Ruth Nanda Anshen (New York: Harper & Row, 1963).

[61] New York: Harper & Row, 1963. The final two chapters first appeared in book form in *The Protestant Era*; second edition with a foreword by William Schweiker in the Library of Theological Ethics (Louisville: Westminster John Knox Press, 1995).

any story, is scientifically true or not is irrelevant to the myth whose only goal is not objective truth but participatory meaning. Up until a certain age, children believed in Santa Claus literally, and college age students remember vividly when they broke the myth of Santa Claus. (I always suggest to my students that breaking *through* the myth is what Tillich means by "breaking" the myth; "break" does not mean destroy.) The transition from natural literalism to the deeper meaning of the story is virtually effortless.[62] Since virtually all college age students are either in love, seeking someone to love, or would like to be in love, they are struck by the fact that authentic love must be mythically true and any scientific analytical evidence is virtually irrelevant to what authentic love is. Failing to break the myth of love, as I tell students in a course on relationships and marriage, is one of life's great mistakes.

People of every time and place must confront the absolute question of the meaning of life in the face of love and lovelessness, joy and sorrow, and suffering and death. These questions, while not limited to young people, are prevalent and powerful in the minds of the young. For this reason, the writings of Paul Tillich—especially, his method of correlation, his existential foundation, and his treatment of Protestant principle and Catholic substance—are still relevant to young people wherever they are. Tillich continues to answer their existential questions. His three volumes of sermons continue to open their hearts and minds to broader theological insight and greater spiritual wisdom. Tillich's thought offers a desirable alternative to the theological polarization of our time: between a secular modernity devoid of transcendence on one side and an uncritical, anti-intellectual, fundamentalist neoorthodoxy on the other. Indeed, Tillich's writings are more than relevant; they are still essential in helping the young find their "guiding stars."

[62] The class considers the pathology in still believing in Santa Claus while in college! It is then very simple to make the leap from the Santa Claus story to political, social, moral, and, most important, theological myths that many adults accept without question, without "breaking through." The pathology in this situation is obvious and is visible in our current culture.

Rethinking *The Courage to Be* for American Culture Today

Mary Ann Stenger[1]

The Courage to Be has been one of Paul Tillich's most widely read books, clearly addressing people's religious interests decades after its original publication in 1952. For me and for many other scholars of religion, that book served as our introduction to Tillich. It is a good introduction to his thought, as he grounds his terms philosophically and historically, sets up his argument ontologically, offers a theological analysis of culture, incorporates his approach to existentialist thinking, and concludes with his radical theology rooted in the God above the God of theism. Students and scholars have applied elements from the book in a variety of ways, many of which I expect Tillich could not have imagined when he gave the Terry Lectures at Yale University that served as the basis for the book.

The book appears to have passed the test of time, with a second edition published in 2000 and a third in 2014. Peter J. Gomez and Harvey Cox, the authors of the introductions to the later editions, raise the question of whether Tillich's arguments are dated or irrelevant.[2] Both argue that the book has something to say to their own time period even though Tillich wrote in a different context. Cox states, "yes, Tillich still speaks to the current generation. Even though the challenges to faith may be different ones, his fearless way of facing the challenges in his day still provides a compelling example."[3]

In my view, what gives *The Courage to Be* staying power to address challenges to faith and to life decades after its first publication is Tillich's broad ontological analysis of anxiety and courage, especially his serious treatment of doubt and faith. Readers connect with the argument that courage is necessary to be, to live. In spite of undergraduate students' difficulty with Tillich's ontological language, many still respond positively when they are introduced to

---

[1] First published as Mary Ann Stenger, "Rethinking *The Courage to Be* for American Culture Today," *International Yearbook for Tillich Research* 13 (2018): 197-216.

[2] Peter J. Gomez, introduction to *The Courage to Be*, 2nd ed., by Paul Tillich (New Haven: Yale University Press, 2000), xxxii; Harvey Cox, introduction to *The Courage to Be*, 3rd ed., by Paul Tillich (New Haven: Yale University Press, 2014), xiii.

[3] Cox, introduction, xxiv.

the book in Introduction to Religion courses. Undergraduate students certainly relate to anxiety and can connect easily to doubt and even perhaps guilt and fate, and so can many readers outside the university. Its broad approach to basic facts and experiences of life, with many supporting examples, allows the analysis to be applied decades after its first publication.

My purpose in this essay is to discuss challenges to faith and to life in the current American context and to assess the extent to which Tillich's analysis in *The Courage to Be* is helpful in understanding and/or addressing those challenges.

Shortly before the Terry lectures at Yale University that Tillich revised for *The Courage to Be*, he published the first volume of his *Systematic Theology* where he articulates his method of correlation "as a way of uniting message and situation."[4] In so many writings, even when he does not reference this method, he employs it. Especially in his more philosophical and ontological writings, such as this book, we may not recognize its use. But Tillich still uses it, addressing the deep questions that he finds in the particular cultural and historical context.

Tillich's Context for *The Courage to Be*

Elliott Harvey Shaw argues that Tillich was addressing, at least in part, the American cultural and political situation of the early 1950s in *The Courage to Be*.[5] Shaw not only shows that "*The Courage to Be* is principally a work of contextual theology" but also argues that Tillich's context leads him to change certain points from the Terry lectures to the published book. Specifically, Shaw recognizes the influence of the McCarthy era in post-World War II American politics. The rise of the Cold War between the United States and the Soviet Union enabled Senator Joseph McCarthy to raise the specter of major communist infiltration in the US government as well as in other areas of American culture, such as the entertainment industry. Not only communism but socialism and left-wing ideologies became suspect. Shaw notes that Tillich's political engagement during World War II (activities with the Fellowship of Socialist Christians, led by Reinhold Niebuhr, and with the Voice of America broadcasts to Germany, and with the Council for a Democratic Germany) ended in the postwar period. Shaw argues: "As the national atmosphere became increasingly inimical to left-wing politics, Tillich moved

[4] Paul Tillich, *Systematic Theology*, vol. 1 (Chicago: University of Chicago Press, 1951), 8.

[5] Elliott Harvey Shaw, "The Politics of *The Courage to Be*," *Marburg Journal of Religion* 4, no. 2 (December 1999): 1-10.

away from religious socialist prescriptions to a more privatized form of theology whose concern was to address the situation of the individual in an age when anxiety was becoming a major area of cultural concern."[6]

Anxiety centers Tillich's arguments in *The Courage to Be*, but his analysis of the forms of courage people live by expresses his understanding of cultures, both past and present, in the West and partially in the East. Shaw observes that Tillich expanded the lectures and edited them for a broader audience. In analyzing the differences between the transcript of the lectures and the book, Shaw focuses on Tillich's treatment of communism and Marxism. He argues that Tillich "strengthen[s] the anti-Soviet tone" and "downplays the importance of Marxism as a significant historical force."[7] Shaw also points out differences in Tillich's treatment of American intellectual approaches, with the book "less bluntly anti-American than in his lectures of 1950 and 1951."[8] But Shaw also shows that Tillich's critique of American conformism is stronger in the book than in the lectures.[9] Shaw attributes these changes in part to the growing McCarthyism of the 1950s even though Tillich states in the 1960s that he had not been worried about that movement.[10] Still, Shaw's analysis is important for focusing on the context for Tillich's arguments in the book and for recognizing Tillich's sensitivity to his American readers.

Shaw does not address other elements of the early 1950s in the United States, but Tillich was probably aware of the strong economy, rising productivity, and a baby boom—all of which signaled prosperity for many and fit with Tillich's discussion of American democratic conformism. An aspect that Tillich may have been aware of but did not address was a nascent civil rights movement. The landmark school desegregation case of *Brown v. Board of Education* was decided by the US Supreme Court in 1954. Definitely a significant decision, yet it certainly did not end segregation or racist policies, a fact that I address later.

Present American Cultural Context

Peter Gomes, in his introduction in 2000, describes the American cultural context as showing "superficial signs of religious vitality," "unprecedented economic growth and material prosperity," and lifestyles of people working hard and playing hard in order to avoid underlying anxieties and fears.[11] Harvey

[6] Shaw, 2.
[7] Shaw, 6.
[8] Shaw, 8.
[9] Shaw, 8.
[10] Shaw, 9, 10.
[11] Gomes, introduction, xxxii.

Cox, in his 2014 introduction, focuses on the "resurgence of fundamentalisms" and "its opposite: a vague spirituality, the merchandizing of shallow religiosity, and a kind of 'whatever' indifference."[12] He also notes that the Western tradition of philosophy no longer dominates, as people are more aware of the many world religions and of diverse cultures with which we can engage.[13]

Cox's description of the American spiritual and cultural context holds true today. But I would add some elements to it that need attention today and that should be a part of our rethinking Tillich's analysis in *The Courage to Be*. Important cultural issues today include racial justice (in relation to the killing of Blacks as well as broader issues raised by the Black Lives Matter movement) and sexual justice (brought out by the Me Too movement but also by rights issues raised by gays, lesbians, and transgender people). Both of these issues point to earlier critiques of *The Courage to Be*.

Feminist Mary Daly incorporated elements of *The Courage to Be* in *Beyond God the Father* (1973) with an incisive, stinging critique of patriarchy in religion and in Western culture.[14] She argues that Tillich's thought is "potentially liberating in a very radical sense" but is also inadequate in failing to recognize or to address the oppression of sexual hierarchy.[15] Still, she incorporates and applies critically Tillich's concepts of anxiety, nonbeing, courage, and power of being.[16]

Ethicist Franklin Sherman suggested that Tillich's typology of anxieties needed a fourth anxiety: the anxiety of injustice and oppression.[17] His suggestion stemmed from his experience in South Africa where he encountered people struggling between aristocratic and egalitarian interests. He argued that the anxiety of injustice and oppression was not just felt as an individual anxiety but by individuals as part of a struggle to find a new way of being as a people.

Feminist theologian Carter Heyward offers a related but slightly different critique of *The Courage to Be* in *Touching Our Strength*.[18] She argues that

---

[12] Cox, introduction, xix.

[13] Cox, xxi.

[14] Mary Daly, *Beyond God the Father: Toward a Philosophy of Women's Liberation* (Boston: Beacon Press, 1973).

[15] Daly, 20.

[16] For an extensive discussion of Daly's use of Tillich, see my discussion in "Tillich and Mary Daly's Feminist Theology," in *Dialogues of Paul Tillich*, Mary Ann Stenger and Ronald H. Stone (Macon: Mercer University Press, 2002), 98-134.

[17] Franklin Sherman made this suggestion in a banquet speech in 1985 for the North American Paul Tillich Society meeting in Anaheim, California, held in conjunction with the American Academy of Religion.

[18] Carter Heyward, *Touching Our Strength: The Erotic as Power and the Love of God* (San Francisco: Harper & Row, 1989).

Tillich failed to recognize "the *theological* significance of the material, embodied, and economic grounds of human being."[19] She sees him focusing on the anxiety of the well-educated Euromerican male rather than addressing the social, relational basis of both human beings and divine being.[20] For her, the "God above God" is "finally indifferent to the details of how we live together on the earth."[21] What Heyward sees missing is an adequate analysis of power that would provide a moral basis to his theology and connect more fully with the real experiences of humans.

While these three critiques can be faulted for expecting a book published in 1952 to address the issues of the 1970s and 1980s, they do raise issues that impact the viability and influence of the book for today. It is interesting to note that Tillich did address power and justice in his 1954 book, *Love, Power, and Justice*, although his critics would probably see that book as too abstract for their concerns.[22] Yet still today, these three critiques resonate as they relate to continuing issues of racial justice and sexual justice in American society.

Implicitly, and sometimes explicitly, these critiques point to two interconnected dimensions: the importance of our human bodies in how we live and relate to each other in American culture and issues of justice and power in American culture.

Tillich did recognize the biological elements of both anxiety and courage, although, he is often interpreted as ignoring human embodiment. He assumes our embodiment rather than directly discussing it, and he does not address specific aspects of our embodiment, such as sex or race or disability.[23] Today, of course, these have taken on great significance in American culture and politics. If Tillich were writing today, he might address these dimensions specifically. But given his ontological grounding of analysis, it is just as likely he would have seen these particular bodily aspects as examples of ontological concepts, not requiring separate analysis.

Still, in responding to American cultural-political issues, we must address specific aspects of embodiment. Much more than in Tillich's time, psychologists recognize that factors of race, gender and ethnicity can increase

[19] Heyward, 64.

[20] Heyward, 63-64.

[21] Heyward, 67.

[22] Paul Tillich, *Love, Power, and Justice: Ontological Analyses and Ethical Applications* (New York: Oxford University Press, 1954).

[23] For a broad discussion of issues of embodiment related to Tillich's thought, see Adam Pryor and Devan Stahl, eds., *The Body and Ultimate Concern: Reflections on an Embodied Theology of Paul Tillich* (Macon: Mercer University Press, 2018).

stress and harm the body. A fact sheet from the American Psychological Association, connects "perceived discrimination" as leading to "chronic stress-related health disparities among ethnic/racial and other minority groups."[24] The report also indicates that "Lesbian, Gay, Bisexual, and Transgendered (LGBT) individuals are at increased risk for psychiatric morbidity compared to heterosexuals due to stigma resulting from perceived discrimination."[25] Clearly, chronic stressors include more than the biological facts of race, sexual identity, or disability, but those bodily facts often engender stigma and experiences of perceived discrimination.

What do we see when we see other people? Do we not notice specific aspects of another's body and consciously or unconsciously make assumptions about the person? We are taught to see these differences by our culture. Sometimes these assumptions are directly modeled by political, cultural, or religious leaders; and sometimes indirectly through news reports, films, magazines, and books. The problem is not just that we see bodily differences but that we act and treat people unequally based on those differences. Laws against such discrimination in the workplace or in public places help reduce this, but reports of discrimination indicate that much more needs to be done.[26] In a 2017 survey of a "nationally representative sample" of Muslim adults, forty-eight percent of respondents reported being subjected to at least one discriminatory event, eight percent more than in 2007. Several respondents referenced the travel ban that focused on predominantly Muslim countries and negative media coverage of Islam and Muslims.[27] The report of the American Bureau of Labor Statistics for 2017 shows higher unemployment for persons with a disability, roughly double that of those without disability.[28] These statistics illustrate the reality and extent of discrimination or perceived discrimination based on bodily characteristics. I am not using these facts to argue that Tillich's analysis should have placed more emphasis on particular embodiments but

[24] American Psychological Association, "Health Disparities and Stress," 2012, http://www.apa.org/topics/health-disparities/fact-sheet-stress.aspx.

[25] American Psychological Association.

[26] Pew Research Center, "4. Race, Immigration and Discrimination," in *The Partisan Divide on Political Values Grows Even Wider*, October 5, 2017, https://www.pewresearch.org/politics/wp-content/uploads/sites/4/2017/10/10-05-2017-Political-landscape-release-updt..pdf. The majority of whites, Hispanics, and blacks agree that "more needs to be done to give blacks equal rights."

[27] Abigail Hauslohner, "Discrimination against Muslims is Increasing in U.S., Pew Study Finds," *The Washington Post*, July 26, 2017.

[28] US Department of Labor, Bureau of Labor Statistics, "Persons with a Disability: Labor Force Characteristics News Release," June 21, 2018, https://www.bls.gov/news.release/archives/disabl_06212018.htm.

rather to emphasize the experiences of discrimination and injustice for many in American culture today.

In Tillich's experience, discrimination against Jews dominated German culture leading up to World War II. His response in *The Socialist Decision* was to emphasize the common humanity of all and to denounce the emphasis on blood and soil put forth by the Nazis. In *The Courage to Be*, his analysis is more ontological, describing what he sees as characteristics of all humans. Tillich calls us to focus on our common humanity, with all the anxieties that we share in spite of our differences. The strength of Tillich's approach is that anxieties and forms of courage belong to all humans.

Embodiment in all its particularities and the anxiety of injustice and oppression need to be added to Tillich's analysis today, and more needs to be said about the biological dimensions of anxiety and courage than what Tillich offered. If one's own body stimulates negative responses from other people, one's courage has to involve affirmation of one's body in spite of the ongoing discrimination. The anxiety of injustice and oppression raises the question of the courage to counter unjust structures and policies.

Another key element of American culture today involves our cultural, religious, and political polarization. Political polarization has been growing in recent years and "dwarfs demographic, religious and education differences."[29] These other differences continue to be important but have not grown as much as the political division. The partisan divide between Republicans and Democrats manifests in their views about racial discrimination, government help for the needy, global policy, economic fairness, and more. One's political identification often says more about one's values and social connections than other social-cultural factors. To the extent that people affiliate religiously, they are likely to choose a religious community where their political views will not be challenged.

Two additional and significant factors in our present context have been identified by Harvey Cox: the polarization between fundamentalists or evangelicals and people with no religious affiliation, and the religious pluralism in a country in which Christianity is less dominant.[30] I will follow the structure Tillich employs in the book, highlighting what is helpful for the issues Cox identifies.

---

[29] Carroll Doherty, "Key Takeaways on Americans' Growing Partisan Divide over Political Values," Pew Research Center, October 5, 2017. https://www.pewresearch.org/fact-tank/2017/10/05/takeaways-on-americans-growing-partisan-divide-over-political-values/

[30] Cox, introduction, xix and xxii.

Existential Anxiety as Normal

Stress may be an ordinary part of life, and many external and internal factors that cause stress relate to the types of anxiety discussed by Tillich. Both stress and anxiety have biological and psychological qualities that make people aware of "threats" in their lives and stimulate responses to protect themselves. Tillich describes such responses as forms of courage, with courage also involving biological and psychological dimensions.[31]

Tillich's analysis of the anxiety of fate and death focuses more on the ultimate threat of death than on the everyday experiences of one's "fate." He describes this anxiety as the "most basic, most universal, and inescapable."[32] Both fate and death, and the anxiety associated with them, are part of being human. "For existentially everybody is aware of the complete loss of self which biological extinction implies."[33]

The threat of death is always present and underlies all concrete anxieties, for Tillich. Fate, on the other hand, is seen as contingent, unpredictable, and particular. Fate concerns where each individual is in time, place, and circumstance. The fleeting quality of time connects with death, and he focuses on "weakness, disease, and accidents" as contingent threats to our body and soul.[34] But if we see one's specific bodily characteristics as part of one's fate, we must recognize that qualities such as skin color, race, ethnicity, and sex are given with birth. While some physical disabilities result from weakness, disease, or accidents, many others come with birth or through one's genetic makeup. And unfortunately, these do not just affect individuals as individuals in how they relate to the world, but they especially impact how others see them and respond to them.

It is this element of public response that points to anxiety over injustice and oppression. Perhaps Tillich would have considered such an anxiety as part of the anxiety of fate and death, but I think Franklin Sherman was right to point to it not only as a distinctive anxiety experienced by individuals but also in relation to one's identity with a specific group of people. Stress resulting from discrimination experienced by many non-majority peoples points to the reality of the anxiety of injustice and oppression. Whether we are talking about race, ethnicity, sex, or disability, this anxiety relates to social structures of power that are found in every area of society—churches, governments, schools, housing, employment, and more. The basis of the discrimination may

[31] Paul Tillich, *The Courage to Be* (New Haven & London: Yale University Press, 1952), 78. All following references to *The Courage to Be* will be to this first edition.

[32] Tillich, 41.

[33] Tillich, 41

[34] Tillich, 45.

not be changeable for many, but these structures are contingent and capable of reform. Today, perhaps more than in Tillich's time, we need to recognize the presence of this anxiety in our society.

Turning to the anxiety of guilt and condemnation, we may question how strongly that is experienced today in the United States. A 2015 Pew Research Center report on Religion and Public Life states that almost twenty-three percent of Americans indicate no religious affiliation.[35] So at least for that group, guilt would not connect to religious moral expectations. But, of course, guilt can arise in relation to family, friends, and other social groups. Tillich mostly uses the term "condemnation" in relation to the absolute form of this anxiety, but he also suggests "self-rejection" as an absolute form.[36] That does not depend on religious affiliation but on one's own sense of what one ought to do, and most people would seem to have that moral sense even if views of what is right or what is expected vary greatly across individuals and social groups.

Tillich points to the "profound ambiguity between good and evil" that affects one's personal being, with awareness of that ambiguity connected to the feeling of guilt. When one's awareness of guilt moves toward "self-rejection," then despair can result.[37] Tillich notes that people can try to avoid guilt and despair by rejecting moral norms and judgments or by trying to act as perfectly as possible.[38] In recent years, we seem to have more examples of the former than of people focusing on perfect moral living.

Recent political and cultural movements in the United States suggest that there are people who live outside of the anxiety of guilt and condemnation. Political lies and illegal cover-ups have not led to moral confessions of guilt or a sense of shame. The scandal of the sports doctor who deceived and sexually assaulted young female gymnasts comes to mind. He never expressed guilt for what he did, despite the number of accusers. Instead, many of the young girls responded that they had felt guilt.[39] Similarly, the sex scandals of pedophilia, assault, and rape by Roman Catholic priests reveal "religious" men who were sometimes cited for "moral failure" but who often continued to find

---

[35] "America's Changing Religious Landscape," Pew Research Center, May 12, 2015, https://www.pewforum.org/2015/05/12/americas-changing-religious-landscape/.

[36] Tillich, *The Courage to Be*, 52.

[37] Tillich, 52-3.

[38] Tillich, 53.

[39] "Who Is Larry Nasser?: A Timeline of His Decades–Long Career, Sexual Assault, and Prison Sentences," *Lansing State Journal*, https://www.lansingstatejournal.com/pages/interactives/larry-nassar-timeline/.

other victims for their sexual activities; if they felt any guilt, it did not seem to arise in their dealings with these young victims.[40]

These cases are in American news, but if "leaders" show this lack of anxiety of guilt, we can expect other examples from people not so well known. The anxiety of guilt and condemnation seems to require moral depth within persons, a sense of moral expectation for oneself, and self-judgment. Tillich does mention "anomism" as an effort to avoid the anxiety of guilt, but he argues that "the anxiety of guilt lies in the background and breaks again and again into the open, producing the extreme situation of moral despair."[41] But the examples I have given suggest some people do live without such despair, serving their immediate desires. The result is often injustice for others that may bring on despair for them as victims rather than despair for the perpetrator. But, of course, neither direction can finally remove guilt for those who feel it.

Do people today live deeply enough to feel guilt? If people simply move from one activity to another, escaping in momentary pleasure of drugs or sex, from what would guilt arise? Or, do some live on the "surface" precisely to escape feelings of guilt about not having lived up to personal or social expectations? These are complex questions that I cannot answer here. Rather, I point out that Tillich *assumed* a depth dimension not only in culture but in individual's lives. He also *assumed* processes of self-reflection and self-assessment, shaped by the kinds of people Tillich encountered in the university and seminary settings where he spent most of his academic life.

Similarly, Tillich assumed that "ordinary" people search for deep meaning in life, with doubt often motivating them to a deeper level of meaning and understanding. Tillich saw religious meaning in secular, cultural activities such as the creative arts or politics or psychology.[42] He considered the experience of "depth" to be an integral part of being human. Yet we need to ask whether people do experience "depth" or sufficiently doubt the value of the surface activities in their daily living to search for deeper meaning. Do sports events, political rallies, "hook-up" sex, shopping, etc. offer "religious" meaning for some people?

---

[40] Laurie Goodstein and Sharon Otterman, "Catholic Priests Abused 1000 Children in Pennsylvania, Report Says" *The New York Times*, August 14, 2018, https://www.nytimes.com/2018/08/14/us/catholic-church-sex-abuse-pennsylvania.html.

[41] Tillich, *The Courage to Be*, 53.

[42] See Tillich's discussions in "On the Idea of a Theology of Culture," in *What Is Religion?*, trans. William Baillie Green (New York.: Harper & Row, 1969), 155-81; and Paul Tillich, *Theology of Culture*, ed. Robert C. Kimball (London: Oxford University Press, 1959).

Tillich's assumptions raise questions with respect to the anxiety of emptiness and meaninglessness. As long as people are satisfied by pleasurable but fleeting activities, they may not experience doubts about meaning. Tillich thought most people would seek something deeper, but he recognized that some people can live with "spiritual indifference and emptiness" although he sees that as potentially leading to meaninglessness and to threatening their very existence.[43]

The philosophy, usually attributed to Ayn Rand, that self-interest is good and altruism is destructive, has been popular with some political and cultural leaders in recent years. They are not indifferent to meaning but follow self-interest as the dominating value and basis of behavior. Examples include personal sexual pleasure above the rights of victims and lack of concern for low-income or unemployed people or for children in those families. Self-interest affects not only person-to-person interactions but also business values (bottom line as the only thing that matters) and political values (America First).

Doubts and questions about institutions have been increasing in recent years, with revelations of sexual abuse by previously respected leaders, both in churches and schools. As it has happened many times before with political leaders, the disgrace and fallout appears to be less. But for the Roman Catholic Church, with the report from the Grand Jury in Pennsylvania that outlines a thousand victims over several decades, and for the evangelical Willow Church near Chicago where the pastor resigned over charges of sexual harassment,[44] the cases of sexual abuse often raise questions for members who are totally surprised by the reports. Their personal Christian faith may not be destroyed by these cases, but their respect for and faith in the churches themselves has diminished.

Also, there has been a loss of faith in experts, particularly academic experts and previously respected news sources. In an article in *Foreign Policy*, James Traub argues that Americans "lack not only a sense of shared citizenry or collective good, but even a shared body of fact or a collective mode of reasoning toward the truth. A thing that we wish to be true is true; if we wish it

[43] Tillich, *The Courage to Be*, 51.

[44] Laurie Goodstein, "How the Willow Creek Church Scandal Has Stunned the Evangelical World," *The New York Times*, August 9, 2018, https://www.nytimes.com/2018/08/09/us/evangelicals-willow-creek-scandal.html.

not to be true, it isn't."[45] Selective social media can simply support one's existing views and lead people to dismiss other views as false or "fake news." This suggests that many (both liberals and conservatives) can only accept truth that serves their viewpoint and can keep at bay doubts and questions. This approach to "truth" fits Tillich's analysis of sacrificing self to maintain certitude, often resulting in a "fanatical self-assertiveness."[46] Tillich sees this behavior as demonstrating the reality of the anxiety of meaninglessness because fanatics must suppress the questions both in themselves and others, sometimes "attacking with disproportionate violence those who disagree."[47] This analysis connects directly with the increased polarization in the United States, not only politically but religiously, morally, and culturally.

In discussing the three main forms of anxiety, Tillich provides examples of how people cope. He argues that these coping mechanisms often manifest underlying anxiety. He also recognizes that socially accepted forms of coping with anxiety may fail to work for some people, often resulting in what he calls pathological anxiety that can develop into neurosis, "*the way of avoiding non-being by avoiding being*."[48] Pathological anxiety is possible for anyone "when changes of the reality to which he is adjusted threaten the fragmentary courage with which he has mastered the accustomed objects of fear."[49] He argues that people suffering from pathological anxiety and neurosis need medical help, while spiritual help relates to ordinary existential anxiety. Today's opioid "epidemic" is a medical crisis that appears to fit Tillich's description of avoiding nonbeing by avoiding being. According to the Centers for Disease Control and Prevention, "drug overdose deaths and opioid-involved deaths continue to increase in the United States … up among both men and women, all races, and adults of nearly all ages."[50] Although only a small percentage of the population is addicted to opioids, the increase in use and overdose deaths affects millions of families. Tillich's emphasis on the medical character of pathological anxiety and neurosis supports efforts to respond medically to people who

---

[45] James Traub, "The United States of America Is Decadent and Depraved," *Foreign Policy*, December 19, 2017, https://foreignpolicy.com/2017/12/19/the-united-states-of-america-is-decadent-and-depraved/.

[46] Tillich, *The Courage to Be*, 49.

[47] Tillich, 49-50.

[48] Tillich, 66. Italics in the original.

[49] Tillich, 69.

[50] Centers for Disease Control and Prevention, "Understanding the Epidemic", "Data Overview", https://www.cdc.gov/drugoverdose/epidemic/index.html. Updated August 30, 2017.

overdose.[51] Spiritual help may be important to the families that are affected by this crisis of substance abuse, as they experience the normal existential anxieties.

Courage in the Face of Anxiety

Courage is necessary for dealing with all forms of anxiety, both existential and pathological. Tillich centers his analysis of courage in the polarity of self and world, with critiques that aim toward a deeper understanding of courage rooted in the power of being-itself. While he focuses on one side of the polarity and then the other, his goal is "a courage to be which unites both forms by transcending them."[52] There are three kinds of courage: to be as a part, to be as oneself, and religious.

The courage to be as a part focuses on participation in something beyond oneself, often a social or political group. Tillich's insightful analysis of the dominant American form of courage in the early 1950s as the courage to be as a part focused on the conformism Americans exhibited in spite of their sense of individualism as essentially American. Certainly, in the post-World War II era, productivity and seeming prosperity were found in cities and suburbs. And productivity was not only industrial but social, with the early stages of the baby boom and the social support for starting over after personal defeat. Tillich also recognized the American approach to death that often worked to avoid its reality and focused on immortality as ongoing participation in the productive process rather than on Christian resurrection.[53] But given the shuttering of many factories and the move of much production outside the United States today, to what extent does Tillich's analysis of democratic conformism still hold?

A dominant political and cultural characteristic of American culture today is polarization. To the extent that we conform, we often do so with a sense of belonging to one group and opposing another. As mentioned earlier, the increasingly polarized divide between Republicans and Democrats also involves polarization over issues of race, economy, government programs, and

---

[51] A major drug company, Walgreens, announced that it would make the antidote drug, narcan, available in the pharmacy section without prescription in forty-five states that allow it. Peter Martinez, "Narcan Available at more than 8,000 Walgreens Locations Nationwide," *CBS News*, October 26, 2017, https://www.cbsnews.com/news/narcan-available-at-all-walgreens-locations-nationwide/.

[52] Tillich, *The Courage to Be*, 154.

[53] Tillich, 110.

more. Thus, the polarization is over values that divide people socially and often religiously. People mostly choose to spend time with those who share their values.

We can see this as exemplifying elements of the courage to be as a part. Political identification, and a sense of social belonging that goes with that, do not exactly fit the patterns of neo-collectivist courage that Tillich presents. Nor do they exemplify fully the qualities of democratic conformism he analyzes. While democratic conformism still plays a role in American society, the current phenomena of either strong loyalty to a leader and his policies or intense rejection of that leader and his political actions do not connect to the value of productivity that Tillich identifies with American democratic conformism. Instead, these qualities carry elements of collectivism while verbally affirming individuality.

Both sides of this polarization require either/or thinking, rather than more creative both/and approaches. The courage to be as a part means that one knows to which group one belongs and who the "enemy" is on the other side. However, belonging to the group is seen as a personal choice, not something imposed by totalitarian methods as in neo-collectivist societies.

The "blood and soil" mythology and the idolization of the leader that Tillich observed in Nazism have parallels in the rallies that candidate, and then president, Trump has held. Emphasis on "making America great again" by getting rid of or preventing immigrants connects with the "blood" of a white supremacism and the "soil" of being born in America while ignoring the status of African Americans or Native Americans. Can we see this political identification with Trump, his party, and his policies connecting to the three existential anxieties? I would argue that the courage people find in belonging to this political group does help people cope with the anxiety of fate and fears of the "other." President Trump offers people a vision of a society that looks like most of the people attending his rallies. He connects illegal immigrants to criminals and promises to remove those who have mostly come from south of the border. This gives people hope for their own future and for that of their families. The slogan of "make America great" provides meaning for many as they envision a strong, somewhat monolithic society that holds their values. Since many evangelical leaders have supported President Trump and this movement, some may consider these values as Christian values, even if other more liberal minority Christians disagree. The experience of belonging to this political movement helps many counter the anxiety of doubt or emptiness. They know who they are, who they want to socialize with, and what American values they believe.

On the other side in polarized America, we find people who also socialize mostly with those who share their political views and values. Some of them may show up at protests to express their views that counter President Trump's policies and actions. These political gatherings reject the "blood and soil" mythology while affirming American pluralism and acceptance of "others." People connecting with this political side may include those with no religious affiliation as well as liberal Christians, Jews, and Muslims. Their vision and hope for the future includes diverse groups, but participants often have a hard time talking with or including the other political side. The anxiety of fate stems in part from their fears associated with the current political administration. The anxiety of doubt manifests in their questioning of President Trump's political policies and approaches. Their meaning comes from connecting with others who share their pluralist, inclusive political approach. Thus, this too has elements of the courage to be as a part.

I have not discussed the anxiety of guilt for either side of the polarization, since I do not see guilt as strongly felt in the United States today. Both sides have questioned the norms and values of the other side and can take comfort in seeing their own values and actions as right. Accordingly, the anxiety of guilt and condemnation in themselves is suppressed in both political movements. Individualism or the belief in oneself functions psychologically and spiritually even while one gains meaning and hope from participating with like-minded people. Internally, people think of themselves as individuals who choose how, when, and where they act. To the extent to which they are acting in conformity with others in their political group, they exemplify the courage to be as a part more than the courage to be as oneself.

Both sides affirm individualism as a "given" American value. But as Tillich pointed out in his discussion of American democratic conformism, the individual "as an individual, is a unique representative of the universe."[54] He saw individualism in relation to being a part of the creative process of the universe, with one's productivity as central. He particularly notes the American value of starting again if one fails. "The typical American, after he has lost the foundations of his existence, works for new foundations. This is true of the individual and it is true of the nation as a whole."[55] He sees Americans accepting failure but affirming production as more important than *what* is produced or *how* it is produced.

Today there is less emphasis on productivity because employment today connects less to manufacturing and more to service jobs. Also, many unemployed people rely on government support for their housing, food, and medical care. Yet Americans espouse their individualism as an important psychological and spiritual value. Internally, people think of themselves as individuals

[54] Tillich, 105.
[55] Tillich, 108.

who choose how, when, and where they act. But to the extent that they act in conformity with others in their political group or rely on others for support, they exemplify the courage to be as a part more than the courage to be as oneself.

The second type of courage is the courage to be as oneself. Tillich begins the chapter on this form of courage with this statement: "Individualism is the self-affirmation of the individual self as individual self without regard to its participation in its world."[56] Individualism is the polar opposite of collectivist forms of courage, but he sees many examples in history of the courage to be as oneself that include some elements of participation (in reason, in nature, and in the universe). His emphasis in these examples is on the freedom of the individual to determine their own being,[57] but none of these forms is as radical as the twentieth century development of Existentialism.

In part, what makes Existentialism radical is that "it has experienced the universal breakdown of meaning."[58] Even in the midst of meaninglessness and despair, the existentialist shows courage in expressing this breakdown in meaning. What centers that experience of meaninglessness, in Tillich's view, is the "loss of God in the 19th century."[59] In his survey of Existentialist art, literature, theatre, and philosophy, he points to the expression of the courage to be as oneself, "to make of oneself what one wants to be."[60] He contrasts that meaning with cynics who accept no answers and try to undermine all expressions of meaning, resulting in a "noncreative courage to be as oneself."[61]

In present American culture, one can find examples of the courage to be as oneself in some arts, poetry, and literature. But one cannot point to any recent artist whose work expresses the courage to be as oneself who is as widely known in American culture as some Existentialist artists and writers were. Instead, recent artistic expressions in literature, poetry, and art have focused more on identity that connects one to others of similar race, ethnicity, gender, sexuality, etc. Today, the courage to be as oneself does mean finding one's individual freedom to be one's self, but it does not mean doing that apart from others like oneself.

The courage to be as a part dominates much more than the courage to be as oneself. Movements focused on ensuring individual rights for minority groups (such as Black Lives Matter or the Me Too movement or Lesbian,

---

[56] Tillich, 113.
[57] Tillich, 119.
[58] Tillich, 139.
[59] Tillich, 142.
[60] Tillich, 150.
[61] Tillich, 151.

Gay, Bisexual, Transgender, and Queer efforts) recognize that they need broad political participation to achieve individual benefits. These political movements express the courage to respond to the anxiety of injustice and oppression. Dominant culture is not so much countered by individual expression but rather by group expression and action.

What about noncreative courage to be as oneself? Is the "surface" living I described earlier an example of noncreative individual courage? It could be, I think, if it stayed individual courage, but more often, the individual finds courage through connecting with others in their surface living rather than asserting one's individuality. Surface living, in general, is noncreative, not expressing new ideas or new actions to develop oneself or one's social group. Such people have enough courage to live but not enough to engage deeply in life or in their world.

The third type of courage is religious, or transcendent, courage. Tillich's overall critique of both forms of courage is that taken to extremes each form leads to the loss of a balanced self-world relationship. Collectivist forms of the courage to be as a part lead to the loss of one's individual self, and radical forms of the courage to be as oneself lead to the loss of one's world. Tillich looks toward a religiously rooted form of the courage to be that can unite *and transcend* both forms.

Tillich's connection of the courage to be with the power of being-itself shows the religious grounding of his philosophy. Transcendent courage unites and transcends the courage to be as a part and the courage to be as oneself because it is religious courage, grounded in the experience of faith in the power of being-itself that is always present. Tillich balances his use of abstract concepts like being-itself, power of being, ground of being, and the God above the God of theism with his emphasis on the experience of being grasped by the power of being-itself and on participating in the power.

As noted above, both feminist philosopher Mary Daly and feminist theologian Carter Heyward criticize Tillich for a theology that is too abstract and disconnected from sexual oppression and from recognizing the importance of *embodied* human life. While I agree with the need for more attention to issues of oppression and to our embodiment, I also see value in Tillich's more abstract expressions of ultimacy for both feminist and pluralist theology. The abstract quality of the "God above the God of theism" or of the "power of being-itself" allows for diverse concrete religious expressions that are seen as relative rather than absolute. By taking radical doubt seriously in his discussion of absolute faith, Tillich relativizes all concrete religious content and yet also allows for the restitution of concrete meanings that will always be relative to the absoluteness and ultimacy of the power of being-itself. "The God above the God of theism is not the devaluation of the meanings which doubt has thrown into the abyss of meaninglessness; he is their potential restitution."[62] The God above the God of theism is the power of being in which specific meanings participate as fragmentary expressions.[63] Tillich's understanding here opens the possibility of diverse concrete expressions of ultimacy whether in feminist expressions (such as Mary Daly's "Verb" or later "be-ing in the Triple Goddess, who is, and is not yet"[64] or Elizabeth Johnson's "She Who Is"[65]) or in a pluralist expression (such as John Hick's "the Real"[66]). The abstract expression of ultimacy also can legitimate terms like "God," "Brahman," or "Allah" as symbols for ultimacy itself.

Of course, the point of Tillich's use of the "God above the God of theism" is to ground the most basic courage to be in the midst of radical questioning or radical guilt. The God above the God of theism or the power of being-itself is the source of all forms of courage, enabling acceptance and participation and affirmation of the individual as individual.[67]

To be and to live requires courage—courage to face fears and anxieties. While Tillich focused on guilt and doubt in the modern world in *The Courage to Be*, today the more widely experienced anxieties are fate and death and the related anxiety of injustice and oppression. Today, one needs transcendent courage rooted in the power of being-itself. Living that out requires that we focus on our embodied lives with concrete actions to face our individual experiences of anxieties and to help others cope and work to counter the injustices in our present society. *The Courage to Be* can still resonate with Americans even if we require somewhat differing analyses of present situation than what Tillich saw in the early 1950s. We must ground our approach to life and our actions in the ever-present ground of being that enables us to live at all. We must experience its empowerment as providing a deep basis to deal with both our own fate and death, and also the shared task working to challenge injustice and oppression. This enables us to deal with the anxiety of fate and death, the anxiety of doubt and meaninglessness, and the anxiety of guilt and condemnation. The ultimate ground of the courage to be enables action and provides hope in the midst of our challenging times.

---

[62] Tillich, 186.

[63] Tillich, 189.

[64] Mary Dally uses "Verb" in *Beyond God the Father*, 33-4 and offers the later phrasing in *Gyn/Ecology: The Metaethics of Radical Feminism* (Boston: Beacon Press, 1978), 14.

[65] Elizabeth Johnson, *She Who Is: The Mystery of God in Feminist Theological Discourse* (New York: Crossroad, 1992).

[66] John Hick, *An Interpretation of Religion: Human Responses to the Transcendent* (New Haven and London: Yale University Press, 1989).

[67] Tillich, *The Courage to Be*, 187-90.

TILLICH & THEOLOGY

The Significance of Paul Tillich's Christology for Contemporary Discussions

Christian Danz

In his magnum opus, *Systematic Theology,* Paul Tillich starts his considerations on Jesus as the Christ with remarks about the Christian event as fact and reception. He wrote: "For the event on which Christianity is based has two sides: the fact which is called 'Jesus of Nazareth' and the reception of this fact by those who received him as the Christ."[1] The Christian event is neither the sole fact of Jesus of Nazareth, nor the sole reception of Jesus by his followers, but rather, both are aspects of this same event. Tillich rejects both the historical Jesus and the so-called kerygma as the starting point of Christology. Christology deals neither solely with Jesus of Nazareth, nor just simply with the interpretation given to him by his followers. The Christian faith is always both fact and reception.

Tillich's meaning is clear if we take into account the methodological construction of his *Systematic Theology*, namely the so-called theological circle,[2] and also the development of his theological thinking from his earlier years. The main-structure of the later *Systematic Theology* is already in his draft of a *Systematic Theology* in 1913.[3] Tillich structured the conception of the *Systematic Theology* from 1913 in three parts: intuition, reflection, and the theological standpoint.[4] The late *Systematic Theology* takes this up in the differentiation of

---

[1] Paul Tillich, *Systematic Theology*, vol. 2 (Chicago: The University of Chicago Press, 1957), 97.

[2] Paul Tillich, *Systematic Theology*, vol. 1 (Chicago: The University of Chicago Press, 1951), 8-11.

[3] Paul Tillich, "Systematische Theologie von 1913," in *Frühe Hauptwerke*, eds. Gerd Hummel and Doris Lax (Berlin/New York: de Gruyter, 1998) EW IX, 278-434.

[4] Cf. Folkart Wittekind, "Allein durch Glauben. Tillichs sinntheoretische Umformulierung des Rechtfertigungsverständnisses 1919," in *Religion – Kultur – Gesellschaft. Der frühe Tillich im Spiegel neuer Texte (1919-1920)*, eds. Christian Danz and Werner Schüßler (Wien: LIT 2008), 39-65; Stefan Dienstbeck, *Transzendentale Strukturtheorie: Stadien der Systembildung Paul Tillichs* (Göttingen: Vandenhoeck & Ruprecht 2011).

essence, existence, and life.[5] Tillich's Christology and his theological circle-structure must be understood against this background. Behind this stands his conviction that the task of theology is not to give a foundation of the Christian faith, but to give explanation and interpretation of the Christian message.[6] And this always has its place in the theological circle.

It is exactly this, namely the circle-structure of theological thinking, that we find not only in the *Systematic Theology,* but also Tillich's writings before World War I. It is also in these pre-World War I writings that he denies the possibility for a foundation of the Christian faith through the historical Jesus. In *The Christian Certainty and the Historical Jesus* (1911), Tillich wrote that Christian certainty is not based on the historical Jesus.[7] Against the background of the theological debates around 1900 on the one hand, and the historical Jesus research on the other, the young Tillich works out his own understanding of Christology. As a result, he does not understand the task of Christology as a theological description of the historical Jesus, but rather Christology as a reflexive function. This means that Christology is a description of the act of faith and not a description of a historical person. Jesus Christ is a picture of the Christian faith itself as an act that happens in history. Tillich calls this the "real picture"[8] in his dogmatics lectures that were held in Marburg and Dresden during the 1920s, as well in his later *Systematic Theology.*

But how does Jesus function for Tillich's Christology, and how is his Christology constructed? Is his Christology a Christology without Jesus?[9] And what exactly is the function of Tillich's doctrine of Christ in his *Systematic Theology*?

Answers to these questions are only possible if we look at the development of Tillich's Christology in his entire work. We can see that he is working out a doctrine of the Christ that takes up the problems of Christology under the conditions of modernity. More than this, he works out Christology as a

---

[5] Tillich, *Systematic Theology*, vol. 1, 66-7: "A third part is based on the fact that the essential as well as the existential characteristics are abstractions and that in reality they appear in the complex and dynamic unity which is called 'life'."

[6] Tillich, 10.

[7] Paul Tillich, "Die christliche Gewißheit und der historische Jesus" in *Briefwechsel und Streitschriften. Theologische, philosophische und politische Stellungnahmen und Gespräche*, eds. Renate Albrecht and René Tautmann (Frankfurt a. M.: Evangelisches Verlagswerk, 1983) EW VI, 31-50.

[8] Tillich, *Systematic Theology*, vol. 2, 115; Paul Tillich, *Dogmatik-Vorlesung (Dresden 1925-1927),* eds. Werner Schüßler and Erdmann Sturm (Berlin/New York: de Gruyter, 2005), EW XIV, 339.

[9] Cf. Gunther Wenz, "Theologie ohne Jesus? Anmerkungen zu Paul Tillich," in *Kerygma und Dogma* 26 (1980), 128-39.

theological description of the act of faith. Jesus represents in and for faith the reflexive structure of the act of faith and the event-character of faith. Both aspects are also important for the contemporary debates of Christology against the background of the so-called third quest of historical Jesus research and global religious pluralism.

The first part of the following considerations looks at the development of Tillich's Christology from the early writings until his late *Systematic Theology*. The second part discusses the Christology of Tillich's dogmatics. Finally, I will show the significance of his doctrine of the Christ for the Christological debates of our time.

The Development of Tillich's Christology

In 1911, the young Tillich had discussed with friends 128 theses about *The Christian Certainty and the Historical Jesus*. Later, in his autobiographical sketch *On the Boundary,* he calls these theses not only very important for his theological development but also considers them to be radical.[10] Why? In his theses from 1911 Tillich claims that the certainty of the Christian faith is independent from the historical Jesus. We also find this position in Tillich's philosophical dissertation from 1910 with the title *The Religio-Historical Construction in Schelling's Positive Philosophy*. Here he criticizes Schelling's attempt to connect the revelation of God in Christ with empirical history.[11] It is only a matter of intuition (*Anschauung*) in which empirical history consists for the inner history of the self-consciousness, and Christian faith as well. What are the foundations and systematic basis for Tillich's position?

First, the contemporary historical Jesus research leads to a difference between the historical Jesus and Christianity. Johannes Weiß and other theologians from the so-called religio-historical school like William Wrede had all shown that Jesus of Nazareth must be understood in the apocalyptic horizon of the ancient Judaism. Albert Schweitzer, in his famous book about the history of Jesus research, declared that the historical Jesus plays no role for the Christian religion.[12] The result for the theological debates is a diminution of the historical Jesus in Christology. Christology doesn't start with the Jesus of

---

[10] Paul Tillich, "Auf der Grenze," in *Begegnungen. Paul Tillich über sich selbst und andere*, ed. Renate Albrecht (Stuttgart/Frankfurt a. M.: Evangelisches Verlagswerk 1971), GW XII, 33.

[11] Paul Tillich, "Die religionsgeschichtliche Konstruktion in Schellings positive Philosophie, ihre Voraussetzungen und Prinzipien," in *Frühe Hauptwerke*, eds. Gerd Hummel and Doris Lax (Berlin/New York: de Gruyter, 1998), EW IX, 272.

[12] Albert Schweitzer, *Geschichte der Leben-Jesu-Forschung*, vol. 2, (Hamburg: Siebenstern, 1966), 620-30.

history, but rather, Jesus is a part of the Christian religion. Both Ernst Troeltsch and the young Tillich reveal such a construction of Christology.

Second, the framework in which Tillich's Christology is understood in the context of speculative theology. Following Fichte and Schelling, Tillich believes that the foundation of the theological system is the absolute truth or the absolute identity. Tillich calls this principle the identity of self-consciousness, which is at the same time the principle of certainty and autonomy.[13] It is important to see that this principle means an identity of the universal and the concrete. This is the structure of the absolute spirit or the absolute truth. The main principle is *spirit* that is characterized through a relation to itself. The concrete is true only insofar as it is a representation of the universal. If the concrete something exists for itself, then the concrete stands in contradiction to the absolute truth.[14]

Tillich constructs not only his theology and philosophy of history but also his Christology against this background. The concrete is a medium that represents the absolute. In this sense, Jesus Christ is a picture that is produced from the spirit, namely the relation between the universal and the concrete. "The autonomous version of the Christological problem has to replace the two-nature-doctrine through a doctrine about the relation between the absolute and the concrete spirit who it is to be viewed in Christ and through him realized."[15] Tillich identifies the dialectical structure of the absolute spirit with his realization in history with Jesus Christ. Only in this way does Jesus play a role in Christology as the individual spirit who knows himself as the realization of the absolute spirit. But the localization of this event in history remains doubtful.[16]

In Tillich's early Christology, Jesus Christ is a picture of the faith from itself, as an identity between the absolute and the concrete spirit. The foundation of the Christian certainty is the faith in this sense, and not the historical Jesus. He is an element of the Christian faith and produced from the spirit as a picture from itself.

During and after World War I Tillich had transformed his early Christology within the framework of the speculative construction of absolute truth and identity. Absoluteness is no longer a subordinate frame of the construction of history, but rather, absoluteness is a part or an element of the act of self-disclosure of the concrete existence. In his writings after the war Tillich

---

[13] Tillich, *Die christliche Gewißheit und der historische Jesus*, 43, thesis 102.

[14] Tillich, 41, thesis 87.

[15] Tillich, 45, thesis 125. I express my appreciation to Joshua Ramos (Denver) for help in this and all translations.

[16] Tillich, 42-3, thesis 100.

calls this breakthrough a metaphorical description of revelation. Tillich speaks now from the unconditioned instead of the absolute. Religion is an act in the human consciousness. What happens in religion is that we become aware of the unconditioned as the presupposition of all acts of consciousness. But this presupposition is not a content as such, because the unconditioned is the condition of all contents. On the one hand, this structure must be disclosed to an individual as revelation. Otherwise knowledge of God is not possible. On the other hand, insofar as one can *talk* about this breakthrough, namely the disclosures of the unconditioned as a presupposition of all acts of the consciousness, this is only possible by using cultural forms. These are used by the unconditioned and negated at the same time. Every concept of God is both necessary and totally wrong.[17]

This understanding of religion leads to important transformations of his Christology. Christology is now a symbolic description of the reflexive structure of the religious act, and within another aspect, it is connected with soteriology.[18] The doctrine of Jesus Christ doesn't start with the historical Jesus. The historical Jesus is not the foundation of the Christian faith. Jesus Christ is a structural description of the event of faith as an act. We could say that Tillich describes the symbolic appropriation of the faith through the individual as an act in history. Jesus is a part or an element within the Christian faith and not a foundation of the faith, which is given independently from faith.[19] If Christology explains the structure of the act of faith then Christology must begin with the act of faith as the breakthrough of the unconditioned in the human consciousness. Tillich called this salvation-revelation, as differentiated from ground-revelation.[20] The latter is the disclosure in the consciousness that the unconditioned is the presupposition of all acts of the consciousness. This general revelation is the condition of the salvation-revelation but at the same

---

[17] Cf. Paul Tillich in "Die Überwindung des Religionsbegriffs in der Religionsphilosophie," in *Ausgewählte Texte*, eds. Christian Danz, Werner Schüßler, and Erdmann Sturm (Berlin/New York: de Gruyter, 2008), 374.

[18] Wittekind, "Allein durch Glauben", 46-52.

[19] Tillich, *Dogmatik-Vorlesung* EW XIV, 328. "The decision about the Christological judgement strikes on the dogmatic level, i.e. in the sphere of faith independent from the historical knowledge."

[20] To this differentiation see Paul Tillich, "Rechtfertigung und Zweifel," in *Ausgewählte Texte*, eds. Christian Danz, Werner Schüßler, and Erdmann Sturm (Berlin/New York: de Gruyter, 2008), 124-37. Cf. Folkart Wittekind, "Grund- und Heilsoffenbarung. Zur Ausformung der Christologie Tillichs in der Auseinandersetzung mit Karl Barth," in *Jesus of Nazareth and the New Being in History*, International Yearbook for Tillich Research 6 (2011): 90-119.

time is always ambiguous.[21] The general or ground-revelation is part of the theological circle, namely a moment in the structural description of the Christian faith. The ground-revelation has a teleological orientation to the salvation-revelation.

The starting point of Tillich's Christology is the *picture* of Jesus Christ.[22] That means an interrelation of both the historical Jesus and the faith of his followers. The picture of Jesus Christ is a real picture of the structure of the act of faith.[23] But what is symbolized by this picture? Nothing other than the reflexive structure of the religious act. Christology describes the salvation-revelation. In this act the consciousness becomes aware that all of its contents are at the same time both necessary and wrong. Only this reflexive structure is the content of the picture of Christ that is focused on the cross. This act always depends on concrete history, but in this reflexive act the human consciousness becomes aware that the unconditioned is the presupposition of the consciousness and could only be expressed in the dialectic form of critique and formation.[24] The content of the true religion is also the negation of this content. It is the *picture* of the Christ in and for the Christian faith.[25]

There is a further development of Tillich's Christology in his first lectures in New York from 1936 with the title *Advanced Problems in Systematic Theology*.[26] What is new in these lectures is not the construction of Christology as such. Tillich's Christology still doesn't deal with the historical Jesus.[27] Jesus is still a picture produced from faith which is not dependent upon the

---

[21] Tillich takes this up in the *Systematic Theology* in his conception of the ambiguity of life. Paul Tillich, *Systematic Theology*, vol. 3 (Chicago: The University of Chicago Press, 1963).

[22] Tillich, *Dogmatik-Vorlesung*, EW XIV, 332-35.

[23] Tillich, *Dogmatik-Vorlesung*, EW XIV, 339.

[24] Christian Danz, "Critique and Formation: Paul Tillich's Interpretation of Protestantism," in *The Courage to Be*, International Yearbook for Tillich Research 13 (2018): 237-44.

[25] Tillich gives a short summary of his Christology in "Christology and the Interpretation of the History from 1930." Paul Tillich, "Christologie und Geschichtsdeutung", in *Ausgewählte Texte*, eds. Christian Danz, Werner Schüßler, and Erdmann Sturm (Berlin/New York: de Gruyter, 2008), 238-53.

[26] Paul Tillich, *Advanced Problems in Systematic Theology: Courses at Union Theological Seminary, 1936-1938*, ed. Erdmann Sturm (Berlin/Boston: de Gruyter, 2016), EW XIX.

[27] Paul Tillich, "The Significance of the Historical Jesus for the Christian Faith," in *Advanced Problems in Systematic Theology: Courses at Union Theological Seminary, 1936-1938*, ed. Erdmann Sturm (Berlin/Boston: de Gruyter, 2016), EW XIX, 317-21.

historical Jesus.[28] Christology remains an explanation of the reflexive structure of faith. However, Tillich now connects Christology as the act of faith with the doctrine of man or anthropology.[29] What is new in the dogmatics courses at the Union Theological Seminary is that a shift has occurred to a more general structure of human being. This relates to Tillich's doctrine of man.[30] We also find this focus on general structures of human being articulated in an existentialist manner. One could say that the Christological conception in the dogmatics courses from New York is an intermediate stage on the way to the Christology of the *Systematic Theology*.[31]

The Christology of the *Systematic Theology*

As we have seen, the task of Christology for Tillich is not to give a description of the historical Jesus. The man from Nazareth is not the founder or the foundation of the Christian religion. Rather he is an element and a part in the Christian faith. This is exactly the content of Tillich's formula that the Christian event is both "a historical fact and a subject of believing reception."[32] We also find this structure in his Christology before World War I, and as well in dogmatics lectures in Germany in the 1920s and New York in the 1930s. The starting point for the Christological construction in the *Systematic Theology* is that the Christian faith as an act in history and theology has the task to explain the faith. We must now deal with the construction of Tillich's Christology in his magnum opus. Here Tillich first explains the interrelation between fact and reception in the Christian event, then considers the function of the historical Jesus for the Christian faith, and at last the function of Christology as an expression of the reflexive structure of the act of faith.

The fact of the Christian event and the believing reception of this fact are not two separate parts. The one is not the presupposition of the other. To

---

[28] Tillich, EW XIX, 319. "The content of our faith is a picture which is created by faith—namely, the picture of Jesus given in the whole New Testament."

[29] Tillich, *Advanced Problems in Systematic Theology*, EW XIX, 115. "The method of our lecture is to show the correlation of the theological concepts with anthropological concepts. ... Christology in correlation to the doctrine of man."

[30] Paul Tillich, *Frühe Vorlesungen im Exil (1934-1935)*, ed. Erdmann Sturm (Berlin/Boston: de Gruyter, 2012), EW XVII.

[31] Cf. also Paul Tillich, "Existential Questions and Theological Answers," First Series: *Existence and the Christ*, Syllabus of Gifford Lectures 1953, University of Aberdeen, 1953.

[32] Tillich, *Systematic Theology*, vol. 2, 98.

be sure, there are some phrases from Tillich that sound as if he meant an historical assumption,[33] but this is not correct. The historical fact as an aspect in the Christian event is not a presupposition of the faith. Rather the historical fact is a presupposition which only exists in the act of faith, with the believing reception consisting not of a separated element. The Christian event, namely the act of faith, is both fact and reception. Tillich constructs his Christology as an expression of the act of faith, and this means an act of appropriation. Faith is for him a personal act, and for this act Jesus represents the personal dimension. But this act is always an act that is bound to a history. Jesus is the *picture*, used by faith to describe a personal act of appropriation. Tillich's differentiation between fact and reception exemplified the structure of the faith or the Christian event. It is at all times both fact and believing reception.

Tillich's formula of the Christian event as fact and reception is not a historical thesis but rather a systematic thesis about the beginning of Christianity. The Christian religion begins neither with Jesus nor with the kerygma of the early Christians.[34] It starts with an interrelation between Jesus and his followers or—as we could call it with a contemporary terminology which is used in the historical research—with the remembered Jesus.[35] The interrelation between *factum and reception* is the structure of the faith as an act, which is bound to a concrete history. This act produces a picture from itself, and without this act no faith is possible. Christianity is what it is only through this act, namely the individual appropriation of the remembered Jesus as a picture of the act of faith. This reception is an act of interpretation and new creation, which leads to its relation to Jesus Christ.[36]

Tillich clearly distinguishes two meanings in the concept of the historical Jesus. On the one hand, the term 'historical Jesus' is defined as the result of

---

[33] Tillich, 98. "If theology ignores the fact to which the name of Jesus of Nazareth points, it ignores the basic Christian assertion that Essential God-Manhood has appeared within existence and subjected itself to the conditions of existence without being conquered by them."

[34] Tillich, 97. "Christianity was born, not with the birth of the man who is called 'Jesus,' but in the moment in which one of his followers was driven to say to him, 'Thou are the Christ.'"

[35] James D.G. Dunn, "Remembering Jesus: How the Quest of the Historical Jesus Lost Its Way" in *The Historical Jesus: Five Views*, eds. James K. Beilby and Paul Rhodes Eddy (Downers Grove: IVP Academic, 2009), 199-225.

[36] Tillich, *Systematic Theology*, vol. 2, 100. "Corresponding to this beginning, the end is the moment in which the continuity of that history in which Jesus as the Christ is the center is definitely broken."

historical research. Historical knowledge, however, is not simply a contemporary construction. It is also ever "fragmentary and hypothetical."[37] In this sense the term 'historical Jesus' is a methodological construct. Yet, there is another meaning of the term 'historical Jesus' that differs from this conceptual usage. Here the term is used as "the factual element in the Christian event."[38] This is very different from the first sense used in historical research. As an element in the interrelation in which the Christian faith is composed, the term 'historical Jesus' doesn't mean the man from Nazareth behind the sources of the New Testament. Rather the term refers to the personal act in which the faith consists, and which occurs in history. Tillich's distinction between the two meanings of the 'historical Jesus' is very helpful for contemporary Christological debates. Historical research is important for an understanding of the history of the Christian religion, its sources, and their relation to the ancient Judaism, but historical research gives us no foundation for the Christian faith. The questions of historical research and Christology are not identical but are, rather, two independent questions. The picture of faith from its own history is, we might say, not only different from the image of Jesus as history, but also the picture of faith independent from history. While there are interrelations between both dimensions, faith "cannot even guarantee the name 'Jesus' in respect to him who was the Christ."[39]

What follows is that faith has its foundation not in the historical Jesus as a result of historical research, but in an historical event. This is only momentarily a paradox, because the historical event means that faith arises without historical foundations in history. Tillich's main thesis is that faith has its foundation and its worth in itself. "And the inevitable answer is that faith can guarantee only its own foundation, namely, the appearance of that reality which has created the faith."[40] There is no ground or principle through which one could give a justification of faith as a personal act which has happened in history. But does that not mean that faith is its own creator and, in this sense, only another name for sin?[41] That's not the case, because faith is justified as a construction of the theological circle. All justifications of the Christian religion are circular. So the task of theology is not to give reasons for faith, but

---

[37] Tillich, 107. Cf. Tillich, "The Significance of the Historical Jesus for the Christian Faith", EW XIX, 317.

[38] Tillich, *Systematic Theology*, vol. 2, 107.

[39] Tillich, 107

[40] Tillich, 114.

[41] Wolfhart Pannenberg criticizes such a construction of the Christian faith in Wolfhart Pannenberg, *Systematic Theology*, vol. 3 (Göttingen: Vandenhoeck & Ruprecht, 1993), 175.

rather to explicate the theological circle. Christology gives no reason for faith but interprets the event of faith. The doctrine of Jesus the Christ is not a *content* of faith. Rather, Christology has a reflexive function for faith, namely, to give a description of the structure of the act which faith is. This is what is meant when Tillich calls Jesus as the Christ a real picture of faith.

Tillich connects, in the *Systematic Theology,* his Christology with soteriology.[42] This is not really surprising because the Christology is an expression of the act of faith that is at the same time salvation. But what exactly expresses the Christology if it is a description of the act of faith? Even in his early writing from the late 1920s, Tillich named the reality of faith the "new being."[43] The "new being" in history is a happening in the human consciousness which finds its representation in the picture of Jesus as the Christ. In this event the consciousness becomes aware that the unconditioned is the ground, abyss, and presupposition of all acts of human consciousness. Tillich always defined this reflexive disclosure of the human consciousness as "religion" or the breakthrough of the unconditioned. It's the basis for all conscious acts in culture. Religion designates with its forms the breakthrough of the unconditioned. On the one hand, it's only possible by using cultural forms to designate the awareness that the unconditioned is a presupposition in the consciousness. But on the other hand, every cultural form is at the same time wrong and must be denied. It is exactly this, the position and the negation of form, which is the content of the picture of Jesus as the Christ. He represents a concrete personal life that negates his own life. Only in this act is Jesus the Christ or the final revelation.[44] Jesus as the Christ is a picture of the faith and the reflexive structure of the act of faith. The content of the true religion is the negation of the content. Tillich calls this content final revelation or salvation-revelation because it conquers both demonization and profanation of religion.

Christology describes the reflexive structure of the act of faith. Therefore, Tillich focused his Christology on the cross and the resurrection of the Christ.[45] Cross and resurrection are on both sides of the act of faith, namely

---

[42] Tillich, *Systematic Theology*, vol. 2, 150. "Christology is a function of soteriology. The problem of soteriology creates the Christological question and gives direction to the Christological answer."

[43] Paul Tillich, "Die Gestalt der religiösen Erkenntnis," in *Dogmatik-Vorlesung* (Dresden 1925-1927), ed. Erdmann Sturm (Berlin/New York: de Gruyter, 2005) EW XIV, 428-29.

[44] Tillich, *Systematic Theology*, vol. 1, 134. "Jesus is the religious and theological object as the Christ and only as the Christ. And he is the Christ as the one who sacrifices what is merely 'Jesus' in him. The decisive trait in his picture is the continuous self-surrender of Jesus who is Jesus to Jesus who is the Christ."

[45] Tillich, *Systematic Theology*, vol. 2, 150-65.

the negation of the form and the affirmation of the form. In this dialectic of critique and formation, which constitutes the act of faith as a reflexive consciousness in the awareness of the unconditioned, lies the realization of true religion in history. In short, Jesus as the Christ is the real picture of the faith.

Christology had a reflexive function and doesn't deal with a historical content or person. The doctrine of Jesus as the Christ is a theological description of the act of faith as a happening in history. To this extent, Christology has a reflexive function of a critique of religion within religion.

The Significance of Tillich's Christology for the Contemporary Christological Debates

As we have seen, Paul Tillich works out his Christology as a theological description of the act of faith. The historical background of Tillich's doctrine of the Christ are the debates in the first half of the twentieth century, especially the historical Jesus research on the one hand, and the Christological debates in Protestant theology on the other hand. One could say that Tillich's Christology is a child of his own time. But what is significant about Tillich's Christology for the debates of the twenty-first century? There are two aspects of his Christological conception that are significant for a Christology in our time.

The first is his starting point: the theological circle. The second is what follows from this regarding the debates about a theology of religions. Tillich proceeds from a conception of religion as a breakthrough of the unconditioned in the human consciousness. But this is a presupposition that is not at all plausible today. In contrast to Tillich we must reject a general concept of religion and work out religion as communication.[46] Religion is not an essential part of human being. Rather, religion is an extension of being human, a particular form of communication in culture which is not strictly necessary for being human. Religion is contingent on history and underlies an evolution in culture. Religion is an interpretation of the world in symbolic forms and the knowledge of religion must be a part of religion. There is no unconscious religion. Tillich's presupposition of religion is inadequate in a pluralistic world. However, Tillich's Christology can still be relevant in the context of a new understanding of religion as communication. First, we must deal with his formula for the Christian event as both factum and reception, and then with the implications of this formula for a theology of religions.

Tillich presupposes the historical Jesus research from the first half of the twentieth century. In his time historical research stood in the shadow of the

[46] Christian Danz, *Gottes Geist: Eine Pneumatologie* (Tübingen: Mohr Siebeck, 2019).

so-called form-history, and the general opinion was that there could be no certain knowledge about the historical Jesus.[47] Further development in historical research, especially in the so-called third quest since the 1980s, leads to a methodological change. On the one hand it becomes clear that the historical Jesus is a methodological construct of science, and on the other hand that it is not possible to go behind the sources in a methodological way. Today, the historical Jesus behind the sources is no longer the aim of the historical research, but rather the remembered Jesus in the sources.[48] Memory is always a construction of the past and not merely a photographic record.[49] That means we could only uncover the interrelation between Jesus and his followers, but not a Jesus for himself. This is the remembered Jesus.[50]

The third quest for the historical Jesus is not unlike Tillich's initial formulation of Christology. Both begin with an interrelation between fact and believing reception. Christology deals neither with a historical Jesus that stands behind the interpretations of his followers, nor simply with these interpretations alone. Historical Jesus research is different from the task of Christology. The first deals with history, while the second deals with the actual Christian faith and explains its structure. This is why Tillich distinguishes two meanings of the term 'historical Jesus.' The historical Jesus as a historical question is a construct of science, but as such it is not the basis or foundation of the Christian faith. The historical Jesus as an element of faith is understood quite differently. Jesus exists as Christ only in and for the act of faith. So it is not merely the remembered Jesus that constitutes the act of faith, but only the religious *use* of the memory of Jesus Christ as expression of the Christian religion. Therefore, Tillich's Christology is important for the contemporary debates because his conception could be connected with the historical Jesus research of the third quest and its methodological program of the remembered

---

[47] See the overview about the historical Jesus research by Paul Rhodes Eddy and James K. Belby, "The Quest for the Historical Jesus: An Introduction," in *The Historical Jesus: Five Views*, eds. Paul Rhodes Eddy and James K. Belby (Downers Grove: IVP Academic, 2009), 9-54.

[48] See, for example, James D.G. Dunn, and in Germany, the New Testament scholar Jens Schröter.

[49] Jan Assmann, *Das kulturelle Gedächtnis. Schrift, Erinnerung und politische Identität in den frühen Hochkulturen* (München: Beck, 2013).

[50] Dunn, "Remembering Jesus", 203. "The fact that Jesus made disciples is generally recognized. What has not been given sufficient recognition or weight, however, is the effect of his impact. These disciples encountered Jesus as a life-transforming experience: they followed him;...Why? Because they had believed Jesus and what he said and taught."

Jesus. His Christology allows for a theological interpretation of the remembered Jesus of historical research.

There is yet another aspect in Tillich's Christology that is significant for contemporary debates, namely his construction of Christology as a reflexive description of the act of faith. Jesus is only in and for the act of faith as the Christ. One could say Jesus is the origin of faith in the Christian religion and is not an assumption outside of the Christian religion. This has consequences for a theology of religions. Contemporary debates about theology of religions, and especially so-called pluralistic theology, demand a reduction of Christology. If Jesus as the Christ is the one and only incarnation of God as objective historical fact, then all other religions are wrong. Contemporary pluralistic theology argues that in traditional Christology there is no recognition of the possibility of other religions.[51] Therefore, the doctrine of the Christ must be reduced. Jesus Christ is like other religious heroes: an appearance of the absolute Real, but neither identical with the Real nor the only one who manifests the absolute. The pluralistic model is not only a realistic approach, naming Jesus as historical person and content of Christology, but also a general concept of religion that reduces religious diversity.[52] Thus, pluralistic theology envisions the equality of the world-religions in the dimension of theology differently than each particular religion. Such a model neither explains how religions function nor recognizes the distinctiveness of concrete religions. All religions are fundamentally the same.

Against the pluralistic model of a theology of religions we must explain how religions function, and also how religions legitimately differ from each other. It here that Tillich's understanding of the Christian event as fact and reception is most significant. It allows us to reject a general concept of religion that assumes religion is intrinsic to being human, and at the same time explain the distinctiveness of Christianity in contrast with other religions. The peculiarity of the Christian religion lies in Christology.[53] Yet the doctrine of the Christ is neither a *content* of the Christian religion, nor is Christology related to other religions. Christology is a picture of the Christian faith for Tillich. Christian religion describes its distinctiveness, namely that the individual appropriation of God is a part or an element of the understanding of God.

[51] John Hick, *An Interpretation of Religion: Human Responses to the Transcendent* (New Haven: Yale University Press, 1989); Perry Schmidt-Leukel, "Religious Pluralism & Interreligious Theology" in *The Gifford Lectures – An Extended Edition* (New York: Orbis, 2017), 26-7.

[52] Hick, *An Interpretation of Religion*, 235-36.

[53] Christian Danz, *Grundprobleme der Christologie* (Tübingen: Mohr Siebeck, 2013), 223-40.

Christology has a function for the description of religion in Christianity and doesn't refer to a historical person. Jesus as a man of history is both a part of ancient Jewish and Christian religion. Only, in the latter, he is the Christ. This significant insight of Tillich's Christology opens a new perspective on the contemporary debates of Christology in the age of religious pluralism. It allows recognition of other religions as distinct religions and explains the distinctiveness of the Christian religion.

Recovering Community: Living Beyond the Symbolic God

Daniel Boscaljon

By defining God as Ultimate Concern, Paul Tillich invited thinkers from culturally marginalized populations to use theological language in ways that provided new symbols of meaning. James Cone, Mary Daly, and other theologians directly influenced by Tillich have examined how contemporary communities symbolize God and how new symbols of God might offer an escape from socio-historically determined circumstances or, at the very least, provide hope for individuals in communities characterized by despair. This produced a panoply of theologies—including disability and queer theologies—that provide compassionate ways to explore meaning among those marginalized within mainstream society. This empowers the marginalized to develop new and nuanced models and ideas of the Gods symbolized within those communities.

This chapter focuses on a marginalized community that has remained underexplored by theologians: addicts. Addiction emerges from the confluence of a capitalist marketplace that profits on consumption and a series of oppressive, traumatic social conditions. It is an increasingly serious fact of life in America. A theological humanism that reckons with addiction provides more widespread and meaningful modes of empowered recovery.

Additionally, a theology anchored in the human suffering caused by addiction opens a new understanding of what God might mean. To argue this, I begin by contrasting *religious* symbols with *theological* symbols within Tillich's theology. I then explore communities that self-organize around twelve-step recovery programs and describe how Tillich's theology accounts for their success. Finally, I describe how the anonymous "higher power" in twelve-step groups operates as a *theological* symbol, allowing the presence of an anonymous Community to serve as a secular, non-hierarchical analogue of the Kingdom of God.

Symbolic Modes of Theology

Tillich's *The Courage to Be* contrasts two overlapping ways that humans interact with God. God is typically received through faith in a religious symbol that anchors a community. The alternative mode of experiencing God—absolute faith—arises in being grasped by the God beyond gods. This is an experience of the power of being-itself unmediated by language, symbol, cult, or concept. Such liminal experiences are difficult to intend or to describe, which is why interactions with God generally work through symbols.[1] Tillich distinguishes six qualities that allow symbols to express ultimacy:

> Like signs, symbols point beyond themselves but cannot be replaced.
> Symbols participate in that which it points.
> They open a level of reality otherwise closed to us.
> They unlock a corresponding dimension of the soul.
> They cannot be produced intentionally.
> They age, grow old and die.[2]

Religious symbols, predicated in specific narratives and rituals that transcend cultural moments as well as concrete elements that remain tied to historical situations, introduce humans into non-temporal spaces of meaning. Rather than being limited to resolving questions constrained within a contemporary moment, religious symbols are both anchored in finite, historical conditions and equally fixed in a non-historical potentiality toward which participants in that community are directed.

Not all symbols are ultimate. Cultural symbols, like those spawned by sports teams or political parties, create communities of interest in which individuals can participate and feel some larger sense of corresponding meaning and corresponding dimensions of reality otherwise closed. Cultural symbols are natural human productions and are only destructive (idolatrous) when humans treat them as ultimate. Determining how their respective communities relate to time distinguishes religious from cultural groups. Social groups anchored in cultural symbols tend to follow narratives predicated on causal logic, from a determined past into a certain future, while religious communities focus on the "presentness" of an eternal that interrupts the temporal structure.

Theological symbols go beyond religious symbols by symbolizing the way that religious symbols function. For Tillich, the Cross was an important *theological* symbol insofar as it represented the Protestant Principle. It symbolized both ultimacy *and* incompleteness or lack of ultimacy.[3]

---

[1] Paul Tillich, *The Courage to Be* (New Haven: Yale University Press, 1980), 186-87.

[2] Paul Tillich, *Dynamics of Faith* (New York: Harper & Row, 1958), 42-43.

[3] Tillich, *Dynamics*, 96-98.

Cultural theologies interpret these levels of symbols even if Tillich is not directly named. Thus, Tillich's thinking can be summarized and deployed as a general heuristic to identify commonalities that connect cultural theological approaches:

The theologies speak to a social issue created by a culture that exercises its dominance and an affected community that comes into being as particularly aggrieved by that issue.

Christianity is reinterpreted through a lens that articulates a future in which that issue no longer harms the affected community. In particular, the figure of the Christ is reconceived as a vision of an "impossible" future that is freed from the kinds of sin exacerbated by the social forces that disenfranchise and destroy the lives of the groups in question.

The theological symbol becomes a mirror that fuses the oppressive and restrictive dimensions of the affected community, in which the general human conditions of finitude are exacerbated by external social forces, with a vision of the world in which these factors are overcome. This is true whether Christ is shown as impoverished, as militant, or as dead.

The reconstitution of a theological symbol (or alteration of an extant symbol to reflect a specific community) is necessary to allow marginalized communities to see themselves when they feel excluded from the Kingdom of God. It also allows a new sense of God to emerge relative to the communities that come into being as a result of the symbol. While a symbol's life remains tied to a community and while theological symbols cannot be "created," the ways theological symbols are *deployed* reflect the finite, historical situations of their communities. Mary Daly argues that a symbol that does *not* engage in this kind of reflection is largely irrelevant.[4]

The Symbolic Dimensions of Addiction

Americans tend to assign addiction into a space between crime and disease, often using race or class to declare the first and diagnose the second. Addiction, however, cuts through all other kinds of identity markers ("white"/"non-white," rich/poor, queer/straight, Christian/Jew, educated/ignorant) to create a group continually at risk. As the pharmaceutical industry expanded opioid addiction to white homes, the problem has gained renewed attention from mainstream media outlets. Addiction rates are chronically underreported, but twelve-step programs now are estimated to serve over one million Americans

[4] Mary Daly, *Beyond God the Father* (London: Women's Press, 1995), 19-33.

yearly, divided into roughly sixty thousand groups focused on over three hundred kinds of addictions and psychological disorders.[5]

Addictive behaviors operate like secular analogues of religious belief. The object of addiction (alcohol, heroin, marijuana) points beyond itself to the experience of a "high" but, like a religious symbol, are instrumental in mediating the experience. Objects of addiction participate in that to which they point even at a biochemical level and open up a level of reality that is otherwise closed.[6] Moreover, the fetishization and celebration of objects of addiction, glamorizing even the tragedies that they invite, suggests that such objects acquire the symbolic depth of non-intentional production. As the object of choice vacillates relative to cultural trends, one can see the drugs that symbolize addiction aging and dying.[7] American culture generally has at least one object of addiction that symbolizes all others (alcohol in the 20s, cocaine in the 80s, meth in the early 00s, opioids at present), keeping a structured space for the symbol of addiction to be continually reborn. While these drugs may symbolize "addiction" at a social level, actual use is non-symbolic: being "high" offers a direct *experience of*, rather than a mediated *encounter with*, ultimacy.

Religious symbols provide structure and vocabulary to order daily life and describe God's presence. In a secular world, addictions provide one secular alternative to religious symbols. They provide users with a sense of daily ritual, common vocabulary, and experiences that interrupt the banality of ordinary time in the everyday world. Generally, objects of addiction are encountered and embraced in communal spaces alongside others who normalize the behavior. Most stories of addiction, before describing individual isolation, are marked by large social scenes. What becomes an object of addiction is often initially encountered in a liminal space of celebration (as enhancement) or mourning (as consolation). These are times when overindulgence is deemed socially acceptable.

---

[5] Jake Flanagin, "The Surprising Failures of 12 Steps," *The Atlantic*, March 25, 2014, https://www.theatlantic.com/health/archive/2014/03/the-surprising-failures-of-12-steps/284616/.

[6] Beyond even psychotropic drugs that allow for a "trip" to another level of reality (e.g. LSD, DMT, peyote, etc.), legal drugs such as alcohol or marijuana also provide users with enhanced or altered experiences of reality that were previously closed.

[7] Addictions themselves are not intentionally created. See Leslie Jamison, *The Recovering* (New York: Back Bay Books, 2018), 121. "Stories of addiction are full of this insistence that addiction can't be fully explained...In resisting definitive explanations, [stories] testify to the way addiction creates its own momentum, its own logic...the ways it can seem autonomous and untethered, born of itself. ...There is no simple key to turn the lock of *why*."

Like an ultimate concern, addictions organize experience around a central modality. As J. Jeremy Wisnewski states in his phenomenological account of addiction, "every other care and concern is subordinated to a central obsession: consumption of the object of addiction...the intelligibility of other things becomes indexed to what one craves."[8] Leslie Jamison corroborates: "my whole life [contracted] around booze: not just the hours I spent drinking, but the hours I spent anticipating drinking, regretting drinking, apologizing for drinking, figuring out when and how to drink again."[9]

The language of addiction is honest about its capacity to induce a limited, temporary sense of ultimacy through an ecstatic "high," and the eventual lack of ultimacy as the "high" is unsustainable. There's nothing idolatrous about the object of addiction, which is shorn of any pretense of universality beyond the diminishing experience of the high. Objects of addiction allow access to a different experience but remain grounded in the matrix of desire from which they emerge. Eventually, as tolerance builds, the addict's craving transitions from a desire for a high to a desire to avoid withdrawal. It becomes a desire for a semblance of normality. In Tillichian language, objects of addiction anchor addicts to a ground of non-being, the experience of negation, loss, and finitude, rather than the experience of Being-itself.

The desire to *control suffering* beats at the heart of addiction. A similar aversion to feeling pain motivates prayer and other forms of interacting with religious symbols. Whether one was introduced to an object of addiction through a desire to escape in the thrill of a "high" or through a desire to temporarily suspend trauma is unimportant. Until it becomes a problem that defines one's life, an ultimate concern, addictions are the means to control and/or avoid all other problems.

The Symbolically Mediated Community of Recovery

Tillich's description of religious symbols helps explain the power that objects of addiction can wield. It is not surprising, then, that twelve-step communities function as thinly secularized Christianity that substitutes a "higher power" for the "destructive power" of the object of addiction. The feeling of helplessness is an existential experience. These communities have their own version of sacred text and rituals that are constituted and reconstituted based on the needs and personalities of organizers, regulars, and occasional visitors.

---

[8] J. Jeremy Wisnewski, "Being Powerless to Change," in *Sobering Wisdom*, eds. Jerome A. Miller and Nicholas Plants (Charlottesville: University of Virginia Press, 2014), 22.

[9] Leslie Jamison, *The Recovering*, 112.

The first three steps, written in the first-person plural, presume a sense of community that persons join by virtue of repeating the phrases. Each repetition recreates a moment of initiation into the group, similar to the Christian rite of communion.[10]

> We are powerless over alcohol and our lives have become unmanageable.
> We believe that a Power greater than ourselves can restore us to sanity.
> We decide to turn our will and our lives over to the care of God as we understand Him.

This "God," a "Him," is a bland but beneficent "power" that replaces the destructive object of addiction. The second step provides hope for restoration rather than any definitive sense that this has happened or will happen. The third step emphasizes *decision* but suggests that, at most, one can choose a central entity that remains beyond one's control but offers a sense of *consolation* that is at least *something* in control. The decision made in step three will restore one to a life that becomes managed. This *power* is *anonymous*, shorn of the Christian identity important to the founders and architects of twelve-step groups.[11] The more complex symbol of "God" from religious tradition is converted into a purely functional, utilitarian role that offers possibility without making promises and the consolations of control within a mythology of re-creation.

This God does *nothing*. Even its existence is unnecessary. It serves as a placeholder, the site of something that "we" came to believe. Lives are turned over to this God, who receives admissions of moral failure. The group is ready to "have God remove" defects of character. Participants "humbly ask God remove our shortcomings." God remains an object of contemplation, but without any mechanism of external salvation. Thus, for twelve-step groups, God (as a shared site or symbol of belief) becomes "something" *greater than* each

[10] Different groups will adjust the wording as needed, changing the language of "alcohol," "sanity," and/or "God" based on the particular needs of the group.

[11] In particular, founder Bill Wilson was inspired by The Oxford Group and its American spokesperson, Samuel Moor Shoemaker, Jr. This group, formed in the 20s as a response to dwindling participation in official churches, had six principles that Wilson explicitly found useful in creating AA. Also notable is Wilson's equally explicit decision to secularize the language of the twelve steps in order to make them available to atheists and agnostics. Ron and Valeria Halvorson, "The Twelve Steps and Their Relationship to Christianity," in *Living Free* (Curtis: RPI Publishing, 1992), accessed through The National Association of Christian Recovery at https://www.nacr.org/living-free/chapter-2-the-twelve-steps-and-their-relationship-to-christianity.

individual and the sum total of individuals within the group, but still does "nothing" more than "exist" as an anonymous name. In this way, the function of "God" in twelve-step programs is powerful even though its "God" remains inactive. It allows recovery groups to form communities around a central symbol of a Higher Power that is *actually* nothing,

Tillich's concept of symbols helps to explain why groups become meaningful for members. The community provides a ritualistic sense of repetition, return, and renewal around a higher power that recurs in religious traditions as well as in addictive behaviors. Most cities have multiple chapters of AA that meet throughout the day, every day. They mark anniversaries of sobriety, tell stories of struggles, and share wisdom. Testimonies refer to the cycle of life between meetings: a space of constant struggle in which one is never recovered but always in recovery. This recalls some Protestant visions of salvation, in which humans are sinful, constantly stray, and continually require the redeeming power of Christ.

Tillich's theological framework shows other important work undertaken by 12-step groups. Tillich's description of courage interprets life in and between meetings. Addicts can have the courage to be individually sober and part of a group. Every vocal contribution is simultaneously an expression of self and a way to identify with the group. Additionally, with its emphasis on the higher power, and the notion of "God as we understand Him," groups encourage people to work through issues of fate, guilt, and meaninglessness. Steps one through three, admitting powerlessness and turning over one's will and life to God, introduce members to the struggle between freedom and determination and the extent of one's responsibility. Steps four through nine work through the process of guilt and condemnation and the need to accept acceptance. The question of how to find meaning in meaninglessness is often the paradox at the heart of recovery. The object of addiction is an idol that simultaneously made life meaningful and unbearable.

The effectiveness of this mode of recovery shares the virtues and limitations of Tillichian religious symbols. Recovery groups *do* offer truly life changing support: gathering community is crucial for millions who struggle with various forms of addiction. Problematically, this *type* of functionality requires the diminution of human autonomy relative to a shared central symbol that maintains control. In groups, "God" or "Higher Power" fulfills the role that Tillich assigned to the Cross, as both a religious and theological symbol.

Twelve-step groups retain a longing for the consolation of divine providence, where everything is under control. The logic of overcoming and control, which is part of what phenomenologists have identified as ingredients to addiction, persists within even a secularized version of a symbolically mediated community.[12] Even if the "higher" power remains a convenient but effective fiction, it still provides believers with the consolation of being-determined by an external authority that remains in control.[13] The dialectically mediated sense of nothing that inheres within this secularized, symbolic god provides a notion of *a* "nothing" that is in control, but a nothing to which members cede their own sense of control. In this way, the god of twelve-step programs offers determinism without returning autonomy, the blank apotheosis of the human inability to control.

The Non-Symbolic World where Nothing is in Control

The secularized "Higher Power" can be reconstituted as a theological symbol freed from its function of consolation and control, especially as present within the *anonymity* central to recovery groups. Anonymity is not just a relational term: as a theological symbol it shows a vision of the world in which *no social force at all*—including the object of addiction—*is in control.* "Anonymity" offers a new theological vision for the Community that comes after the Kingdom of God.

Jane Bennett's *Vibrant Matter* is a particularly lucid guide to thinking about a world where *nothing* is in control. Her description of neo-materialism redefines how power and control operate in terms that are emergent, generative, and participatory. There is no depth in this world. There is no central symbol, governing plan, sense of above, "higher," or beyond. All things participate in this world with different degrees of strength relative to particular contexts. As Bennett puts it in the introduction, her perspective frames the world "on a less vertical plane than is common."[14]

Bennett's exploration of alternate materialisms and vital forces, anchored in a Spinoza-like sensibility, imagines how humans can participate in our environments with a limited, finite sense control. Describing the power in "mere" matter, Bennett offers an alternative to a "higher" power to supplement human agency. Instead of a God, *distributive* events occur through the combined participation of varied actors, and *emergent* causalities have no clear

---

[12] Jerome A. Miller, "Addiction and Tears," in *Sobering Wisdom*, eds. Jerome A. Miller and Nicholas Plants (Charlottesville: University of Virginia Press, 2014), 53-64.

[13] Paul Ricoeur, "Religion, Atheism, and Faith," in *Conflict of Interpretation* (Evanston: Northwestern University Press, 2007). Ricoeur describes our cultural situation in terms of Nietzschean nihilism in ways that correlate with Tillich's existential awareness of the crisis of meaninglessness. However, Ricoeur would purge any particularization of God after the critiques of atheism.

[14] Jane Bennett, *Vibrant Matter* (Durham: Duke University Press, 2010), ix.

point of origin. There is no *higher power*. No one thing, no thing, nothing is in control.[15]

"Distributive" agency opens up a world of assemblages in which simple bodies have only the power of stubbornness or inertia, and complex bodies retain their specific relation of movement and rest in relation to other entities....An assemblage entails "ad hoc groupings of diverse elements, of vibrant materials of all sorts."[16] For example, the electric grid is an assemblage of a "volatile mix of coal, sweat, electromagnetic fields, computer programs, electron streams, profit motives, heat, lifestyles, nuclear fuel, fantasies of mastery, static, legislation, water, economic theory, wire, and wood" in which no single one entity has the power to *control*. Power is distributed among vibrant materials. Because power is distributed among vibrant materials, things happen without any "power" intending or controlling them. [17]

Bennett provides the framework for understanding how questions of addiction do not actually hinge on willpower or intentionality. While Bennett does not explore the particularities of chemical addiction to substances (her account discusses our relation to food), scientific accounts show that the operational relationship would be far more nuanced and complex. The following is an example of how new materialism shows how one might be powerless over an object of addiction and allow no thing to take control instead:

> [The brain] can be seen as material flow...part of the assembly of addiction (its emergent objects, technologies, publics) and its particular logics of agency and belonging...its operations cannot be prejudged or neatly circumscribed. Instead, these operations are dependent on its enmeshment in whole bodies, in social relationships, policy and legislative entities, and beliefs. In this way, no claims can be made based on 'the' brain, and no responses can target the brain alone. In turn, the social and political processes that indivisibly give drug use and addiction shape, meaning and effects cannot be marginalized or downplayed, as is so common in addiction as 'brain disease' approaches. Likewise, no stable formulation of the brain and its action can be constituted in the service of a common world. The brain may still figure in public debate, but not as an autono-

---

[15] Bennett, 28-29. Bennett offers an overview of Kant and Augustine, who both posit the will as something vexed, to clarify the problem with assuming the efficacy of intentionality.

[16] Bennett, 23.

[17] Bennett, 25.

> mous delegate seeking inclusion rather as a liminal material entanglement. Put simply, 'the brain' cannot be cited here as the independent source, site or outcome of any activity or event.[18]

In addition to whatever biochemical factors create addictive relationships, other factors such as politics, economics, etc. are also contributors. The "I" of an addict is not necessarily even an operator (or relatively influential actor) within the larger, impersonal schema of competing powerful forces.

Nothing as a Theological Symbol

Tillich speaks about "nothing" as a theological experience when discussing the God beyond the God of theism and how absolute faith emerges when one is grasped by this god. Unlike symbolically mediated faith, absolute faith "never is something separated and definite, an event which could be isolated and described," nor is it "a place where one can live, it is without the safety of words and concepts," because "it is without a name, a church, a cult, a theology." At the same time, one can sense it "when traditional symbols…have lost their power" to combat anxieties of fate and guilt. Most importantly, however, Tillich adds that this God appears in the face of meaninglessness:

> The courage to take the anxiety of meaninglessness upon oneself is the boundary line up to which the courage to be can go. Beyond it is mere non-being. Within it all forms of courage are re-established in the power of the God above the God of theism. The courage to be is rooted in the God who appears when God has disappeared in the anxiety of doubt.[19]

From a Tillichian perspective, the experience of nothing transforms into a powerful expression of absolute faith. Often, addictions make confronting anxieties of death, guilt, and meaninglessness a regular occurrence.

Thomas J. J. Altizer and John Caputo provide theological possibilities for an anonymous god—the god after the god who disappears—that use *anonymity*, rather than the *cross*, as a theological symbol for Tillich's second god, experienced as nothing. Both of these theological visions are compatible with Bennett's decentralized worldview, which allows this god to be nameless and nothing, not in control.

---

[18] Suzanne Fraser, Kylie Valentine, and Mats Ekendahl, "Drugs, Brains and Other Subalterns: Public Debate and the New Materialist Politics of Addiction," *Body & Society* 24, no. 4 (2018): 58–86, https://doi.org/10.1177/1357034X18781738.

[19] Tillich, *Courage*, 190.

John Caputo's "Weak Theology" begins by contrasting *name* and *event*. Caputo argues that *names* "are historically constituted or constructed" and can "accumulate historical power and worldly prestige." In other words, names function as symbols that anchor conceptual constellations whose preservation of the past obscures the kind of openness that it wishes to introduce to being. Caputo's alternative to name is *event*, which reflects the "uncontainable and unconditional." Caputo argues: "An event refers neither to a being or entity nor to being itself, but to an impulse or aspiration simmering within both the names of entities and the name of being, something that groans to be born...an event is...a distance within the heart of being, within the names for being, that makes being restless."[20] An event is unnamed, anonymous, with no *thing* presenting itself as a symbol—it involves a shift in how the present organizes itself, or in how we perceive its organization.

Tom Altizer reaches similar conclusions, allowing namelessness to become the hinge connecting the existential and the ontological. Like the *event*, Altizer's *anonymous* provides a point of view made possible only after one displaces the kind of symbolic god favored by Tillich and twelve-step recovery programs. The result provides an immanent theological worldview consistent with Bennett's discussion of distributive causality and the work of assemblages. Altizer writes that

> anonymity does name God, and it names God if only because it embodies a total presence, and a presence which we can not only actually see, but can see only because we can no longer see or envision what we once named as God. Just as a purely anonymous vision is impossible apart from the loss or dissolution of an interior and immanent center, so likewise is it impossible apart from the loss or reversal of a transcendent ground or center.[21]

A symbol cannot have a *total presence*. Its appearance is always limited by a sense of identity and difference. Names would limit a total presence and restrict its restless activity. Seeing this total presence requires relinquishing the consolation that would allow a personal relationship with this thing.

At least one recovering addict understands the higher power in this sort of way. Leslie Jamison distinguishes her first time of sobriety from her second. She describes the "Higher Power" as "simply *not me*. ...It was a force animating the world in all of its particular glories: jellyfish, the clean turn of line

[20] John Caputo, *The Weakness of God: A Theology of the Event* (Bloomington: Indiana University Press, 2008), 5.

[21] Thomas J. J. Altizer, *Total Presence: The Language of Jesus and the Language of Today* (New York: Seabury Press, 1980), 35-36.

breaks, pineapple upside-down cake, my friend Rachel's laughter." It becomes an assemblage: "God wasn't faceless omnipotence but proximate particulars, grout and soap—the things that had always been there, right in front of me."[22] This sense of god as nothing in particular, the wholeness that animates the trivial particularities that we overlook, is not a powerful god. It is an anonymous God.

Anonymous Assemblages and the Community of God

A theological symbol summons a new sense of God alongside an emergent community. The resulting "Kingdom of God" symbolizes this ideal way of organizing relationships between humans and their world. Entering this community requires that people reconfigure their foundational understanding of the world. Thus, for Altizer, eschatology is negative as well as positive as it erases what pre-exists it:

> The Kingdom of God is fully present, yes, but its presence effects a full negation of everything which otherwise stands forth as world… the redemption of the world is simultaneously the end of the world.[23]

Altizer argues that Jesus' parables make distinctions such as "here" or "there" that distract from the actual full presence of the Kingdom of God. Faith in a transcendent God also does this. A total presence is immanent. It *is*.

Caputo argues that the world "stands for the business as usual of the powerful…the oppressive order of presence…while the Kingdom contradicts the world, which means that it calls for something contrary to the world."[24] Rather than a transcendent view of God put in terms of a Sovereign Good, Caputo invites us to think of "God" as an event of "solicitation, an event of deconsolidation, an electrifying event-ing disturbance."[25] Oppressive power structures depend on hierarchical forms of symbols. Caputo's Kingdom interrupts centralized power and restores a sense of equality.

Bennett's discussion of emergent publics provides an account of a Community that merges these theological visions without relying on God. This iteration of an assemblage contains a version of total presence without immanence, and a vision of interruption and contradiction. She writes:

---

[22] Jamison, *The Recovering*, 304.

[23] Altizer, *Total Presence*, 48

[24] Caputo, *The Weakness of God*, 37.

[25] Caputo, 39.

> A public is a cluster of bodies harmed by the actions of others or even by actions born from their own actions as these trans-act; harmed bodies draw near each other and seek to engage in new acts that will restore their power, protect against future harm, or compensate for damage done—in *that* constitutes their political action, which, fortunately or unfortunately, will also become conjoint action with a chain of indirect, unpredictable consequences.[26]

The human bodies involved in this public, whose autonomy is already circumscribed by the other actants that stimulate, depress, and otherwise affect it, are collected not by a symbol of strength, but by a sense of shared harm. Coming together occurs as an opportunity for new behaviors that may look different for different individuals. Nothing defines or compels this collective. Publics are always contingent, always in flux, and always engaged in negotiations. There's no hierarchy and no central authority or power. Publics are collections of beings, some of whom are aware that they participate in a larger pattern.

Like an assemblage, publics are neither caused nor circumscribed by intentionality. They emerge from a generative field. They are neither summoned nor governed by a symbol, they are not held together by a strong force, but they remain theological. A theological symbol operates in such publics: they are similar to what Tillich, Caputo, and Altizer called the "Kingdom of God" even if they remain indifferent to a vision of "God" and resist the hierarchy of a "Kingdom." It persists as "Community (of God)," an impersonal "life" present only within the bodies of what is assembled as a total presence. The totality of anonymity humbles the individual, now integrated into the larger Community. Entering this Community requires that one relinquish a need for an entity that controls and thus embrace the uncertainty of an event that provides a different view of both God and addiction.

Jamison demonstrates this sense of impersonal Community throughout *The Recovering*, as she integrates her own story of sobriety relative to those of famous authors who struggled with addiction. Jamison writes:

> The obsession I'd described was exactly what she'd felt…it was what a million other people had felt, too. It wasn't anything original, our yearning—and our conversation wasn't original either. I could have been anyone, and she could have been anyone…It wasn't new, our talk. It was just new for us.[27]

---

[26] Bennett, *Vibrant Matter*, 101.
[27] Jamison, *The Recovering*, 402.

In part, this interchangeability functions through the logic of AA's Big Book in which the second person "you" becomes the first person plural, "we," encompassing the variety of individual selves as well as the stories of all addicts, "which effectively turned assumptions into collective confessions," as Jamison puts it—"you were supposed to relinquish your ego by authoring a story in which you also starred."[28]

Within this emergent collective, this anonymous public, addicts and those who care about addicts are able to find the courage of participation, retaining an *impersonal* sense of identity within a shared sense of human fallibility and suffering. This notion of the impersonal is opened in the wordless moment of understanding that someone's story matches your own. Stories of recovery are as diverse as addictions. They do not attend to the kinds of divisions maintained by central symbols of power in a hierarchical culture but upend and upset them.

Once symbols of control have shattered, this impersonal Community overcomes the anxieties of fate, guilt, and meaninglessness that cripple those in recovery. It emerges, like a public, as a response to harmful actions. The Community interrupts the legal apparatus of policing and incarceration that isolates and criminalizes certain forms of addiction, as well as the economic and medical apparatus that thrives on the assumption of broken lives. This Community takes things a day at a time, but it doesn't take things personally. It keeps trudging on through the monotony. Anonymity, as a theological symbol that does not depend on centralization, finally allows for a reorganized perspective of recovering that echoes how Jamison concludes her book: "It's not just a question of policy, but a question of radically restructuring how we think about addicts as villains…worthy only of punishment. It's not just about compassion, but pragmatism: What will help people get better? It's about adjusting our vision."[29]

[28] Jamison, *313*.
[29] Jamison, 452.

New Materiality, Spirituality, and Leadership

Jari Ristiniemi

Meteorologist Allan Pounds, observing the changing fauna in Amazonas since the beginning of 1980s, claims that today's world needs "spiritual leaders who are able to show the way."[1] During the last two decades conceptions of spiritual leadership have been appearing in leadership literature.[2] Goleman, Boyatzis, and McKee claim that many leaders "bring to their work life the thoughtful mode of self-reflection that they cultivate in their spiritual lives."[3] Today we find "spiritualized Feminism", and different forms of "Artivism" where art is used as means for social, cultural, and environmental change.[4] More and more activists, cultural and political thinkers, philosophers, and theologians have turned to Gilles Deleuze, Félix Guattari, and Michel Foucault, following them into new materiality and radical immanence.[5] Michel Foucault suggested that the Iranian revolution at the end of 1970s might be

---

[1] Henrik Ennart, "Smarta kolibrin hotad i molnes regnskog," *Svenska Dagbladet*, December 13, 2015. My translation.

[2] Richard Bolden, Beverley Hawkins, Jonathan Gosling and Scott Taylor, *Exploring Leadership: Individual, Organizational and Societal Perspectives* (Oxford: Oxford University Press, 2012), 157ff; Gary Yukl, *Leadership in Organizations* (Boston: Pearson, 2013), 350; Lee G. Bolman and Terrence E. Deal, *Nya perspektiv på organisation och ledarskap*, (Lund: Studentlitteratur, 2015), 471; Lee G. Bolman and Terrence E. Deal, *Reframing Organizations: Artistry, Choice and Leadership*, (Hoboken: John Wiley and Sons Ltd, 2013).

[3] Daniel Goleman, Richard Boyatzis, and Annie McKee, *Primal Leadership: Unleashing the Power of Emotional Intelligence*, (Boston: Harvard Business Review Press, 2017), 40.

[4] Leela Fernandes, *Transforming Feminist Practice: Non-violence, Social Justice, and the Possibilities of a Spiritualized Feminism* (San Francisco: Aunt Lute Books, 2003); and Peter Weibel, *Global Activism: Art and Conflict in the 21st Century* (Cambridge: MIT Press, 2014).

[5] Considering the position of radical immanence, see Gilles Deleuze, *Pure Immanence: Essays on A Life* (New York: Zone Books, 2001); and Sharon Peebles Burch, "Response," in *Bulletin of the North American Paul Tillich Society* 44, no, 2 (2018): 11-14.

the birth of "a *political spirituality*."[6] Behrooz Ghamari-Tabrizi suggests that Foucault "gives spirituality a corporeal meaning."[7] One of the representatives of modern China, Jiang Shigong, proposes the synthesis between China's historical heritage, emphasizing the Confucian "Learning of the Heart," and "the Socialism with Chinese Characteristics," which would elevate "communism to a kind of ideal faith or a spiritual belief."[8] He also writes that communism "is also the highest ideal that will be absorbed into current political practice, a vibrant spiritual state. Communism is not only a beautiful future life, but is also, and more importantly, the spiritual state of Communist Party members in their practice of a political life."[9] He also says that the president of China, Xi Jinping, led his people through "a spiritual baptism" in his 2016 July 1 address.[10]

Western philosophy has separated the political from the spiritual for the past 500 years. That separation is being challenged today from many directions (political, environmental, and psychological to name a few). While our understanding of spirituality is diversifying, so also our understanding of materiality is broadening. In this essay I understand the *old* materialism as an ontologically reductive, closed, one-dimensional category: there is only matter and nothing else. *New* materiality means that the materiality of anything and the potentiality of anything are interwoven. There is interaction between matter and spirit. This is a shift in thought that Paul Tillich anticipated and encouraged. I understand spirit in the widest possible sense as value- and meaning-orientation that is congruent with self-awareness.[11] We become aware of our spiritual/material nature.

Since the idea of spiritual leadership is emerging in many disciplines, it is important to discuss what spirituality and spiritual leadership might be. I think we can explore this from two sources. First, we can discuss spirituality

---

[6] Janet Afary and Kevin B. Anderson, *Foucault and the Iranian Revolution: Gender and the Seductions of Islamism* (Chicago: The University of Chicago Press. 2005), 203ff.

[7] Quoted in Jeremy R. Garrette, "Prologues to a Confession of the Flesh," in *Religion and Culture: Michel Foucault* (New York: Routledge, 1999), 1.

[8] Jiang Shigong, "Philosophy and History: Interpreting the 'Xi Jinping Era' through Xi's Report to the Nineteenth National Congress of the CCP," Reading the China Dream, 2018, 21, accessed January 22, 2019, https://www.readingthechinadream.com/jiang-shigong-philosophy-and-history.html.

[9] Shigong, 21ff

[10] Shigong, 22.

[11] Tillich made a distinction between the human spirit and God's Spirit by capitalizing Spirit when it comes to God's Spirit. The main focus, initially, in this article is on the human spirit.

in the light of the new materiality, when spirituality has corporeal meaning. Second, we can discuss Paul Tillich's understanding of spiritual leadership. His ideas of personal, creative, and spiritual leadership are congruent with ideas from the new materiality. Spirituality is about how we encounter and cope with potentials in life: the essences or potentialities of both organic and inorganic things. It is our connection with the radical immanence of spirit.

Evolving Interactional Life

New materiality is anchored in life. Life in Tillich's view is the interaction in which potentialities realize and actualize themselves: "the movement of reality as a whole enables some potentialities to become actual," Tillich wrote.[12] All life is needed for the realization of individual life processes: human life would not be there without the activity of atoms, plants, bees and ants, sun, and the particles crossing the universe. Life is a unity. This unity cannot be restricted to humankind: "in order to understand the unity of life in humankind we must understand the unity of life in all its dimensions and levels."[13] The inorganic and the spiritual are two sides or dimensions of evolving life. Tillich wrote: "Certainly, in the inorganic realm, there is nothing actually organic, or actually psychological or actually spiritual. But potentially these other dimensions are present."[14] Life evolves from the inorganic dimension to others with a growing complexity as a result. All beings are a part of that evolving or evolution.

Interaction between spirit and matter also suggests interaction between culture and nature or cultural evolution and natural evolution. Today's neurophysiology lifts this interaction up: "Biology and culture are thoroughly interactive. …There is growing evidence that cultural developments (for example in learning and art) can lead to profound modifications in the human genome."[15] Culture affects biology. It is not only biology that affects culture, as we usually think. There is the affective loop or influence between the two. On the physiological level, "scientists describe the open loop as 'interpersonal limbic regulation,' whereby one person transmits signals that can alter hormone levels, cardiovascular function, sleep rhythms, and even immune function inside the body of another."[16] This signalizing happens mostly in unconscious

[12] Paul Tillich, "Dimensions, Levels, and the Unity of Life," unpublished typescript, 1958, 7, Paul Tillich Papers, Andover-Harvard Theological Library, bMS 649/82 (17).

[13] Tillich, 1.

[14] Tillich, 7

[15] Antonio Damasio, *Self Comes to Mind: Constructing the Conscious Brain* (London: Vintage Books, 2012), 294.

[16] Goleman, Boyatzis, and McKee, *Primal Leadership*, 7.

levels. The interpersonal limbic regulation focuses what kind of people we are and how we relate to each other and to our surroundings, including the more-than-human world.

Life processes are co-dependent. Spirit (potentiality) and matter (materiality) are two sides of the unity of life: "the spiritual is the fulfillment of the organic and its potentialities, not its distortion."[17] As life evolves, higher animals and humankind might reach centered self-awareness, even to the point of "reaching the spiritual dimension," congruent with self-consciousness in humankind.[18] Materiality, including things, plants, animals, and humankind, has a spiritual dimension.

Self-awareness and Leadership

Initially, self-awareness is precipitated by the clash of the ideal self (some call it the grand self) and the real self. There is "*discontinuity*—the glaring gap between ... [the] ideal self and the reality."[19] The ideal self is no relational self, as it is immersed with feelings of excessive self-importance. To transform the discontinuity, mental labor is needed. Through mental labor we might get connected with our emotions, and through emotions get in tune with other people, reaching a new stage of self-awareness compared with the preceding self-centered stages. Goleman and others speak about "*attunement*—alignment with the kind of resonance that moves people emotionally as well as intellectually."[20] This attunement "requires direct connection with people's emotional centers."[21] To be able to get in tune with people, not only with oneself, is an emotional competency, and emotional competence or skills are today in the center of leadership.[22] Leadership in terms of the ideal or grand self is unbearable for a team, as mixed emotions and twisted meanings make many of today's working places into madhouses.[23]

Affect or affection has started to play such a central role in understanding organizations. People are "resonant" with each other, leading to what

---

[17] Tillich, "Dimensions, Levels, and the Unity of life," 11.

[18] Tillich, 9.

[19] Goleman, Boyatzis, and McKee, *Primal Leadership*, 108.

[20] Goleman, Boyatzis, and McKee, 208.

[21] Goleman, Boyatzis, and McKee, 208.

[22] Gerard J. Puccio, Marie Mance, and Mary C. Murdock, *Creative Leadership: Skills That Drive Change* (Los Angeles: Sage, 2011), 174.

[23] Gervase R. Bushe, *Clear Leadership: How Outstanding Leaders Make Themselves Understood, Cut Through the Mush, and Help Everyone Get Real at Work* (Mountain View: Davies-Black Publishing, 2001).

Goleman and others call "resonant leadership."[24] In resonant leadership the emotional "tune" we are in affects other people. In working places it is an inherent part of the organizational climate and culture.[25] Spiritual leadership is the very opposite of leading through the ideal self. It is leadership that emerges from the "resonance" of participants with each other. We might understand resonance as the ground of "the politics of affect."[26] The politics of affect is about how we are in relation to each other; it is about wholeness.

I think more is needed for wholeness than the cognitive and the emotional competence (head and heart). There is also physicality (body) and the center of personality (self-realization). Spirit is in all these aspects flowing from the center. We cannot treat the center of personality as one more ingredient of wholeness, but as the center that permeates all the others. An individual is a person or personality through and through. Spiritual leadership is exercised from the center of personality onwards. In Tillich's view it is "the radiation into the world of him who is united in himself," a radiation of which we all are capable.[27]

The awakening of self-awareness and self-consciousness gives the possibility of subjectivity positing itself. This might be understood as the act in the center of personality in which the individual abandons itself to itself and then finding itself in that very abandonment. The abandonment is the very opening of the self to that which is beyond the self, it has a passive/active character. Giorgio Agamben writes: "But this abandonment of the self to itself is precisely what destines humankind to tradition and to history."[28] I think it destines the individual to his or her local and global tradition and to individual and collective history. I think that the constitutive act of subjectivity positing itself is for the individual as individual. In Tillichian terms, to abandon the self to itself is the pole of individualization, the other pole being that of participation. Tillich thought that both individualization and participation happen in the power of potentiality: "The most individualized being is the most unapproachable and the loneliest one. But, at the same time, he has the greatest potentiality of universal participation."[29] Only a person is capable of

---

[24] Goleman, Boyatzis, and McKee, *Primal Leadership*, 19ff.

[25] Goleman, Boyatzis, and McKee, 208.

[26] Brian Massumi, *Politics of Affect* (Cambridge: Polity Press, 2015).

[27] Paul Tillich, *Theology of Culture* (London: Oxford University Press, 1964), 195.

[28] Giorgio Agamben, "*Se: Hegel's Absolute and Heidegger's *Ereignis*," in *Potentialities: Collected Essays in Philosophy*, ed. Daniel Heller-Roazen (Stanford: Stanford University Press, 1999), 131.

[29] Paul Tillich, *Systematic Theology*, vol. 3 (Chicago: The Chicago University Press, 1976), 33.

her/his aloneness. A person recognizes estrangement, but also strives toward a new connectedness. Tillich thought that the polarity of individualization and participation is a structural element in life.

Spiritual Leadership and Self-Transcendence

Thus far we have been focused exclusively on the human spirit, seeing the act of subjectivity positing itself as that of spirit coming into being: the personality is born. Tillich goes further. The humanist ideal is the realization of human potentiality. Spirituality is about how we discover potentials in life. Yet there are stages in these discoveries. Tillich thought that at the stage of estrangement (personal, societal, cultural, and environmental) there is "the infinite distance between the individual and the species" and "no one can fulfill the humanist ideal, since decisive human potentialities will always remain unrealized."[30] The humanist ideal is the realization of the potentialities of the human species, unattainable for many human beings under the present societal and cultural conditions. Tillich thought that some of the potentials are realized, but even these realizations are mixed with opposition and contradiction. Tillich proposes a way forward. He talks about "self-transcending humanism."[31] The self now attains to itself in the power of that what is beyond the self.

When it comes to self-transcendence there are two possibilities: We actively take the steps of self-transcendence or we are drawn into a process of self-transcendence. I understand self-transcendence from the second perspective. Tillich claimed that the "basic character of life, of all life" is "self-transcendence and return to itself in one and the same act."[32] From this basic character he derived: "the three main life processes which can be distinguished: Life integrating itself, life producing itself, life manifesting itself."[33] Life is experienced as self-integrating, self-producing and self-manifesting, but the conflicting and contradictory trend is present as well. Life integrating itself is threatened by disintegration, production by destruction, and manifestation by concealment.[34] Life is characterized by ambiguity and contradiction, in short, by its finiteness. Spirituality, while anchored in life-experience, is the oscillation between life integrating itself and disintegrating itself; life producing itself and inhibiting itself; life manifesting itself and hiding itself. We think that spiritual leaders are trustworthy if they speak of life itself based on correct understanding of lived life, giving a realistic vision of life. A spiritual leader

[30] Tillich, 86.
[31] Tillich, 86.
[32] Tillich, "Dimensions, Levels, and the Unity of Life," 12.
[33] Tillich, 12.
[34] Tillich, 12.

might be aware of the spiritual oscillation in life. David Livermore notes, while outlining cultural leadership, that "life is about things that transcend us."[35]

Individuals do not only affirm themselves in the act of subjectivity positing itself. This happens also in relation to God through the working of God's Spirit in the human spirit:

> The Spiritual power works … through man's total personality, and this means, through him as finite freedom. … The Spiritual power gives a center to the whole personality, a center which transcends the whole personality and, consequently, is independent of any of its elements. And this is ultimately the only way of uniting the personality with itself.[36]

I think it would be better to say that this is the ultimate way of uniting the personality with itself but not the only way. The abandonment of the self to itself brings along, even if fragmentarily, the unity of the personality with itself. When the self abandons itself to itself, the personality is born. The needful distance in relation to the external world is created, making both the *cognitive* and the *emotional differentiation* possible. Both in relation to the outer world and the inner world a certain distance is needed, otherwise the mechanism of psychological projection distorts the relation: "When I am my wants I am self-centered and driven by my needs for gratification. Differentiating myself from my experience [being separate from it but still connected to it] makes it easier to be less reactive and more choiceful in how I respond to others. It helps me to differentiate myself from other people."[37] The self or total personality is so much more than immediate wants. In estrangement, only the personal needs are admitted. It seems that both the cognitive and the emotional differentiation are necessary conditions of leadership.

Self-transcendence might open the self to that which is beyond the self: the field of singularities or potentialities. It is here, it seems to me, that Tillich finds the integration of the human spirit with the divine. God's Spirit works in the human spirit:

> The "in" of the divine Spirit is an "out" for the human spirit. The spirit, a dimension of finite life, is driven into a successful self-transcendence; it is grasped by something ultimate and unconditional.

---

[35] David Livermore, *Leading with Cultural Intelligence: The Real Secret to Success* (New York: AMACOM, 2017), 63.

[36] Paul Tillich, *Love, Power and Justice: Ontological Analyses and Ethical Applications* (London: Oxford University Press, 1960), 120.

[37] Bushe, *Clear Leadership*, 117.

> It is still the human spirit; it remains what it is, but at the same time, it goes out of itself under the impact of the divine Spirit.... Ecstasy does not destroy the centeredness of the integrated self.[38]

This is important, as we tend to think in either/or terms, giving no place for the humanity of humans or materiality, nor for the spirituality of the more-than-human world. The centeredness of the integrated self is there. The self sees its continuity in tradition and in history, but also in relation to that which is beyond the self. This is in opposition to a modern definition of self as an autonomous non-relationality. The self is relational through and through.

Spiritual Leadership and Moral Imperative

The individual has a relationship with God or the ground of all being: "Justice, power, and love towards oneself is rooted in the justice, power, and love which we receive from that which transcends us and affirms us. The relation to ourselves is a function of our relation to God."[39] Love, power, and justice are the main ethical categories in Tillich's ethics.

Tillich was one of the founders of Religious Socialism. He accepted the Marxian analysis of the capitalist/bourgeois society, but he also saw that Socialism had become a collective ideology with no place for the individual. In collectivism the individual is missing. And if the individual is missing in Jiang Shigong's understanding of spirit or spirituality, emphasizing the pole of participation, then he misses the pole of individualization and the act of subjectivity positing itself as such. Tillich, on his side, claimed that personality is the bearer of spirit. Awareness of the spirit is born in the human-to-human encounter:

> Each person, in being a person, makes the demand not to be used as a means. We can run ahead in the world of knowing and acting, in every direction, in every dimension. We can make use of all kinds of things in order to do this. But suddenly we encounter a person, a being who says without words, simply by being a person, "Just to this point and not beyond! Acknowledge me as a person. You cannot use me as a means." And we say the same thing to him. Both of us demand acknowledgment as persons. My demand on him is as unconditional as his demand on me.[40]

---

[38] Tillich, *Systematic Theology*, vol. 3, 112.

[39] Tillich, *Love, Power, and Justice*, 122.

[40] Paul Tillich, *My Search for Absolutes* (New York: Simon & Schuster, 1984), 94-95.

The moral imperative is grounded in the human-to-human encounter. We should treat each other as ends (valued for themselves) and not as means (valued for our selfish purposes and desires).

According to Tillich, the moral imperative is the *modus operandi* of the law. However, the law based on the moral imperative demands something of me that I cannot fulfill. Tillich thought that the law is ambiguous. It is "good" as far as it expresses the essential human nature, yet "the law as law expresses man's estrangement from himself."[41] Prior to self-realization "in the state of mere potentiality or created innocence ... there is no law."[42] The law emerges as such only when subjectivity finds itself in estrangement. The resulting situation of ambiguity and contradiction is the port of entry into ethics.

Tillich's thinking is part of a larger shift in philosophy in the first half of the twentieth century. This was a shift from phenomenology and structuralism to post-phenomenology and post-structuralism, in short, to historicity of thinking. One of the main philosophers in the move to the historicity of thinking was Emmanuel Levinas. Instead of the universalizing, totalitarian and colonial trend of Western philosophy and metaphysics, which he saw in Western thinking as the motivating force leading to the Holocaust, he understood thinking as an ethico/political project which aims to restore the alterity of the Other. The other person is there on his or her own.[43] Thinking is to be done with the Other; it takes place with the Other in the human-to-human encounter; how we are and how we act in that very encounter is essential: "Through morality alone are I and the others produced in the universe."[44] In Levinas' view "the alienable subjectivity of need and will ... claims to be already and henceforth in possession of itself."[45] Perhaps that is the state in which the grand self finds itself? In Tillich's view the relation to the Other shows that the individual is estranged from her/his nature (essence or potentiality). He wrote: "Actualization of one's potentialities includes, unavoidably, estrangement; estrangement from one's essential being, so that we may find it again in maturity."[46] Only those who are estranged and experience alienation are capable of return and reunion. Spiritual existence is awareness of the oscillation between individualization and participation. In extreme forms of in-

[41] Tillich, *Systematic Theology*, vol. 3, 48.

[42] Tillich, 48.

[43] Emmanuel Levinas, *Totality and Infinity: An Essay on Exteriority*, (Pittsburg: Duquesne University Press, 2007).

[44] Levinas, 245.

[45] Levinas, 245.

[46] Tillich, *Love, Power, and Justice*, 112.

dividualization, one loses the world; in extreme forms of participation, individuality is out of sight. In spirituality one has courage in both poles of existence.

Spiritual Leadership and the Ontology of Love

Tillich's ethics is the ontology of love. In Tillich's view it is love that fulfills what the law demands. This love, being ontological, is not emotional or sentimental love but it is a *dialectical* element of life driving through and among other things as a dynamic of participation and individualization. It is the original power of potentiality and of life. Ontological love is not limited to humankind and the human heart only. Tillich wrote: "We see love in all beings and even the inorganic realm is full of analogies of love. [Love] is essential to life."[47] The main ethical categories of the ontology of love have "their source in the nature of man and beyond this in the nature of life itself."[48] It is not a question of different *sources* but rather of different dimensions of life in which ethical elements come to expression. Tillich wrote: "Justice is the form in which power of being actualizes itself."[49] Form I take here as a form-of-life.[50]

Tillich talks of the inherent justice in the individual: "The inherent claim of a thing is that it is reunited with that to which it belongs."[51] This means, from the human point of view, that the estranged individual is reunited with the human species and we become aware of our common humanity. For all reunion, including the reunion of personality with itself, love is essential: "Love is the ultimate criterion, because it is the movement of life itself, power is that which gives reality to life, and justice is that what gives structure to life."[52] And if love is the movement of life itself, then its source is somewhere prior to the individual. In Tillich's view, love fights against that which is against love in the individual, society (including its organizations), culture, and the entire universe: "This strange work is necessary. For it destroys what tries to destroy love. Love destroys what is against love."[53] I think we should

---

[47] Paul Tillich, "Love, Power, and Justice," in Sprunt Lectures, 1954, 1, Paul Tillich Papers, Andover-Harvard Theological Library, bMS 649/69 (8).

[48] Tillich, "Love, Power, and Justice," 1.

[49] Tillich, 1.

[50] Giorgio Agamben, following Gilles Deleuze, finds a way past the dualistic constellations while focusing on forms-of-life. Such forms come from life itself, and they are an integral part of life and life-processes. See Giorgio Agamben, *Homo Sacer: Sovereign Power and Bare Life* (Stanford: Stanford University Press, 1998), 188.

[51] Tillich, "Love, Power, and Justice," 6.

[52] Tillich, 7.

[53] Tillich, 4.

take this as an expressive language of ethics, language born from life-experience from the below.

Martin Luther King was among those whose leadership was influenced by Tillich's ethics: "Power at its best is love implementing the demands of justice. Justice at its best is love correcting everything that stands against love."[54] Western political thinking has not mixed politics and love with each other. The only power recognized since Hobbes and Machiavelli seems to be a pyramid of power over others. There is the leader at the top of the pyramid subordinating all others. The leader alone is responsible to "god above." In the ontology of love, power is shared equally. It is power with and for others. It is the power of potentiality which each thing possesses, sustaining itself in the context of empowering the Other.

Justice requires that we join in the struggle of "love correcting everything that stands against love." The present has several kinds of injustices. Love fights the injustices through "the demands of justice," for example, in saying No to human and animal exploitation in industrial and/or governmental "strategies"; it is unjust for animals to "serve against their inherent justice as food or working power."[55] Considering ideologies, King wrote:

> Truth is found neither in traditional capitalism nor in classical Communism. Each represents a partial truth. Capitalism fails to see the truth in collectivism, Communism fails to see the truth in individualism. Capitalism fails to realize that life is social. Communism fails to realize that life is personal. The good and just society is neither the thesis of capitalism nor the antithesis of Communism, but a socially conscious democracy which reconciles the truths of individualism and collectivism.[56]

Collectivism and individualism can be integrated. Collectivism (participation) and individualism (individualization) might be seen as aspects of the *differentiated* unity of life, they meet each other in justice as a form of life.

According to Tillich, we are part of the evolving life process through participation and individualization: "Life individualizes in every leaf of the same tree as well as in every human face."[57] Evolution is not just about the human species. It is also about differentiation and individualization for all creatures. Even an ant in an ant colony is still an individual! As humans we

---

[54] Martin Luther King, Jr., *Where Do We Go from Here: Chaos or Community?* (Boston: Beacon Press, 2010), 38.

[55] Tillich, "Love, Power, and Justice," 6

[56] King, *Where Do We Go from Here*, 197.

[57] Tillich, "Love, Power, and Justice", 1-2.

are both the species (through participation) and individuals (through individualization). I think Kierkegaard expressed this well: "the essential characteristic of human existence, that a humankind is an individual and as such is at once herself or himself and the whole species, in such wise that the whole species has part in the individual, and the individual has part in the whole species... Every individual has the same perfection... Perfection in oneself means therefore perfect participation in the whole."[58] In our common humanity we partake of something that transcends our individuality.

Spiritual Leadership as Creative Resistance

We live in a time when "people are treated as numbered units, interchangeable parts of no interest or value in themselves, empathy is sacrificed in the name of efficiency and cost-effectiveness."[59] We might call this opposition to the ontology of love "organized lovelessness."[60] Organized lovelessness is synonymous with a dominating "entrepreneurial leadership" model based on calculation and measurable values starting in the 1980s.[61] The old materiality of Western culture that separated the physical world from spirituality turned basic relations upside down: economy stands above politics; calculation above life; greed above other values. It is no longer understood that politics is a form of culture and an existential concern of the soul. No wonder Foucault turned his gaze from the present Western culture to a possibility of a spiritual culture and politics in Islamic culture (two cultures which have common roots and common grounding philosophers). In Tillich's view, a culture that loses its existential depth becomes empty. Today, culture in many contexts has become an empty decoration and a "reality" television show.

Our modern world denies that things have inherent value that is independent of subjective opinion. It thinks that values are merely subjective and that all talk about essential nature is abstract nonsense. Our world might

---

[58] Sören Kierkegaard, *The Concept of Dread* (Princeton: Princeton University Press, 1973), 26. The translator uses the word *race*; I think *species* is better. I have made the citation gender neutral.

[59] Daniel Goleman, *Social Intelligence: The New Science of Human Relationships* (New York: Bantam Books, 2006), 252. Cited in Jeffrey A. Raffel, Peter Leisink, and Anthony E. Middlebrooks, eds., *Public Sector Leadership: International Challenges and Perspectives* (Cheltenham: Edward Elgar, 2009), 252.

[60] Aldous Huxley, *The Perennial Philosophy* (New York: Harper & Row, 1945), 96. Cited in Jeffrey A. Raffel, Peter Leisink, and Anthony E. Middlebrooks, eds., *Public Sector Leadership: International Challenges and Perspectives* (Cheltenham: Edward Elgar, 2009), 252.

[61] Raffel, Leisink, and Middlebrooks, *Public Sector Leadership.*

acknowledge potentiality, but not with any metaphysical or spiritual significance. Yet the human being is not a laboring animal who gets her/his value or worth from what she/he does but an agent in building up others and the common world out of life producing itself. However, overcoming organized lovelessness is possible only if we introduce another kind of value-theory based on reuniting materiality and spirituality.

Instead of a subjective value-theory, Tillich had an ontological one. Tillich suggests that "the [empirical] intuition of values" should be balanced with an "ideating element." Values emerge from human encounters that combine "an ideating and an empirical element."[62] In Tillich's view, and here we come to an alternative value-orientation, each thing (inorganic and organic things, animals and human beings) has value in itself through the power of their potentiality or inner nature: "We judge the value of a tree, not from the point of view of its wood or shade value for us, but from the point of view of its potentialities as a tree for itself."[63] The value is objectively present, not dependent on our opinion. Given this value theory, spirituality might be defined as *the sensitivity for the multiple.* That is, we are capable of intuiting the value/potentiality inherent in the thing. Given this value theory, it is no longer possible to treat people as numbers or as productive units, as has been familiar since the beginning of modernity and industrialism.

This is no easy work when the world culturally and socially is run by utilitarian values and love of profit. Today, spiritual leadership is leadership of creative resistance. To be a person is to be capable of self-transcendence beyond just ego. Creativity means providing novel goals for a collective. Spirituality means sensitivity to the potential of each and every thing. Some forms of leadership move in this direction, some follow old value-orientations. What is called servant leadership is still a Western way of thinking about value. It is not the values of altruistic love creating commodity value for the stakeholders that is the foundation of the spiritual leadership.[64] A political analysis of the local/global world is missing in this form of leadership. When we learn to respect other cultures and religions and their value-orientations, for example, the rights of the indigenous people, we might land in the following: "The

[62] Paul Tillich, "Is a Science of Human Values Possible?," unpublished typescript, 1959, 6, Paul Tillich Papers, Andover-Harvard Theological Library, bMS 649/82 (13).

[63] Tillich, 6.

[64] It is not possible to conclude from the spiritual leadership, here in the form of the servant leadership, that it would necessarily promote the business and create value for the investors. This position is forespoken by the International Institute for Spiritual Leadership, see "What is Spiritual Leadership," accessed February 21, 2019, https://iispiritualleadership.com/spiritual-leadership/.

conventional, Anglo-Saxon, corporate forms are challenged, redefining spiritual and religious belief as ends in themselves, perhaps means to a good life, but certainly not as technologies that should be mobilized to improve organizational efficiency or stimulate positively deviant performance."[65] Spiritual leaders proclaim love in the situation of organized lovelessness. When cost-effectiveness is normative behavior and determines how people relate to each other, spiritual leaders create a momentum of creative resistance by introducing new value-orientations where both materiality and spirituality of things is affirmed.

Tillich's understanding of authentic spirituality starts with the human situation and human experience of estrangement, ambiguity, and contradiction. Critical thinking has two tasks: to analyze the present and to conjure alternatives for the future. In leadership we start "first by looking at the reality and then at the ideal vision."[66] Both sides are needed. Justice, and with it spirituality, includes struggle and risk. The higher the risk (and the more discontinuities justice must overcome), the higher the intensity of the spirit. In spiritual leaders we see the intensity of the spirit. This is why spiritual leaders are not found solely in religion. They emerge in other public sectors (including art, science, and politics). I think that Paul Tillich would applaud Michel Foucault, Leela Fernandes, and other adherents to the new materiality as they try to "articulate a vision of spirituality that is linked to material transformation in this world."[67]

[65] Bolden, Hawkins, Gosling, and Taylor, *Exploring Leadership*, 163.
[66] Goleman, Boyatzis, and McKee, *Primal Leadership*, 206.
[67] Leela Fernandes, *Transforming Feminist Practice*, 16.

TILLICH & RELIGIONS

The Utopian Seed of Modern Chinese Politics in Ruism (Confucianism) and its Tillichian Remedy

Bin Song

A substantial intellectual interaction between Paul Tillich's thought and the Ru[1] tradition started from Liu Shu-hsien (1934-2016), a contemporary Ru philosopher who completed his dissertation on Tillich at Southern Illinois University in 1966 and then compared Tillich's conception of religion as "ultimate concern" to the religiosity of Ruism. Liu was born in a transformative period of modern China, when traditional Ruist values were radically doubted by Chinese intellectuals. Liu's comparison of Tillich's thought and Ruism has two major motifs.

Firstly, it rediscovers the transcendent dimension of Ruism that makes it more relevant to the modern era. Secondly, Liu presents the wisdom of Ruism to a global audience to enrich global conversation about religion. Ru scholars' work on Tillich shares largely the same concerns, and broadens the conversation into topics such as metaphysics, spirituality, religious ethics, and political philosophy.[2]

My interest in Tillich is also influenced by Liu and related global discussions. I am exploring how Tillich's theology can inform my practice of Ruism to make this tradition more meaningful in modern society. Moreover, Tillich's theological reflection on human destiny in the twentieth century also drives me to re-examine the intellectual, social, and political transition of modern

---

[1] "Confucianism" is a misnomer devised by early Christian missionaries to refer to the Ru tradition with a primary purpose of religious comparison and conversion, just as Islam was once called "Muhammadanism" in a similar historical context. A detailed explanation of the history on the nomenclature of "Confucianism" can be found at Swain Tony, *Confucianism in China: An Introduction* (London: Bloomsbury, 2017): 3-22; and Anna Sun, *Confucianism as a World Religion: Contested Histories and Contemporary Realities* (Princeton: Princeton University Press, 2013): 45-76. Following the reflective scholarly trend upon the nomenclature, "Confucianism" will be written as "Ruism" or the Ru tradition, and "Confucian" or "Confucianist" will be written as "Ru" or "Ruist" in this chapter. Accordingly, "Neo-Confucianism," which normally designates new developments within Ruism during the Song and Ming Dynasties (960-1644 CE), will be referred to as Ruism in the concerned period.

[2] A most recent example of the scholarship is Keith Chan Ka-fu and William NG Yau-nang, *Paul Tillich and Asian Religions* (Boston: De Gruyter, 2017).

China. There are two central questions. Firstly, why is there such a strong utopianism in modern Chinese politics? Secondly, in order to understand and avoid the disturbing consequences of political utopianism, how can Tillich's thought illuminate our answer to the first question?

I argue that the history of radical modernization in China from 1840 until the 1970s bears a striking resemblance to the revival of Ruism as a dominant intellectual trend of medieval China.[3] We can discern a utopian seed of modern Chinese politics in traditional Ruist spirituality. Tillich's thought on "Spiritual Presence," which is articulated mainly in the third volume of his *Systematic Theology*, can be taken as a remedy for contemporary Ru scholars to recognize the unfortunate nature of utopianism so that Ruism in this modern era can stay more reflective.

The Radical Modernization of China

Tillich's theological reflection on "Spiritual Presence" is concerned with the political history of humankind in the twentieth century, a major feature of which is the ebb and flow of totalitarian ideologies and regimes. Similarly, in order to apply Tillich's thought to an investigation of modern Chinese politics, we need to briefly recount the process of China's modernization around the same time period.

There are roughly three phases of China's modernization between the 1840s and the 1970s: technological, institutional, and cultural.[4] They all share the same goal to save China from national crisis that was triggered by aggressive western powers. Each phase was launched by its supporters because they thought their predecessors had failed to achieve this goal. Altogether, the unfolding of these phases yields an overall feature of China's modernization: this is an intensifying process of internalization, idealization, and radicalization.

The first phase, or the Self-Strengthening Movement (1860-1894), was technological. It prioritized the acquisition of western arms and technologies for modernization in order to sustain the traditional ideology and institutions

---

[3] "Medieval China" in the chapter refers to the long period of Chinese history from Tang to Ming Dynasty (618-1644 CE), when Ruism had gradually established its dominant influence in the intellectual world.

[4] Similar ways to periodize China's modernization can be found in Yu Ying-Shih, "Radicalization and Conservation in Modern Intellectual History of China," in *Qian Mu and Chinese Culture* (Shanghai: Shanghai Yuandong Chubanshe, 1994), 194-97; and Edmund S.K. Fung, *The Intellectual Foundations of Chinese Modernity: Cultural and Political Thought in the Republican Era* (New York: Cambridge University Press, 2010), 4.

of imperial China. It ended with the defeat of Qing dynasty (1644-1912) in the Sino-Japanese War (1894-1895).[5]

The second phase focused on institutional modernization starting from the Hundred Days' Reform (1895) and the New Administration of the post-Boxer decade (1901-1911). These movements tried to adapt the old Chinese imperial system into a British-style constitutional monarchy using a form of progressive reformation. The former was thwarted by conservative power in the royal court, and the latter was too late to resolve the problems that had been forming for centuries. In contrast, the Xinhai Revolution in 1911 led by Sun Yat-sen intended to establish a French-style republic through violent revolution. Although it succeeded in overthrowing the Qing dynasty and ended China's millennia-long imperial epoch, the revolutionaries lost their power. China subsequently experienced an extremely chaotic warlord period. Even if the revolutionaries had regained power and established the Nanjing national government in 1927, the resulting polity was a party-state system following the example of the Soviet Union and thus, far from its original, revolutionary, ideal.

The New Cultural Movement started in the 1910s, and it initiated the third and last phase of China's modernization as cultural transformation. Proponents of the New Cultural Movement claimed that neither technological nor institutional modernization would be effective unless it were grounded in the transformation of individual human minds. Since culture was taken to be the greatest influence upon human mind, active intellectuals in this phase strived to select and promote what they considered to be the most advanced modern ideas from western culture to transform the soul of Chinese people. The process included radical antagonism against traditional Chinese culture, especially Ruism.[6]

In this cultural phase, three intellectual trends can be distinguished: liberalism, cultural conservatism, and socialism. Liberalists were convinced that democracy and science are the most modern ideas in the West. They typically

---

[5] Details of the historical events mentioned in this section, especially those in the first two phases of China's modernization, could be found in J.M. Grasso, J.P. Corrin, and M. Kort, *Modernization and Revolution in China: From the Opium Wars to the Olympics* (Armonk: M.E. Sharpe, Inc., 2009).

[6] Analyses of the idealization and radicalization of the New Cultural Movement and its influence on the modern intellectual history of China could be referred to Fung, *The Intellectual Foundations*, 37-57; Lin Yu-sheng, *The Crisis of Chinese Consciousness: Radical Antitraditionalism in the May Fourth Era* (Madison: The University of Wisconsin Press, 1979), 17-40; and Yu Ying-shih, "The Crisis of Chinese Culture and its Background in the Intellectual History," in *Historical Figures and Cultural Crisis* (Taipei: Sanmin Shuju, 2004), 165-66.

entertained a radical anti-traditional belief that these modern ideas could be gradually imprinted into the Chinese zeitgeist only after the traditional ones had been wiped out. Cultural conservatives felt the same urgency to improve traditional Chinese culture. However, they did not think westernization subsumed modernization. Some values present in Chinese traditional culture were considered as universal and eternal. Hence, they maintained that China's modernization ought to cautiously learn from the West and adapted to preserve Eastern culture. Comparatively, most Chinese socialists were much less patient, and this was particularly true for the Marxist revolutionary socialists. They believed that democracy and science would not function well if grafted onto capitalistic institutions. Instead, communism should be the consummation of human history towards which all societies are striving.[7]

The cultural phase of China's modernization can be divided into two sub-phases. From 1919-1949, all three trends competed and intermingled with each other. An intellectual could be politically liberal and culturally conservative, while simultaneously remaining sympathetic with socialist ideas. However, after 1949, the Marxist revolutionary socialism, culminating in Maoism, overwhelmed all the others.

In my view, the crystallization of China's modernization from the 1840s to the 1970s into Maoist Marxism as its intellectual kernel is characteristic of the whole process. Maoist Marxism is a theory of holism. It categorizes human history into one scheme, uniformly depicts the historical and national identity of modern China, and provides a package of policies intended to resolve the most fundamental issues of Chinese society. Because of this holistic approach, it is radically antagonistic towards both traditional Chinese culture and any element of western culture other than its own version of socialism. Maoist Marxism is also a theory of voluntarism. The key factor for social transformation is not objective reality (traditionally considered by Marxists as necessary for any change of social superstructures), but the knowledge and will of each individual.

Maoist Marxism has a distinct utopian character. Its utopianism not only projects a perfect future as the end of human history that can be finally and fully realized. It also asserts that China can rely on the correct knowledge and will of each individual. And this can be achieved mainly through ideological inculcation and organized mass movements.[8] The latter point speaks to the

[7] See Fung, *The Intellectual Foundations,* 62-127, 145-58, and 200-55.

[8] About the utopian nature of Maoist Marxism, please refer to Arif Dirlik, *Marxism in the Chinese Revolution* (New York: Rowman & Littlefield Publishers,

most influential utopian element of Maoist Marxism, and its consequences were ferociously revealed in the decade of the Cultural Revolution (1966-1976).

After the 1970s, when Deng Xiaoping called for the suspension of ideological controversy and concentration upon the development of national economy, his reform intended to acquire the most advanced technologies and economic policies from the West while maintaining the solidarity of the Chinese Communist Party's leadership, ideology, and institutions. Deng's reform had much in common with the Self-Strengthening Movement, painstakingly repeating the cycle.[9]

The Revival of Ruism in Medieval China

As inspired by Tillich's spiritual approach to explaining the mechanism of political utopianism (which we will discuss later), our inquiry into the overall features of the process of China's modernization attempts to discover its deeper spiritual drive. While doing so, we find that China's modernization bears a striking resemblance to the revival of Ruism as the dominant intellectual trend in medieval China.

There are three phases to the revival of Ruism in Medieval China that parallel the process of China's modernization: literary (technological to a certain extent), institutional, and intellectual.[10] These were driven by similar concerns. Ruist literati needed to tackle with dynastic crises which were caused by deteriorating domestic political environments and the aggression of the ethnic minority groups from northern China. Internalization and idealization are responses in both. In its last phase, there was even a hint of moral utopianism. The three phases can be briefly described as follows.

2005), 19, 47, 120-33; Maurice Meisner, *Marxism, Maoism, and Utopianism* (Madison: The University of Wisconsin Press, 1982), xi, 18, 22-25, 38-61, 59-72, 89-109; Fung, *The Intellectual Foundations*, 262; and Lin, *The Crisis*, 4.

[9] Dirlik has a similar observation in Dirlik, *Marxism*, 232.

[10] This way of periodization is mainly inspired by Yu Ying-shih, *The Historical World of Zhu Xi: A Research of the Politics and Culture of Scholar-Officials in Song Dynasty*, vol. 1 (Beijing: Sanlian Shudian, 2004), 39-56, 328-46; and its vol. 2, 411-22. It can also be verified by Peter Bol's narrative of the medieval revival of Ruism in Peter K. Bol, *"This Culture of Ours:" Intellectual Transitions in T'ang and Sung China* (Stanford: Stanford University Press, 1992). I name the third phase of China's modernization as "cultural" in order to stay in tune with the New Cultural Movement and the Cultural Revolution which are both hallmarks of this phase. However, as analyzed before, the greatest influence of this phase is to import new ideas from the West and thus, intellectual.

In the early Tang Dynasty (618-907), Chinese culture was syncretic and balanced. The royal court sponsored the compilation and annotation of a magnificent collection of classics from different traditions, including Ruism, Buddhism, and Daoism. It also encouraged expression of these substantial ideas in various refining artistic forms.[11] Tang's culture valued the Ruist ideal of the virtuous person: "to blend properly one's substance and refinement."[12] Tang's decline was caused by the An-Shi Rebellion in 755, when local warlords captured the capital and ousted the emperor. This dynastic crisis triggered the Movement of Ancient Prose, the first phase of Ruist revival in medieval China.

The Movement of Ancient Prose, launched by Han Yu (768-824), affirmed that the prevalence in early Tang of the Buddhist, Daoist, and other similar ideas had deviated from the Way of ancient sage-kings, contaminated people's morality, and hence, led to Tang's declination. In order to revitalize the dynasty, people, especially the literati, needed to recapture and internalize the original Ru ideas which had achieved their paradigmatic expressions in the Pre-Qin period (before 221 BCE) and the Han Dynasty (202 BCE - 220 CE). The concrete method to achieve this goal was to re-adopt the literary craft of "ancient prose" which was much plainer and more philosophically grounded than the flowery "rhythmical prose" popular in Han's time.[13]

The Movement of Ancient Prose in the early Song period (960-1279 CE) maintained the same motif and methodology as its predecessor in Tang. Its proponents searched for ideas in Ruist classics in order to bring peace and order to Song's politics and strived to develop the correct way to compose literature in order to transmit these ideas. Although this movement had its political appeals, they had not yet been put into practice in the institutional level. Its investigation into early Ruist classics touched some philosophical topics, but the movement had not delved into the nature of human heartmind (xin) and its metaphysical foundation as later Ruist reformers did.[14] In this sense, the Movement of Ancient Prose was a reformative movement of literary technique led by the literati elite,[15] and merely involved the initial and surface aspects of Ruism's revival. As technological reform, it is analogous to the first

[11] See Bol, *This Culture of Ours*, 84-107.

[12] Analects 6:16, 1n, in *A Source Book of Chinese Philosophy*, trans. and ed. Wing-Tsit Chan (Princeton: Princeton University Press, 1963), 29.

[13] See Bol, *This Culture of Ours*, 130-36.

[14] A detailed explanation of Ru philosophy in its Song and Ming period will be presented in the next section.

[15] See Peter K. Bol, *Neo-Confucianism in History* (Cambridge: Harvard University Asia Center,
2008), 52-55; and Yu, *The Historical World of Zhu Xi*, vol. 1, 39, 95, 328-38.

phase of China's modernization. It transformed Chinese culture from a syncretic balance between substance and refinement to the preponderance of idea over its artistic expression.[16]

Several major defeats by the northern regimes of ethnic minority quickly deepened Song's dynastic crisis. This triggered the second phase: the political reform of Wang Anshi (1021-1086). Based upon a philosophical re-interpretation of Ruist classics, especially the *Zhou Book of Ritual*, Wang Anshi proposed various political, economic, military, and educational reformations under the aegis of his emperor. He also attempted to ground institutional reformations on his understanding of human nature and its cosmological conditions. However, political reformation failed to overcome the imperial court's conservative power.

In the view of Cheng Yi (1033-1107), the inability of both the Movement of Ancient Prose and Wang's reform to deal with the crisis was due to an inadequate moral philosophy that was too adulterated by Buddhist and other non-Ruist elements. Cheng argued that the dynasty ought to concentrate upon rectifying people's heartmind, thus equipping each individual with the right moral ideas, before any political reform could succeed. The idea of "pattern-principle" (li) in Cheng's philosophy refers to the way that a set of cosmic and human realities dynamically and harmoniously fit together, upon which an individual's moral behavior depends. Accordingly, Cheng defined "Learning of Way" as a process of internalizing right moral ideas through an investigation of the pattern-principles of things. In contrast with the "Literary Learning" of the previous movement, the "Learning of Way" devalued the necessity of cultural refinement for understanding moral ideas.[17] With this new idea of learning, the medieval revival of Ruism embarked upon its final phase: intellectual.

According to the traditional historiography of Ruist thought, this intellectual phase can be further divided into two sub-phases: the Cheng-Zhu school of pattern-principle and the Lu-Wang school of heartmind. Wang Yang-ming (1472-1529), argued that access to innate goodness does not come from the cumulative investigation of many pattern-principles in external things, but from the momentary attainment of the innate "conscientious knowing" within human heartmind.[18] Later, a more left-wing school of Wang

---

[16] See Bol, *Neo-Confucianism*, 56.

[17] See Yu, *The Historical World of Zhu Xi*, vol. 1, 45-52, 108; Bol, *This Culture of Ours*, 305-26; and Bol, *Neo-Confucianism*, 163-67.

[18] About the Difference between Zhu Xi and Wang Yang-ming, please also refer to Barry C. Keenan, *Neo-Confucian Self-Cultivation* (Honolulu: University of Hawai'i Press, 2011), 13.

followed his teachings of the completeness and the continuous presence of the conscientious knowing, but held that there is one dimension of human heartmind which has the potential to encompass all the pattern-principles of things in the cosmos, and which enables humans to respond appropriately to all cosmic and human events.[19] More importantly, the potentiality of this dimension of human heartmind can be fully realized at any moment of everyday life.[20] This left-wing school of Wang resonates with Mao's voluntarist Marxism as a way of moral utopianism.

The Utopian Seed in the *Great Learning*

Why did China's modernization from the 1840s to the 1970s and the revival of Ruism in medieval China experience very similar phases: technological, institutional, and intellectual? Why were both processes equally oriented to internalization, idealization, and in varying degrees, utopianism? And why did both of them, if assessed by their own initial motives, ultimately fail? We can best answer these questions by analyzing one of the most important Ruistic canons, the *Great Learning,* because this reveals the spiritual root of holistic thinking. In doing so, we discover the relevance of Tillich's thought to contemporary Chinese politics and culture.

Han Yu, the originator of Ruism's medieval revival, used the text of the *Great Learning* to denounce the infringement of Daoist and Buddhist ideas on the literati. After the annotation by Cheng Yi and Zhu Xi, the text was considered "the gate through which beginning students enter into virtue" and occupied a foundational position in the Ruist canonical system of Four Books.[21] Until 1905, when the Ruist civil examination was officially abrogated, this Chen-Zhu interpretation of the *Great Learning* was received as orthodoxy. Most of the active intellectuals in early modern China, including opponents of Ruism, studied the text as part of their early education. Given the centrality of the *Great Learning* to Chinese intellectual life, the text is, therefore, the best choice for analyzing the spiritual rationale undergirding both the medieval revival of Ruism and China's modernization.

---

[19] See Ji Wenfu, *The Left-wing School of Wang Yang-ming* (Taipei: Wanjuanlou Chubanshe, 1990), 17.

[20] See Qian Ming, *The Formation and Development of the School of Wang Yang-ming* (Nanjing: Jiangsu Guji Chubanshe, 2002): 172-76; and Peng Guoxiang, "A Debate of the Ready-Madeness of the Conscientious Knowing in Middle and late Ming," *The Sinological Studies* 11 (2003/06): 15-46.

[21] See Daniel K. Gardner, *Chu Hsi and the Ta-hsueh: Neo-Confucian Reflection on the Confucian Canon* (Cambridge: Harvard University Press, 1986), 4, 18-19.

The *Great Learning* was originally written for the ruling class, although it was considered later to be a general guideline of education for all people. The two paragraphs that epitomize the holistic mode of thinking are as follows:

> 4.1 If an ancient person wished that all people under Heaven manifest their luminous virtues, he would first govern his state well. 4.2 If he wished to govern his state well, he would first regulate his family. 4.3 If he wished to regulate his family, he would first cultivate himself. 4.4 If he wished to cultivate himself, he would first rectify his heartmind. 4.5 If he wished to rectify his heartmind, he would first make his intentions sincere. 4.6 If he wished to make his intentions sincere, he would first extend his knowledge. 4.7 The extension of knowledge consists in the investigation of things.
>
> 5.1 When things are investigated, knowledge is extended. 5.2 When knowledge is extended, intentions are sincere. 5.3 When intentions are sincere, the heartmind is rectified. 5.4 When the heartmind is rectified, the person is cultivated. 5.5 When the person is cultivated, the family will be regulated. 5.6 When the family is regulated, the state will be governed well. 5.7 When the state is governed well, there will be peace under Heaven."[22]

[22] This translation is adapted from Chan, *A Source Book*, 86; Keenan, *Neo-Confucian Self-Cultivation*, 38; and Gardner, *Chu Hsi and the Ta-hsueh*, 91-92. The original text according to Zhu Xi is in Zhu Xi, *The Complete Works of Master Zhu*, vol. 6 (Shanghai : Shanghai Guji Chubanshe, 2002), 17, in compliance with which I mark the order of each sentence by the first number representing the paragraph and the second for the sentence. The use of "he" highlights the importance of individual and keeps in line with the historical context, rather than showing any sexual bias of mine. My philosophical interpretation of the text is based upon Zhu Xi's and Wang Yang-ming's common understanding. However, in case there is a significant discrepancy between them, I will explain it explicitly. Zhu Xi's understanding of the *Great Learning* could be found mainly in these texts: *The Great Learning in Chapter and Verse*, in Zhu, *The Complete Works*, 13-28; *Further Questions about the Great Learning*, in Zhu, *The Complete Works*, 505-47; the fourteenth to eighteenth rolls of the *Classified Conversations of Master Zhu*, in Zhu Xi, *Classified Conversations of Master Zhu* (Beijing: Zhonghua Shuju, 1998): 249-427. Wang Yang-ming's mature understanding of the text which pivots upon the term "the extension of knowledge" could be found mainly in *Letter in Reply to Gu Dongqiao*, in Wang Yang-ming, *The Complete Works of Wang Yang-ming* (Shanghai: Shanghai Guji Chubanshe, 1992): 41-57; *Letter in Reply to Vice-Minister Luo Zheng-an*, in Wang, *The Complete Works*, 75-78; *A Preface to the Ancient Version of the Great Learning*, in Wang, *The Complete Works*, 242; *Inquiry on*

The pivotal term in this textual chain is in 4.5, *cheng yi*, to make one's intentions sincere. *Yi* implies an intentional response of human heartmind[23] to external things when they affect it. The standard by which to judge the sincerity of intentions is whether they can be held in public as in private. The teaching about *cheng yi* is related to a specific method of moral discipline: *shen du*, vigilant solitude. A person with vigilant solitude is able to live by moral rules even in private. Their pursuit of morality would be voluntary, i.e., for the sake of oneself rather than for the sake of others.

Nevertheless, although sincere intentions are usually attached to spontaneous emotions, the sheer spontaneity of emotions does not guarantee that the accompanying intentions are sincere. This is because people's judgement of the nature of affecting things could be wrong, and their following emotions would be consequently inappropriate. Therefore, the text teaches that *cheng yi* should be premised upon *zhi zhi*, to extend one's knowledge. The knowledge to be extended is about pattern-principle, which, as mentioned above, designates the way that a set of cosmic and human realities dynamically and harmoniously fit together. Because no pattern-principle of anything can be fully clarified without a comprehensive grasp of all the pattern-principles of its related things, the process of extending one's knowledge must lead to an ecstatic fulfillment of human spirituality, i.e., a penetration of human heartmind into the One pattern-principle of all under Heaven. For Zhu Xi, this ecstatic fulfillment is characterized by a sagely omniscience through which all the qualities of the things in the world and all the operations within human heartmind are thoroughly understood.[24] For Wang Yang-ming, the fulfillment is a feeling of mysterious union of the human heartmind with all under Heaven, and consequently, manifested as a sagely omnipotence through which all evolving things in the cosmos can be appropriately responded.[25]

In short, one's intentions would be sincere if spontaneous emotions were grounded upon the knowledge of the pattern-principles of things. One would thus find their genuine self, or, in terminology of the *Great Learning*, a person would manifest their luminous virtue. One would also be dedicated to helping others to manifest their luminous virtue as well. The *Great Learning* instructs

---

the Great Learning, in Wang, *The Complete Works*, 967-73. An analysis of the development of Wang Yang-ming's thought of the *Great Learning* in contrast with Zhu Xi could be found in Qian, *The Formation*, 38-84.

[23] Since Ruist philosophy typically espouses intelligence is inseparable from emotion, the center of human consciousness is termed as (xin) and translated as heartmind.

[24] Zhu, *The Complete Works*, 20.

[25] Wang, *The Complete Works*, 966, 972.

one to "love and renew the people" in order to "regulate one's family," "govern one's state well," and ultimately, "bring peace throughout all under Heaven." The process can be envisioned as expanding concentric circles through which a cultivating virtuous person at the center helps to transform the moral characters of their neighbors by the method of *shu. Shu* means "to help the others to establish what one establishes oneself, and to help the others to accomplish what one accomplishes oneself," and "do not do to others that one does not want to be done."[26] In the *Great Learning*, this method is called the Way of Measuring-Square, because it is taken to be the measure of human relationship.[27]

Although Zhu Xi and Wang Yang-ming disagree significantly on their understandings of the last two terms of the quoted text: *zhi zhi* (extension of knowledge) and *ge wu* (investigation of things), they both share an ecstatic optimism, either in the way of a cognitive (Zhu) or a performative (Wang) penetration of human heartmind into all the pattern-principles of all under Heaven. They also share the belief that peace between states and order within a state are ultimately dependent on the moral self-cultivation of either the individual as a sagely emperor who orchestrates society from above or as ordinary people sustaining the Way from below.

In general, the *Great Learning* grounds moral rules on the knowledge of cosmic realities in each individual's mind so as to construct an "anthropocosmic" worldview.[28] We can interpret the first five steps, from "investigation of things" in 5.1 to "cultivate one's person" in 5.4, as religious because moral rules are based on the knowledge of cosmic realities. It is during the process of human interactions, rather than in the introspective self-cultivation of a solitary person, that ethical problems actually arise. Therefore, the sixth step in 5.5 to "regulate one's family" is ethical. The seventh step in 5.6 and 5.7 to "govern one's state well" and "bring peace throughout all under Heaven" is political. In this way, the *Great Learning* establishes one spiritual fulcrum in each individual's mind which fulfills their religious, ethical, and political concerns all at once. We can now answer our original questions.

Why does China's current modernization in question reflect its past medieval revival of Ruism in its orientation towards internalization and idealization? It is because under the influence of the *Great Learning*, major participants of these two historical events shared the same belief that the solution of

---

[26] *Analects* 6:28, 15:23, in Chan, *A Source Book*, 31, 44.

[27] Zhu, *The Complete Works*, 24.

[28] See Tu Wei-ming, *Centrality and Commonality: An Essay on Confucian Religiousness* (Albany: State University of New York Press, 1989), 9.

political crises at the state level depends upon a thorough grasp by each individual of a single correct doctrine about how to tackle those crises. Why does the current modernization have similar radical and utopian phases? It is because both historical events share the same belief that there is a single correct doctrine that enables humans to fulfill multiple goals and resolve disparate problems all at once.

Both contemporary and past movements assumed that the way of spiritual life can be fully realized through individuals' voluntary efforts regardless of the contextual restraints. Both movements ultimately failed. The obstacle for Ruism's medieval revival was that unruly elements of the state could not be managed by a moralistic statecraft. The obstacle for contemporary Maoist Marxism is that voluntaristic holism denies the possibility of progressive reformation through the cooperation of people with their pluralistic ideas and diverse backgrounds.

The text *Great Learning* affirms that we can fulfill our political and ethical concerns if and only if we have fulfilled our religious concerns. There may be good reasons to believe that the peace among states and the order within a state are ultimately dependent upon voluntary moral practice of each individual which can be enhanced by their religious belief. Nevertheless, it is overly optimistic and unrealistic to think that this is the only means to bring peace and order to states. By the same token, a well-cultivated virtuous person cannot guarantee that their family members will become equally virtuous merely because of their moral influence and religious charisma. In other words, politics, ethics, and religion should be seen as three intricately interconnected, yet fundamentally different areas of human life. Their relationship is not as simple and monolithic as the *Great Learning* envisioned.

This misguided form of holism, so to speak, implies that we people could fulfill our multiple concerns and resolve our disparate problems all at once if and only if we adopt in our mind one single, correct, all-encompassing doctrine. In my view, this explains the extreme reaction of Chinese intelligentsia to dynastic and national crises, and the erroneous assumption that the overall transformation of individual minds is the best way to resolve those challenges. This form of spirituality, with its misguided conception of pluralistic and changing social realities, explains both past and current dilemmas facing China.

Ultimate Concern and Preliminary Concerns

Paul Tillich's theology, and especially his pneumatology, helps us understand and correct the unfortunate impact of Ruism on Chinese politics and culture.

Tillich's definition of religion as Ultimate Concern is based on his ontology. He affirms that the philosophers' absolute (*logos)* and religionists' absolute (*pathos)* ought to be identical. Therefore, the concept of Ultimate Concern involves two series of conditions. First, there are conditions of reality. Ultimate reality conditions all other realities without itself being thus conditioned. Second, there are conditions of human concerns. The unconditionality of ultimate reality implies that the concern about it is also ultimate. Hence, ultimate concern places an unconditional demand upon all preliminary concerns so that if a person has to make choices about their concerns at crucial moments of life, the ultimate concern is the one thing they should never surrender.[29]

The process of moral self-cultivation in the *Great Learning* is easily aligned with Tillich's understanding of Ultimate Concern. The Ruist thinkers tried to ground the demand of political and moral rules on the pattern-principles of things generated by the all-encompassing, and constantly creative, cosmic power. In the *Great Learning*, the One pattern-principle of Heaven, which includes and coheres with the many pattern-principles of things, is ultimate reality. On the other hand, individuals can satisfy ethical and political concerns if and only if they grasp the pattern-principles of things. "Extension of knowledge" is the way the fulfillment of all other preliminary concerns is conditioned.

However, although Tillich maintains that religion as Ultimate Concern provides "depth, direction and unity" to all preliminary concerns,[30] he never asserts, like the Ruists did in the *Great Learning*, that the fulfillment of Ultimate Concern is both the necessary and sufficient condition for fulfilling preliminary concerns. In other words, what the fulfillment of Ultimate Concern could furnish is the "meaning," but not the "means" of the fulfillment of preliminary concerns. In this sense, Tillich does not oversimplify the interconnection between piety, morality, and earthly happiness.

For Tillich, the fulfillment of ultimate concern takes a form of momentary and ecstatic religious experience during which the divine Spirit is manifested in the spiritual dimension of human life. In this moment, humans as finite beings are grasped by the infinite creative power of God as the ground of being. As a consequence, they will be transformed into their New Being as an essential union with God without removing their own existences and enliven themselves in a dynamic and harmonious communion with all other

---

[29] See Paul Tillich, "The Two Types of Philosophy of Religion," in *Theology of Culture* (New York: Oxford University Press, 1959), 1-2, 22, 105; and Paul Tillich, *Systematic Theology*, vol. 1 (Chicago: University of Chicago Press, 1951), 11-14.

[30] Tillich, "The Two Types," 105.

creatures without losing their own uniqueness. Spiritual Presence, as the consummation of humanity's deepest concern, reveals the ideal for human life while simultaneously offering assurance that the ideal could become actual.[31]

According to Tillich, human life is a "multidimensional unity," and therefore, the fulfillment of ultimate concern can never be full and complete. Unity has five dimensions: inorganic, physical, psychological (together, these two constitute the organic dimension), personal and spiritual. Because each of these dimensions is indispensable to and coexists within an individual's life, changes in one dimension will not necessarily block the intrinsic qualities of another dimension. Therefore, if Spiritual Presence grasps a person in the spiritual dimension of life, creating an unambiguous presence of meaning, this can impact, but not abolish, the nature of the other dimensions. The subject-object split in all dimensions other than the spiritual guarantees that human life is never divested of ambiguities, including even those most unambiguous ecstatic life moments. As a consequence, Tillich argues that the presence of divine Spirit in human life is always fragmentary. The perfection of human personality should not be envisioned as full realization of the unambiguous presence of meaning at ecstatic moments of life. Rather, a person ought to, under the guidance of the ideal informed by the unambiguous manifestation of Spiritual Presence, continue to fight the ambiguous, transform the ambiguous, and create new manifestations of the unambiguity within ambiguities, despite the fact that any success in this process will only take place fragmentarily and anticipatorily.[32]

Another important dimension to human life is historical. Tillich's thought about the fragmentary manifestation of divine Spirit in the ecstatic moments of an individual's life is brought into his reflection on the destiny of human history based on themes in traditional Christian eschatology. For Tillich, since Spiritual Presence is the actual, albeit incomplete, realization of the ideal of life, the aim of human history is also revealed through it. It is unnecessary, however, to interpret traditional Christian symbols of eschatology as "the last" in any temporal sense. Instead, the eschaton of human history which could be fragmentarily realized in the form of Spiritual Presence is the aim of history in the normative sense. Tillich believes that there is no perfect temporal state of human history for which all humans should strive. Otherwise, the state of human history, concrete and finite, would be unduly considered infinite, and thus, become a false and demonic object of ultimate concern. According to Tillich, what humans should pursue is to fully devote themselves

---

[31] See Paul Tillich, *Systematic Theology*, vol. 3 (Chicago: University of Chicago Press, 1963), 11-128, 137, 143, and 222.

[32] See Tillich, 11-30, 71, 222-41, 276.

to realizing a better state of human society under the guidance of the already experienced ideal of Spiritual Presence. Nevertheless, since the realization of the ideal is always partial and fragmentary, we should acknowledge that even if a better state of human society can be accomplished, it would not be worshiped but criticized, and if necessary, rejected.[33]

In general, Tillich envisions human history as a two-dimensional dynamic process. The vertical dimension, as momentary realization of an ideal in the form of Spiritual Presence, needs to be manifested as actual improvements of human conditions in the horizontal dimension. Meanwhile, the development of human society on the horizontal dimension requires the continuous guidance and infusion of prophetic power from the fulfilled ultimate concern on the vertical dimension.[34] Therefore, the unambiguity of the fulfillment of ultimate concern can only be manifested in the ambiguities of the fulfillment of preliminary concerns either for an individual or for human history. The condition of ultimate concern upon preliminary concerns is at best necessary, but absolutely not sufficient.

Tillich's thoughts about fragmentary Spiritual Presence in an individual's life is a powerful antidote to the Ruist type of moral utopianism that affirms the complete realization of an ideal of human life for specifically cultivated persons and at specific life moments. Correspondingly, his philosophy of history through his reinterpretation of Christian eschatology is also a powerful corrective to the Maoist-Marxist type of historical utopianism that affirms the full realization of a perfect state of human history relying upon the inculcated knowledge and will of each individual.[35] The moral type of utopianism in Ruism is an intellectual and psychological preparation for the process of China's radical modernization. However, the Maoist-Marxist historical type of utopianism is only possible once the spiritual dimension of Ruism is misunderstood or jettisoned. Now that the revival of Ruism is becoming a noticeable social phenomenon in contemporary China and other areas of the globe, Ruist scholars would be inspired by Tillich's reflection on spirituality and politics. They can advance the self-transformation of Ruism in a more mindful way. In particular, I believe Ru scholars' work can focus upon the following

---

[33] See Tillich, 307, 320, 358-59, and 373; and Paul Tillich, "The Political Meaning of Utopia," in *Political Expectation* (New York: Harper & Row, 1971), 177-78.

[34] See Tillich, *Systematic Theology*, vol. 3, 420; Tillich, "The Political Meaning," 179.

[35] Scholarly reviews on Tillich's thought of utopianism can be found in Raymond F. Bulman, *A Blueprint for Humanity: Paul Tillich's Theology of Culture* (New Jersey: Associated University Press, 1981), 69, 78; and Ronald H. Stone, "On the Boundary of Utopia and Politics," in *The Cambridge Companion to Paul Tillich*, ed. Russell Re Manning (Cambridge: Cambridge University Press, 2009), 208-21.

two facets so as to constructively reconsider the Ruist legacy as inspired by Tillich's thought. First, resources within Ruism which are more conducive to the critique of moral utopianism can be uncovered.[36] Second, the contemporary revival of Ruism should promote religious and cultural pluralism, and thus contribute to more inclusive domestic or international politics. To the latter facet, the cross-cultural study of world religions and philosophies will remain essential.

[36] I made an endeavor to uncover some of these resources in my dissertation "A Study of Comparative Philosophy of Religion on 'Creatio Ex Nihilo' and 'Sheng Sheng' (生生, birth birth)," Boston University, 2018. Recently, I also find one contemporary Ruist philosopher, Tang Junyi (1909-1978), shares a similar view of philosophy of history to Tillich's. Please see Thomas Frohlich, "The Challenge of Totalitarianism: Lessons from Tang Junyi's Political Philosophy," in *Confucianism for the Contemporary World: Global Order, Political Plurality, and Social Action*, eds. Tze-ki Hon and Kristin Stapleton (Albany: State University of New York Press, 2017), 131-66. My review of this book can be found at the journal of *Philosophy East and West,* issue of July 2019.

Shin Buddhism and the New Being

Kirk R. MacGregor

Shin, or True Pure Land, Buddhism claims that Amida Buddha, while still a bodhisattva named Dharmākara (or Hōzō), made forty-eight vows to create a Pure Land paradise and then fulfilled these vows in order to achieve Buddhahood. The tradition's leading teachers, Shinran (1173–1262) and his predecessor Hōnen (1133–1212), emphasized the depravity of all human beings and their consequent inability to acquire sufficient merit to enter the Pure Land. Shinran thus mourned, "I am false and untrue, and without the least purity of mind....Since greed, anger, evil, and deceit are frequent, we are filled with naught but flattery. With our evil natures hard to subdue, our minds are like asps and scorpions."[1] Indeed, as Tillich put it, there was an unbridgeable gap between each person's essential being (what that person can and should be) and existential being (what that person actually is).[2] For both Shin Buddhism and Tillich, we suffer estrangement from our essential nature. What must overcome this gap is New Being, a reality where essential being is manifested under the conditions of existence without being conquered by them.[3] This piece will argue that in Shin Buddhism, the bearer of the New Being is Dharmākara or whatever historical figure stands behind the legend of Dharmākara. The Shin conception of Amida's grace stands functionally equivalent to Tillich's conception of God's grace. Continuing along this path, Tillich's proclamation of the New Being in Jesus as the Christ is paralleled by the Shin proclamation, using Tillichian language, of the New Being in Amida as the Buddha. The redemptive work of Amida fulfills the principles of the doctrine of the atonement articulated by Tillich. When the Shin adherent accepts that s/he is accepted by Amida exactly as s/he is by reciting the *nembutsu* ("I pay homage to Amida Buddha") in faith and embarks in compassionate service to all sentient beings, s/he participates in New Being.

---

[1] Quoted in Alfred Bloom, *Shinran's Gospel of Pure Grace* (Ann Arbor: Association for Asian Studies, 1965), 29.

[2] Paul Tillich, *Systematic Theology*, Three volumes in one (Chicago: University of Chicago Press, 1967), 2:21-22.

[3] Tillich, 2:118-19.

Dharmākara (or His Historical Referent) as Bearer of the New Being

It is historically doubtful that a bodhisattva named Dharmākara actually lived. However, it is equally clear that Shin Buddhists experience and participate in what Tillich called New Being. According to Shinran, everyone possessing true faith has "attained the adamantine true mind," transcends "the five destinies" (i.e., birth in a hell, as a hungry ghost, animal, human being, or god), transcends "the eight difficulties" (i.e., eight hindrances to seeing a Buddha), and attains "assuredly in this life ten blessings," including "the protection of spiritual power," "possession of highest virtue," "transforming evil into good," being "always protected by the light of the mind," "always having a joyous mind," "requiting virtue," "always practicing great mercy," and "entrance into the company of the truly assured."[4] This forms an excellent description of the "unlimited power of self-transcendence" that New Being facilitates.[5] As Tillich emphasized while lamenting the alleged failure of the quest for the historical Jesus, faith in New Being ensures its own foundation, "namely, the appearance of that reality which has created the faith."[6] Participation therefore secures the reality of the event upon which Shin Buddhism is based, namely, "a personal life in which the New Being has conquered the old being" regardless of that person's name or historical particulars.[7] Tillich therefore maintained that even if Jesus of Nazareth never existed, there would still be some person underlying the Jesus myth who definitively transformed reality. Reasoning analogously, Shin Buddhism then presents us with a person, whether Dharmākara or the individual whose life inspired his legend, in whom New Being found actualization. For Shinran, when this person "performed bodhisattva practices…in profound compassion for the ocean of all sentient beings in pain and affliction…there was not a moment, not an instant, when his practice in the three modes of action [,bodily acts, verbal acts, and mental acts,] was not pure, or lacked this true mind." He therefore "brought to fulfillment the perfect, unhindered, inconceivable, indescribable, and inexplicable supreme virtues."[8]

As interpreted by Hōnen and Shinran, Dharmākara's Eighteenth Vow guaranteed that faithful recitation of the *nembutsu* (*Namu Amida Butsu* = "I

---

[4] Quoted in Bloom, *Gospel*, 67.

[5] Tillich, *Systematic Theology*, 2:120.

[6] Tillich, 2:114.

[7] Tillich, 2:114.

[8] Shinran, *The Essential Shinran: A Buddhist Path of True Entrusting*, ed. Alfred Bloom (Bloomington: World Wisdom, 2007), 133.

pay homage to Amida Buddha") ensures one's rebirth into the Pure Land, regardless of one's previous deeds. As Hōnen wrote:

> There is power enough in the Nembutsu, even if pronounced but once, to destroy all the sins whose effects have persisted through eighty billions of kalpas. And so you ought to bear in mind that Amida has the power to come forth to welcome to his land those oppressed by the very worst *karma*, and you ought to believe that by simply calling upon his name you will be born there, quite irrespective of whether you have merit inherited from former lives or not, and no matter whether your sins be light or heavy.[9]

During the interim between reciting the *nembutsu* and being reborn in the Pure Land, the believer "remains in the state of non-retrogression" and abides "in the rank of the company of the truly assured."[10] Alfred Bloom points out that, for Shinran, "the Pure Land shares all the traits of Nirvana. It is infinite and incomprehensible in its nature.... Birth in the Pure Land means freedom from the endless repetition of births and deaths. All illusions disappear, and beings, becoming as pure as the land itself, achieve spiritual freedom and union with the Buddha."[11] Shinran indeed equated the Pure Land with nirvana: "When we say that to enter the Pure Land of Bliss is to realize the Great Nirvana, or to attain the Highest Enlightenment, or to arrive at Extinction, [these terms,] though differing, all refer to the gift for going to the Pure Land."[12] Hence rebirth in the Pure Land conquers the Tillichian gap between essential being and existential being.

Hōnen depicted the bridging of this gap—even for the persons whose gap is largest—through faith in Amida. Shinran emphasized that, in Tillich's words, such faith "is the state of being grasped by an ultimate concern."[13] Shinran declared, "needless to say, our Buddha Amida grasps beings with his Name."[14] Faith occurs "when we encounter the profound Vow of the gift of Amida's Other Power and our minds which rejoice at being given true faith are assured."[15] Notice for Shinran that the believer is seized by Amida; the believer does not conjure up faith through self-power (*jiriki*), but the other-

---

[9] Quoted in Bloom, *Gospel*, 22.

[10] Quoted in Bloom, 62, 61.

[11] Bloom, 79.

[12] Quoted in Bloom, 79.

[13] Tillich, *Systematic Theology*, 3:130.

[14] Shinran, *Kyōgyōshinshō*, trans. Dennis Hirota, Hisao Inagaki, Michio Tokunaga, and Ryushin Uryuzu (Kyoto: Hongwanji International Center, 1987), 1.128.

[15] Quoted in Bloom, *Gospel*, 61-2.

power (*tariki*) of Ultimate Reality generates faith (*shinjin*) in the believer without in any way opposing the believer's will. Shinran explained the effect of the Eighteenth Vow as follows: "Amida's vast Vow always, of itself, grasps and holds beings. This is the necessary way of its working.... True and real *shinjin*, which is given by Amida Tathagata...is the very cause for attainment of supreme enlightenment."[16] Stressing that no amount of education would enable humans to self-sufficiently generate faith, Hōnen told the story of the profoundly educated Tendai Buddhist priest who became a scholar of Pure Land theology and still could not obtain a faithful spirit: "There used to be a priest of the Tendai sect, who was very diligent in the study of the Jōdo (Pure Land) doctrines. With a sigh he once remarked, 'I have already come to understand the main points in this teaching, and yet somehow a believing heart has not yet been stirred within me. What can I do to awaken such faith?'" Upon perceiving that he could do nothing of himself, the priest prayed to Amida, who immediately seized his spirit and infused the gift of faith therein: "My doubts all disappeared in a trice, and a settled faith laid hold of me...Perfect and skillful must be the art of Amida Nyorai in saving humans."[17]

The Tillichian Grace of Amida Buddha

The divinely initiated relationship between the Shin Buddhist and Amida proves analogous to the Tillichian relationship between the Christian and God. Cognizant of the gulf between essential and existential being (represented by the theological symbol of depravity), Shinran stressed that faith, which overcomes the gulf, originates in the grace of Amida. Bloom explains: "With an acute sense of human depravity, Shinran developed his theory that even faith, the will to believe, is a gift of Amida Buddha. Once this faith is aroused, salvation is assured. There need be no anxiety for the future, nor any frustrating religious disciplines calculated to close the gap between our real and ideal selves."[18] Similarly, Tillich maintained that grace undergirds the divine-human encounter: "The term 'grace' (*gratia*, *charis*) qualifies all relations between God and man in such a way that they are freely inaugurated by God and in no way dependent on anything the creature does or desires."[19] As with the grace of Amida, Tillich held that God's grace completes rather than violates creaturely freedom: "Grace does not create a being who is unconnected

[16] Shinran, *Kyōgyōshinshō*, 2.255.

[17] Hōnen, *Hōnen the Buddhist Saint: His Life and Teaching*, eds. Harper Havelock Coates and Ryūgaka Ishizuka (Kyoto: Society for the Publication of the Sacred Books of the World, 1949), 374.

[18] Bloom, *Gospel*, 88.

[19] Tillich, *Systematic Theology*, 1:285.

with the one who receives grace. Grace does not destroy essential freedom; but it does what freedom under the conditions of existence cannot do, namely, it reunites the estranged."[20] Shinran would thus agree with Tillich's words that grace "gives fulfilment to that which is separated from the source of fulfilment, and it accepts that which is unacceptable."[21]

Shinran stipulated that the all-encompassing nature of Amida's grace leads to eventual universalism. While recognizing that some persons do not place faith in Amida during their present lifetime, Shinran held that Amida would arouse faith in these persons during some future life. Hence the doctrine of reincarnation couples in Shin Buddhism with grace to preclude eternal condemnation. Shinran grounded the idea that at some point in the cycle of transmigration, all sentient beings, including the evil reprobates and the proud good people, will receive salvation, in his interpretation of Dharmākara's Seventeenth Vow.[22] According to Shinran's reading, Dharmākara promised:

> When I attain Buddhahood, people...whether they have listened to my Name with evil intentions in previous lives or whether they indeed aspire to be born in my land for the sake of enlightenment—will be kept from returning once more to the three evil courses...They will instead all attain birth in my land, which is the desire they cherish in their hearts. If it not be so, may I not attain Buddhahood.[23]

Since Dharmākara is now Amida Buddha, it follows that all will, in time, be reborn into the Pure Land and so realize Buddhahood. Bloom discloses the inclusive hope Shinran provided his followers: "The final destiny of beings is Buddhahood. Based on the understanding of what Buddhahood means, he imparted a strong sense of hope to his disciples, not an egoistic hope, but one which looked forward to the eventual realization of Buddhahood by even the lowest creatures, and in whose realization believers all share as they become Buddhas."[24]

The Shin account of eventual universalism is mirrored by Tillich's reasoning that everyone will attain to eternal life. Like Shin Buddhism, Tillich began by acknowledging that "not everyone is prepared to accept saving grace.

---

[20] Tillich, 2:79.

[21] Tillich, 1:285.

[22] Kirk R. MacGregor, *A Comparative Study of Adjustments to Social Catastrophes in Christianity and Buddhism: The Black Death in Europe and the Kamakura Takeover in Japan as Causes of Religious Reform* (Lewiston: Mellen, 2011), 299.

[23] Shinran, *Kyōgyōshinshō*, 1.75-76.

[24] Bloom, *Gospel*, 88.

This raises the problem of the relation of divine love to man's ultimate destiny; this is the question of predestination."[25] For Tillich, this question can be resolved in one of two ways: "The doctrine of the ambiguity of all human goodness and of the dependence of salvation on the divine grace alone either leads us back to the doctrine of double predestination or leads us forward to the doctrine of eternal essentialization."[26] Tillich ruled out the first possibility: "It cannot be understood as double predestination, since that violates both the divine love and the divine power. Ontologically, eternal condemnation is a contradiction in terms."[27] For "everything as created is rooted in the eternal ground of being. In this respect non-being cannot prevail against it."[28]

Consequently, Tillich subscribed to the doctrine of eternal essentialization: "This corresponds to the assertion that everything temporal comes from the eternal, and it agrees with the Pauline vision that in ultimate fulfilment God shall be everything in (and for) everything. One could call this symbol 'eschatological pan-en-theism.'"[29] Eschatological panentheism is accomplished for Tillich by divine grace: "Grace, as the infusion of love, is the power which overcomes estrangement....Grace is the effective presence of love in man. The very term 'grace' indicates that it is not a product of any act of good will on the part of him who receives it but that it is given gratuitously, without merit on his side. The great 'in spite of' is inseparable from the concept of grace."[30] Grace can effectuate eternal life for all persons without contravening their wills because those wills choose from the beneficent options supplied by the Spiritual Presence, which stands above and beyond the subject-object relationship that plagues causal determinism. As Tillich explained:

> The solution is that the determining subject is determined by that which transcends subject and object, the Spiritual Presence. Its impact on the subject which is existentially separated from its object is called "grace"...."Grace" means that the Spiritual Presence cannot be produced but is given. The ambiguity of self-determination is overcome by grace, and there is no other way of overcoming it and of escaping the despair of the conflict between the command of self-

[25] Tillich, *Systematic Theology*, 1:284.
[26] Tillich, 3:408.
[27] Tillich, 1:284.
[28] Tillich., 3:415.
[29] Tillich, 3:420-21.
[30] Tillich, 2:49; 3:274.

> determination and the impossibility of determining oneself in the direction of what one essentially is.[31]

Shinran and Tillich would therefore concur that Ultimate Reality (Amida or God) alone is the cause of salvation. While faith constitutes the act of human reception, this act is itself a divine gift.[32] For both Shinran and Tillich, "the ultimate end of religion is the salvation of all beings."[33]

The New Being in Amida as the Buddha

At this juncture we need to ask: what is the Shin Buddhist equivalent to New Being? The answer is Buddha nature or Buddha mind, namely, "the inherent nature that exists in all beings" which is "identical with transcendental reality."[34] This quotation reveals that Buddha nature simultaneously participates in both existence and essence. As I have argued elsewhere, Hōnen maintained that Buddha nature did not eternally exist in the past. Rather, Buddha nature emerged when Amida, by becoming the avatar Dharmākara and, over long eons, fulfilling his forty-eight monastic vows to create the Pure Land, produced in his own person a divine-human reality or Buddha nature.[35] What Tillich said of Christ is thus equally true of Amida: "the eternal God-Man unity has appeared under the conditions of existence."[36] Similar to the accounts of Jesus in the Gospels, the *Muryōjukyō*, *Amidakyō*, and *Kammuryōjukyō*—the three prominent scriptures of Shin Buddhism—contain no hint of estrangement between Dharmākara and the ground of his being. For Shinran, Dharmākara lived in complete unity with the power of being-itself:

> No thought of greed, anger, or harmfulness arose in his mind; he cherished no impulse of greed, anger, or harmfulness. He did not cling to objects of perception—color, sound, smell, taste. Abounding in perseverance, he gave no thought to the suffering to be endured. He was content with few desires, and without greed, anger, or folly. Always tranquil in a state of samādhi, he possessed wisdom that knew no impediment. He was free of all thoughts of falsity or deception. Gentle in countenance and loving in speech, he perceived people's thoughts and was attentive to them. He was full of

---

[31] Tillich, 3:211.

[32] MacGregor, *Comparative Study*, 268-72; Tillich, *Systematic Theology*, 3:224.

[33] Bloom, *Gospel*, 88.

[34] Hsing Yun, *Being Good: Buddhist Ethics for Everyday Life*, trans. Tom Graham (New York: Weatherhill), 152-53.

[35] MacGregor, *Comparative Study*, 170.

[36] Tillich, *Systematic Theology*, 2:169.

> courage and vigor, and being resolute in his acts, knew no fatigue. Seeking solely that which was pure and undefiled, he brought benefit to all beings.[37]

Dharmākara showed the depth of his reliance on the ground of being, and so the ground of everything personal, by making his own supreme enlightenment contingent on the benefits he would bestow upon all persons. The Eleventh Vow in the *Muryōjukyō* asserts that Dharmākara will not attain greatest enlightenment if those who believe in him fail to gain psychological wholeness, namely, not being "definitively settled in the group of the faithful before their entrance into Nirvana."[38] The Twelfth Vow states that Dharmākara will not receive the highest enlightenment if "my light should be limited and not be able to illumine hundreds of thousands of kotis (an enormous number)."[39] Such a vow guarantees the universal accessibility of his Buddha nature.

As a free gift, Amida accordingly implanted this quality of his own being within the nature of all humanity, thus rendering it universal. Shinran disclosed the particulars of Amida's work, on account of which he is rightly accorded the status of Tathagata (the one beyond all coming and going and so transcending all dualities):

> The mind of the Buddha is difficult to understand, but if we may infer concerning his mind, (we might say) that the whole sea of sentient beings, from the beginningless past even until the present time, are defiled, impure and stained. Their minds are not pure, and being false, they do not have a mind of truth. For this reason the Tathagata had compassion on the whole sea of suffering sentient beings. For incomprehensibly infinite kalpas he performed the disciplines of a Bodhisattva, and never for even a single moment were his practices of the mouth, mind or body, impure, or untrue. By his pure, sincere mind, the Tathagata perfected his completely harmonious, unimpeded, mysterious, inexpressible, incomprehensible, supreme virtue. *He transferred the sincere mind of the Tathagata to all the sea of sentient beings who are passionridden, evil in deed and in mind.*[40]

However, this universal Buddha mind is not self-actualizing but remains a mere potency until humans freely choose to avail themselves of it.

---

[37] Shinran, *Essential*, 133.

[38] Quoted in Bloom, *Gospel*, 3.

[39] Quoted in Bloom, *Gospel*, 2.

[40] Quoted in Bloom, *Gospel*, 46; emphasis in original.

Since one cannot access a gift without first acknowledging the giver, faith in Amida becomes the true path through which individuals tap into their indwelling Buddha nature and so realize the same level of transcendence as Amida.[41] At the pivotal moment when one is led to faith, Amida "saves the believer suddenly and in a crosswise action."[42] This action is crosswise because the individual, moving in the horizontal or created plane from fruitless path to fruitless path and from reincarnation to reincarnation, is saved by the unilateral action of Amida, who from the vertical or divine plane snatches the person out of the estrangement that enslaved her or him and so instantaneously liberates her or him.[43] Because faith is the means by which individuals gain contact with the Buddha nature, Shinran equated faith with Buddha nature: "Buddha nature is denominated great faith.... All beings will truly attain great faith eventually. So it is taught that all beings possess Buddha nature. Great faith is itself Buddha nature."[44] This notion resonates perfectly with Tillich's three elements of faith, which essentially delineate participation in New Being. As Tillich wrote, faith's first element is "being opened up by the Spiritual Presence;" its second element is "accepting it in spite of the infinite gap between the divine Spirit and the human spirit;" and its third element is "expecting final participation in the transcendent unity of unambiguous life."[45] By experiencing liberation from estrangement, the Shin Buddhist is opened up by the Spiritual Presence. By placing faith in Amida, the Shin Buddhist accepts Spiritual Presence despite the infinite gap separating one from essential being. By possessing full confidence that one will be reborn in the Pure Land, the Shin Buddhist expects final participation in the transcendent unity of unambiguous life.

The Tillichian Atonement of Amida

Tillich posited, "the doctrine of atonement is the description of the effect of the New Being in Jesus as the Christ on those who are grasped by it in their state of estrangement."[46] Tillich delineated six principles of atonement, all of which are satisfied by Amida's redemptive work. For Tillich, "the first and all-decisive principle is that the atoning processes are created by God and God alone.... the bearer of the New Being...mediates the reconciling act of God

[41] MacGregor, *Comparative Study*, 170-71.
[42] Shinran, *Kyōgyōshinshō*, 2.250.
[43] MacGregor, *Comparative Study*, 269.
[44] Quoted in Bloom, *Gospel*, 40.
[45] Tillich, *Systematic Theology*, 3:133.
[46] Tillich, 2:170.

to man."[47] Amida as the Buddha mediates the reconciling act of himself to humanity by accruing the infinite merit which created the Pure Land, bestowing his own nature on humanity, and eventually awakening in all persons faith by his grace. As Amida promised in the Twenty-Second Vow: "After my obtaining Buddhahood...all beings might establish themselves in true peerless enlightenment, and further be led on beyond the ordinary stages of Bodhisattvahood, even indeed to the virtues of Samantabhadra."[48] In other words, Amida will lead all persons not merely to partial fulfillment of their ontological potential but indeed to eternal essentialization and complete self-actualization.

Tillich maintained that "the second principle for a doctrine of atonement is that there are no conflicts in God between his reconciling love and his retributive justice."[49] Hōnen explained the harmony between Amida's love and justice through a creative reappropriation of the transfer of merit doctrine, which had historically allowed laypeople who could not finish the Eightfold Path to access the excess merit of bodhisattvas and other righteous humans in order to attain nirvana. But owing to Amida's status as a divine-human Buddha, Hōnen stipulated that persons could now procure a transfer of merit from Amida, namely, the endless merit he earned during his impeccably compassionate earthly sojourn and fulfillment of his forty-eight vows. Hōnen proclaimed the transfer mechanism to be faith. Since Pure Land adherents are in this way clothed with the perfect merit of Amida, they may be reckoned as fully just in his sight and therefore deserve no retribution. Instead, no matter how evil they had previously been, they possess Amida's righteousness and stand before Amida as morally entitled to the Pure Land.[50] Accordingly Hōnen daringly announced:

> It matters not how great a sinner may be, he should not give way to doubts; for...Amida does not hate a man, however deeply stained with sin he might be....Even the man who is so sinful that he has committed the ten evil deeds and the five deadly sins may be born into the Pure Land....And if a sinful man may thus be born into that land, how much more a good man![51]

---

[47] Tillich, 2:173-74.

[48] Quoted in Bloom, *Gospel*, 3-4.

[49] Tillich, *Systematic Theology*, 2:174.

[50] MacGregor, *Comparative Study*, 171.

[51] *Hōnen*, 402-3.

Thus Amida proves himself to be just and blameless as well as the one who lovingly justifies and makes blameless everyone who believes in him.[52]

For Tillich, "the third principle for a doctrine of atonement is that the divine removal of guilt and punishment is not an act of overlooking the reality and depth of existential estrangement."[53] Amida did not overlook existential estrangement but fully analyzed it, consequently experiencing compassion for all who suffered it and deep longing for their restoration. Shinran reports Amida's assessment as follows: "I find that all beings, an ocean of multitudes, have since the beginningless past down to this day, this very moment, been evil and defiled, completely lacking the mind of purity. They have been false and deceitful, completely lacking the mind of truth and reality."[54] Hōnen reported that, as a result, "Amida vowed not to achieve enlightenment until all who would chant his name would be reborn in his country."[55] In order to effectuate this promise, Amida brought the possibility of existential estrangement upon himself by entering into the created sphere as Dharmākara, experiencing its temptation. Since he did not succumb to it, Amida overcame the gap between existential and essential being. He can therefore victoriously proclaim, "I have appeared in the world and expounded the teachings of the way of enlightenment, seeking to save the multitudes of living beings by blessing them with the benefit that is true and real."[56] In this manner, Amida fulfilled Tillich's fourth principle for atonement theology, namely, "that God's atoning activity must be understood as his participation in existential estrangement and its self-destructive consequences."[57]

Tillich expressed the fifth principle of atonement theology in Christian terms: "in the Cross of the Christ the divine participation in existential estrangement becomes manifest."[58] Transposing this principle into a Shin Buddhist key, we can say that Amida's participation in existential estrangement proves clear in the renunciation of his earthly throne and giving worship to the Buddha Lokeśvararāja, who walked the earth during the time of Amida's incarnation. The *Muryōjukyō* explains this event:

> At that time there was a king who, having heard the Buddha's exposition of the Dharma, rejoiced in his heart and awakened aspiration for highest, perfect enlightenment. He renounced his kingdom

[52] MacGregor, *Comparative Study*, 172.

[53] Tillich, *Systematic Theology*, 2:174.

[54] Shinran, *Essential*, 133.

[55] *Hōnen*, 688.

[56] Shinran, *Essential*, 68.

[57] Tillich, *Systematic Theology*, 2:174.

[58] Tillich, 2:175.

and throne, and became a monk named Dharmākara....He went to see Tathāgata Lokeśvararāja, knelt down at his feet, walked around him three times keeping him always on his right, prostrated himself on the ground, and, putting his palms together in worship, praised the Buddha.[59]

Amida's renouncing of glory and humbling himself to the lowest point resembles Jesus' decision to lay aside his glory and humble himself to the ignominious point of death on a cross (Phil. 2:6-8). Amida's action constitutes, in Tillichian terms, "the effective manifestation" of Amida's "taking the consequences" of human estrangement upon himself.[60] Moreover, Tillich remarked that the process of atonement encompasses the "subjective side," namely, the human experience that the numen "is eternally reconciled."[61] In their spiritual journeys, both Hōnen and Shinran had this experience. Despite his realization of personal unfitness for the Pure Land, Hōnen professed: "The fact is that it is only...because he himself comes for us, to bring us to that Pure Land, that we are able to get there at all."[62] That Amida is reconciled to the sin of humanity is evident in Shinran's pronouncement:

> However good a man may be, he is incapable, with all his deeds of goodness, of effecting his rebirth in Amida's Land of Recompense. Much less so with bad men....Being so, good deeds are of no effect and evil deeds of no hindrance as regards rebirth. Even the rebirth of good men is impossible without being helped by Amida's specific Vow issuing from his great love and compassion which are not at all of this world.[63]

Accordingly, Tillich's objective and subjective sides of atonement are met in Amida's renunciation and its effects upon its human beneficiaries.

Tillich's sixth principle of atonement theology "is that through participation in the New Being...men also participate in the manifestation of the atoning act of God."[64] According to Bloom, Shinran utterly disclaimed "the possibility of birth in the Pure Land for one who is merely attracted to it because of its pleasures and bliss." Rather, he insisted that the Shin devotee "seek

---

[59] *The Three Pure Land Sutras*, trans. Hisao Inagaki with Harold Stewart, rev. 2nd ed. (Berkeley: Numata Center for Buddhist Translation and Research, 2003), 9.

[60] Tillich, *Systematic Theology*, 2:176.

[61] Tillich, 2:176.

[62] *Hōnen*, 409.

[63] Quoted in Bloom, *Gospel*, 32.

[64] Tillich, *Systematic Theology*, 2:176.

the salvation of all beings" in "this world."[65] The Shin Buddhist must share in the salvific labor of Amida, working "selflessly and unhindered for the salvation of beings" and displaying "pure and perfect altruism."[66] The very essence of reality—or in Tillichian language, structure of being-itself—"operates to bring beings to enlightenment despite their sin and ignorance."[67] As Shin Buddhists work in and through the power of being-itself by achieving the enlightenment of others, they fully take part in New Being.

Shin Buddhist Participation in New Being

Shin participation in New Being is functionally equivalent to what Tillich described as justification. The way of life displayed by Shin Buddhists is often termed "naturalism," and the phrases describing it are *kono mama* (just as I am) and *somo mama* (just as you are). Resembling ideas from Christian hymnody, the Shin Buddhist accepts that s/he is accepted by Amida just as s/he is. Alfred Bloom explains that, as a result, "one can take life just as it is, as one finds it, and in the midst of this life find the ultimate reality."[68] Such acceptance furnishes the necessary empathy to work for justice and transformation in the world. On Tillich's reckoning, to be justified a person "must accept that he is accepted; he must accept acceptance."[69] While for Tillich this occurs through Christ, for the Shin Buddhist this occurs through Amida. Tillich held that the Christian life that follows justification takes the persons and affairs of this life—"both the individual Christian and the church, both the religious and the secular realm"—and in them finds absolute significance through the sanctifying work of the divine Spirit.[70]

The life of Shin Buddhists is one of compassion (*karuna*), derived from their attitude to accept everything as it is not so that it can stay as it is but so that it can participate in Buddha nature, overcoming its existential estrangement. With their eternal destiny secure, Shin Buddhists are free to work selflessly and unimpeded for the liberation of all beings. When one stands in the company of the truly assured, "compassion becomes the essence of one's existence and not a means to an end."[71] Bloom observes that, for Shinran, "compassion is the essence of religion, history and reality, and it confronts beings at every turn in great individuals, in the tradition of the Pure Land and as the

[65] Bloom, *Gospel*, 82.
[66] Bloom, 84.
[67] Bloom, 85.
[68] Bloom, *Gospel*, 43.
[69] Tillich, *Systematic Theology*, 2:179.
[70] Tillich, 2:180.
[71] Bloom, *Gospel*, 84.

name and Light from Amida Buddha which arouses the awareness of sin and the humble attitude of faith in beings."[72] Tillich famously identified the essence of religion as ultimate concern, which necessarily has an all-encompassing quality: "The ultimate concern is unconditional, independent of any conditions of character, desire, or circumstance. The unconditional concern is total: no part of ourselves or our world is excluded from it; there is no 'place' to flee from it."[73] It therefore demands compassion for every being in the world. This type of compassion Tillich calls *agapē*, which is universal in scope, excludes no one, and "affirms the other unconditionally, that is, apart from higher or lower, pleasant or unpleasant qualities."[74] As Tillich continues, "*Agapē* accepts the other in spite of resistance. It suffers and forgives. It seeks the personal fulfilment of the other."[75] Consequently, the altruistic Shin *karuna* and Tillichian *agapē* seemingly amount to interchangeable concepts.

For Shinran, the actualization of the Buddha nature or mind in Shin Buddhists guarantees compassion as their rule of life, with occasional sin amounting to the exception that proves this rule. As the very nature of Amida, the Buddha mind most strongly desires good and other-centered actions but detests evil and purely selfish actions. While Shin Buddhists are free to choose between good and evil, their choices are unequally motivated in favor of good, such that they will live in virtually continual compassion to their fellow human beings.[76] Bloom comments that in the Buddha mind, "the gratification of the ego is set aside for praise of the divinity and for altruistic aspiration for all humanity."[77] Shin Buddhists therefore occupy what Tillich denominated the Spiritual Community, which "is New Being, created by the Spiritual Presence...a manifestation of unambiguous life."[78] Moreover, Tillich emphasized that,

> as the community of the New Being, the Spiritual Community is a community of love. As the Spiritual Community contains the tension between the faith of the individual members, with their indefinite variety of experiences, and that of the community, so it contains the tension between the indefinite variety of love relations and the *agapē* which unites being with being in the transcendent union of unambiguous life. And as the variety of conditions of faith does

[72] Bloom, 85.
[73] Tillich, *Systematic Theology*, 1:12.
[74] Tillich, 1:280.
[75] Tillich, 1:280.
[76] MacGregor, *Comparative Study*, 277.
[77] Bloom, *Gospel*, 88.
[78] Tillich, *Systematic Theology*, 3:150.

> not lead to a break with the faith of the community, so the variety of love relations does not prevent *agapē* from uniting the separated centers in the transcendent union of unambiguous life. Nevertheless, it is multidimensional love, fragmentary in view of the separation of everything from everything else in time and space, but an anticipation of the perfect union in Eternal Life.[79]

At the heart of this multidimensional love, claimed Shinran, stood gratitude to Amida Buddha and Gautama Buddha. This gratitude entails that "we must repay the grace of Tathagata's great compassion, though our bodies are (ground) to powder."[80] In Bloom's words, the gratitude proclaimed by Shinran "awakens us to our true self and our potentiality to contribute positively to the world and society as bearers of compassion and wisdom, which are the essence of Buddhahood."[81]

For Shinran, the application of compassion must be without partiality. Thus he defined the Shin Buddhist as "*not discriminating at all between the poor and the rich and well-born*: *Not discriminating* means not choosing, not rejecting. *Poor* means impoverished and in need. *At all* is for emphasis."[82] Shinran underscored the unconditional nature of compassion in the following instructions regarding its beneficiaries to his disciples: "The amount of evil one has committed is not considered; the duration of any performances of religious practices is of no concern. It is a matter of neither practice nor good acts, neither sudden attainment nor gradual attainment, neither meditative practice nor non-meditative practice, neither right contemplation nor wrong contemplation.... It is like the medicine that eradicates all poisons."[83] The ethic of compassion inspired in Shin Buddhists by the Buddha nature resembles the ethic of love inspired in Christians by grace. Since the Buddha nature is a gracious gift of Amida to his followers, the following words of Tillich apply equally to Shin Buddhism and Christianity: "Morality in the Spiritual Community is determined by grace."[84] By virtue of its inherent inclination toward other-centered actions, the Buddha mind furnishes Shin Buddhists with precisely those ethical acts it requires. This observation evokes Tillich's description of how grace accomplishes the implementation of the moral law:

[79] Tillich, 3:156.
[80] Quoted in Bloom, *Gospel*, 73.
[81] Alfred Bloom, in Shinran, *Essential*, 183.
[82] Shinran, *Essential*, 185; emphasis in original.
[83] Shinran, 185.
[84] Tillich, *Systematic Theology*, 3:159.

> Grace is the impact of the Spiritual Presence that makes the fulfilment of the law possible—though fragmentarily. It is the reality of that which the law commands, the reunion with one's true being, and this means the reunion with oneself, with others, and with the ground of one's self and others. Where there is New Being, there is grace, and vice versa. Autonomous or heteronomous morality is without ultimate moral motivating power. Only love or the Spiritual Presence can motivate by giving what it demands.[85]

Shinran and Tillich agreed that all moral systems without what Tillich called "Spiritual Presence" lack the power to motivate their adherents and therefore eventually collapse. Only communities driven by *karuna* or *agapē*—created by the Spiritual Presence—successfully discharge the moral imperative.[86]

Conclusion

Although Tillich never investigated the Shin modality of Mahayana Buddhism in *Christianity and the Encounter of World Religions*, I submit that if he had, he would have been pleasantly surprised, if not overtly enthusiastic, at the cross-cultural applicability of his theological ideas. Tillich hinted at such a possibility concerning what he knew of Mahayana, namely, "that in Mahajana Buddhism the Buddha-Spirit appears in many manifestations of a personal character, making a nonmystical, often very primitive relation to a divine figure possible."[87] Indeed Tillich would have found that, for Shin Buddhism, this is a remarkable understatement. Far from primitive, the Shin relation between Amida Buddha and his devotees is extremely sophisticated and evinces the essential facets of a valid manifestation and presentation of New Being.

---

[85] Tillich, 3:274.

[86] Tillich, 3:274-75.

[87] Paul Tillich, *Christianity and the Encounter of World Religions*, reprint ed. (Minneapolis: Fortress, 1994), 67.

Pantheism and Paul Tillich: Mystical Immanence and Divine Involvement in an Evolutionary World

Bradford McCall

Whether Ultimate Reality is conceived as personal God or impersonal principle somehow at work in the world is an issue that divides major world religions into opposing camps. Eastern philosophies are commonly considered non-dualistic, while Western philosophies are commonly considered dualistic, relying on Greek-derived intellectual standards. Dualism is a deep-seated habit of thinking in binary opposites which can result in paralyzing practical and theoretical difficulties.

Many Christian scholars think that the Western mindset is necessarily dualistic and, by extension, committed to dualistic theism. Yet the West already contains a pre-philosophical form of non-dualism within one of its more marginalized roots, that of ancient Hebrew culture, which makes possible a new form of non-dualism, one to which the West can subscribe. Paul Tillich suggests that the natural world can have no being itself without the underlying ground of being, that is, God (the Spirit). Indeed, the infinite is precisely the finite, for if it were not, it could not be infinite in truth; as John Thatamanil says, the infinite is precisely what it is: not other than the finite.[1]

Tillichian Nonduality

The focus of Christian nondualism is to bring humans closer to God and the realization of "oneness" with the Divine.[2] According to David R. Loy, the concept of nonduality is usually associated with various kinds of absolute idealism, or mystical traditions in the East—and as a result, many modern philosophers are poorly informed on the topic. Increasingly, however, nonduality

---

[1] John J. Thatamanil, *The Immanent Divine: God, Creation, and the Human Predicament* (Minneapolis: Fortress, 2006), 140, 184.

[2] James Charlton, *Non-dualism in Eckhart, Julian of Norwich and Traherne: A Theopoetic Reflection* (New York: Bloomsbury Academic, 2012), 2.

is finding its way into Western philosophical debates.[3] Loy in fact distinguishes five different conceptions of nonduality:

> The negation of dualistic thinking in pairs of opposites. The Yin-Yang symbol of Taoism symbolizes the transcendence of this dualistic way of thinking.
>
> *Monism*, the nonplurality of the world. Although the phenomenal world appears as a plurality of "things," in reality they are "of a single cloth."
>
> *Advaita*, the nondifference of subject and object, or nonduality between subject and object.
>
> *Advaya*, the identity of phenomena and the Absolute, the "nonduality of duality and nonduality."
>
> *Mysticism*, a mystical unity between God and mankind. [4]

John J. Thatamanil seizes upon Tillich's idea of ecstatic experience as the closest one gets to close the gap between immanence and transcendence. An important characteristic of the ecstatic experience is that it is an "inbreaking" of the divine into existence: not vice versa.

Tillich's dynamic vision denies that ultimate reality is an unchanging absolute that resists change and leads inevitably to an immanence that might itself be called "nondual."[5] A dualistic conception of God is at least problematic for, if not devastating to, twenty-first century theology because it "transforms the infinity of God into a finiteness which is merely an extension of the categories of finitude."[6] What Tillich means by this is that using a dualistic notion of God subjects God to the categories of time and space, along with substance ontology.[7] Indeed, the God of dualism is an entity that has his "home" in heaven above, but nevertheless acts within time, interacts with other beings causally, and is merely one substance among others. Such a God "is just one item in a universe that proves to be more encompassing than God is."[8]

---

[3] David R. Loy, *Nonduality: In Buddhism and Beyond* (Somerville: Wisdom, 2019), 6.

[4] David R. Loy, *Nonduality: A Study in Comparative Philosophy* (New Haven: Yale University Press, 1988), 17–25.

[5] Thatamanil, *The Immanent Divine*, 23.

[6] Paul Tillich, *Systematic Theology*, vol. 2 (Chicago: University of Chicago Press, 1957), 6.

[7] Thatamanil, *The Immanent Divine*, 19.

[8] Thatamanil, 19.

Although Tillich views naturalism as the preferable option over and above supernaturalism (what he terms supra-), it is nevertheless problematic in part because it "denies the infinite distance between the whole of finite things and their infinite ground, with the consequence that the term 'God' becomes interchangeable with the term 'universe' and therefore semantically superfluous."[9] Tillich indicates that God's life is life as spirit. He distinguishes between the abyss of the divine and the fullness of its content, that is, between divine depth and divine *logos*. The first of these, divine depth, has historically been applied to the Father (which makes God, "God"), and the second of these—divine logos—is generally assumed to be the Son. Tillich writes:

> "The first principle is basis of Godhead....It is the root of his majesty, the unapproachable intensity of his being, the inexhaustible ground of being in which everything has its origin....The classical term *logos* is most adequate for the second principle, that of meaning and structure....Without the second principle the first principle would be chaos, burning fire, but it would not be the creative ground....As the actualization of the other two principles, the Spirit is the third principle. Both power and meaning are contained in it and united in it. It makes them creative. The third principle is in a way the whole (God *is* Spirit), and in a way it is a special principle (God *has* the Spirit, as he has the *logos*). It is the Spirit in whom God 'goes out from' himself, the Spirit proceeds from the divine ground. He gives actuality to that which is potential in the divine ground and 'outspoken' in the divine *logos*. Through the Spirit the divine fulness is posited in the divine life as something definite, and at the same time it is reunited in the divine ground."[10]

Tillich is clear that the meaning of transcendence must be conceived differently in our modern era, since God does not inhabit a spatiotemporal realm that is different than the natural world in which we live.

I follow Thatamanil in his development of a thorough Christian nondualism by applying his insights from the human predicament, using Tillich, to the concepts of immanent creativity and macroevolution. Spirit, manifest by immanent creativity in the macro-evolutionary process, already participates in the natural world all of the time. There is not a time when the Spirit is not embedded and embodied within this natural world. In fact, for Thatamanil, the divine life necessarily includes human life insomuch as God (the Spirit) is

---

[9] Tillich, *Systematic Theology*, vol. 2, 7.

[10] Paul Tillich, *Systematic Theology*, vol. 1 (Chicago: University of Chicago Press, 1951), 250–51.

the creative ground of human life.[11] I agree, but would like to expand it to the entire temporal and natural world, not just human beings per se. As such, the Spirit is not alien to the natural world; rather, it is the very depth of the natural world, the depth to which the Spirit inhabits. God as Spirit does not stand over against the natural world. Tillich explicitly states that God is infinite because he has the finite…within himself united with his infinity."[12]

Spirit is never—ever!—separate from the finite natural world. I assert that *pan/en/theism* is directly implicated. Indeed, the infinite power of the creative Spirit is forever and always present to the natural world, driving it toward greater complexity in and through the processes of macroevolution. Thus, there is, within the natural world, an infinite drive toward self-transcendence, whether that "self" be electrons, atomic nuclei, atoms, elements, bacteria, cats, dogs, mushrooms, or people (and so forth, as it were). Entities are never at rest. They are never content with being what they are for the present moment. Instead, they forever "strive" to become more than they are through macroevolution, and this in and of itself testifies to both the presence and power of the infinite within the finite, whether that finite entity be atoms or animal species.

Despite all this, Tillich's thought retains a residual dualism that fails to explain mystical immanence as being expressed in macro-evolutionary processes in and within the natural world. We need to look elsewhere, for example, to the non-substantialist theological ontology of Joseph Bracken in which ultimate reality is perceived to be an overriding activity (or, in my language, "involvement") versus being a substance. Tillich's work has made the path easier to arrive at this mystically immanent, nondualistic macroevolution mediated by divine involvement, for he has set forth the thesis of an internal relationship between being itself and other beings. He appeals, for example, to Paul the apostle's pneumatology.

In Romans 8:26, divine immanence is experienced as an immanently ecstatic event accomplished by the work of the Spirit that grasps and prays through us when we know not how to pray. I would like to extend this thought to "creation" in general and macroevolution in particular by claiming that it is the Spirit who is the immanent principle of creativity throughout the natural world. In Tillich's theology of Spirit, God approaches humans when they are "grasped" by the power inherent in being-itself and thereafter driven beyond

[11] What Thatamanil here applies to God generically, I would like to—as indicated by my parenthetical addition—apply to the Spirit specifically. Cf. Thatamanil, *The Immanent Divine*, 147.

[12] Tillich, *Systematic Theology*, vol. 1, 252.

themselves into ecstatic union with divinity.[13] The result of this endeavor is the "mutual immanence" that Tillich so eloquently speaks of in his third volume of *Systematic Theology*.[14] I would like, further, to generalize this Tillichian "mutual immanence" idea and extrapolate it to all of reality.

Instead of the conceptual terms causality and substance, Tillich prefers "a more directly symbolic term, 'the creative and abysmal ground of being.' In this term both naturalistic pantheism, based on the category of substance, and rationalistic theism, based on the category of causality are overcome."[15] "Ground," for Tillich, serves to incorporate the best elements of both causality and substance, but at the same time rejects their literal adequacy. God can be imagined as a substance inasmuch as beings cannot exist without and apart from God, just as brick mortar cannot exist apart from sand granules. But at the same time, God cannot literally be a substance, or the natural world (and other beings) would not be marked by freedom. Similarly, God can be imagined as a cause amongst other causes, since it is the involvement of God that causes the natural world and hence other beings to be, but God cannot literally be thought a cause because of the freedom of the natural world and other beings.

God (the Spirit) is the ground of being as well as its depth of being. God (the Spirit's) involvement as the ground of being is neither contingent nor provisional. Tillich states that there "is no divine nature which could be abstracted from his eternal creativity."[16] Indeed, for Tillich, the ground is the very source from which everything emerges: "The ground of being has the character of self-manifestation; it has *logos* character. This is not something added to the divine life; it is the divine life itself."[17] Tillich's God, then, cannot be conceived apart from the world (again, I assert, *panentheism* is directly implicated).[18]

As Bracken states, "the grounding activity is not an entity, and the entity is other than the grounding activity. At the same time, they are not two since only together, namely, as grounding activity and that which exists in virtue of the grounding activity, are they one concrete reality. This grounding activity, moreover, is infinite because it serves as the ontological ground for literally everything that exists....It transcends them all since it is their common ground

---

[13] Cf. Thatamanil, *The Immanent Divine*, 11.

[14] Paul Tillich, *Systematic Theology*, vol. 3 (Chicago: University of Chicago Press, 1963), 114.

[15] Tillich, *Systematic Theology*, vol. 1, 238.

[16] Tillich, *Systematic Theology*, vol. 2, 147.

[17] Tillich, *Systematic Theology*, vol. 1, 157–58.

[18] Thatamanil, *The Immanent Divine*, 145.

or source of existence and activity. Whereas entities are inevitably limited or defined by their relations to one another, this grounding activity is strictly unlimited and therefore infinite."[19] The being of being itself is *becoming* itself.[20] Thatamanil suggests that the way forward, building on and perhaps correcting some of Tillich's contentions, is to go the route proffered by Bracken: infinite reality must be understood as activity (or, in my terminology, "involvement") and not as a substance.[21] Thatamanil argues along with Bracken that viewing being-itself as ontological creativity makes theological sense.

This has direct implications for the immanence versus transcendence of God debate, for God cannot be transcendent if by that one means that there is a separation between God and the world. Assuming this latter point, Tillich redefines the terminology of transcendence by purging it of its supranaturalistic overtones. As such, there is no antagonism between God's transcendence and immanence. God's immanence does not come at the price of his transcendence, nor vice versa. William Placher calls such a dynamic the "contrastive" account of the debate between transcendence and immanence, one that makes "divine transcendence and involvement in the world into a zero-sum game."[22] Placher analyzes the history of the transcendence versus immanence debate back to the fundamental error of thinking God to be one being among others. He argues: "If God were one of the things in the world—as implied by the contrastive account of transcendence—then it would be natural to ask where God is located—in the world or outside it?"[23] And, as Thatamanil notes, either answer negates the other. Tillich denies this sort of duality and the reified concept of divinity that it necessitates.

It is my assertion that nondualistic macroevolution rejects the oppositional account of the transcendence versus immanence debate. Tillich's God does not need to intervene in nature or history to be present there, for in his theology, symbolically speaking, God *is* the power of being in everything and as such is "the source of all particular powers of being."[24] The volcano, the earthquake, the rogue nation, the nation championing justice, the sinner and the saint—all are ultimately empowered by the source of all being, which is God's creative power (which, as we have previously noted, *is* the Spirit). It is

---

[19] Joseph A. Bracken, "Infinity and the Logic of Non-Dualism," *Journal of Hindu-Christian Studies* 11 (1998): 41.

[20] Thatamanil, *The Immanent Divine*, 188.

[21] Thatamanil, 188.

[22] William C. Placher, *The Domestication of Transcendence: How Modern Thinking About God Went Wrong* (Louisville: Westminster John Knox Press, 1996), 111.

[23] Placher, 112.

[24] Tillich, *Systematic Theology*, vol. 3, 385.

in this sense that God can be spoken of as "Almighty."[25] Indeed, for Tillich, all power, understood as "the eternal possibility of resisting non-being," ultimately comes from God. Therefore, "since God as *the* power of being is the source of all particular powers of being, power is divine in its essential nature."[26]

Tillich's theology of transitory dualism contains the proverbial seeds of a Christian nonduality. It is Thatamanil's contention that a Christian nondualism in which God is understood to be all in all is a potent vision for twenty-first century theology. For God to be anything less than that means that God is no god at all. Christian nondualism both asserts and achieves a deep coincidence between immanence and transcendence. Tillich contributes to this view of Christian nondualism by explicating how traditional theism yields impoverished and inadequate views of transcendence and immanence. In their stead, Tillich proffers a vision of God in which he is at once qualitatively transcendent in power, yet also—at the same time—radically immanent by being the ground of being itself. This is especially applicable to a mystical understanding of macroevolution.

Tillich, Panentheism, and Mysticism

I assert a radical panentheistic immanence, bordering on pantheism. But it is not truly pantheism, for, as Tillich says, God is neither alongside things nor even "above" them; rather, he is nearer to them than they are to themselves; "He is their creative ground, here and now, always and everywhere."[27] Tillich is an important conversation partner here because his theology "amounts to a twentieth-century distillation of the history of Christian mystical theology."[28] It is more accurate therefore to speak of the "reality of God," which points to his true nature as being-itself. This insight, says Tillich, enables us to take a first step towards solving the problem of the transcendence and the immanence of God, for "as the power of being, God transcends both every being and also the totality of being. Being-itself infinitely transcends every finite being. There is no proportion or gradation between the finite and the infinite."[29] Indeed, within Tillich's corpus, one can discern the footprints (or shadow), or even voices, of such great historical mystics as Meister Eckhart and Nicholas of Cusa, who themselves propagated and "kept alive a radical

[25] Paul Tillich, *Love, Power, and Justice* (London, Oxford University Press, 1954), 110–11.

[26] Tillich, *Systematic Theology*, vol. 3, 385.

[27] Tillich, *Systematic Theology*, vol. 2, 7.

[28] Thatamanil, *The Immanent Divine*, 9.

[29] Paul Tillich, *Ultimate Concern* (London, SCM, 1965), 263.

sense of divine presence."[30] Therefore, Tillich's theology incorporates one of, if not the most robust accounts of divine immanence on tap today.

I assert that *creatio ex deo*, creation out of God, can be made consistent with a nondual, panentheistic, perspective upon divine involvement in an evolutionary world. This *creatio ex deo* removes the stumbling block of the seemingly unbridgeable chasm between God and the world, particularly in and through the work of the Spirit. As a Process theologian, I assert that this panentheistic concept of divine involvement in an evolutionary world envisions a God and natural world relationship that is not based upon duality. God's Spirit is everywhere present and pervasive within the natural world, but also exceeds it, though this is no duality, for the reality of God's Spirit is supraspatial (i.e., God's Spirit is beyond spatiality) and supranatural (i.e., God's Spirit is beyond naturality).[31] As such, the natural world is not external to the divine reality in any way. Rather, God's reality is determined by his relation to the natural world insomuch as his involvement (or activity) therein is based upon being the very ground of creativity and *being* itself. And that itself *is* mystical. Tillich again is useful here, in part because he understands being-itself to be a "dynamic creative power" that "gives rise to what it grounds."[32] Giving rise to what it grounds, I submit, is an apt metaphor for how God "creates" (if I may use such a loaded word) through the processes of macroevolution and also permeates the natural world thereafter.

Several Process-oriented thinkers, myself included, are quite content to think of God not as an entity but as a unifying activity immanent within the cosmic process. Bernard Meland, for example, refers to God not as a transcendent person but as "the Efficacy within relationships."[33] Similarly, Bernard Loomer identifies the world with God in the following passage:

---

[30] Thatamanil, *The Immanent Divine*, 9.

[31] Note that whereas Tillich uses the term supranatural to refer to what is ordinarily called supernaturalism, I use the term as being referent to what is beyond nature, but not wholly outside of it. In fact, Tillich claims that the entire and "basic intention of my doctrine of God" is to go beyond the naturalism and supranaturalism (again note his distinctive meaning for supra-) in his second volume of *Systematic Theology*, 5. Indeed, according to Tillich, whatever conception of divinity that portrays God as intervening from the outside into causal networks within the world is "supranatural" (cf. Tillich, *Systematic Theology*, vol. 2, 5). This supernaturalism, as I refer to it (but supra- according to Tillich) is problematic because it is not only contra science, but also because it pictures God as regularly disrupting the "inviolability of the created structures of the finite" (Tillich, *Systematic Theology*, vol. 2, 6).

[32] Thatamanil, *The Immanent Divine*, 11.

[33] Bernard Meland, *Fallible Forms and Symbols: Discourses on Method in a Theology of Culture* (Philadelphia: Fortress, 1976), 152.

> The world is God because it is the source and preserver of meaning; because the creative advance of the world in its adventure is the supreme cause to be served; because even in our desecration of our space and time within it, the world is holy ground; and because it contains and yet enshrouds the ultimate mystery inherent within existence itself.[34]

In a more recent publication Gordon Kaufman likewise refers to God not as a world transcendent entity but as a "serendipitous" creativity (i.e., that which I designate "involvement") at work in our own lives and in the natural world around us.[35] Indeed, within *In Face of Mystery,* Kaufman proposes the concept of "serendipitous creativity" as a metaphor more appropriate for thinking of God today than such traditional image/concepts as creator, lord, and father. In another essay, Kaufman more fully elaborates and more carefully nuances that concept: it is no longer possible, he argues, to connect today's scientific cosmological and evolutionary understandings of the origins of the universe and the emergence of life (including human life and history) with a conception of God constructed in the traditional anthropomorphic terms in an intelligible way.[36] However, the metaphor of serendipitous creativity—directly implied in and by the idea of evolution itself—has resources for constructing a religiously pertinent and meaningful late modern/postmodern conception of God. Indeed, it is apropos for naming God because it preserves—and indeed even emphasizes—the ultimacy of the *mystery* that God is, even while it connects God directly with the coming into being-in time-of the new and the novel.

In sum, affirming nonduality does *not* eviscerate transcendence.[37] Thatamanil states that it is possible, in nonduality, to have immanence without forgoing transcendence. For me, God and the natural world are thoroughly interdependent as manifest in the processes of macroevolution. God *is* the (serendipitous) creativity everywhere expressed by and within the macro-evolutionary process. Because God is the creativity of the macro-evolutionary process, God is forever linked with entities, both inanimate and animate,

---

[34] Bernard M. Loomer, "The Size of God," in *The Size of God: The Theology of Bernard Loomer in Context*, eds. William Dean and Larry E. Axel (Macon: Mercer University Press, 1987), 42.

[35] Gordon D. Kaufman, *In Face of Mystery: A Constructive Theology* (Cambridge: Harvard University Press, 1993), 390–401.

[36] Gordon D. Kaufman, "On Thinking of God as Serendipitous Creativity," *Journal of the American Academy of Religion* 69, no. 2 (2001): 409–25, especially 410.

[37] John J. Thatamanil, "Ecstasy and Nonduality: On Comparing Varieties of Immanence," *Journal of Hindu-Christian Studies* 22 (2009): 19–24, cf. 21.

while they advance in complexity. God is both encountered and experienced through the processes of macroevolution. If this be not mysticism, what else could it be?

Tillich and Mysticism

Gilles Deleuze and Félix Guattari, in *What Is Philosophy?*, state: "Immanence can be said to be the burning issue of all philosophy because it takes on all the dangers that philosophy must confront, all the condemnations, persecutions, and repudiations that it undergoes."[38] Immanence and mysticism, seemingly, go hand-in-hand. Or, rather, nonduality and mysticism do. Or, perhaps, a decidedly *nondual* version of immanence and mysticism do. I will, for lack of better terminology, still hesitantly employ the term immanence. I suggest that the processes of macroevolution together imply mystical experience, as they exhibit and manifest the profundity of the Spirit's creativity within the physical realm through my newly coined terminology of "divine involvement."

My definition of mysticism is based on Ralph Inge's comments that it is "the attempt to realize the presence of the living God in the soul and in nature."[39] A critical component in this definition is the admission that in order to know God, humanity must partake of the divine nature itself. If this definition is accepted, among many other feasible and possible ones—notes Julio Savi[40]—the goal of mysticism is the same as the purpose of human life described by Baha'u'llah: "to know [one's] Creator and to attain His Presence."[41] I would like to expand this concept to the entirety of the natural world, particularly pneumatologically.

The assumptions of mysticism, as described by Inge, and those of the Baha'i Faith, according to Julio Savi, are the same: human beings have a divine nature whose development through practicing the love of God allows their inner vision to become acuter, leading thereby to perceive the presence of God. This perception of the presence of God is usually referred to by mystics

---

[38] Gilles Deleuze and Félix Guattari, *What Is Philosophy?* (New York: Columbia University Press, 1994), 45.

[39] William Ralph Inge, *Christian Mysticism* (Whitefish: Kessinger, 2012), 5.

[40] Julio Savi, "The Baha'i Faith and the Perennial Mystical Quest: A Western Perspective," *Baha'i Studies Review* 14 (2007): 5.

[41] Shoghi Effendi, trans., *Gleanings from the Writings of Baha'u'llah* (Wilmette: Baha'i Publishing Trust, 1952), 70.

and students of mysticism as "mystical experience."[42] The world religious literature is rich in descriptions of mystical experience. Based on these descriptions, scholars have listed a number of its characteristics as follows:[43]

A consciousness of the oneness of everything:

Walter Terence Stace describes this consciousness as arising from the exclusion of "all the multiplicity of sensuous or conceptual or other empirical content...so that there remains only a void and empty unity."[44]

In this condition, the mystic "attains to complete communion with the Absolute Order, and submits to the inflow of its supernal vitality,"[45] and thus experiences what Nicholas of Cusa called "*coincidentia oppositorum*"[46] or "coincidence of contradictories."[47]

Timelessness:

Frank C. Happold explains that, during a mystical experience, the relationships between events "are not capable of being adequately described in terms of past, present, and future, or earlier than, later than. These experiences have a timeless quality."[48]

Sense of objectivity or reality:

Happold writes that mystical experiences "are states of knowledge,"[49] a knowledge characterized by a high degree of certitude.

Feelings of blessedness, joy, peace, happiness, etc.

A feeling that what is apprehended is holy, sacred or divine.

Ineffability:

---

[42] Savi, "The Baha'i Faith," 7.

[43] Note that I am indebted to Savi for this list, and I acknowledge such forthrightly, even though I have "massaged" it for my own purposes. See Savi, "The Baha'i Faith," 10–11.

[44] Walter Terence Stace, *Mysticism and Philosophy* (London: Macmillan, 1961), 79.

[45] Evelyn Underhill, *Mysticism: The Preeminent Study in the Nature and Development of Spiritual Consciousness* (New York: Image Classics: 1990), 432–33.

[46] Nicholas of Cusa, "Apologia Doctae Ignorantiae," in *Nicolai de Cusa Opera Omnia*, ed. Raymond Klibanski, two volumes (Leipzig/Hamburg: F. Meiner Verlag, 1932), 2:15.

[47] Jasper Hopkins, *Nicholas of Cusa's Debate with John Wenk: A Translation and an Appraisal of De Ignota Litteratura and Apologia Doctae Ignorantiae*, 3rd ed. (Minneapolis: The Arthur J. Banning Press, 1988), 470.

[48] Frank C. Happold, *Mysticism: A Study and an Anthology*, 3rd ed. (Harmondsworth: Penguin, 1990) 47–48.

[49] Happold, 45.

Mystical experience resembles a feeling and "it is not possible to make a state of feeling clear to one who has not experienced it."[50]

Paradoxicality:

Mystics frequently feel an urgent need to share their experience with others, and they try to overcome its ineffability through such "linguistic devices as simile, metaphor and paradox, however inadequate these may be for the task."[51]

Transience:

Mystical experience, with its feeling of timelessness, is seldom prolonged. And yet, some mystics are wholly immersed in their spiritual condition, so that their mystical experience "can become so frequent, so much a way of life, that, in the words of St. John of the Cross ... 'the soul has it in its power to abandon itself, whenever it wills, to this sweet sleep of love'."[52]

Passivity:

The mystics perceive themselves as the object of their own experience, as deprived of any will, as being seized by an outward power.

Nonreality of the ordinary self:

Usually there is a strict connection between the perception of the self, on the one hand, and sensory perception, awareness of time and the feeling of being willingly active, on the other. In a mystical experience all of that disappears, and, in the words of Rudolf Otto, the mystic perceives "the self... the personal 'I', as something not perfectly or essentially real, or even as mere nullity."[53] The perception of the self is expanded to bring the individual closer to her inner self, a reality that mystic Meister Eckhart calls "*scintilla animae*" (the spark of the soul).[54]

Side phenomena:

That is, "special altered states—visions, locutions, raptures and the like—which admittedly have played a large part in mysticism but which many mystics have insisted do not constitute the essence of the encounter with God."[55]

---

[50] Happold, *Mysticism*, 45.

[51] Robert Andrew Gilbert, *The Elements of Mysticism* (Shaftesbury: Element, 1991), 89.

[52] Happold, *Mysticism*, 55.

[53] Rudolf Otto, *The Idea of the Holy: An Inquiry into the Non-Rational Factor in the Idea of the Divine and its Relation to the Rational*, trans. John W. Harvey (Oxford: Oxford University Press, 1959), 21.

[54] Meister Eckhart, *Passion for Creation: The Earth-Honoring Spirituality of Meister Eckhart*, ed. Matthew Fox (Rochester: Inner Traditions, 2000), 277.

[55] Bernard McGinn, *The Foundations of Mysticism: Origins to the Fifth Century* (New York: Crossroad, 1997), xvii–xviii.

Many scholars agree with Dom Cuthbert Butler—whose text on Western mysticism has been described as "a masterly exhibition of the religious and psychological normality of the Christian contemplative life, as developed by its noblest representatives"[56]—on the opinion that "Essential mysticism should not be identified with occasional accidental concomitants, as visions, revelations, raptures, or other psycho-physical phenomena', and that 'the title mystical' should not be given 'to curious experiences and manifestations bordering on those of Spiritism; to intimations, second sight, telepathy; or religious "queer stories." For all such phenomena there is an accepted scientific term: they are "psychic" not "mystic'."[57] "True mysticism" is described as a state of communion between a believer and the soul of the Manifestation of God that conveys the Spirit of God unto him or her, bringing "such ecstasy of joy that life becomes nothing." This communion is identified with "the secret, inner meaning of life" and with "the core of religious faith."[58] Through their studies of the descriptions of the mystics, scholars have inferred that many factors may contribute to bringing about mystical experience:[59]

> A personal predisposition, which may also be ignored by the subject.
>
> An act of will on the part of the subject, which may express itself as an active search for God before her experience begins.
>
> Specific stimuli, whose nature depends on the mystic's personality, upbringing, and religious, social and cultural background. These stimuli are synthesized by Robert Andrew Gilbert as follows: aspects of nature (commonly water, trees, flowers and their scent, sunrise and sunset), music; poetry; creative work; sexual love; natural beauty; sacred places; prayer, meditation and worship; the visual arts; literature in various forms; and personal relationships.[60]

Conclusion

The panentheistic, mystical non-dualism, directly inspired by Buddhism but not identical to it, proposed by this paper is an epistemological, ontological,

[56] Underhill, *Mysticism*, xi.

[57] Dom Cuthbert Butler, *Western Mysticism: The Teaching of Augustine, Gregory and Bernard on Contemplation and the Contemplative Life*, 2nd ed. (Eugene: Wipf and Stock, 2001), lxii.

[58] Savi, "The Baha'i Faith," 16.

[59] Cf. Gilbert, *Elements of Mysticism*, 87–88.

[60] Gilbert, 87.

metaphysical, and praxical middle way[61] both for the West (within the West) and also between East and West.[62] It is, itself, ecstatic. For Tillich, the Spirit is no forgotten God but the reality of God present to our own spirit, the one who makes the new being of Christ alive in both life and history. Tillich's theology of Spirit, comprising the largest section of the three-part *Systematic Theology*, is the constitutive element of his understanding of God and the human person, and completes the Trinitarian structure of his system. The Spirit is a dimension of life that unites the power of being with the meaning of being; in fact, according to Tillich, spirit can be defined as the actualization of power and meaning in unity.[63]

The last volume on the Spirit is the least examined and discussed of his *Systematic Theology*, but it is vital to an interpretation of the whole. Tillich is in truth a theologian of being, but what he means by being is misunderstood if he is not also seen as a theologian of the Spirit. Tillich considered in brief the divine Spirit in the first and second volumes of his *Systematic Theology*: in volume one, when spirit was described as "the most embracing, direct, and unrestricted symbol for the divine life;"[64] in volume two, when the divine Spirit became the Spirit of Jesus the Christ, constituting him as the Christ and making the power of the New Being effective.[65] While Tillich also considers the Spirit in many places, it is only in the third volume of his systematics that a full picture of the divine Spirit can be found.

In this closing paragraph, I would like to set-out a preliminary "link" between Eckhart's "divine presence" and Tillich's "spiritual presence" with my own conception of "divine involvement" in an evolutionary world. I assert, boldly, that Eckhart's "divine presence" and Tillich's "spiritual presence," are both constituted by the Spirit of God through my terminology of "divine involvement." Tillich notes that "the Spiritual Presence is fully experienced only when the grades are left behind and the mind is grasped in ecstasy. In this radical sense, mysticism transcends every concrete embodiment of the divine by transcending the subject-object scheme" of a person's "finite structure, but

[61] Cf. Amos Yong, *Pneumatology and the Christian-Buddhist Dialogue: Does the Spirit Blow Through the Middle Way*?, Studies in Systematic Theology (Leiden, Netherlands: Brill Academic, 2012).

[62] Cf. Milton Scarborough, *Comparative Theories of Nonduality: The Search for a Middle Way* (New York: Continuum, 2011).

[63] Tillich, *Systematic Theology*, vol. 3, 111.

[64] Tillich, *Systematic Theology*, vol. 1, 249.

[65] Tillich, *Systematic Theology*, vol. 2, 156-57.

for this very reason, it is in danger of annihilating the centered self, the subject of the ecstatic experience of the spirit."[66]

For Tillich, "Ecstasy is the classical term" for being "grasped by the spiritual presence." As such, it describes the human situation under the spiritual presence exactly. The Spiritual Presence creates an ecstasy in both of them which drives the spirit of a person beyond itself "without destroying the essential, i.e., rational, structure....[As such,] ecstasy does not destroy the centeredness of the integrated self....[Indeed,] the ecstatic character of the experience of spiritual presence does not destroy the rational structure of the human spirit and does something the human spirit cannot do by itself." When it grasps a person, "it creates unambiguous life." By the very nature of their self-transcendence, humanity "is driven to ask the question of unambiguous life, but the answer must come to him through the creative power of the Spiritual Presence."[67] The activity of the Spiritual Presence, for Tillich and for me, is the guide of all human activity and change according to the telos of God's Kingdom, and which facilitates the movement toward life eternal, meaning that the Spirit is the power of being itself to effect and realize essentialization. May we, then, pursue the Spirit with reckless abandon, for she is already pursuing us.

[66] Tillich, *Systematic Theology*, vol. 3, 143.
[67] Tillich, 112

TILLICH & POPULAR CULTURE

Tillich and the Rise of Personal Religions

Thomas G. Bandy

The difference between religion and spirituality today is simply this. In religion, we say *I believe in God.* In spirituality, we exclaim *Oh, my God!* The bridge between statement and exclamation is what might be described as "personal religion." It is a broad spectrum of spiritual ideas, attitudes, and behavior patterns, prompted not only by alienation from religious institutions and traditions, but also by the blurring of once well-defined boundaries between sectors (health, education, social service, business, entertainment, military, government, etc.) and disciplines (theoretical and applied sciences, ecology, psychology, pop culture, self-help literature, etc.) It may be broad and ill defined, but it is the fastest growing "religious" movement in Western culture, and is permeating and transforming Protestant, Evangelical, and Catholic memberships.

While it is difficult to define "personal religion," I think two seminal authors capture the essence and urgency of this diverse movement. Evelyn Underhill introduced the average person to contemplative literature in the midst of post-World War I cynicism about institutional religion. She was the first widely read lay person to focus on the "inner life," by which she meant "all that conditions the relation of the individual soul with God; the deepening and expansion of the spiritual sense; in fact, the heart of personal religion."[1] Paul Tillich crossed boundaries between theology, existential philosophy, and depth psychology and linked religion and culture as two sides of the same coin. He wrote that "religion is the substance of culture, culture is the form of religion."[2] In sermons popularized in the midst of post-World War II secular skepticism about God he articulated what many had already intuited, that there were hidden depths in daily life, including "the feeling for the inexhaustible mystery of life, the grip of an ultimate meaning in existence, and the invincible power of an unconditional devotion."[3] Religion could no longer be

---

[1] Evelyn Underhill, *Concerning the Inner Life with The House of the Soul* (London: Methuen & Co., 1956), 1.

[2] Paul Tillich, *Theology of Culture* (New York: Oxford University Press, 1959), 42.

[3] Paul Tillich, *The Shaking of the Foundations* (New York: Pelican, 1962), 181.

contained by institutional dogmas solely interpreted by professional clergy. It was within everyday life and could be interpreted by any individual.

Tillich was very sensitive to the ethical and religious challenges of globalization as an émigré between two continents and dialogue partner across major religious traditions. However, he still spoke in the context of relative demographic homogeneity in America. Yet the year of Tillich's death (1965) was also the year in which participation in religious institutions and church denominations peaked, and subsequently experienced accelerated decline to the present day. It was also the year when psychographic and lifestyle research began tracking the exploding heterogeneity of America. Perhaps, if Tillich had lived another two decades, his attention would have shifted from globalization to more regional demographic trends and the cultural origins for the rise of "personal religion" that rapid demographic change and exploding lifestyle diversity have encouraged.

Extreme diversity in personal religion parallels accelerated demographic and lifestyle diversity in America. We often point to the impact of globalization on religious faith, but it is in the four great demographic trends toward urbanization, centralization, isolation, and consolidation that the explosion of personal religion in America is best understood.

> *Urbanization* is the advance of cultural diversity along major transportation corridors that redistributes populations, alters business and retail patterns, transforms small towns, and challenges social norms and religious practices.
>
> *Centralization* is the migration of older, poorer, and non-traditional households from rural areas to county seats and mid-market cities as health care and social service, food distribution, and education are concentrated, transforming housing and changing neighborhoods, and challenging the privileges and traditional liturgical habits of church members.
>
> *Consolidation* is the relocation of upper- and middle-class households away from urbanization and centralization for greater privacy, security, family and financial stability, and class consciousness, often in pursuit of recreational or retirement opportunities. Christendom often lingers in these areas, and churches are on the defensive in confrontation with culture. The meaning of "traditional religion" is reshaped by personal angst.
>
> *Isolation* is the legacy of declining and aging populations, stalled economies, limited social services and unsustainable churches, and the sense of marginalization left behind by urbanization and centralization and often in conflict with both. Religion is precious, but the unsustainability of churches encourages personalized spiritualties.

These demographic and lifestyle trends create social tensions and challenge communities of faith and religious practices. It is the breeding ground for "personal religion." For "personal religion," unlike traditional or institutional religion, is highly mobile, inexpensive, private and protected from criticism, and free to accept or reject any belief or value that is specifically relevant or irrelevant to their lives at any given time. Just as there are visible trends in lifestyle diversity, so also there are visible kinds of personal religionists. Their quest for meaning and purpose emerges from a sense (or "life threat") of abandonment or displacement generated by the four major demographic trends. Within that broad context, each kind of personal religionist shares particular anxieties and exhibits particular behavior patterns and spiritual yearnings that would be familiar to Tillich.

The Categories of Personal Religion

If Tillich were present to study the diversity in lifestyle and personal religion, I suspect his perspective on personal religions would be similar to that of psychotherapists on personalities. (Indeed, the "lifestyle segments" in current demographic research are often described as "lifestyle portraits.") The stance of a therapist is one of *acceptance*, which is often described as *empathy, non-judgement,* or *unconditional positive regard.*[4] The theologian's study of lifestyle portraits is not about agreement or approval, but neither does it aim to preserve the status quo. Perhaps Tillich might call it a prophetic critique of love.

My years in consulting and coaching with churches and faith-based nonprofits all across the US and Canada has been grounded in Tillich's understanding of the dynamics of religion and culture and leads me to suggest the following five portraits of personal religionists.[5]

Spiritual Dilettantes: They have thrived in the relative peace, economic prosperity, and climate of opportunity that America has enjoyed in the latter half of the twentieth century. They publicly claim church memberships and privately consider church non-participation. They revisit religion at life-cycle events in their extended families. Religion is something of a hobby in which they non-contextually collect ideas from various faiths. They dabble in religion insofar as it satisfies their curiosity and assuages their personal discomforts. Their spirituality is often dismissed as shallow, self-serving, and materialistic, but there is a depth and urgency that lies beneath the surface. The

[4] Lucy Bregman, "Psychotherapies," in *Spirituality and the Secular Quest*, ed. Peter H. Van Ness (New York: Crossroad, 1996), 261.

[5] I first wrote of this in my book *Talisman: Global Positioning for the Soul*, a book aimed at airport bookstores rather than academic libraries. See the second edition, (Eugene: Wipf and Stock, 2006), 15-19.

context of their quest for God is shaped by a pervasive or chronic depression. Life-cycle events of birth, maturity, marriage, or death peak their anxieties over emptiness and meaninglessness. They long to discover patterns of meaning or mythologies that explain personal behavioral traits or world events. If they read Tillich at all, they mainly value quotations in which he refers to "Kairos Moments," hoping that Spirit will somehow interrupt the monotony of daily living. But they can also be drawn to Tillich's more complex understanding of symbols as both representations of, and portals to, deeper meaning and purpose.

Divining Spiritualists: This is a somewhat smaller, but growing population. Some disparage religion and look for the magical in life. They gravitate to new religious movements, aboriginal practices, psychic communications, and supernatural phenomena. Others manipulate religion in order to anticipate or control spiritual energies through direct or personal relationships with God, often using mediums like crystals or objects of nature, Bibles or crucifixes. Both claim to access hidden knowledge through personal enlightenment. They resemble ancient Gnostics, but without the self-denial. They may be very liberal or very conservative. Many claim local church memberships, but frequently quarrel with traditional dogma or denominational policy. The context of their quest for God is shaped by a pervasive sense of dread of the ominous unknown. They are prone to believe conspiracy theories. Their preoccupation with the supernatural is often driven by anxieties about fate and death. If they read Tillich at all, they mainly value his critiques of Catholicism and Protestantism as they search for a more intimate connection with God. But they can also be drawn to Tillich's interpretation of religious ecstasy and his nuanced sense of divine presence and love.

Seriously Experimenting: Many of these have opted out of the church altogether or are people who have grown up with no formal religious experience whatever. Their pragmatism makes them suspicious of abstractions and dogmas. For them church participation is an eccentric habit that is only occasionally useful to promote generational harmony or political policies. They are often associated with students, professionals or entrepreneurs in corporate or retail business, influencers in sports or entertainment sectors, and struggling middle-class households keen on self-help literature and addiction intervention. They invest significant time, energy, and money exploring spiritualties. They are active seekers but are unclear about what they seek. They invest a lot of time searching for God but are hesitant to commit to any specific faith or spiritual discipline. Despite strong egos, they chronically second guess themselves, which often results in frequent changes in personal relationships, careers, and religious preferences. The context of their quest for God is shaped by a sense of estrangement from the meaning of life, and their failure to build authentic relationships. They may connect with Tillich indirectly through media or online influencers. They may take special interest in Tillich's later work in comparative religions and biographies of his eclectic lifestyle.

Rationally Reserved: I often find people in this group on church and non-profit boards, and among professionals in public sectors for education, health, and social service, as well as government and legal services. They are products of the Enlightenment, confident in education, and committed rationalists. They are skeptical of supernaturalism, and confident that there is an explanation for every seeming miracle. While they may have liberal or conservative ideologies, they believe that education, dialogue, and progress will achieve peace, happiness, and prosperity. Religion must be reasonable and shaped around what they assume are sophisticated tastes. God's presence is felt through responsible human behavior.

Some understand religion as a form of psychotherapy that seeks wholeness, guarantees acceptance, and perceives religious figures as archetypes. If they still participate in church, they prefer small churches because they resemble therapy groups. Others understand religion as cosmic harmony that reveals the order of the universe, honors creation and reconciles enemies. If they still participate in church, they prefer larger churches that resemble schools with parallel programs in both applied and theoretical science. They are often passionate to "make a difference," but tend to be low risk-takers.

The context of their quest for God is often shaped by a pervasive sense of guilt, inadequacy, or failure. Their ideals of truth, goodness, and beauty contrast with flawed relationships, global crises, and chronic injustice. They may have already read Tillich in the context of a liberal arts education, most likely examples of his sermons, or books like *Courage to Be, Dynamics of Faith*, or *Love Power and Justice.* They may read the first volume of *Systematic Theology*, skim the second, and ignore the third because they believe in progress or progressive thinking and imagine Tillich to be out of date. They may be less comfortable with Tillich's political and prophetic work, and more comfortable with holistic "life" philosophers like Teilhard de Chardin or Whitehead.

Radically Committed: This last category of personal religionists is relatively small. I see them more often outside the US in Canada, Australia, South Africa, and perhaps eastern and western Europe, but they are growing in America especially among millennials with no church experience and outlier baby boomers who are alienated from the church. These people merge theory and practice to choose countercultural lifestyles that show contempt for the current world order and desire for a utopian future. For them, social service is a mystical experience, and mysticism is the ground for moral activism. Although religion is "personal," they tend to travel in small groups that are reminiscent of medieval pilgrim bands that self-consciously traveled geographically and spiritually toward a New Jerusalem. They go to paradoxical extremes of individual self-expression and communal accountability, freedom, and obedience.

Some personalize religion *internally* and are highly committed to meditation, holistic health, naturalistic recreations, globe-trotting cultural immersion, and visual or performing arts. They are more appreciative of Roman Catholic monasticism and Eastern Orthodox ecclesiology than Protestant principles and polities. Others personalize religion *externally* and are highly committed to activism, social or political reform, action/reflection learning, and empathy with marginalized groups. They are appreciative of Protestant protest although not necessarily Protestant preaching. Both groups gravitate to church buildings converted to community centers and spiritual leaders who are heroic figures.

The context of their quest for God is often shaped by a sense of shame and abiding anger. The shame arises from experiences of personal abuse or dehumanizing oppression, and empathy with homelessness and social genocide. The anger arises from experiences of emotional or economic repression, helplessness in political processes, and agony amid environmental destruction. Religion is "personal" because the threat of non-being is personal and survival urgent. The planet is at risk. Perhaps even more importantly, their soul is at risk. Tillich's concepts of the "demonic" and expectations for "New Being" are powerful insights. The "courage to be" is as metaphysical as it is political. The *Radically Committed* are attracted by Tillich's vision of the realm of God and urgency for the life of the spirit.

I want to stress that all five groups of personal religionists are present *within* the church as well as *beyond* the church. This is why the popular demographic description of "Nones" is largely irrelevant to the expression of personal religion. Priests and pastors are increasingly shocked by liturgical idiosyncrasies and doctrinal liberties taken by people who otherwise appear to be loyal church members. Mindful of Tillich's link between religion and culture, I would say that few people in America are truly devoid of spiritual interest. The "secular city" that was so widely expected in 1965 has turned out to be a bubbling cauldron of spiritualties.

The Ground of Expectation and Hope

The categories outlined above suggest a tidiness to personal religion that is far from the messy reality. Regardless of how it manifests itself in behavior, however, it emerges from a sense of personal threat and existential anxiety. In order to understand this, we must build on Tillich to go beyond Tillich.

Tillich identifies the existential anxieties that drive the quest for God (or "absolutes")[6] in three pairings: emptiness and meaninglessness, fate and death, guilt and condemnation.[7] My experiences of immersion in cultural diversity, particularly amid the lifestyle diversity of North America, western Europe, and Australia, reveals these to be helpful but inadequate to the cultural and religious situation today in several ways.

First, Tillich tends to conflate each pairing into a single, broad signification, and attribute all existential anxieties in a general way to an abstract idea of the public who share the same human condition. Today there is no such thing as "the public." Society is fracturing at such a rate that there are currently seventy-one describable, definable "publics" or "lifestyle segments" in the United States alone (with additional variations in other countries).[8] And the elements in each pairing are separated into distinct and unique anxieties that shape the conscious behavior and unconscious motivations of distinct publics. In the absence of demographic and lifestyle data, Tillich defined "four main ways of feeling among the younger and many of the older people" in 1936: *fear, uncertainty, loneliness,* and *meaninglessness.*[9] Today, I think the "human condition" can be better nuanced in at least four ways among the generations. The lives of the Silent Generation, born before 1945, tend to be shaped by a sense of *abandonment*. Baby boomers born between 1946 and 1964 tend to be burdened with chronic *depression*. Baby Busters (Gen X born between 1965 and 1976) and Millennials (Gen Y born between 1977 and 1995) tend to be unconsciously and consistently *angry*. And the emerging Gen Z (born after

---

[6] Paul Tillich, *My Search for Absolutes* (New York: Simon and Schuster, 1967), 124-32.

[7] Paul Tillich, *The Courage to Be* (New Haven: Tale University Press, 1952), 41-54.

[8] The development of lifestyle "portraits" or "segments" has emerged through corporations like Experian (www.Experian.com) that digitally track individual and household behavior patterns and is used for marketing and strategic planning in corporate and nonprofit, social service and health care, and other sectors. Two of their most significant resources (regularly updated) include "Mosaic USA E-Handbook" (2015) and "Mosaic USA: Group and Segment Descriptions" (2013) and are accessible by subscription. They are included by subscription in the church and nonprofit search engine www.MissionInsite.com (a resource of American Church Services Technologies (www.acst.com). MissionInsite research also includes my commentary of religious and ministry expectations of lifestyle groups and segments, "MissionImpact" (2018).

[9] Paul Tillich, *The Protestant Era* (Chicago: University Press, 1948), 245. Originally delivered as an address to the Fiftieth Church Congress of the Protestant Episcopal Church on May 6, 1942.

1996 for whom a convenient label has yet to be widely used) views the world with an underlying sense of *dread*.

Second, the anxieties that Tillich describes as *guilt and condemnation* should be revised as *guilt and shame*. This has been a frequent comment from professional psychoanalysts who occasionally respond to my public presentations and popular publishing. Tillich himself noted that the word "guilt" in American cultural context is also associated with "guilt feeling."[10] The term not only signifies condemnation deserved, but also pervasive undeserved self-condemnation. This latter anxiety is not guilt as much as shame (undeserved victimization that undermines self-esteem). Shame is a relatively new phenomena emerging among Gen X, Y, and Z. It has more to do with courageously addressing what Jung might call one's "shadow" self and facing the frightening ghosts of the unconscious mind. In part, this is a result of the increase of personal abuse (sexual, physical, economic, or political) which has created a culture of trauma and robbed younger generations of self-esteem. And in part, this is a result of global crises like genocide, famine, pandemics, and global warming that have not only generated feelings of moral guilt but also a sense of personal betrayal or temptation to suicide.

Third, the postmodern world of accelerated mobility, changeability, and ambiguity demands a more elaborate interpretation of existential anxiety. The same observation has led others to suggest additional polarities like injustice and oppression.[11] I suggest that a fourth existential polarity might be described as anxiety over oppression and displacement. This is because such anxiety is not actually remedied by legal or political actions. No recompense or policy change can compensate the suffering of refugees, grief for lost homelands, and loss of cultural norms.

Moreover, Tillich suggests that the Kairos of the New Being generates three profound acts of courage: to participate, separate, and accept acceptance. By adding a fourth set of existential anxieties, a new kind of courage is required. It is the courage to trust and be trusted. Contemporary chaos is not a result of lack of leadership, but lack of both professional and mutual trust. The

---

[10] Paul Tillich, "Fifth Dialogue," in *Ultimate Concern: Tillich in Dialogue,* ed. D. Mackenzie Brown (New York: Harper & Row), 120.

[11] Mary Ann Stenger recalls that Franklin Sherman made this suggestion in a banquet speech in 1985 for the North American Paul Tillich Society meeting in Anaheim, California, held in conjunction with the American Academy of Religion. See her article in this book.

quest for God today is an exercise in risk management. It requires confidence in the inner lives of leaders, and dedication to the inner life among followers.[12]

In order to understand contemporary yearnings of "personal religion," we can again build on Tillich to go beyond Tillich. Among personal religionists, "incarnation" is not just a noun, but also a verb. It is a religious affirmation of belief, but it is also a mystical exclamation of experience.

I have always been struck by Jaroslav Pelikan's description of multiple experiences of Christ through the ages. He wrote *Jesus through the Centuries* because he believed that "Jesus is far too important a figure to be left only to the theologians and the church."[13] He traced eighteen images or perspectives on Jesus the Christ from the Apostolic Age through three-quarters of the twentieth century roughly in chronological order, describing the relevance of each not just to the church, but to the changing cultures and spiritual needs in each period. The same method of correlating existential questions and spiritual answers can be applied to contemporary lifestyle diversity. Each lifestyle portrait, shaped as they are by specific life threats, and driven as they are by particular existential anxieties, has the potential to experience incarnation in unique ways. Christ might be variously experienced as teacher, guide, healer, vindicator, rescuer, gatherer, promise-keeper, or apocalyptic transformer. Each of these incarnations is included in what Tillich might call the "New Being."

The relative abstraction of existential anxieties and incarnational hope must be translated into concrete forms of behavior if they are to be discerned and overcome. For personal religionists, it requires more courage to change one's lifestyle than to agree or disagree with a concept. It is here that the pairings of existential anxieties split into distinct contextual motivations for the quest for absolutes. The schema I propose looks like this:

---

[12] This crisis is more visible in the decline of credibility among religious leaders than the decline of relevance in religious programs. Indeed, today the number one reason unbelievers do not participate in the church, and the number one reason church members consider leaving the church, has nothing to do with the style of worship, the form of education, or the friendliness of fellowship. The reason for non-participation is that the public does not trust religious leaders (whether professional clergy or elected laity). See *Quadrennium* research in in www.MissionInsite.com.

[13] Jaroslav Pelikan, *Jesus through the Centuries: His Place in the History of Culture* (New Haven: Yale University, 1985), xv.

Life Threat	Motivational Anxiety	Behavioral Change	Act of Courage	Incarnational Hope
Abandonment	Oppression	Vulnerable, seeking acceptance	Courage to Trust and Be Trusted	Rescuer
	Displacement	Homeless, seeking reunion		Gatherer
Depression	Emptiness	Lost, seeking direction	Courage to Participate	Guide
	Meaninglessness	Lonely, seeking rapport		Teacher
Anger	Guilt	Broken, seeking healing	Courage to Accept Acceptance	Healer
	Shame	Abused, seeking self-esteem		Vindicator
Dread	Fate	Trapped, seeking deliverance	Courage to Separate	Promise Keeper
	Death	Dying, seeking renewal		Transformer

[Table 1 – Bandy]

Unfortunately, tables like this suggest a linear orderliness that is not the case. Lifestyle segments migrate into different lifestyle segments as context constantly changes. Nevertheless, one senses that distinct publics are driven by specific anxieties that shape daily behavior. Behavioral observation of any given public reveals clues to the anxiety that drives their quest for God or the Absolute, and also to the hope that addresses their sense of personal threat.

How one experiences Jesus the Christ is legitimately different from how others experience incarnation; and how one yearns to experience incarnation today might be different than how one needs to experience incarnation tomorrow. A lifestyle "portrait" is in fact a lifestyle "video." Personal religionists of all kinds would appreciate the "life philosophy" of Henri Bergson in which he refers to the "cinematographical character" of existence.[14] This is precisely what makes "personal religion" *personal.* And it provides a more profound understanding of the diminished relevance of established churches and denominations that continue to assume "one size fits all" for dogmatic assent, deployment of clergy, development of liturgy, and presentational preaching.

---

[14] Henri Bergson, *Creative Evolution*, trans. Arthur Mitchell (London: Macmillan, 1911), 322.

What appeals most to personal religionists is Tillich's language around the Ground of Being, Depth of Being, and Power of Being. They do not always represent Tillich's thought accurately, but they are inspired by his vision. They would understand the Ground of Being as a kind of "ground zero" that is the intersection between the finite and the infinite, or, existence as it is experienced concretely rather than defined abstractly. It is the intersection between yearning and expectation or between hope and grace.

Beneath that invisible line lies the Depth of Being. Humanity "reaches up" from the experience of chronological time and the context of life struggle as victor or victim; the potential of intimate relationships pregnant with change; and the desire to find mentors who can guide through the ambiguities of daily living. This is the context of life threats and existential anxieties.

Above that invisible line lies the Power of Being. God-above-gods "reaches down" in Kairos events and infinite beginnings. Incarnation occurs paradoxically as both reasonable order and apocalyptic transformation, describable only in symbols and stories, providing meaning and purpose. Every religion is a "mythology" in the most profound sense of that term.

The Ground of Being, therefore, becomes the context for courage to participate, separate, accept acceptance, and trust and be trusted. It is a combination of mystical reunion and contextual reconciliation that is partially fulfilled and eternally promised. Religion is not about certainty or assent, but about patterns of meaning experienced and interpreted by individual self-awareness.

The most profound "personal religion," which is to say authentically "mystical" spirituality is associated with those categories I characterize as the "Seriously Experimenting" and "Radically Committed." They quest for God in a way that Tillich might have associated with his "dynamic-typological method," and that he later described as "Religion of the Concrete Spirit." The three elements would resonate with many post-modern seekers:

> The "experience of the holy within the finite" as "the universal religious basis"
>
> The critical, "mystical" movement which preserves the sacramental by refusing to allow the Holy to become objectified
>
> The ethical, prophetic element which is the moral imperative.[15]

Each "pop culture" (i.e. lifestyle group or lifestyle segment) seeks the same three things, but with different questions, forms, medias, and methods.

[15] Paul Tillich, "The Significance of the History of Religions for the Systematic Theologian" in *The Future of Religions* (New York: Harper & Row, 1966), 86-87.

The *form* of the search may vary, and even the *content* that is the goal of the search may vary, but the *import* or *urgency* of the search is clear.

Tillich and the Critique of Personal Religion

If Tillich were addressing those I describe as *Spiritual Dilettantes* and *Divining Spiritualists,* he might interpret their quest as rejection of technical "controlling knowledge" of the secular world that separates subject from object and transforms the object "into a completely conditioned and calculable 'thing'," and anticipation of the metaphysical "receiving knowledge" of the later post-secular age.[16] Personal religionists reject both pure objectivity and pure subjectivity, craving to understand through the internal participation of subject and object. "The surface must be penetrated, the appearance undercut, the 'depth' must be reached, namely, the *ousia,* the 'essence' of things, that which gives them the power of being."[17]

Tillich's concept of "Kairos" and his interpretation of "ecstasy" may be attractive to these groups as they have become popularized in culture. In Tillich's own theological system, however, they also suggest what would be his critique of this kind of personal religion. "Kairoi" are associated with "history-shaking power"[18] rather than personal transcendence. As such, they are events that transform society and anticipate the Realm of God which is beyond the power of human beings to create or control. He warns that Kairoi "can be demonically distorted and erroneous."[19] The mystic sensibilities of the *Spiritual Dilettante* and *Divining Spiritualist* are expressions of ego. Either the universe revolves around one's ego, or one's ego tries to control the universe. It is common for personal religionists to criticize established religions as sources of violence and war, but Tillich might say that the competitiveness of personal egos creating religions to suit themselves results in even more violence. Personal religionists *demand respect,* without realizing that "demanding," by its very nature, sacrifices respect. The possibility of peace and reconciliation is even more remote.

If Tillich were addressing those I describe as *Seriously Experimenting,* he might interpret their quest with terms like "inspiration" and "infusion" that are "spatial metaphors and involve, respectively, 'breathing' and 'pouring' into the human spirit....The Spiritual Presence is not that of a teacher but of a

---

[16] Paul Tillich, *Systematic Theology*, vol. 1 (Chicago: University of Chicago Press, 1967), 97.

[17] Tillich, 101.

[18] Paul Tillich, *Systematic Theology*, vol. 3, (Chicago: University of Chicago Press, 1967), 372.

[19] Tillich, 371.

meaning-bearing power which grasps the human spirit in ecstatic experience."[20] Some of the *Seriously Experimenting* are fleeing the dogmatic Christocentrism of conservative evangelicals, and Trinitarian abstractions of mainstream church traditions. Instead of "Christ-centered" living, Tillich might empathize with the "Spirit-saturated" living of Pentecostalism and some aboriginal religions. Tillich's influence on contemporary Pentecostal authors is noteworthy. Peter Althouse refers to Tillich in order to interpret "soaking prayer" in the emerging "Catch-the-Fire" movement originating from the Toronto Blessing. Estrangement is overcome through the "overwhelming presence of the Father's love as mediated through the Spirit."[21] It is what Tillich might call "spiritual presence" ("spirit as a dimension of life [uniting] the power of being with the meaning of being")[22] and what Andreas Nordlander calls "Pneumatological Participation."[23] In response, John Thatamanil says: "[Tillich] is permitted to be what he truly is: a pneumatological theologian who stands ready to be captured by the Spirit, a theologian of grace, who longs for the Spirit's gracious coming, a longing that is even recognized as eschatological."[24]

Tillich considered mysticism and faith to be compatible rather than contradictory. He suggested that the rejection of Protestantism for eastern religions resulted from the loss of "sacred silence" in liturgies and overemphasis of preaching and teaching. Yet if faith requires the depth of mysticism, so also mysticism must lead to the power of faith. Tillich would likely criticize the *Seriously Experimenting* for ignoring (or avoiding) human guilt and divine acceptance revealed in the New Being.[25] The realities of estrangement are ignored, and the ethical and prophetic dimensions of faith are lost. Their sensibility not only threatens the loss of the "centered self", but also the hope of authentic community.[26]

---

[20] Tillich, 115.

[21] Peter Althouse, "Eschatology in the Theology of Paul Tillich and the Toronto Blessing," in *Paul Tillich and Pentecostal Theology*, eds. Nimi Wariboko and Amos Yong (Bloomington: Indiana University Press, 2015), 179.

[22] Tillich, *Systematic Theology*, vol. 3, 111.

[23] Andreas Nordlander, "Pneumatological Participation: Embodiment, Sacramentality, and the Multidimensional Unity of Life," in *Paul Tillich and Pentecostal Theology*, eds. Nimi Wariboko and Amos Yong (Bloomington: Indiana University Press, 2015), 101-14.

[24] John Thatamanil, "A Spirited Encounter," in *Paul Tillich and Pentecostal Theology*, eds. Nimi Wariboko and Amos Yong (Bloomington: Indiana University Press, 2015), 229.

[25] Tillich, *Systematic Theology*, vol. 3, 243.

[26] Tillich, 143.

If Tillich were addressing those I describe as *Rationally Reserved*, he might interpret and critique their quest in two ways. Affirmatively, they live within what Tillich might call a "Philosophical Circle." Their "scientific" approach to religion (whether inductive or deductive) is based "on an immediate experience of something ultimate in value and being of which one can become intuitively aware." It is a "'mystical a priori,' and awareness of something that transcends the cleavage between subject and object."[27] The *Rationally Reserved* concentrate on abstractions which they consider generally valid concepts among all religions. *God is love,* they might say, but nothing more concrete. Negatively, they do not live in what Tillich calls the "Theological Circle," a narrower circle at the center of which is the "unrepeatable uniqueness" of the Christian message.[28] The center is "ultimate concern" in, on, or for which one has surrendered subjectivity. The claim of ultimate concern is total: "no part of ourselves or of our world is excluded from it; there is no place to flee from it …no moment of relaxation or rest is possible."[29] Comforted by the conviction that "God is love," the Rationally Reserved remain forever on the sidelines and rarely on the picket lines.

Ultimate concern determines our being or not-being, but while the *Rationally Reserved* might apply this culturally, they do not take it personally. For Tillich, ultimate concern has the power of threatening or saving *my* being.[30] The believer is constantly torn between faith and doubt, but for the *Rationally Reserved* the believer has settled into constant skepticism. Tillich has in mind a kind of cognition that differs from their rationalism. "It has a completely existential, self-determining, and self-surrendering character and belongs to the faith of even the intellectually most primitive believer. Whoever participates in the New Being participates also in its truth." It is "ecstatic reason" that is "overpowered, invaded, shaken by the ultimate concern ...[;] the contents of faith grasp reason."[31]

Some personal religionists make a profound attempt to cross from the philosophical circle to the theological circle by pursuing process theology under the influence of Bergson and Jung. Their world view is determined by the *potentiality of being*, rather than the stark contrast between *being* and *non-being*. Their sense of ultimate concern is neither transcendent nor immanent, but pervasive in the sense that the internal constitution of all things participates in the essential nature of God. Tillich includes this possibility in his

[27] Tillich, *Systematic Theology*, vol. 1, 9.
[28] Tillich, 10.
[29] Tillich, 12.
[30] Tillich, 14.
[31] Tillich, 53-54.

discussion of dynamics and form.[32] It is impossible to speak of *being* without *becoming*. The vitality of spirit is responsible for the "universal tendency toward self-transcendence."[33] Tillich, however, applies this literally to being human, but only analogically to subhuman nature.[34] His third ontological polarity of freedom and destiny challenges even this confidence. All forms of thought and intuition, moral and social forms, are "simultaneously employed and shattered"[35] by the "form-creating" and "form-bursting" power of being[36] that creates something new. For Tillich, God does not *pervade* creation, but *pulsates* through creation. The *Rationally Reserved* hope in progress and continuing education. Tillich's hope lies in theonomous manifestations of Spiritual Presence through truth and expressiveness, purpose and humanity, and power and justice,[37] or, in essence, revelation and risk.

One suspects that of all the types of personal religionists today, Tillich would be most empathic with the group I describe as *Radically Committed.* D. Mackenzie Brown records an interesting dialogue with a student in 1963. The student describes a friend "radically anti-church in all ways, shapes, and forms" who is excited about Tillich's distinction between estrangement and sin. "'Well,' she said, 'I have never heard anything of this sort in a church.' The student asks Tillich for an example of such a church. Tillich replies: 'No I don't believe that you can name a particular church. But there are many good young ministers everywhere in the country who make the attempt. *And for this very reason they are often dismissed*'"[38] (my italics). The offhand remark in 1963 has great significance nearly sixty years later. The descendants of then "young ministers" are either dropping out of church leadership or have never given it a thought. Church is getting in the way of their quest for God.

Tillich would likely understand how their quest for God has been shaped by anger and anxieties of displacement and oppression. However, he would be concerned that this spiritual force not be subverted in demonic ways toward fascist mythologies or lost in electronic fantasies. The underside of being radically committed is the temptation to be radically resentful. It is an existential, not just a psychological state. "Ressentiment" occurs when the ego creates an

---

[32] Tillich, 179.

[33] Tillich, 181.

[34] Tillich, 185.

[35] Paul Tillich, "The Conquest of the Concept of Religion in the Philosophy of Religion," in *What is Religion?* (New York: Harper Torchbooks, 1969), 144.

[36] James Luther Adams, *Paul Tillich's Philosophy of Culture, Science & Religion* (New York: Schocken Books, 1965, 131.

[37] Tillich, *Systematic Theology*, vol. 3, 252-65.

[38] Paul Tillich, *Ultimate Concern: Dialogues with Students*, ed. D. MacKenzie Brown (London: SCM Press, 1965), 98.

enemy in order to avoid culpability. It is rooted in a sense of inferiority and helplessness but results in assigning blame and factional confrontation.

The sense of urgency and mutual accountability among the *Radically Committed* is laudable. The danger is that small groups might function in closed theological and moral systems with only marginal openness to dialogue and critique. The *Radially Committed* who personalize religion *internally* are liable to reduce faith to an aesthetic philosophy. Those who personalize religion *externally* are liable to reduce faith to political ideology. Both may come to define themselves by who they are not, rather than by who they are. They risk being self-justifying and exclusive. Tillich's hope is that these tendencies can be resisted through the courage to participate in the world, separate from the world, and accept acceptance as a gift rather than an achievement.

I suspect that for Tillich the rise of personal religion in the latter half of the twentieth century, and acceleration in the twenty-first century, would not have come as a surprise. As early as 1957 he anticipated the "end of the Protestant era" and described the essential steps toward revival (italics mine):

> Church leaders must put an end to denial and the pretense of institutional health. They must *reformulate its appeal* for a *disintegrating world* and focus on a message of hope rather than harmony.
>
> Church leaders must cease their confrontation with culture for a conversation with culture and deny the legitimacy of any *cleavage between a sacred and profane sphere.*
>
> Church leaders must *protest every power which claims divine character for itself*, including the institution of the Church.[39]

Personal religions of all kinds are focusing on hope in a disintegrating world, exploring the internal participation of the sacred and secular in a quest for meaning and purpose, and protesting idolatries that are most glaringly apparent in the institutions of religion themselves. Yet he would still be quite critical of the relative success of personal religions in doing so. In the end, the problem with "personal religion" is that it is not what it claims to be. It is *merely* personal and *still* religion. Personal religion falls short of what Tillich describes as "Spiritual Presence."

First, Tillich would challenge their success in replacing superficial harmony with genuine hope. Instead of reaching toward theonomy, personal religionists bounce back and forth between extremes of autonomy and heteronomy. They never fully resolve subject/object dualism that is at the root of Western modernity. "Philosophers, mystics, lovers, seekers of intoxication—

[39] Tillich, *The Protestant Era*, 228-30.

even of death—have tried to conquer this cleavage. In some of these the Spiritual Presence is manifest; in others the desperate and often demonic desire to escape the cleavage by escaping reality is visible."[40] Because personal religions are *merely* personal, they ultimately fail to be agencies of reconciliation.

Second, Tillich would challenge their success in reuniting the sacred and secular. Personal religionists fail to define purpose and defend humanity because they cannot reconcile "the conflicts caused by the unlimited possibilities of technical progress and the limits of his finitude in adapting himself to the results of his own productivity."[41] The assumption of an inherently "good will" ignores the estrangement of the self from the self and cannot ultimately ban the destructive side of humanity. "The 'search for identity' which is a genuine problem of the present generation" can only be achieved "from the vertical direction, out of which reunion is given and not commanded. The self which has found its identity is the self of him who is 'accepted' as a unity in spite of his disunity."[42] Since personal religions are *still* religions, they cannot resolve the dilemma of human self-destruction.

Third, Tillich would challenge their success in resisting demonic power (forms, practices, or persons claiming ultimate authority). Personal religions avoid addressing a fundamental ambiguity about justice. "The justice of social cohesion implies the injustice of social rejection." Tillich argues that only in spiritual *community* can the ultimate equality of everyone be reconciled with the self-actualization of the individual as individual.[43] The power of being of the individual can only be actualized in the power of being of the whole community they represent.[44] Spiritual Presence is manifest in love that surrenders the *personal* for the sake of the *communal.*

Tillich would propose something different than personal religion. He tentatively calls it *Religion of the Concrete Spirit* that includes three elements:

> The "experience of the holy within the finite" as "the universal religious basis;"
>
> The critical, "mystical" movement which preserves the sacramental by refusing to objectify the Holy;

---

[40] Tillich, *Systematic Theology*, vol. 3, 253.
[41] Tillich, 258.
[42] Tillich, 260.
[43] Tillich, 262-63.
[44] Tillich, 263.

The ethical, prophetic element which articulates what "ought to be." [45]

The religion of the concrete spirit is a quest for theonomy rising from the conflict between autonomy and heteronomy under the conditions of existence.[46] Theonomy represents the partial participation of the infinite in the present, and the vision of full participation which lies in the future.

Theonomy is not religion, and neither is it merely personal. It is "what happens to culture as a whole under the impact of the Spiritual Presence."[47] It is a different kind of spiritual community. In spite of the existential estrangement of the children of God from God and from each other, "spiritual community is possible by the working of *agape* as a manifestation of the Spirit within it."[48] It both celebrates and overcomes diversity. "As a consequence, the immense diversity of being with regard to sex, age, race, nation, tradition and character—typological as well as individual—does not prevent their participation in the Spiritual Community."[49]

Culture forces religion to become more personal than institutional, but spirit forces individual spiritualties to become less personal and more communal. The tension itself is theonomous. Tillich might value personal religion as a step toward what he called "Religion of the Concrete Spirit." He wrote: "We can see the whole history of religions in this sense as a fight for the Religion of the Concrete Spirit, a fight of God against religion within religion. And this phrase, the fight of God within religion against religion, could become the key for understanding the otherwise extremely chaotic, or at least seemingly chaotic, history of religions."[50] Yet there is another step. "The Spiritual Presence by which the individual is grasped in the act of faith transcends individual conditions, beliefs and expressions of faith." However, "it is faith, nevertheless, overcoming the infinite gap between the infinite and the finite" in every fragmentary moment that anticipates the "transcendent union of unambiguous life."[51] It is the source and destiny not just of one human being, but of humanity.

---

[45] Tillich, "The Significance of the History of Religions," 86-88.
[46] Tillich, *Systematic Theology*, vol. 1, 83.
[47] Tillich, *Systematic Theology*, vol. 3, 249.
[48] Tillich, 157.
[49] Tillich, 157.
[50] Tillich, "The Significance of the History of Religions," 86-88.
[51] Tillich, *Systematic Theology*, vol. 3, 155.

Paul Tillich and the Method of Correlation

Sharon P. Burch

One answer to the question "Why Tillich? Why Now?" is his development of an insight that he termed the "method of correlation." At the beginning of volume one of his *Systematic Theology*, published in 1951, Tillich explains that the phrase refers to a theological approach that moves "back and forth between two poles, the eternal truth of [the Christian] foundation and the temporal situation in which the eternal truth must be received."[1] By the phrase "temporal situation" he is referring to the ever-changing "scientific and artistic, the economic, political and ethical forms in which human beings express their interpretation of existence.... The 'situation' to which theology must respond is the totality of humanity's creative self-interpretation in a special period."[2] He maintains that this is implicit in systematic theology and always has been.

What could not have been predicted at the time it appeared was how constructive and far-reaching this principle would become. Not only did it anticipate the challenges presented to the theological endeavor by the scientific research, space exploration, and advancements in technology that have occurred over the past hundred years or so, but also it provided a possible strategy for constructive work with the disaffection with organized religion that is represented by the "spiritual but not religious" phenomenon of the late twentieth and early twenty-first centuries. These changes have presented the theological endeavor with the need to reconstruct basic theological assumptions and examine long-standing premises about the nature of the institutional church. Tillich's discussion of the method of correlation elucidates a philosophical framework on which such a reconstruction can be based.

At the time it appeared, Tillich's work with the method of correlation indicated his sensitivity to the increasing recognition within science and philosophy that human perceptions of reality are deeply and inescapably relative. The work of Alfred North Whitehead (1861-1947) in mathematics and process metaphysics described the reality of universal and constant change. Albert Einstein's (1879-1955) theory of general relativity was under scrutiny. The pressure of two world wars and the race to develop atomic weaponry had

---

[1] Paul Tillich, *Systematic Theology*, vol. 1 (Chicago: University of Chicago Press, 1951), 3.

[2] Tillich, 3.

spurred research into the physics of sub-atomic particles, and Newtonian principles once held to be incontrovertible about the nature of matter were in the process of being revamped.

Gradually, the idea that everything was relative was emerging as a new normal. Whatever we had vested with permanence might have merit but not because it was fixed for all eternity. And that included language. It became more and more generally accepted that truths long assumed to be fixed were both expressed and received in accordance with an ever-changing and time-bound linguistic, social, and cultural milieu.

Tillich held that the foundations of Christianity consisted of the revelatory events reported in Scripture and the history of the religious rites and practices of the church. But at the same time he was convinced that there was no way the eternal truth could be expressed or received that wasn't time-bound. The questions may be eternal, but the way they were expressed was, had been, and always would be contextual. This meant that theology, in the process of identifying and accurately describing the questions pertinent to the specific time and context in which they were asked, crafted both the explanations of why they were held to be true and described why they were important to the whole of Christianity using terminology and concepts appropriate to the time they were described. Thus, theology could not insist that these explanations applied in exactly the same way to the current state of affairs.

Tillich explicitly endorsed a panentheistic view of God, meaning that rather than holding that God was a transcendent deity, removed from the world, he held that God was at once both transcendent and immanent. In this view, God is part of everything that is and yet more than any one thing or even the totality of all things.

Tillich was convinced that the theological goal of the method of correlation was to identify the existential questions that emerged at a particular time within a specific context, and to comment on them theologically. He held that the search for the meaning of life is an activity universal to human beings, originating in what he terms the "*mystical a priori*," which he described as "an awareness of something that transcends the cleavage between subject and object."[3]

It is a primal inchoate yearning that human beings share for reunion with that from which they sense they are estranged, to which they recognize they belong, and with which they long to be reunited. The urgency that drives human beings to find the source of meaning in life is evidence of the human quest for what is loosely termed "spirituality." Christianity, as a system of belief, emerged and continues to be important because it offers answers to the

[3] Tillich, 9.

questions that arose from this search. The same is true of other systems of faith and the religions of the world.

One of the most important aspects of Tillich's work with the method of correlation is his identification of two criteria that differentiate a search that is theological from any other investigation. First he specifies that "only those propositions are theological that deal with their object in so far as it can become a matter of ultimate concern for us."[4] And second, he designates Ultimate Concern as "that which determines our being or not-being. Only those statements are theological which deal with their object in so far as it can become a matter of being or not-being for us."[5] Tillich defines God as "Being-Itself," i.e., that about which human beings are ultimately concerned.

Tillich identifies himself as a Christian theologian, by which he means that he (and anyone else who identifies as a theologian) is determined by the faith in which they believe. "The attitude of the theologian is 'existential.' They are involved—with the whole of their existence, with their finitude and their anxiety, with their self-contradictions and their despair, with the healing forces within them and in their social situation."[6]

He amplifies this assertion by saying that being in a state of faith neither means that the theologian has resolved every particularity that Christianity (or any other system of belief) can present, nor does it indicate that a Christian theologian never has moments of doubt. Instead he describes it as meaning that they are "ultimately concerned with the Christian message even if they are sometimes inclined to attack and to reject it."[7]

He also suggests that being open to the new is an important and valid position for Christian theologians. He cites the remarkably improved technology that emerged during his lifetime as facilitating the sharing of knowledge, ideas and information about the world's religions and spiritualties, scientific investigations, and the results of experiments and investigations. These resources have expanded our comprehension of the role of Ultimate Concern to humanity as a whole as well as helping us understand our solar system, the planet on which we live, and the cosmos beyond. He says: "'Open experience' is the source of systematic theology."[8]

Tillich holds that when Christian theologians are asked to identify the existential questions that face the people of their time, they necessarily bring to the task their own particular background. This includes the way they have

---

[4] Tillich, 21.
[5] Tillich, 14.
[6] Tillich, 22-23.
[7] Tillich, 10.
[8] Tillich, 47.

been and are being shaped by the social, cultural, and linguistic assumptions and practices of their personal, social, and cultural situations. This matrix has influenced how they have received historical Christian perspectives, and it is from within this matrix that existential questions emerge. Since the matrix is ever-changing, it must be acknowledged and frequently re-investigated by the theologian undertaking the work. In Tillich's words, "although God in God's abysmal nature is in no way dependent on human beings, God in God's self-manifestation to human beings is dependent on the way human beings receive God's manifestation."[9]

There is, however, a "norm" against which the existential questions have to be evaluated to qualify them as theological. He defines that norm as "the New Being as Jesus as the Christ as our ultimate concern."[10] In Tillich's words, systematic theology develops answers "*from* the sources, *through* the medium, under the *norm*."[11] This formula provides a means by which the received perceptions of the mystical a priori can be checked against the revelatory history of the Christian tradition and thus provides a measure by which a preliminary concern is elevated to ultimacy.

Tillich provided the following example:

> It is not an exaggeration to say that today human beings experience their present situation in terms of disruption, conflict, self-destruction, meaninglessness, and despair in all realms of life. This experience is expressed in the arts and in literature, conceptualized in existential philosophy, actualized in political cleavages of all kinds, and analyzed in the psychology of the unconscious. It has given theology a new understanding of the demonic-tragic structures of individual and social life....
>
> The question arising out of this experience is not, as in the Reformation, the question of a merciful God and the forgiveness of sins; nor is it, as in the early Greek Church, the question of finitude, of death and error; nor is it the question of the personal religious life or of the Christianization of culture and society. It is the question of a reality in which the self-estrangement of our existence is overcome, a reality of reconciliation and reunion, of creativity, meaning and hope. We shall call such a reality the 'New Being in Jesus as the Christ.'[12]

---

[9] Tillich, 61.
[10] Tillich, 50.
[11] Tillich, 64.
[12] Tillich, 49.

The implications of the method of correlation have become ever more pertinent over the course of the mid-to-late twentieth and early twenty-first centuries. Diana Butler Bass contends that the 1970s were characterized by "a time of profound change, a rearrangement of social relationships, a time of cultural upheaval and transformation....And Americans began an extended experiment in reordering faith, family, community, and nation."[13]

This shift has turned out to require hard work, diligently undertaken, and often reflects exploratory efforts that morph and develop as they are investigated. Studies began to be published that described in detail how Christian truths, often thought to be "eternal," have been and are variously received by specific populations. Scholars undertook to examine how linguistic, cultural, and social differences affected the understanding of long-held Christian truths. The term "contextual theology" was coined to designate these studies.[14]

Mary Daly, a now well-known feminist theologian who credited Tillich's insights as generative of her own, began to write about how women and their insights have been affected by a social system that presumed male dominance was normal.[15] As other women joined her, they alerted the theological community to the awkward truth that by refusing to validate the insights of women, the definition of God, the understanding of the Gospel accounts of Jesus and his teachings, and assumptions about the church leadership had been limited by masculine gender assumptions. Intimations about the nature of God perceived and reported by women over the centuries had been ignored or relegated to second-tier status, although the profound validity and clarity that women achieved as they struggled with the "mystical a priori" and matters of ultimate concern had provided and were providing sensitive and informative insights into the nature of God and the practices of Christianity. Some of these proved to be quite different from interpretations that had long been held by a male, largely white minority.

Black and womanist theologians followed, contributing to the discussion by framing the existential questions that characterized their communities, clarifying the quality of their insights not only for their own people and com-

---

[13] Diana Butler Bass, *Christianity After Religion: The End of Church and the Birth of a New Spiritual Awakening* (New York: HarperCollins, 2010), 3.

[14] See Angie Pears, *Doing Contextual Theology* (Routledge: New York, 2010) for a comprehensive overview of the major contributions to the field and an excellent commentary on the contribution made by each of those discussed.

[15] Mary Daly, *The Church and the Second Sex,* (New York: Harper & Row, 1968).

munities but also for what was considered at the time to be "the white establishment."[16] Latin American Liberation theologians eloquently presented the case of the economically disadvantaged. They point out how marginalization interfered with their experience of the grace described and promised by the revelatory teachings of Jesus of Nazareth. Their experience is historically similar to the marginalized poor for whom the social stratifications that characterized the rule of the elite Temple authorities at the time of Christ prevented healing and wholeness for a full range of people.[17] Interfaith dialogue is yet another resource that has usefully contributed to the efforts to describe the "mystical a priori" and accurately assess existential questions.[18] Attention to the discipline of Practical Theology increased. Pastoral care, Christian education, preaching, and church administration have emerged as particularly vital disciplines that provide an entry into the existential situations out of which theological questions emerged.[19] Congregational Studies provides fruitful avenues of investigation using sociological assessment tools and strategies. The approaches it has developed are helpful in analyzing a congregational setting or community milieu and provide the tools a faith leader needs to identify and interpret factors affecting the people who are part of the church.[20]

Each of these efforts is an application of the method of correlation at work and develops more clearly its implications, but I can't help but wonder if Tillich would have been taken aback by today's demands that theology itself, as well as the institutional church, thoroughly embrace the principles he laid out.

Philip Clayton suggests that "an effective answer to the current situation will require us either to breathe new life into existing institutions or to invent radically new forms of Christian community."[21] He further postulates that

> these efforts amount to nothing less than a re-structuring of academic theology as well as the institutional church as it has been

[16] See Grace Ji-Sun Kim and Susan M. Shaw, *Intersectional Theology: An Introductory Guide* (Fortress: Minneapolis, 2018) for a look at contemporary work in this area.

[17] See works by Paolo Friere, Gustavo Gutierrez, Juan Luis Segundo, and Oscar Romero, among others.

[18] See works by Ninian Smart, Rita Gross, and Masao Abe, among others.

[19] See works by Don S. Browning, Thomas Groome, and Edward Farley, among others.

[20] See works by Nancy Ammerman, Jackson Carroll, Carl S. Dudley, and James Wind, among others.

[21] Philip Clayton, *Transforming Christian Theology: For Church and Society* (Fortress: Minneapolis, 2010), 2.

> known and experienced in the past. Professional theologians are not trained to pay a lot of attention to what ordinary Christians think. We dialogue mostly with other theologians and academics (sort of like God listening only to the angels). Traditionally, theology has been modeled on a Greek and medieval understanding of God. At its most extreme, this leads to the belief that God could not interact with the world without compromising God's omnipotence.[22]

The result of paying attention to "what ordinary Christians think" is to expect clergy to invest time and energy listening to the intelligent, thinking people around them, some of whom are already part of the worshipping community, and others who have recognized that their own intuitions and experiences do not fit what they have heard from the pulpit and who are no longer or have never been part of a worshipping congregation.

Clayton invites us to

> imagine what will happen when pew-sitting Christians and those who have gradually drifted away from the institutional church—together with pastors, denominational leaders, and directors of social justice ministries—begin to share their personal faith stories and talk openly and passionately about their faith journeys. Imagine a church where every member is thinking deeply about the core Christian question in light of our contemporary world.[23]

Diana Butler Bass suggests: "What the world needs is better religion, *new forms* of old faiths, religion reborn on the basis of deep spiritual connection—these things need to be explored instead of ditching religion completely. We need religion imbued with the spirit of shared humanity and hope, not religions that divide and further fracture the future."[24] She goes on to say that "the world cannot afford the sort of religion that we have had for the last two or three centuries. People are searching for something new. That something new…is actually something quite old: *faith*, the profoundly personal response to the 'terror and splendor and living concern of God.'"[25]

Mark Richardson, President of Church Divinity School of the Pacific in Berkeley, California, in the course of an address to the Pacific Coast Theological Society said that seminary graduates "cannot be sent out into ministry solely as the administrative oil in the machinery of congregational life. They must be sent out to lead congregations to participate in God's mission outside

[22] Clayton, 59.

[23] Clayton, 7.

[24] Butler Bass, *Christianity After Religion*, 96.

[25] Butler Bass, 98.

the parish gates with an attitude of generosity and trust that this is the place of God's presence."[26]

As a theologian, adjunct professor in a Doctor of Ministry program at a local seminary, and pastoral counselor, I ask myself how I see Tillich's method of correlation being incorporated into the life and ministry of the church—how has it affected biblical interpretation, rites and rituals, prayer books and liturgies? For example, I have a friend who recently lost a child. As she worked with her pastor about the memorial service, she found herself disturbed by liturgical passages that described her child as now happier and living in a much better place where all was perfection. She found that she could no longer accept notions of a hierarchical heaven available only to the properly faithful and devout. She felt alienated from those traditional passages and came close to refusing to have a memorial service if it meant that those prayers had to be used. Fortunately, the faith leader was flexible and together they reworded the liturgy to be more relevant to her existential situation. Such experiences of disappointment and alienation challenge seminaries and the theological community as a whole.

Another instance of the impact of the ideas introduced by the method of correlation occurred during a class discussion about church signage and accessibility. One of the students was describing how well located her church was—it occupied one corner of a busy intersection directly across from a shopping mall. As she talked, she became newly aware that the church did not face the mall—it faced the intersecting street. It had stained glass windows that could be seen from the mall, but there was no easily seen sign that indicated the name of the church, no informational billboard that carried an inspirational saying or an invitation to attend—just lawn. The more she reflected, the more she realized that the "good location" did nothing to make the community aware of the presence or mission of the church.

In addition, she realized that church parking was parallel to the sanctuary and social hall and the short walkway from the parking lot led to a breezeway that connected the entrance of the sanctuary to the entrance to the social hall. The front door of the church could not be seen from the street or the parking lot. To her dismay, she realized that it was attractive, functional—and insular. The welcome mat may have been out, but it could not be seen. What would it take to open up the entrance to the church so that it could offer, through its physical layout, an invitation to participate?

[26] Mark Richardson, "Transforming Theology at the Graduate Theological Union in Light of the Church's Changing Mission," Address to the Pacific Coast Theological Society, November 2, 2013.

That question led to speculation about what it would mean for the congregation if people who shopped at the mall did begin to come to services. What questions would they have, and why did they bring them to a church setting? Students recognized that often the expectations of the people in their congregations were that people came to a church service, hopefully, to become just like the people who already gathered there. But what if the newcomers brought with them insights, outlooks, and expectations that differed from those of the current members? How would the congregation discover, explore, accommodate, and value the newcomer's perspectives as constructive assets?

One of the class members was experiencing such implications. He pastored a church that was located across a roadway from a university campus. His parishioners were interested in inviting students to come to worship, hopefully to interest them in joining the church, and possibly having them help with outreach projects. However, they were finding it awkward and difficult to find common ground with the students, so they initiated a program that was designed to help them get acquainted.

They put together a series of screenings that dealt with themes of existential anxiety and difficulty, invited students to come to see the movies and enjoy good coffee, and dedicated themselves to exploring with the students what the role of the church might be in their lives. What they discovered was the dynamic accuracy of Clayton's insight that the church was facing the need to invent new forms of Christian community. The students had no interest in coming to a service on Sunday morning, listening to a sermon, singing hymns from a hymnal, and visiting over refreshments. If they talked about faith in any way, it was to share a vital and deeply personal experience that they had had at one time, and to hear about similar experiences from others. This was not what the parishioners wanted to hear, and their pastor was in the process of pondering what that might indicate about the future of his church.

In all three of these situations, the work of Thomas Bandy would be helpful. He presents a creative, instructive, and unique approach that is based on insights into the existential needs of specific groups. These insights are based on "lifestyle portraits," which are the products of multi-national corporations that track attitudes, world views, and behavior patterns. They can be used for strategic planning in education, social service, health care, politics, business, and other public sectors. This same data can be used to illustrate both the expectations of church members for stability and continuity and to describe the sectors of the public that are disaffected, rebellious and/or disinterested in church.

His books deal with training theologians, faith leaders and seminarians in the use of demographic and lifestyle research to track and analyze the digital "footprints" of distinct publics in specific contexts. His analysis reveals a range of attitudes and behaviors that indicate how congregational members and community residents relate to particular spiritual assumptions and practices. He argues that in light of this research, established religious institutions have become "sideline" churches and are out of touch with the situation and religious questions of congregations and the communities in which their churches reside.[27]

Using this practical application of Tillich's method of correlation, he explores the anxiety, fear, and reaction to threatening incidents that drive human beings to search for meaning and purpose. Lifestyle portraits are an invaluable aid because they help reveal the existential questions that cannot be easily put into words. Bandy describes how both lay leaders and clergy can learn to listen empathetically to the publics that comprise their neighborhoods or communities and creatively design relevant ministries that address the needs of people within their reach. "Really listen for the way in which different people think, the way people live, and how they identify the priorities in their lives. Listen to how they express themselves, and explore the hidden but all-important dances of their daily lives. Look behind dogmas to discern passions. Look beyond ideologies to decipher core values and bedrock beliefs."[28]

These efforts reflect the seriousness with which the field of theology takes the challenge to respond to the existential questions of our time. Just as Tillich's method of correlation redefined the task of systematic theology in light of process philosophy and theories of relativity, the advent of contextual theologies, congregational studies, and digitally advanced demographic and lifestyle research are ways to adapt Christian theory and practice to shifting human patterns of thought and behavior that have taken place in the past seventy-five years.

Given the rapid and profound changes that have occurred and are occurring, is it any wonder that the quest for God has become both urgent and bewildering? What are ways that faith leaders can support the efforts of congregations to free themselves from dogmatism and traditionalism and assure diverse and multi-cultural publics that their experiences of the mystical a priori are legitimate moments of communion with the Divine that have been addressed by other human beings in the course of history? How can theology rigorously hold to the norm that assures humanity that Ultimate Concern really is being identified and explored, and not some preliminary concern that current impressions have elevated to sacred proportions?

---

[27] Thomas Bandy, *Sideline Church: Bridging the Chasm Between Churches and Cultures* (Nashville: Abingdon, 2018), (among others).

[28] Bandy, xvii.

Ministry is responsible for speaking a word of hope to the existential anxiety of human beings and alleviating the loneliness and despair of historical existence—with the assurance that the "something further" that they intuit, and in some sense know they belong to, is indeed worthy of faith. Tillich's method of correlation describes that task and, most importantly, provides criteria by which the theological endeavor can judge its own efforts to remain faithful to the enduring truths of the Christian faith without creating an idol by disavowing change as a constant in humanity's efforts to receive the eternal truths of the Christian message or by becoming enthused about a particular change to the point of promoting a preliminary concern to ultimacy.

Playing with God? Theological Depth in Video Games after Gamergate[1]

Benjamin J. Chicka

During his lifetime, Tillich located depth of meaning and theological import in both religious and secular art. Tillich's theology of culture is replete with references to Raphael, Dürer, "The School of Athens," Grant Wood's "American Gothic," Michelangelo, Shakespeare, Kafka, and Goethe.[2] When looking at such a list today it may be hard to remember that these were popular figures making a large impact on their societies through art. Yet there is no reason to restrict his views about the importance of art only to those classics. Given Tillich's interest in the arts, it is a natural fit to apply his theology of culture to the video game industry.

No contemporary pop culture art form has as large a social impact today as the video game. For the past ten years, video games have earned more than the movie and music industries combined. Gross revenue for the industry in 2019 has not been released at the time of writing, but was projected to top 150 billion dollars.[3] Even if you do not identify as a "gamer," but play *Candy Crush Saga* or some other game on your phone, you contribute to the enormity of the industry. You may have played video games growing up or know of them as a frivolous way your children or younger relatives pass the time with friends. I suspect you are familiar with at least one of these names: Pac-Man, Super Mario, Sonic the Hedgehog, Zelda, and Lara Croft. I also suspect you have heard of immensely influential game franchises like *Call of Duty*, *Grand Theft Auto*, *Mortal Kombat*, and *Halo*.

Even if you recognize these games, you may not consider them relevant to theological reflection. At best, you might think of these games as harmless

---

[1] An extensive exploration of the ideas in this article will be available in the author's forthcoming book, *Playing God: Tillich, Levinas, and Video Games*, published by Baylor University Press.

[2] James Luther Adams, *Paul Tillich's Philosophy of Culture, Science, and Religion* (Washington, D.C.: University Press of America, 1982); Raymond F. Bulman, *A Blueprint for Humanity: Paul Tillich's Theology of Culture* (Lewisburg: Bucknell University Press, 1981).

[3] "Global Games Market Report 2019," Newzoo, 2019, https://newzoo.com/insights/trend-reports/newzoo-global-games-market-report-2019-light-version/.

forms of entertainment. At worst, you might associate some of these games with controversies over whether violent video games lead to real-world violence. Note that claims about such a causal link have been roundly debunked[4] and linked instead with journalistic and political manipulation.[5] This alone would likely attract Tillich's passion for justice. Beyond these controversies, however, it is less likely you have heard of the character Sam from *Gone Home*, independent game developer Lucas Pope's *Papers, Please*, or a game made by an Iranian born Muslim, *1979 Revolution: Black Friday*. Video games like these represent the lives and plights of individuals from various minority groups often ignored or actively repressed in society. The interactivity provided by video games can provide powerful lessons in listening to, accepting, and helping those who are so ignored. For those facing social oppression and isolation, these games can become a means to personal fulfillment and desire for justice. These are video games full of political and moral significance and theological depth.

Tillich and the Political Significance of Gaming

The political significance in the emergence and proliferation of video games is a somewhat recent phenomenon provoked in large part by one event that launched a movement: Gamergate. Gamergate began in August 2014. At the center of media attention was a game called *Depression Quest*, an interactive text-based game about the experience of living with depression. This game is quite unlike the commercialized, fast-paced, action-based video games full of shooting and explosions. However, the developer of the game had a personal relationship with a member of the media, and this led to accusations that undue publicity was used to try and push "real" video games out of the industry in favor of alternatives such as *Depression Quest*. Gamergate became the canary in the coalmine for a world in which facts do not matter when hate can be weaponized to achieve goals. The developer experienced extreme harassment,

---

[4] Andrew Fishman, "Blame Game: Violent Video Games Do Not Cause Violence," *Psychology Today*, July 16, 2019, https://www.psychologytoday.com/us/blog/video-game-health/201907/blame-game-violent-video-games-do-not-cause-violence. This article contains a summary of relevant research, including a well-vetted list of studies providing more in-depth explanations of the research.

[5] American Psychological Association Task Force on Violent Media, *Technical Report on the Review of the Violent Video Game Literature*, 2015, https://www.apa.org/pi/families/review-video-games.pdf; American Psychological Association's Society for Media Psychology and Technology, "News Media, Public Education and Public Policy Committee," *The Amplifier Magazine*, June 12, 2017, https://div46amplifier.com/2017/06/12/news-media-public-education-and-public-policy-committee.

including death threats. It does not take much imagination to notice connections to similar acts of ideological or physical violence against LGBTQ+ individuals, immigrants, members of non-Christian religions, and other minorities that have spread across the various countries since Gamergate.

What is more interesting is what happened in the wake of Gamergate. As Gamergate and right-wing politics aligned against anyone non-white, non-male, non-cis, and non-Christian, those being rejected refused to be silent. New opportunities opened within the video game industry to affirm identities the real world does not always allow to be realized. Games about coming out as gay in high school are now made by development teams including LGBTQ+ members, for example. The interactive nature of video games provides players an environment in which they can actively express themselves when interacting with characters sharing their identity. For those whose identities are not pushed to the margins of society, interacting with these others in video games is an opportunity to empathize with the experiences of others. In response to a reactionary movement designed to suppress minorities and their perspectives, new sorts of video games emerged. Those games provide spaces where alternative identities can be explored, developed, and affirmed.

There is already evidence that virtual affirmation of minorities can lead to better representation and ethical treatment. As Gamergate became a culture war, the video game industry noticeably changed. The Penny Arcade Expo (PAX) held yearly in Boston (PAX East), Seattle (PAX West), and San Antonio (PAX South) is the largest US gaming convention held explicitly for fans rather than industry professionals. Well over seventy-five thousand people attend PAX East over the course of four days each year, but organizers introduced their first "Diversity Lounge" at PAX East in 2014. It is a safe space where under-represented people can join with friends and allies. Anyone can explore the space and learn more about topics they may not understand. Businesses catering to gay and lesbian fans of games can also easily connect with that audience. TakeThis.org began hosting AFK (away from keyboard) rooms at all PAX conventions that same year. They are quiet safe spaces staffed by health care practitioners and volunteers for those overwhelmed by the size or culture of PAX. At every PAX convention there are panels running in dozens of rooms throughout every day of the convention. In the wake of Gamergate, interest in talking about video games differently increased within the industry. There have been more panels at each PAX about being a woman in gaming, being a transgender gamer, and generally why diversity matters. Large groups of people were beginning to see the depth of meaning in video games for the first time.

Social disruption in the form of two world wars and their aftermath was the fire in which Tillich's theology was forged. Similarly, Gamergate and its aftermath provided the fire for developers to forge new kinds of video games. In his introduction to *Political Expectation*, James Luther Adams outlines some features of Tillich's situation that may be familiar to those who have followed the video game industry since 2014: nationalism, militarism, class division, and capitalist resistance of big industry versus a more popular socialist spirit.[6] A theology in such situations, according to Tillich, must have two dimensions, the vertical and horizontal. The former is a critical standpoint that brings every position, including religious ones, to judgment and calls them to responsibility. The latter reflects Tillich's insistence that theology cannot be dogmatically confined to church hierarchy and handed down from on high.

Tillich and the Moral Significance of Video Games

Tillich explicitly distanced himself from Heidegger's philosophy because he thought it was too detached from culture and seeking something supposedly pure behind it, for ignoring the ways in which culture inevitably shapes human thought.[7] Tillich believed that the truth of religion should embrace and be found in the entire world, and that it is not merely a separate thing given to that world. "Religion is the substance of culture, culture is the form of religion."[8] For theology to be engaging for and accepted by people, it must be true *for them*. If a theological message is simply a rejection of someone's ideas, beliefs, and culture in favor of a complete alternative, such theological claims will almost never be embraced.[9] Religious answers do not need to be reduced to culture, but they cannot be alien impositions.

Tillich did not simply embrace cultural creations as the key to saving humanity, however. He identified strongly with the strand of existentialism from Marx to Nietzsche that spoke to and challenged, in quite a Biblically prophetic way, the current situation. Culture should be embraced not as it is, but when it is transparent to depths of meaning through theological critique. Tillich's terms for the critique and embrace of culture are heteronomy, autonomy, and theonomy. A heteronomous theology is what is found in supernatural religion, a form of religion that will force God on the world whether the

---

[6] James Luther Adams, introduction to *Political Expectation*, by Paul Tillich (New York: Harper & Row, 1971), vii.

[7] Paul Tillich, "Die Theologie des Kairos und die gegenwärtige geistige Lage," *Theologische Blätter* 13, no. 11 (November 1934), 305-28.

[8] Paul Tillich, *The Protestant Era* (Chicago: University of Chicago Press, 1948), 57.

[9] Paul Tillich, *Systematic Theology*, vol. 1 (Chicago: University of Chicago Press, 1967), 59-66.

world wants it or not. A theological embrace of cultural autonomy has lost its critical edge and simply accepts the world as it is. It is a view that seeks redemption in the finite world, no other source needed. In more traditional theological language, heteronomy is about transcendence while autonomy is about immanence. The opposite of theonomy is heteronomy that destroys autonomous creativity by external force. Theonomy is Tillich's paradoxical embrace of both, affirming both positions and also neither, in that it is a position affirming divine transcendence in the immanence of our world: "Theonomy is autonomous reason united to its own depth."[10]

The concept of theonomy is directly related to Tillich's position that God is not a being with specific attributes and intentions, but the ground of being. God is the ground, the support, giving meaning to everything that exists. Therefore, God is not found in some other heavenly realm, but in the depths of reality here and now. The problem is when the piece of reality in which God is encountered is elevated to an ultimate status, turning God from the ground of being into a finite being. This is the problem of idolatry. Religious symbols need a transcendent *import* that goes beyond their materiality and an immanent *form* which allows them to be encountered by finite humans. Tillich peppered his writings with reminders that the non-symbolic element of God is a safeguard against elevating any finite symbol into an idol, "namely, that he is ultimate reality, being itself, ground of being, power of being; and the other, that he is the highest being in which everything that we have does exist in the most perfect way."[11]

Thus, God is and is not a symbol. Religiously meaningful *content* (e.g. sermons about God as the highest perfect being) is a symbol for that which is not symbolic, God as the ground of being. We need symbols that personalize God because God is for us and can make our lives meaningful now, but such symbolization should not be taken literally. As Adams describes the proper religious attitude toward finding God in the world, it is always a matter of affirmation and denial, always saying no even when saying yes to the ultimate meaning of anything.[12] Without the no, the yes becomes impossible. If theological meaning is bestowed, but never qualified, that meaning is lost as something is elevated above its status. Such improper elevation transforms part of reality from a window through which God can shine into a closed door leaving us alone to deal with the world. In religion "one is confronted with the ultimate seriousness of existence, its support and threat and promise: the support

---

[10] Tillich, *Systematic Theology*, vol. 1, 85.

[11] Paul Tillich, *Theology of Culture*, ed. Robert C. Kimball (New York: Oxford University Press, 1959), 61.

[12] Adams, *Paul Tillich's Philosophy of Culture, Science, and Religion*, 207.

of (intimacy and community with) an infinite and inexhaustible reality, the threat of the blindness that comes from the [*Hubris*] or blasphemy of claiming absolute truth, and the promise of new, concrete, meaningful fulfillment."[13] Theonomy is pointing, intuiting, and affirming meaning in the moment, but not fully bringing it out into finite existence. The latter move would rob the ground of being of its eternal power to empower all moments.

The theological significance of Tillich's concept of theonomy for popular art in general, and video games in particular, is that it encourages the hope of overcoming estrangement. With God understood as the ground of being, estrangement is separation from God and one's true nature. Estrangement is separation from what is really true unity, from one's essence.[14] However, because everything that exists can never be separated from that which grounds its existence, feelings of estrangement and separation can be overcome. "In every religion the experience of the holy is mediated by some piece of finite reality. Everything can become a medium of revelation, a bearer of divine power."[15] Meeting a stranger, by contrast, is to encounter a reality necessarily separated from you, a God apart from the world.[16] In such a supernatural theology, ultimate identity with God may never be realized. In heteronomous culture, God is the problem. The issue is how to go about finding the stranger. Tillich's approach is the reverse. We are the problem. God is everywhere already present, and we just need to realize this truth.[17] "*God is the presupposition of the question of God*: This is the ontological solution of the problem of the philosophy of religion, God can never be reached if he is the *object* of a question, and not its *basis*."[18] The way to overcome estrangement is to realize that God is already present. God is the ground of being, not a being, even an ultimate one. Out of this paradoxical situation of the transcendent in the immanent, with its potential for distortion, comes the problem of human estrangement.

Estrangement manifests culturally in terms of polar opposites, and the supposed need to choose either one or the other. As Adams summarizes the

---

[13] Adams, 207.

[14] Paul Tillich, "The Philosophical Background of My Theology," in *Main Works*, vol. 1, *Philosophical Writings*, ed. Gunther Wenz (Berlin; New York: Walter de Gruyter, 1989), 418.

[15] Paul Tillich, *Biblical Religion and the Search for Ultimate Reality* (Chicago: The University of Chicago Press, 1955), 22.

[16] Paul Tillich, "The Two Types of Philosophy of Religion," in *Main Works*, vol. 4, *Writings in the Philosophy of Religion*, ed. John Clayton (Berlin; New York: Walter de Gruyter, 1987), 292-94.

[17] Tillich, *Systematic Theology*, vol. 1, 204-6.

[18] Tillich, "The Two Types of Philosophy of Religion," 290.

situation, the problem arises when anyone "attempts to place himself at the depth or the center of being rather than relate himself to it; when man, who is dependent upon the primal 'given' creativity of being, sets up his own creaturely and conditioned character as unconditioned."[19] Heteronomy is perhaps most easily associated with cultural forces that impede the realization of personal desires. Religious institutions can behave in this way, forcing sets of rules and beliefs on people. Indeed, they have often prevented gay, lesbian, and transgender individuals from realizing their essential selves. Autonomy is a natural reaction to such forces, seen in widespread millennial critiques of neoliberalism and late-stage capitalism, as well as in atheistic reactions to harmful work performed by religious institutions. Theonomy, on the other hand, supports cultural autonomy. People are allowed to be themselves but are understood as fulfilled in their ultimate depths.

A theonomous society is one in which one group will not latch onto one polar tension in life and use it as a force with which to bludgeon other groups. A demonic heteronomous society is what happened in Nazi Germany, and the heteronomous forces of Gamergate similarly tried to reduce people to objects to be used and manipulated. The "demonic" is not a definite entity or set of entities working for evil in the world, but a power inherent of the structures of existence right alongside the sacred. Just like moral transformation that comes from a divine encounter, heteronomous distortions demand unconditional adherence. In what Tillich calls their prophetic role, churches and theologians should critique culture so that its powers are revealed rather than perverted or made opaque.[20]

Tillich and the Theological Depth of Video Games

I have described three Tillichian themes highly relevant to video games as an art form of contemporary pop culture: the concept of theonomy over against both heteronomy and autonomy, the resulting hope to overcome estrangement, and the demonic forces (external forces often including the institutional church) that try to undermine both. Viewed in light of these three themes, we see the art of video games in a new light.

Tillich's categories for a theology of culture are form, content, and import. In a sense, the content does not matter. A picture of an everyday object could convey theological meaning while a religious painting fails in that regard.[21] The key issue is whether different cultural forms have divine import,

[19] Adams, *Paul Tillich's Philosophy of Culture, Science, and Religion*, 32.

[20] Tillich, *Theology of Culture*, 50-51.

[21] Paul Tillich, *The Religious Situation*, trans. H. Richard Niebuhr (Cleveland; New York: Meridian Books, 1956), 57.

whether they point beyond themselves to ultimate meaning. If they do, we have a case of Tillich's theonomous transcendence in immanence. Tillich identified two theological reactions to culture, both of which he found lacking in favor of his alternative hybrid approach. Conservative "defenders of the faith" reject cultural advancements and trends in favor of a separate supernatural realm, and I agree with Tillich that the irrelevance of that approach to culture should be obvious. Tillich also thinks liberal approaches that too eagerly embrace culture on its terms make a critical mistake, however. Such approaches stop challenging culture in terms of a new reality it could make manifest, if only reunited with its ultimate depth.[22] Any piece of culture, any art form can, in principle, be charged with ultimate importance.

Grounded in Tillich's theology of culture, the theologian can now turn a "critical eye" on video games, and the content of those games as a form of art. I argue that some video games point beyond themselves to ultimate meaning, divine import. Any component of form, content, or import can come to dominate a given game, or the perspective a player takes toward a game. Some games are very challenging and contain little to no plot, and some players just care about becoming skillful at playing games like some people are skillful at a sport. In such cases, form is dominant, with no regard to content or import. Such games and players have little to no interest in compelling storylines. Others care more about story and enjoy games with the same focus, containing little to no challenging gameplay. Neither should be thought of as opposed to import though, to ultimate meaning, as theonomous import is impossible without the concrete forms. However, video games are different than other cultural productions in being an interactive form that engages the person beyond a mere act of interpreting art. Because the person is involved, video games strongly connect with the entirety of Tillich's theological system relating to estrangement and overcoming estrangement by realizing one's essence. Video games can help individuals realize their essential ultimate identity.

Tillich helps us see the potential of any cultural form, and especially the potential of art and video games, by viewing it in relation to the ultimate. We cannot simply take culture at face value—this painting is pretty, that game is fun, but no further questions are asked about them or meaning sought within them. Video games can be demonic, at worst, and revelatory, at best, in Tillich's sense of those traditional symbols. Consider how Tillich might describe the video game industry before and after Gamergate. The ultimate truth revealed in a novel situation does not destroy or reject what is given there, but transforms what has been corrupted. "Therefore we can speak of the New in terms of a *re*-newal: The threefold "re," namely, *re*-conciliation, *re*-union, *re*-

[22] Tillich, *Theology of Culture*, 45-47.

surrection."[23] As Adams notes, Tillich relates theology and culture through a sense of the right timing, a moment in which God both employs and shatters cultural forms, neither restricting theology to an isolated realm nor making it an imposition on culture for which human history is irrelevant.[24] Tillich's theology is one for the here and now, not a retreat to conservative dogmas or the naïve assertation of a liberal utopia. For Tillich, we are estranged from what we are essentially, and only in protest against that distortion is ultimate truth found. Estrangement is simultaneously the problem and solution. For Tillich, there are no theological answers divorced from the situation of the people asking questions.

No religion can be completely separated from culture and the society in which it exists. This also means that theology is engaged in the risky business of meaningful living, not the protector of eternal truths detached from the changes of concrete existence. Only by being so engaged, rather than defending a list of dogmatic statements, can theology actually critique the situation in which it finds itself. "Intellectual and spiritual life, no matter how vital it may be, is doomed to fruitlessness and emptiness if it does not receive new impulses from the actual social situation and the challenges which it presents."[25] While Tillich could not have conceived of video games playing such a large role in societies worldwide today, they reveal ultimate depths of meaning that are at the core of his theology. These depths of meaning can be discovered in the autonomous work of video game developers rather than forced upon them by external forces. At the same time, there is a symbolic aspect in video games that has infinite significance—they do not create what they reveal but are the created forms in which something new breaks into concrete existence. The power of a video game is not that it offers an escape to an alternate digital reality, but that it is another way to discern ultimate meaning.

A growing segment of the video game industry, just like Tillich, does not want the existing video game culture to continue unchallenged. Developers like Rami Ismail explicitly bring a religious critique to the video game status quo. At the 2015 Game Developers Conference, Ismail gave a talk in which he noted one of the biggest games from 2011, *Battlefield 3*, a game with a one hundred million dollar budget in which all enemies are brown, heroes white, and Muslims terrorists, could not be bothered to spell an Arabic word correctly in one of its major scenes. "One hundred million dollars to make sure

---

[23] Paul Tillich, *The New Being* (New York: Charles Scribner's Sons, 1955), 20.

[24] James Luther Adams, foreword to *A Blueprint for Humanity: Paul Tillich's Theology of Culture*, by Raymond F. Bulman (Lewisburg: Bucknell University Press, 1981), 19.

[25] Paul Tillich, *Political Expectation* (New York: Harper & Row, 1971), 8.

you can kill my people, and nobody took the time to make sure the text on this enormous set-piece was right.... This isn't just a translation error, it's a gross disrespect towards an entire culture, to spend tens of millions of dollars on rag-dolls, but not have courtesy to have someone review the writing."[26] *Battlefield 3* was a distortion of deeper meanings that can be manifest in cultural creations. National pride has meaning, but when its meaning harms millions of lives, it has become demonic. Both Ismail and Tillich represent unapologetic prophetic voices about what it is to be truly human, and how that truth can burst forth in cultural products. Those who would deny such expression, who prefer the status quo, are not simply expressing personal preference for one type of game over another. They are demonically distorting human life.

Theonomy does not reject the free choices of individuals or cultures, but indicates how ultimate meaning shines through, or distorts, the autonomous choices of individuals and cultures. In light of this line of argumentation, consider the following video games as examples of theonomy.

In *Papers, Please* players control an immigration officer on the border of a fictional, Cold War era, Eastern Bloc country. Gameplay involves players inspecting the forms immigrants provide them with at the border. Only if players admit those allowed and turn away individuals with invalid credentials will the player's character receive full pay. If players do not make enough money, family members may have to go without heat, food, and could eventually die. The most interesting aspect of the game is that immigrants explain their reasons for crossing the border while you inspect their documents. Players can admit people with invalid papers because they are trying to visit dying relatives, smuggle in medicine for sick loved ones, or escape sex trafficking and almost certain death.

1979 Revolution: Black Friday was created by Iranian born game developer Navid Khonsari, who used the game to tell the under-represented cultural history of the Iranian Revolution. Players control Reza Shirazi, a young photographer who wants to document the revolution, but not get involved. However, neutrality does not remain an option for long, and turning to or away from Islam as a means of coping with the situation becomes an option in game. Players can properly go through all the steps of praying during a call to prayer, with Reza saying "Allāhu akbar!" out loud with others taking part in the prayer. In stark contrast to the mistakes of *Battlefield 3*, Muslims are

---

[26] Rami Ismail, "We Suck at Inclusivity: How Language Creates the Largest Invisible Minority for Games," *GDC Vault*, 2014, https://www.gdcvault.com/play/1022362/We-Suck-at-Inclusivity-How.

depicted uttering a phrase at the heart of their religious lives during prayer instead of shouting it while being depicted as stereotypical terrorists.

Gone Home is arguably the game responsible for elevating gaming to an activity beyond entertainment. Players control Katie, a college-age girl returning to an empty home from an overseas trip. Players learn what Katie's parents and sister Sam have been doing through discovering notes, journals, and audio messages. By exploring the house in this way, players experience how Sam came to grips with her own sexuality, struggled with family acceptance, was bullied, and met the girl she loves. Some notes are vague and imply Sam may have committed suicide or at least be contemplating self-harm. However, the ending reveals Sam is now confident in herself and spending a weekend away with her girlfriend. Sam is fine. She does not need saving. She just needs people to let her be herself. Such an expression of being accepted in spite of other mitigating factors can be transformative for LGBTQ+ players still experiencing real-world harassment instead of acceptance. There is even proof that *Gone Home* is directly responsible for converting some players from being against gay rights to being for them.[27] This sort of focus on emotionally salient aspects of different people's lives aligns with Tillich's focus on realizing true personal identities in concrete cultural situations.

Theonomous Video Games

It is also the communities and culture that have developed around such games that matter. Just as Tillich noted "like everything spiritual, religion is supported by a community,"[28] the communities developing around these alternative styles of video games are perhaps even better examples of Tillich's theology of culture at work. Seeing the potential in video games, they have pushed developers to bring forth their meaningful depths rather than block the way to meaning with outdated and incorrect tropes and representations of minority groups in games. Objections like the one offered by Ismail are becoming more common when developers make mistakes. People are starting to hold developers accountable rather than proceeding with business as usual. God's universal presence as the ground of being is realized by particular historical communities, just like there is a paradoxical affirmation of transcendence in immanence. When gay rights are being openly debated, for example, interacting with or playing as a gay character can be a genuine source of relief and

[27] Gita Jackson, "The Video Games That Made People Question Their Beliefs," *Kotaku*, July 2, 2019, https://kotaku.com/the-video-games-that-made-people-question-their-beliefs-1836045401.

[28] Paul Tillich, *What is Religion?*, trans. James Luther Adams (New York: Harper & Row, 1969), 117.

validation. When communities develop around such issues represented in video games, people in minority communities will engage. As would happen in a theonomous culture, people are thirsting for deep meaning in video games, rather than just taking them at face value as nothing more than a fun hobby.

The theological significance of video games is not just that they can help marginalized people affirm their essence, but that people who are less marginalized can learn to be more accepting and loving by playing video games. In a forthcoming book from Baylor University Press, I discuss Tillich in context with Emmanuel Lévinas and his focus on the ethical responsibility toward the other. Tillich believed Christian theology could provide "the courage to be" to those experiencing existential meaninglessness during his lifetime. A theological assessment of video games in our time reveals the same power among marginalized groups often dismissed as "the other" in societies around the world. For players whose identities are nearer to the center of society, encountering LGBTQ+, non-Christian, immigrant, and other marginalized characters in touch with their power of being in games can transfer that courage to players encountering those others in games. As referenced briefly regarding the ability of *Gone Home* to change minds regarding gay rights, this is not just a theory but is really happening. Individuals who experience daily marginalization can draw courage from these virtual experiences. And for those in the dominant center of a culture, these games put them face to face with ethical calls from others in a more immediate way than any book or lecture on the ethical responsibility toward others could possibly achieve.

Video games are at the center of protests among younger people over a lack of meaning in the myriad of ways people have distorted their lives. Video game development after Gamergate is in a position similar to Tillich's postwar hope for Christian socialism, as it represents people in need of redemption who are also the means to that redemption. It is possible to identify at once the religious aspect of culture, even while that aspect is being distorted by the very culture in which it is identified. The possibility to make such an identification is what makes Tillich's approach to culture theological—placing culture in the context of that which is beyond it, both judging it and saving it in that very judgment. The popularity of video games, the communities that have developed around them, and the changes they have brought to the industry, are all expressions of people calling out for depth, and demanding that their own depth be affirmed. While worldwide protests struggle to move the giants of late-stage neoliberalism, video games allow for temporary yet real change and genuine affirmation of the depth of one's being. As I write this, some politicians in the United States are working to strip gay and lesbian individuals of existing rights that have only barely been achieved and block efforts that would allow the possibility of transgender, bi, and other LGBTQ+ individuals to experience fullness of being. However, in video games they can be fully human, and encounter others like them who live without prejudice and discrimination heaped upon them. They can be victors in spite of political structures of this world.

Conclusion

The Gamergate situation revealed that video games cannot be ignored as mere entertainment. They possess real power and potential. Nevertheless, just as every cultural form participating in the ground of being is ambiguous, Gamergate did this only in part. Gamergate's defenders tried to deprive the cultural form that is video games of its deeper potential meaning. They defined video games in such a way as to be wielded as a possession of only certain sorts of video game fans against all others who criticize Gamergate for hindering unconditional deeper meaning from bursting forth through video games.

Gamergate revealed the potential demonic distortion of video games. Because it lacked existential depth, the situation Gamergate created lacked proper moral direction. The result was culture against culture, one free autonomous group against others, the demonic distortion of both culture and how meaning is found in culture. Such tragic failure aligns with Tillich's description of the pitfalls and promises of the demonic. However, video games, as everything finite, participate in God as the ground of being. The demonic, while a distortion, must contain a promise of fulfillment, or else it would not tempt people. On the other hand, if it did not participate in the structures of reality in which Tillich locates ultimate meaning, it would be non-existent.[29] The demonic (in Tillich's sense not of an evil being but the distortion of truth) clearly exists, but because it exists it draws its power of being from the ground of being.

Gamergate resulted in a situation in which its defenders wanted to stay at the surface level, incorrectly elevating it to the level of ultimate concern. Like many historical failures, Gamergate could be viewed as a sign that there is still a thirst for transcendence and infinite meaning, something that transforms the meaning of the present even when history has been a mixed success. Tillich's God may break into the world as a violent disruption of given structures. But such a divine breakthrough is also a productive burst of energy from which the ultimate depths of humanity can shine through because demonic coverings that distort such potential for infinite meaning have been removed.

[29] Adams, foreword, 20.

Video games possess real political power and moral potential, and it is important that power and potential be properly directed. Such disruptions of given structures ultimately serve to prevent distortions of God as the ground of being. Even when truth shines through the medium with a message, neither the medium nor the message can be identified with *the* truth. If it is, religion becomes demonic. Truth is revealed through the forms of culture. However, while cultural forms may reveal truth, they cannot be identified with *the* truth. Otherwise, meaningful reactions to Gamergate could eventually result in the same ideological tendency toward distortion and persecution they protested.

TILLICH & SCIENCE

Paul Tillich's Enduring Relevance to Ecophilosophy and Environmental Ethics

Jeremy D. Yunt

> Is nature not completely subject to the will and willfulness of man? This technical civilization, the pride of mankind, has brought about a tremendous devastation of original nature, of the land, of animals, of plants. It has kept genuine nature in small reservations and has occupied everything for domination and ruthless exploitation. And worse: many of us have lost the ability to live with nature. We fill it with the noise of empty talk, instead of listening to its many voices, and, through them, to the voiceless music of the universe. Separated from the soil by a machine, we speed through nature, catching glimpses of it, but never comprehending its greatness or feeling its power. Who is still able to penetrate, meditating and contemplating, the creative ground of nature?"—Paul Tillich, "Nature, Also, Mourns for a Lost Good" (1948)[1]

As an undergraduate student in the early 1990s at the University of California at Santa Cruz (UCSC), I had the good fortune of meeting Dr. Paul Lee. Lee was Paul Tillich's last teaching assistant at Harvard, and he came to UCSC to teach philosophy after having taught at Harvard and MIT. He eventually founded the Religious Studies Department at UCSC, and then the Homeless Garden Project—a social and ecological program that fed the Santa Cruz community with organic produce, while also helping homeless people find meaning in their life and get off the streets and into permanent housing. In my time with Lee, he would often repeat what he said was one of Tillich's favorite mantras: "We are living in the late stage of the self-destruction of industrial society, as a world above the given world of nature." These words encapsulated for Tillich the spiritual and ecological urgency that industrialization had foisted upon humanity.

Tillich's life coincided with the rise of industrialization, and he witnessed how the worldwide commodification of the natural world—the packaging of nature into "goods" for consumption—had led to what he called a "second

---

[1] Paul Tillich, *The Shaking of the Foundations* (New York: Charles Scribner's Sons, 1948), 79.

nature," or "Frankenstein," above given, organic nature.[2] While Tillich appreciated the creative spirit at work in industrial inventiveness, he also knew the vast power of this ascendant synthetic world to bend humans to its unnatural, stultifying, and often dehumanizing demands. This destruction of nature at the hands of humans was for Tillich a clear symbol of our existential estrangement—from ourselves, from other humans, from nature and nonhuman animals, and ultimately from the creative Ground of Being itself, i.e., God. Of course, Tillich had his own particular, non-objective understanding of the creative source of nature, and one scholar elucidates it perfectly: "Instead of looking outside nature for a supernatural being called God, Tillich looks through nature to the transcendent depth and ground of nature. God, says Tillich, is not a being, he is ... the power of being which enables all things that are to be."[3]

Were he alive today, I have no doubt Tillich would be one of the most outspoken Christian thinkers advocating for a more humane and compassionate appreciation of nature and all its nonhuman beings. For Tillich, to be religious was to be deeply concerned about humanity's impact on the natural world, for nature is an expression of Being-Itself. Although he never developed a systematic "theology of nature," he was far ahead of other Western religious thinkers in understanding and expressing the dialectical role the material world plays in the human existential drama, including how the fate of humanity and nature are shared: "Nature is not only glorious; it is also tragic. It is subjected to the laws of finitude and destruction. It is suffering and sighing with us."[4] For this reason, Tillich never hesitated to use strong religious language to decry the real danger underlying humanity's troubled relationship with nature, as well as the spiritual impoverishment issuing from the industrial process:

> I would say the most universal expression of the demonic today is a split between the control of nature by man, and the fate of man to fall under the control of the product of his control. He produces and then falls under the power of what he has produced, the whole system of industrial existence. It has liberated him, it has given him

[2] Paul Tillich, "The World Situation," in *The Spiritual Situation in Our Technical Society*, ed. J. Mark Thomas (Macon: Mercer University Press, 1988), 6.

[3] James A Carpenter, *Nature and Grace: Toward an Integral Perspective* (New York: Crossroad, 1988), 52.

[4] Carpenter, 81.

> control over nature and now it puts him into a servitude in which he loses more and more his being, his person.[5]

Tillich stood out amongst the theologians of his day because he took seriously the material world's role in aiding or distorting our spiritual lives. As such, he challenged common anthropocentric viewpoints and placed intrinsic ethical value not only on nonhuman animal and plant life, but even on the inorganic dimension that makes all of organic nature possible in the first place. In his well-known *Saturday Evening Post* article from 1958, "The Lost Dimension in Religion," Tillich framed this lost dimension—the dimension of depth—in terms of our relationship with nature:

> Modern man is neither more pious nor more impious than man in any other period. The loss of the dimension of depth is caused by the relation of man to his world and to himself in our period, the period in which nature is being subjected scientifically and technically to the control of man. In this period, life in the dimension of depth is replaced by life in the horizontal dimension.[6]

Here Tillich uses the spatial metaphor "horizontal" to characterize humanity's evolving consciousness during the rise of industrialization. Ceaselessly driving forward and transforming the world (the horizontal) with a newfound form of reasoning he alternately calls "controlling," "scientific," or "technical," humanity's concerns in this period shifted toward the process of objectifying the world, withdrawing any sense of sacredness from nature: "Beginning with Galileo the mathematically-oriented natural sciences banished the supernatural. Nature becomes purely objective, rational, and technical."[7] In contrast to this quite rational way of understanding and shaping the world, Tillich points out that life until the Renaissance was characterized more by ontological or existential concerns (the vertical), where "world-consciousness is still embedded in a mystical or ecstatic God-consciousness… [Any] distinction between nature and the supernatural is abolished. Nature is supernatural in quality, and the supernatural is nature itself."[8]

Tillich refers to this pre-scientific form of reason as "existential," "participatory," or "ontological," wherein truth is something discovered by being in some sense involved in, and caring for, the "object" of one's relation, e.g.,

---

[5] Paul Tillich, quoted in Tomoaki Fukai, *Paul Tillich—Journey to Japan in 1960* (Berlin: Walter de Gruyter, 2013), 68.

[6] Paul Tillich, "The Lost Dimension in Religion," *The Saturday Evening Post* 230, no. 50 (June 14, 1958).

[7] Paul Tillich, *What is Religion*? (New York: Harper & Row, 1969), 128.

[8] Tillich, 128.

nature. This is a significant distinction, because when technical reason gained dominance during the scientific revolution as a special, and in some cases only, way of truly understanding the world, it had vast implications for humanity's growing estrangement from itself and nature. One particular consequence of this shift in consciousness is the myth of the rational mastery of nature—a myth with clear ecological consequences:

> The analysis and mastery of nature and of society presuppose a power that exercises mastery. In this connection the following questions arise: Who can exercise such rule? How is it possible that human intelligence can know nature and bring it into its service through this knowledge? And how is it possible for society to be rationally structured? Who is to be responsible for the structuring of society, and what guarantee is there that it will be done rationally?[9]

With the rising ecological crises in the world today, it's not difficult to answer these rhetorical questions he poses. For example, a concrete outcome of this myth of rationality is seen in the simple fact that, in the year 2016 alone, around nine million people died worldwide from pollutants created by human technologies. We might imagine Tillich asking, "What rational creature would create products that are known to inadvertently kill millions of other humans?"

Even with his sharp critique of reason, Tillich understood that scientific/technical reason serves a vital function in humanity's need to be creative and better understand its world; science, for Tillich, is an indispensable and valuable element of our species. The problem arises when this limited form of reasoning is employed alone and without the aid of existential or ontological reason as a balancing force. Under these circumstances, he saw technical reason taking on a life of its own, often leading to the objectification and unnecessary destruction of nature, as well as the dehumanization of the individual person. So rather than seeing the human as a thinking mind, in a body, in an objectified world—a vestige of Descartes and the rationalist philosophy he birthed—Tillich instead saw the human's role more in Heideggerian terms, as a being-in-nature, which emphasizes the embeddedness of the human in the world. This form of consciousness allows for proper respect and care for the natural world supporting us, because here we see ourselves as a natural being, in need of the aesthetic and vital powers nature provides to the human spirit that arises out of it.

---

[9] Paul Tillich, *The Socialist Decision*, trans. Franklin Sherman (New York: Harper & Row, 1977), 48-49.

Tillich was prescient in recognizing that the more humans understood nature in technical ways and treated it as such—as a storehouse of resources without inherent value, or as a threatening presence to be dominated—the more we would see our spiritual and environmental problems grow. Therefore, he characterized this relentless and often unquestioned destruction of organic life as "demonic," a "structure of destruction" within humanity capable of tearing apart and profaning a prime bearer of the holy, i.e., nature. For this reason, he characterized our existential estrangement leading to the destructive domination of nature as "sin." And by highlighting a specific element of sin as "concupiscence"—often defined as a lower appetite or desire in the human psyche antagonistic to reason—Tillich spoke of the human's "unlimited desire to draw the whole of reality into one's self. It refers to all aspects of man's relationship to himself and to his world."[10]

Langdon Gilkey brilliantly contextualizes Tillich's broadened understanding of sin in relation to our ecological problems:

> As Tillich would put it, this demonic use and using up of nature bespeaks a deep alienation of human being from itself, from nature, and from its own infinite ground; consequently, it seeks that infinity of meaning, and so seeks itself and its unity, through taking the infinite into itself, by possessing and using the finite infinitely.
>
> Tillich has, in reinterpreting [the category of concupiscence], given it a much wider meaning as the prime symptom of estrangement of human being from the whole world of goods and so of nature—and as the key 'sin' of our technical, commercial culture.[11]

Sin should not be seen primarily in its narrow conception as the breaking of religious or moral commandments. Rather, it should be widened and understood as the inherent existential estrangement in humanity, splitting the self apart from its healthy, centered, essential nature and its source, namely, God.

Tillich captured the danger and significance of this estrangement from nature with two philosophical concepts: "forwardism" and "means-ends distortion." Again framing his insights in the spatial metaphors of the horizontal and vertical, he unveiled the deep spiritual issues surrounding our obsessive scientific and technical drive ahead in the horizontal dimension, producing

---

[10] Paul Tillich, *Systematic Theology*, vol. 2 (Chicago: The University of Chicago Press, 1957), 52.

[11] Langdon Gilkey, *Gilkey on Tillich* (New York: Crossroad, 1990), 184-85.

and consuming the novelties we create out of the natural world, without stopping to ask the vital vertical question: For what?

> [A] more longtime spiritual danger has resulted from the alliance of science and technology. It has caused the perversion of means and ends. It enabled man to produce tools without limits and to make this production into an end itself. In this way it suppressed the question of an end, of the meaning not only of the process of production and consumption (under the control of advertisement), but of life as such. The feeling of emptiness and meaninglessness in innumerable people is a result of this perversion.[12]

Here Tillich anticipates the contemporary "deep ecology" movement, which insistently questions humanity's use of nature to fulfill its needs and desires. The Norwegian philosopher Arne Næss, the "father" of deep ecology, addressing the pointed difference between a *vital need* of humanity and a *nonvital desire*, shows that "the complicated question concerning how industrial societies can increase energy production with the least undesirable consequences is largely a waste of time if this increase is pointless in relation to ultimate human ends."[13] Extending this analysis, Tillich points out that technologies in modern consumer culture often provide for manufactured, shallow desires that have been created through advertising. Many of these desires necessitate massive destruction of organic nature and have concrete, negative impacts on humanity's spiritual being. Therefore, in order to really understand how technology plays such a predominant role in the loss of meaning in human culture—and contributes to innumerable ecological, health, and spiritual problems—it's important to examine Tillich's conception of "spirit" itself.

Tillich is committed to the principle that our relationship to nature is a large determinant of the quality and depth of our spiritual lives, and not just a meaningless backdrop to it. Therefore, every technological problem fundamentally altering our place in nature should be approached, first and foremost, from a spiritual perspective. And since he saw the unique spiritual dimension in our species principally defined as a union of *power* and *meaning*, technology should be understood as a material extension of our power over nature in an effort to not only provide for our needs, but also realize deeper meaning. As

---

[12] Paul Tillich, "Science and the Contemporary World in the View of a Theologian," in *The Spiritual Situation in Our Technical Society*, ed. J. Mark Thomas (Macon: Mercer University Press, 1988), 177.

[13] Arne Næss, "The Deep Ecological Movement: Some Philosophical Aspects," in *Environmental Philosophy: From Animal Rights to Radical Ecology* (Upper Saddle River: Prentice Hall, 1998), 194.

such, technology has an internally projected purpose (meaning) before it has a practical use (power). And Tillich anticipates insights from the somewhat new field of ecospychology when he points out a primary spiritual and psychological danger arising from unquestioned technology: "We aspire to rule nature through the machine. But it would seem that the machine is adjusting us to its reality, instead of man adjusting the machine to his own being."[14]

Tillich alludes to the shifting nature of modern consciousness that accompanies industrialization. In this new technical consciousness humanity often fails to ask ultimate questions behind the technologies it creates, or whether or not these technologies truly serve the psychological/spiritual, ecological, or social/cultural health of itself and its world. Instead, technologies are created simply because they can be, and then the transitory concerns surrounding them demand more and more of our attention and consume our lives in almost religious ways. In the wake of this technological obsession we are left with a multitude of problems to confront, many of which Tillich himself addressed: space exploration and the conquest (and pollution) of space, while deep social, ecological, and economic needs remain unmet on earth; pursuit of "virtual" reality and the colonization of other planets while, or because, actual reality (our planet) is increasingly destroyed by our own hands; the prospect of the annihilation of all life through nuclear war; worldwide computer networking and robotics manufacturing for increased economic efficiency, often leading to mass unemployment and the more efficient destruction of nature.

No matter what realm of existence he is analyzing, throughout Tillich's writings we sense his conviction that empathizing with, and defending, nature is of vital importance to the human spirit, bringing great depth and meaning to our experience of life itself. That's why he often spoke passionately, particularly in his sermons, of the suffering of nature at the hands of humans:

> Sympathy with nature in its tragedy is not a sentimental emotion; it is a true feeling of the reality of nature. Schelling justly says: 'A veil of sadness is spread over all nature, a deep unappeasable melancholy over all life.' According to him this is 'manifest through the traces of suffering in the face of all nature, especially in the faces of the animals.' The doctrine of suffering as the character of all life, taught by the Buddha, has conquered large sections of mankind.

[14] Paul Tillich, "Religious Dimensions of Contemporary Art," in *On Art and Architecture*, eds. John and Jane Dillenberger (New York: Crossroad, 1987), 180.

> But only he who is connected in his own being with the ground of nature is able to see into its tragedy.[15]

This empathy for nature ultimately drew Tillich into developing his unique and holistic *Lebensphilosophie*, which he terms the "multidimensional unity of life."

Tillich credits Albert Schweitzer's radical "reverence for life" as having largely inspired his own life philosophy:

> I have come to the idea that every theology which separates men from nature is completely mistaken. Nature participates in man and men participate in nature, and for this reason I feel now more than in earlier years the impact of Schweitzer's idea of the inviolability of life. I even have a large section in the forthcoming third volume of my Systematic Theology under the title, 'The Inviolability of Life.'"[16]

Of course, we now know that Tillich instead called this section of his system "Life and the Spirit," and it's here he develops his most significant contribution to environmental—and even animal—ethics for us today.

In this part of his system, Tillich attempts to debunk hierarchical understandings of life in the modern age that have led to our increased alienation from, and desecration of, the natural world. Conceived as a challenge to the mechanistic and dualistic theories put forth by Western materialist science, positivist philosophy, and religious fundamentalism—which we see today increasing its attacks on science, reason, and nature—Tillich hopes to unveil the "unity and diversity of life in its essential nature" by examining the evolutionary continuum of the life process. In doing so, he opens us to a more holistic and empathetic approach to *all life*. He starts by fleshing out the objectifying outcome of seeing humanity on a different level "above" nature, something which has created dire consequences for nature and nonhuman beings.

In an effort to counteract the problems of such objectification, Tillich wants to replace the metaphor "level" with the metaphor "dimension." The reason for this replacement, Tillich explains, is that the term "level" is a "metaphor which emphasizes the equality of all objects belonging to a particular level. They are 'leveled,' that is, brought to a common plane and kept on it.

---

[15] Paul Tillich, *The Shaking of the Foundations* (New York: Charles Scribner's Sons, 1948), 82.

[16] Paul Tillich, *The Theological Significance of Schweitzer*, January 11, 1959, 8, transcript, archives of the Albert Schweitzer Institute for Humanities, Quinnipiac University, Hamden.

There is no organic movement from one to the other; the higher is not implicit in the lower, and the lower is not implicit in the higher."[17]

Perhaps the clearest theological expression of this hierarchical view is the "Great Chain of Being." Each existing being is clearly demarcated and assigned a degree of value based on its level, starting at the top with God as the ultimate being, and then descending down to angels, humans, animals, plants, minerals, and so on. This classical religious view was later supplanted during the Enlightenment with another hierarchical vision of life through the rise of scientific knowledge. Replacing God with the human mind or consciousness, reality is here composed of different levels—the physical, biological, chemical, and mental—all of which are thought to be reducible down to the interaction of inorganic processes (scientific reductionism). Tillich sees both these religious and scientific views as mistaken.

He believed that when existence is cognitively arranged according to levels, it is easy for humanity to see everything nonhuman simply as an object for manipulation and commodification. Therefore, Tillich posits the totality of *being* as the primary reality humans must grasp in order to understand and appreciate the fundamental unity and sanctity of all dimensions of life; and in Tillich's holistic vision, all the dimensions of existence intersect in one point, namely, Being-Itself. For this reason, he emphasizes the ontological importance of this symbolic replacement, speaking of a "dimension" as

> a geometrical metaphor which has its merits, and as every metaphor, its limits. I have made a crusade for this metaphor against the other spatial metaphor, levels. Level puts basic realities, body and mind, culture and religion, world and God above each other....
>
> But this imagery is wrong. These basic realities are within each other. And this is what the metaphor dimension conveys, for dimensions cross each other in one point without interfering with each other.[18]

Then Tillich makes explicit the ethical consequences of this metaphorical shift: "The significant thing...is not the replacement of one metaphor by another but *the changed vision of reality* which such replacement expresses."[19] In other words, how we define life conditions how we view, interact with, and

---

[17] Paul Tillich, *Systematic Theology*, vol. 3 (Chicago: The University of Chicago Press, 1963), 13.

[18] Paul Tillich, "Religion and Art in the Light of the Contemporary Development," in *On Art and Architecture*, ed. by John and Jane Dillenberger (New York: Crossroad, 1987), 166.

[19] Tillich, 166, (emphasis mine).

ultimately treat life, and so "it is obvious that the use of the metaphor 'level' is a matter not of inadequacy alone but of decision about the problems of human existence."[20] This is why Tillich's multidimensional unity of life is highly relevant to environmental ethics today; his life philosophy is meant to lead to a shift not only in one's consciousness, but also in one's actions. It is a call to concern for *all life*, not just human life.

In order to confront our conceptualization and treatment of life, Tillich had to address one of the primary scientific, religious, and philosophical problems inherent in hierarchical "levels" thinking:

> The question of the relation of the organic to the inorganic 'level' of nature leads to the recurrent problem of whether biological processes can be fully understood through the application of methods used in mathematical physics or whether a teleological principle must be used to explain the inner-directedness of organic growth.[21]

Tillich rejected the first method of understanding life, which we know as scientific materialism or reductionism, by calling it an "ontology of death." This belief system takes even primary phenomenal experiences like human consciousness—the basis of our comprehending and expressing reality—and reduces it to nothing but chemical and neural processes. It would explain, for instance, psychological depression as nothing but chemical reactions in the human body, leaving out of the equation what the actual *feeling* or *meaning* of depression is—the two components of depression most important to someone actually experiencing it. This is why Tillich was so opposed to the growing drive of scientific reason toward scientism. In scientism, the extension of scientific principles is applied to all matters of life, with the conviction that nothing outside of the purview of science can provide ultimate meanings about the nature or structure of human existence and the universe. Ironically, since science itself cannot either verify or falsify this belief, we can say, with Tillich, that such a position is itself philosophical, or quasi-religious—not scientific.

Tillich's multidimensional approach to life also caused him to reject the second method of levels thinking, which is known historically as *vitalism*. In opposition to scientific reductionism, which seeks to explain the complexity of life by breaking it down to its most basic elements, vitalism instead introduces a supernatural, nonmaterial force into the life process. For Tillich, this method also disrupts the natural, emergent nature of life's multidimensional unity. It creates a worldview in which humans are not seen as a part of nature

---

[20] Tillich, 14.
[21] Tillich, 14.

but are instead above it because they are in some sense imbued with, and controlled by, a supernatural power.

His criticisms of these narrow scientific and philosophical/religious approaches led Tillich to instead conceive of life in a way that has deep significance for our valuation of nonhuman life forms. We see this most fundamentally in his widened redefining of life itself, wherein he rejects the reductionist idea that the inorganic dimension is not a part of life: "Just like every other dimension, the inorganic belongs to life, and it shows the integratedness and the possible disintegration of life in general."[22] Tillich considers this universal concept of life as "unavoidable" and says that it "liberates the word [life] from its bondage to the organic realm."[23] This anticipates future environmental philosophy and ecotheology, and challenges the historical anthropocentric bias of Christian theology that has caused much of humanity to see both nonhuman organic life (e.g., animals) and the inorganic dimension of reality as relatively unimportant or meaningless.

Tillich goes even further and turns anthropocentrism on its head by elevating the ontological status of this dimension: "the inorganic has a preferred position...in so far as it is the first condition for the actualization of every dimension. This is why all realms of being would dissolve were the basic condition provided by the constellation of inorganic structures to disappear."[24] The ecological and religious implications of this statement should not be underestimated. This basic truism—that our species would not even exist without sound inorganic and organic dimensions supporting us—is something now thrust upon us by ecological crises, and Tillich drives this point home forcefully.

When he speaks of the inorganic dimension's "preferred position," Tillich is not saying that the inorganic is more important than humans in a moral, valuational sense—a complaint fundamentalist Christians often make against those who show a deep concern for defending nonhuman animals and the intrinsic value of organic nature. Rather, he is simply highlighting the inorganic's ontological status as the fundamental conditioning dimension of all the others—without it, nothing in the universe would exist. The modern world's lack of insight into these simple scientific and existential facts is quickly contributing to our current ecological troubles, and Tillich wants to show that the "spirit" actualized in our being—a defining, unique component of the human being—is only made possible due to the material of which we

[22] Tillich, 34.
[23] Tillich, 12.
[24] Tillich, 19.

are composed and which supports our being, i.e., nature. In short, Tillich believes that the spirit in humanity cannot be separated from the inorganic and organic dimensions through which this spirit is actualized. Spirit, in other words, arises as a unique dimension of life in an evolutionary and organic way: "In the inorganic, the spiritual is present. In the spiritual, the inorganic is present, and both in the organic. I could say with most of the progressive biologists and neurologists that man's spiritual dimension is present in every cell of his body.... You cannot separate them."[25]

For Tillich, words like "spirit" or "soul" do not denote things that exist in a material sense, and thus he does not see the emergence of spirit as a supernatural act of a divine being who interferes in the laws of the natural world. Instead, spirit is a dimension of life that arises organically through the evolutionary processes of nature. He even suggests the potential of spirit arising in other beings by saying that "within the reach of present human experience, this has happened only in man. The question of whether it has happened anywhere else in the universe cannot yet be answered positively or negatively."[26] Tillich's evolutionary approach to the life process allows him to envision the possible future development of spirit in other beings, thus anticipating what modern science now teaches us about the evolving complexity of nonhuman animal emotions, cognition, and intentionality. For Tillich, the openness of the evolutionary process implies—however difficult it may be to imagine—the possibility of other animal beings gaining new dimensions of consciousness, meaning we cannot set an absolute boundary line between ourselves and other species who led up to the development of our own species, or even those who may come after us. After all, we have to remember our own evolutionary origins.

Tillich's appreciation for nature is fundamentally based on the organic and inorganic continuum holding all life together in an ultimate unity. And today, millions of people share his appreciation for nature and its nonhuman beings by showing serious concern for the psychological and physical suffering of all beings who share in existence. His thought provides a sound philosophical, religious, and scientific grounding for this growing ethical concern for other beings who do not fully embody what he calls the spirit dimension, but who nonetheless approach it.

Tillich even highlights our intuitive, precognitive relation with nonhuman animals when he speaks of our "ability to participate empathetically in

[25] Paul Tillich, "Thing and Self," in *The Spiritual Situation in Our Technical Society* (Macon: Mercer University Press, 1988), 115.

[26] Tillich, 21.

the psychological self of even the highest animals in such a way that, for example, [we] can fully understand psychological health and disease."[27] What he intimates is that while many of the so-called "higher" animals (e.g., dolphins, chimpanzees, elephants) do not fully embody what he terms the spiritual dimension, they do clearly exhibit intentionality and self-actualization, and thus contain the potential for expressing and experiencing a sense of meaning beyond what we've previously thought.

I believe he is correct to remain open on this point. Current neurocognitive data from animal studies show that many animals embody a sense of purposiveness and meaning beyond mere stimulus and response reactions. We have come a long way from Descartes' view of animals as mere machines, and in his 1997 address to the North American Paul Tillich Society, Durwood Foster recounted a fascinating story confirming Tillich's position on this matter:

> Some of us wanted to go fishing.... They were said to be biting over in the bay. We assumed Paulus [Tillich] was coming, and it seemed to be so when we met at the Tillichs' house to deploy. But on hearing the talk of fishing, Paulus' mood changed. One could wonder if this was linked to other reactions of avoidance, or dread, toward the animal world. But the tack he took was to indict, quite vehemently, our Ritschlian attitude of callously exploiting nature, turning everything into a mere thing to be used. He was totally sincere about this, whatever was afoot in the dread. We argued we planned to eat the fish, if we caught any, and harvesting the game was essential for its own well-being. Paulus wasn't impressed. He stayed home. And when we got to the water, no one wanted to fish.[28]

In the end, Tillich's vision of the multidimensional unity of life should lead us to question our personal stances toward the natural world, and thus expand our sense of moral subjectivity beyond the socio-personal to include a valuation of life in its totality. Without the basic dimensions of life actualized within us (inorganic and organic), our life "of the spirit" would remain in a state of mere potentiality. That said, Tillich still believes that our life in the spiritual and historical dimensions warrants some ontological valuation beyond that of other species; for these dimensions arise from *and* comprehend

---

[27] Tillich, 37.

[28] Durwood Foster, "Afterglows of Tillich," *Newsletter of the North American Paul Tillich Society* 23, no. 1 (January 1997).

all the dimensions conditioning them. On face value, this might seem to betray some anthropocentrism in Tillich's thought, but things are not quite so simple:

> Historical man adds the historical dimension to all other dimensions which are presupposed and contained in his being. He is the highest grade from the point of view of valuation, presupposing that the criterion of such value judgment is the power of a being to include a maximum number of potentialities in one living actuality. This is an ontological criterion, according to the rule that value judgments must be rooted in qualities of the objects valuated, and it is a criterion which should not be confused with that of perfection. Man is the highest being within the realm of our experience, but he is by no means the most perfect.[29]

In making this claim Tillich brings together two very significant points: he affirms the ontological significance of humanity, while simultaneously highlighting the moral pitfalls of a prideful anthropocentrism that frequently arises from our unique human dimensions—often causing immense suffering to other humans and the nonhuman beings with whom we share the planet. In short, Tillich lays out the paradoxical essence of humanity's ontological importance and uniqueness, against what he considers the moral perfection of animals: "Perfection means actualization of one's potentialities; therefore, a lower being can be more perfect than a higher one if it is actually what it is potentially. And the highest being—man—can become less perfect than any other, because he not only can fail to actualize his essential being but can deny and distort it."[30]

Tillich's understanding of morality centers on whether or not humans are actualizing their inherent potential, their essential self, through acts of love—what he describes as "the reunion of the separated." And for Tillich, our essential self is revealed when we attempt to overcome existential estrangement and reunite in love, however fragmentarily, with all dimensions of reality—including ourselves, others, God, and the natural world of which we are a part. This explains why he sees the significance of our species not only in the physical and cognitive powers we possess, but also in the moral maturity we are capable of, ultimately forcing us to account for the way we use the unique abilities we've been given. With clear implications for ecological and

[29] Paul Tillich, *Systematic Theology, Volume 3* (Chicago: The University of Chicago Press, 1963), 17.

[30] Tillich, 36.

animal ethics, Tillich highlights this moral challenge inherent in our uniqueness: "Animals...are completely bound to the actual and acting situation in which they find themselves. They are in the bondage of all nature. This bondage makes their special character, their perfection. They cannot destroy themselves in the way that man can."[31]

Tillich never faltered in his calls for humanity to respect and reunite with nature. This makes him the antipode of other-worldly religious thinkers who see nature as insignificant to our spiritual lives, or even insignificant to the creative ground of nature, God. This is largely due to his multidisciplinary approach to reality, utilizing science, theology, philosophy, history, psychology, and aesthetics to analyze human consciousness and action. Through all these lenses, and always with reference to the eternal and our relation to it, he shows us how to see the natural world as a bearer of the holy. His vision is of a deeper understanding of existence, one able to comprehend what is truly meaningful, authentic, and intrinsically worthy across all dimensions of life—not just human life. And while he lifted up and affirmed the spiritual value and ontological significance of our species, he also brought us back down into the realm of nature by issuing stark rebukes of anthropocentrism and anti-evolutionary (in religion) and reductionist (in science) views of life. At a time when humanity is desperately in need of a new vision toward nature and our place in it, this makes his insights relevant, challenging, and deeply useful.

Much more could be said of Tillich's ongoing relevance to our ecological situation, but perhaps it's important to conclude by saying something about the growing number of Christians today who see their salvation [*salvus*: to heal and make whole] as a personal event unrelated to other nonhuman beings and the natural world which supports them. Tillich had strong words against this position, and he asked us to believe, and act, with the conviction that the symbol of salvation inextricably links our fate to the fate of nature: "For there is no salvation of man if there is no salvation of nature, for man is in nature and nature is in man."[32] This idea of universal salvation, which he termed "eschatological pan-en-theism," envisions everything temporal (including nature) as coming from the eternal and returning to the eternal. It's a challenging symbol to those who unnecessarily and wantonly harm others, nature, or its many nonhuman beings, because it emphasizes in both physical and spiritual terms the vital importance of our concrete actions in the world. In a stark and uncompromising warning, Tillich challenges us to believe with him that the quest for salvation has deep significance for the present moment—for us and

---

[31] Tillich, "Thing and Self," 116-17.

[32] Tillich, *The Shaking of the Foundations*, 84.

for all of nature—and not just for some personal spiritual experience or place beyond the world.

> The bodiless spirit...is not the aim of creation; the purpose of salvation is not the abstract intellect or a natureless moral personality. Do we not see everywhere the estrangement of people from nature, from their own natural forces and from nature around them? And do they not become dry and uncreative in their mental life, hard and arrogant in their moral attitude, suppressed and poisoned in their vitality? They certainly are not the images of salvation.[33]

[33] Tillich, 85.

Paul Tillich's Legacy in Psychology and Pastoral Psychotherapy[1]

Pamela Cooper-White

At a meeting of the AAR Psychology, Culture, and Religion Group some years back, we watched a video of Paul Tillich in conversation with Carl Rogers in 1965 at San Diego State College.[2] It struck us at the time—and in rereading the transcript this still comes across—that these two men (known as "great men" and as representatives of the respective traditions of psychology and theology) in the process of their conversation replicated each one's method quite exactly. That is to say that Rogers, while offering his own point of view at times, spent much of his "air time" artfully mirroring Tillich's statements and posing questions, and Tillich in every instance gave a lengthy and somewhat lecture-like answer. So Tillich's correlational method was enacted in vivo, with psychology/the concerns of the world raising up issues and questions, and theology/the Christian message giving authoritative answers!

The Influence of Psychology on Tillich

We know that Tillich's correlational method was groundbreaking during his lifetime, and that in fact he saw it as a much more mutual dialogical process than it has sometimes been characterized to be (although in his essay "Existentialism and Psychoanalysis" he was still insisting that "the interpretation of man's predicament by psychoanalysis raises the question that is implied in man's very existence. Systematic theology has to show that the religious symbols are answers to this question."[3]) Nevertheless, we know that Tillich was

---

[1] This article was first presented to the American Academy of Religion Annual Meeting, Atlanta, GA, November 21, 2015. A transcript of that presentation can be found in *Bulletin of the North American Paul Tillich Society* 42, no. 2 (2016): 28-34.

[2] A transcript of this conversation is published as "Dialogue: Paul Tillich and Carl Rogers," *The Meaning of Health: Essays in Existentialism, Psychoanalysis, and Religion by Paul Tillich*, ed. Perry LeFevre (Chicago: Exploration Press/Chicago Theological Seminary, 1984), 194-202.

[3] Paul Tillich, "Existentialism and Psychoanalysis," in *The Meaning of Health: Essays in Existentialism, Psychoanalysis, and Religion by Paul Tillich*, ed. Perry LeFevre (Chicago: Exploration Press/Chicago Theological Seminary, 1984), 94.

profoundly influenced by psychology—particularly in his earlier life by Freud,[4] later by Jung,[5] and still later— especially after coming to the United States—by a variety of humanist and existential approaches to psychotherapy and psychology, including a deep friendship with the analyst Karen Horney,[6] and on-going, rich interaction from 1941 to 1945 as a member of the New York Psychology Group (which included Erich Fromm,[7] Rollo May, Carl Rogers, the

---

[4] Tillich's early mention of Freud appears in *The Religious Situation*, trans. H. Richard Niebuhr (New York: Henry Holt and Company, 1932), 32, in which he acknowledges Freud's discovery of "the purely psychological" method (as opposed to prior approaches to psychology as physical degeneracy):

> This discovery was important ethically and religiously particularly because it recognized—with questionable over-emphasis, to be sure—the fundamental importance of the erotic sphere for all aspects of psychical life....Speaking in the language of religion, psycho-analysis and the literature allied with it cast light upon the demonic background of life. But wherever the demonic appears there the question as to its correlate, the divine, will also be raised. Speaking psycho-analytically, this is the question as to the power which can sublimate the erotic drive present in all things psychical.

Thanks to Eric Crump, PhD, for this reference. Much later, while at Harvard, Tillich wrote appreciatively about "the depths of Freud" in "Psychoanalysis, Existentialism, and Theology," in *The Meaning of Health: Essays in Existentialism, Psychoanalysis, and Religion by Paul Tillich*, ed. Perry LeFevre (Chicago: Exploration Press/Chicago Theological Seminary, 1984), 151-59. Tillich draws four lines of intersection and even influence from "depth psychology" on theology in "The Theological Significance of Existentialism and Psychoanalysis," in *The Meaning of Health: Essays in Existentialism, Psychoanalysis, and Religion by Paul Tillich*, ed. Perry LeFevre (Chicago: Exploration Press/Chicago Theological Seminary, 1984), 81-95. For a discussion of this relationship between Tillich's theology and psychoanalysis, see also William R. Rogers, "Tillich and Depth Psychology, in *The Thought of Paul Tillich*, eds. James Luther Adams, Wilhelm Pauck, and Roger Lincoln Shinn (New York: Harper & Row, 1985), 102-18.

[5] Cf. Ann Belford Ulanov, "The Anxiety of Being: Paul Tillich and Depth Psychology" in *The Thought of Paul Tillich*, eds. James Luther Adams, Wilhelm Pauck, and Roger Lincoln Shinn (New York: Harper & Row, 1985), 119-36.

[6] Tillich describes Horney as his "great and wonderful friend" and describes their serious debate about the question "Is man essentially healthy?" in "Psychoanalysis, Existentialism, and Theology," in *The Meaning of Health: Essays in Existentialism, Psychoanalysis, and Religion by Paul Tillich*, ed. Perry LeFevre (Chicago: Exploration Press/Chicago Theological Seminary, 1984), 157.

[7] Cf., Guyton Hammon, *Man in Estrangement: A Comparison of the Thought of Paul Tillich and Erich Fromm* (Nashville: Vanderbilt University Press, 1965).

anthropologist Ruth Benedict, several Jungian analysts, several Union Seminary professors, and the pastoral theologian Seward Hiltner, among others.[8]) Earlier, in the years after WWI and on into the 1930s, much of this influence was through personal relationships—in psychiatrist Earl Loomis' words, "his recovery of the idea of the 'demonic' doubtless served him as one major bridge between religio-philosophical and analytical thinking. His circle of 'bohemian' sociopolitical friends put him constantly in touch with analytically informed intellectuals."[9]

The influence of psychoanalysis and psychology on Tillich has been examined in detail by Terry Cooper in his book *Paul Tillich and Psychology*.[10] Cooper carefully analyzes in particular the discussions of the New York group, which in his words "dealt with issues that are very much with us today, such as whether faith can be psychologically explained, the meaning of transcendence, the relationship between psychotherapy and ethics, the appropriateness of self-love, and whether human love is parallel with Divine love."[11] In his interactions with the New York group, Cooper writes:

> In my view, Tillich's involvement in the New York Psychology Group reinforces the notion that he practiced a method closer to the revised correlational approach [e.g., of David Tracy[12]]. Tillich engaged answers as well as questions. He did not assume a privileged position in which other people simply brought up their secular questions. He was quite aware, for instance, that Fromm held a competing worldview with its own answers and resolutions to the problems of human existence. [Fromm was an adamant and articulate atheist existentialist.] Tillich did not simply "answer" Fromm's questions; instead, he disagreed with Fromm's solutions.[13]

---

[8] The group's discussion are detailed in Terry D. Cooper, *Paul Tillich and Psychology: Historic and Contemporary Explorations in Theology, Psychology, and Ethics* (Macon: Mercer University Press, 2005), 99-145.

[9] Earl A. Loomis, Jr., "The Psychiatric Legacy of Paul Tillich," in *The Intellectual Legacy of Paul Tillich*, ed. James R. Lyons (Detroit: Wayne State University Press, 1969), 82.

[10] Cooper, *Paul Tillich and Psychology.*

[11] Cooper, back cover.

[12] David Tracy, *Blessed Rage for Order: The New Pluralism in Theology* (San Francisco: Harper & Row, 1988); see also David Tracy, "Tillich and Contemporary Theology," in *The Thought of Paul Tillich*, eds. James Luther Adams, Wilhelm Pauck, and Roger Lincoln Shinn (New York: Harper & Row, 1985), 260-77; also cited in Cooper, *Paul Tillich and Psychology*, 199.

[13] Cooper, *Paul Tillich and Psychology*, 199.

The influence *on* Tillich of psychology in general, and psychoanalysis in particular, is woven throughout his works. Many of the deep existential themes he revisited in his work over and over have both psychological and theological resonances, particularly, perhaps, in the realm of theological anthropology. In Tillich's words, "Man must be considered under three aspects: first, under the aspect of his created goodness or original innocence; second, under the aspect of the distorted existential situation in which he finds himself actually; third, under the aspect of his rehabilitation through healing or saving powers which he experiences in life and history."[14] The human experiences of fear of death, fear of the unknown, loneliness, and guilt were primary thematic issues during Tillich's lifetime for both psychoanalysts and theologians, and both were deeply interested in healing and change. In Tillich's words, the "Old Being" of estrangement from oneself, others, and life in general, with its attendant risks of cynicism and despair, toward actualization of the "New Being" of "reconciliation and transformation."[15] Tillich reframed the category of "sin" from Augustinian concupiscence to the inescapable human condition of separation and alienation—from self, from others, from life, and from God.[16] Tillich embraced the mid-century language of "human potential,"[17] and saw the aim of pastoral care in particular to assist persons in coming to self-acceptance[18]—not as resignation, but as existential courage in the face of the human condition, the "courage to be."[19]

Tillich's Legacy in Psychology

While it is therefore relatively easy to discern the influence of psychology *on* Tillich, it is somewhat harder to pin down *Tillich's* direct legacy in psychology. In one sense, much of Tillich's influence can be said to be indirect—through

---

[14] Paul Tillich, "Psychotherapy and a Christian Interpretation of Human Nature," in *The Meaning of Health: Essays in Existentialism, Psychoanalysis, and Religion by Paul Tillich*, ed. Perry LeFevre (Chicago: Exploration Press/Chicago Theological Seminary, 1984), 53.

[15] Paul Tillich, "Theology and Counseling," in *The Meaning of Health: Essays in Existentialism, Psychoanalysis, and Religion by Paul Tillich*, ed. Perry LeFevre (Chicago: Exploration Press/Chicago Theological Seminary, 1984), 117.

[16] Paul Tillich, "You Are Accepted," in *The Shaking of the Foundations* (New York: Charles Scribner's Sons, 1955), e.g., 155.

[17] Tillich, "The Theology of Pastoral Care: The Spiritual and Theological Foundations of Pastoral Care," in *The Meaning of Health: Essays in Existentialism, Psychoanalysis, and Religion by Paul Tillich*, ed. Perry LeFevre (Chicago: Exploration Press/Chicago Theological Seminary, 1984), 126.

[18] Tillich, "You Are Accepted," 153-63.

[19] Tillich, *The Courage to Be* (New Haven: Yale University Press, 1952).

years of ongoing intellectual ferment and exchange with such figures as Fromm, May, Loomis, Rogers, and others, Tillich held his colleagues' feet to the fire, keeping the philosophical (if not traditionally theological) foundations of existential therapy and psychological theory at the forefront of these psychologists' thinking about both theory and practice. In *Tillich and Psychology*, Cooper only gives 23 pages out of 281 pages overall to the topic of "Tillich's Ongoing Relevance."[20]

Nevertheless, Tillich's influence is directly discernible in three particular arenas: first, the theory and practice of a branch of psychology called "existential psychotherapy;" second, the theory and practice of *pastoral* counseling and psychotherapy; and third, methodology in pastoral and practical theology through Tillich's method of correlation.

Existential Psychotherapy

A search through *current* existential therapy web sites does not typically name Tillich as a source—more commonly found are Kierkegaard, Camus, Sartre, Nietzsche, and Viktor Frankl,[21] although the Wikipedia article does mention him as having influence through translations from his German works, along with Otto Rank, Swiss analyst Ludwig Binswanger, Karl Jaspers, Martin Buber, and Hans-Georg Gadamer, among others.[22] But one of the most influential existential psychotherapists in the 1970s and 80s, James Bugental, whose books *Psychotherapy and Process* and *The Art of Psychotherapy* were required reading in many humanistic and pastoral counseling programs, was directly influenced by Tillich's *The Courage to Be.* Bugental saw in Tillich's language of "ground of being," and the courage to "overcome" the inherent anxiety of being human, a congenial spiritual (though not explicitly religious) way of thinking about the goals of therapy—therapy as opening a door to greater human freedom and exercise of ethical responsibility.[23] Tillich is also cited by Irvin Yalom throughout his major textbook *Existential Psychotherapy*, particularly in reference to ontological anxiety and the failure to live one's own allotted life. Yalom quotes Tillich saying "neurosis is the way of avoiding non-

[20] Cooper, *Tillich and Psychology*, 195-218.

[21] E.g., "Existential Psychology – History of the Movement," Psychology Encyclopedia, accessed November 14, 2015, http://psychology.jrank.org/pages/229/Existential-Psychology.html.

[22] "Wikipedia: Existential Therapy," *Wikipedia, The Free Encyclopedia*, last modified March 9, 2021, https://en.wikipedia.org/wiki/Existential_therapy.

[23] James F.T. Bugental, *Psychotherapy and Process: The Fundamentals of an Existential-Humanistic Approach* (Reading: Addison-Wesley, 1978); and James F.T. Bugental, *The Art of the Psychotherapist* (New York: W.W. Norton, 1987).

being by avoiding being."[24] For Yalom, such insights did not replace the dynamic insights of Freud and Jung, but reoriented therapy toward the root anxiety of human beings "twisting between two fears—the fear of life (and its intrinsic isolation) and the fear of death"[25]—with the goal of therapy to help individuals inhabit their full potential.

Pastoral Counseling and Psychotherapy

In addition to his intellectual influence on existential psychology, Tillich was closely involved during his years in America with the emerging field of clinical pastoral education and pastoral counseling—on the one hand promoting the importance of pastoral theology among systematic theologians with whom he had great influence, and on the other hand, participating in conferences of pastoral theologians, therapists, and chaplains and serving on the board of the journal *Pastoral Psychology*. While a professor at Union Theological Seminary, he was a strong supporter of the founding of the curricular concentration in "Psychiatry and Religion," and his works have been taught to generations of pastoral theologians and practitioners for decades. Tillich stated that "care, including pastoral care, is something universally human" and "care is essentially mutual: he who gives care also receives care."[26]

Tillich's definition of pastoral care in his address to a very early meeting of the National Conference of Clinical Pastoral Education in 1958 is still relevant today: "*a helping encounter in the dimension of ultimate concern.*"[27] In fact, it may be even more relevant and more widely accepted today, as the whole field of pastoral care—with its longstanding embeddedness in Protestant Christian theology and helping paradigms—is now being challenged by the need for a much wider interreligious and intercultural approach. In the shift in nomenclature from "pastoral care" to "spiritual care" in medical and nursing departments, hospitals, prisons, and military chaplaincy, we see both Tillich's definition and method—grounded in his own Pauline and Lutheran tradition and in "the Christian message," but even more deeply grounded in the ineffable, the Unconditional, the Ground of Being from which all religious and spiritual traditions mysteriously arise.

These insights of Tillich resonate with much more recent developments in pastoral theology, care, and counseling, in which postcolonial notions of

[24] Irvin Yalom, *Existential Psychotherapy* (New York: Basic Books, 1980), 42, 74, 111, 147, 282.

[25] Yalom, 74, citing Otto Rank.

[26] Yalom, 21.

[27] Paul Tillich, "The Theology of Pastoral Care," *Pastoral Psychology* 10, no. 7 (1959), 22.

hybridity and more postmodern, constructivist, and narrative influences are being adopted in pastoral counseling training,[28] with particular attention in my own work to the relational psychoanalytic concepts of intersubjectivity and multiplicity of self—and God.[29] A dialectical, hermeneutical, and intercultural sensibility is in the air in pastoral theological theory and practice!

To test out what actual influence Tillich had on contemporary psychotherapy, I did a bit of "crowd sourcing" among three groups of the practice of contemporary therapists: the International Association of Relational Psychoanalysts and Psychotherapists or "IARPP" (a secular organization of contemporary analysts doing cutting-edge theory and practice), the Society for the Exploration of Psychoanalytic Therapies and Theology or "SEPTT" (an organization that grew out of CAPS, the Christian Association for Psychological Studies), and the American Association of Pastoral Counselors or "AAPC," in which liberal mainline clergy predominate. By email I posed the question: *(How, if at all) has Paul Tillich had an influence on your theory and practice of psychotherapy?* And I added, "Even if your answer is 'Not at all!' or 'Paul who?' I'd like to hear that from you!"

I received no responses at all from the analysts. A few members of SEPTT responded as follows.

Janet Stauffer, Professor of Marriage and Family and Dean of Students at Evangelical Seminary in Myerstown, Pennsylvania, wrote:

> A mentor once said "No is also a yes to life" attributing it to Paul Tillich. I have used that repeatedly in helping persons who are over obligated to others to find permission, indeed the demand that true giving requires both yes and no.

---

[28] E.g., Emmanuel Yarketkwei Lartey, *In Living Colour: An Intercultural Approach to Pastoral Care and Counseling*, 2nd ed. (London: Jessica Kingsley, 2003); Emmanuel Yarketkwei Lartey, *Pastoral Theology in an Intercultural World* (London: Jessica Kingsley, 2006); Melinda McGarrah-Sharp, *Misunderstanding Stories: Toward a Postcolonial Pastoral Theology* (Eugene: Pickwick, 2013); Carrie Doehring, *The Practice of Pastoral Care: A Postmodern Approach* (Louisville: Westminster John Knox Press, 2006); Christie Cozad Neuger, *Counseling Women: A Narrative, Pastoral Approach* (Minneapolis: Fortress Press, 2001); Pamela Cooper-White, *Shared Wisdom: Use of the Self in Pastoral Care and Counseling* (Minneapolis: Fortress Press, 2004); and Pamela Cooper-White, *Many Voices: Pastoral Psychotherapy in Relational and Theological Perspective* (Minneapolis: Fortress Press, 2007).

[29] E.g., Cooper-White, *Shared Wisdom; Many Voices;* and *Braided Selves: Collected Essays on Multiplicity, God, and Persons* (Eugene: Cascade Books, 2011).

Another Christian psychologist and Marriage and Family therapist, Gary Ventimiglia, stated at first that he was more influenced by Buber than by Tillich, but then revised his response, saying:

> Your question stimulated thoughts about Buber and Tillich and also the latter's relationship to Rollo May whose writings have influenced my life very much. In starting to think about all this I remembered my particular beefs with Tillich's most famous work, *The Courage to Be.* This is a really useful book on the development of atheistic existentialist thought and its impact on 20th century theology. My beefs with Tillich are more on the theological side concerning his "God above God," and "absolute faith" concepts. Yet the latter introduces Tillich's love of the importance of an existential response to the real in life. So I remember that he wrote a particularly helpful section in the, "Theology of Culture" entitled, "The Theological Significance of Existentialism and Psychoanalysis." So I looked at that again and saw my notes in it and lo and behold, I really like what he says, and actually do practice according to some of his assertions. I knew this when I first read this book 10+ years ago. I just forgot about it. So you could say that unconsciously, I have been influenced by his thought for many years now!"

In the other (only two) responses from SEPTT, one said "not at all" and the other said he was sure Tillich was there in his background, but he couldn't specifically identify a direct influence.

The happy surprise came from the Pastoral Counselors. I had twenty-four responses. Seven of those took the time to say "not much" or "not at all." One indicated that he had shifted in mid-career from Tillich to Barth as his primary theological resource. The remaining seventeen had very positive responses. Many cited having been profoundly shaped by Tillich's "Ground of Being," and the concepts of existential anxiety, "person-in-environment," and "ultimate concern." *The Courage to Be; Love, Power and Justice;* and "You Are Accepted" were the most often cited texts. One had paired Tillich's theology with Kohut's Self Psychology theory. Several acknowledged Tillich's influence, but considered it indirect, from their early training. Brian Hooper, a pastoral counselor in Nashville wrote,

> We had to read Tillich as part of my training to become an AAPC Fellow. My mentor had done his Ph.D. in Tillich and so even if not widely read in Tillich, I know I was influenced in a "second generation" way. Additionally, the idea of being and non-being together

> with conceiving of God as the "ground of being" has indeed influenced my ability to address my clients' spiritual concerns quite apart from religious agreement or disagreement. And long ago, I was touched by the idea that faith is accepting that we have been accepted; this has assisted me through my own crises of faith. Listening for the existential anxiety and assisting my clients to find hope in accepting self as accepted by God/Ground of Being has been immensely valuable, and I think it has especially assisted me to accept them even as they are undifferentiated from some crisis through which they are journeying.

Scott Sullender, a professor at San Francisco Theological Seminary, wrote more of Tillich's influence on his personal spiritual formation:

> In effect, Tillich and Tillich's thought saved me for the Christian faith. It made sense of the Christian faith, and of the human predicament, in ways that provided me with a map that guided me in my subsequent spiritual and psychological development. His *Courage to Be*, marked up and ragged, still sits on my shelf.

Pastoral counselor Sheryl Marshall stated, "I still find his work centering."

Some of the most elaborated responses came from several senior practitioners in the field.

John Patton, now retired from Columbia Seminary, and past president of AAPC, ACPE, *and* the Society for Pastoral Theology, wrote:

> My Chicago dissertation was entitled "A Theory of Interpersonal Ministry Based on the Systematic Theology of Paul Tillich and the Psychological Theory of Harry Stack Sullivan." Those two writers have clearly influenced my theory and practice of pastoral counseling, which is inclusive of pastoral psychotherapy. The generic way of expressing the thesis is that the practice of care and counseling requires both a conscious expression of what the therapists represents (in Tillich "transparency to the divine") and an explicit theory of the way to practice (sensitivity, the ability to provide security, and an honest and genuine expression of the therapist's self.) In my last little book on pastoral counseling I described this as "relational wisdom," the pastor's speciality in an interdisciplinary context.

Harville Hendrix, a pastoral counselor and founder of Imago Couples Therapy (made popular by Oprah), reflected:

> I wrote my doctoral dissertation on Tillich and Freud's view of anxiety. Tillich was my theological mentor in divinity school and saved

> me from exiting religion and theology all together with his ontology. While I have modified his views from the singularity of being to being as connecting, his Ground of Being as the Source and his theory of anxiety as the imagination of non-being, a terror behind all human suffering, has been a deep guide and source for all my work in psychology and couples therapy. He moved theology from Christian provincialism to inclusiveness, and his view of anxiety included the psychological ground of all suffering. He is beyond contemporary in his depth.

Two respondents also highlighted Tillich's relevance in interreligious and cultural terms: David Augsburger, who wrote *Pastoral Counseling across Cultures* in the 1980s, stated:

> 1) "Communication as participation" initiated exploration of theology of communication, and opened a rich vein for exploration of systems theory and theology. 2) His concept of "Correlation" facilitated dialogue between disciplines--theology, ethics, psychology, anthropology, sociology and offered a model that respected both while compromising neither. 3) A theology that was grounded in a dialectic between the essentialism of classic German philosophy and French existentialism brought Essence and existence into dialogue and synthesis in constructive new ways. 4) Obviously, his equating grace and acceptance became a centering point that allowed dialogue between the Rogerian unconditional positive regard tsunami and a theological understanding of grace as acceptance on multiple levels on a long spectrum that stretches from ultimate concerned depths to the undivided attention/accurate empathy offered in an isolated therapeutic hour; 5) "Love, power and justice" brought together two poles of union and separation in a just synthesis that applied Hegelian dynamics to the center of psychological theory, conflict studies theory, social theory. I could go on for another five topics, and I would especially note how African American Doctoral Students found a home in Tillich's thought which had been suggested by the many uses by Martin Luther King, Jr.

And one of the younger respondents, Siroj Sorajjakool, a professor of religion, psychology, and counseling at Loma Linda University, wrote as follows:

> When I got married my professor gave me a gift, it was Paul Tillich Systematic Theology Vol. 1 – 3. Took me three years to complete reading. When I did my qual, he was one of the theologians I

> picked. Being from a Buddhist country [Thailand], Tillich makes so much sense particularly his concept of non-being and the courage to be in the midst of non-being. I think in many different ways, it takes Buddhism to a different level. In Tillich, it is not just the ability to embrace non-being but the courage to live meaningfully in the midst of non-being. So for me Tillich helps me learn to embrace finiteness, vulnerability, brokenness, mental illness, and even death with courage to maintain goodness and compassion even when confronted with non-being.

It may be worth noting that most of my respondents were pastoral counselors in their 50s or older. Tillich's direct influence was certainly strong among my generation and older colleagues who read Tillich in our divinity and doctoral programs, and existentialism was the exciting intellectual paradigm. With feminism/Womanism, postcolonialism, and the increase of published writings from women and communities of color and the global south, there has been a concomitant increase in the influence of feminist and liberation theologies and indigenous, experiential-based paradigms for pastoral theology and care. Pioneering voices in this move to authorize experience as a source for theology included James Cone's *Black Theology of Liberation* (in which he cited Tillich extensively),[30] and Ada María Isasi-Díaz' *Mujerista Theology*,[31] among a growing number of others. In the postmodern era following the Holocaust, the atom bomb, and the Vietnam war, suspicion of authorities also led to the erosion of influence of heroic "great men" including the great European and American male thinkers of the nineteenth and mid-twentieth centuries. Tillich's influence is probably waning among younger scholars and practitioners in the pastoral field—and yet, Tillich's own path-breaking intuitions about the importance of human experience as a source for truth, and the correlation between theology and life in the world may have also paved the way, with or without direct attribution, for a more experience-grounded systematic and practical theological method in the past two decades or so.

---

[30] James Cone, *A Black Theology of Liberation*, Fortieth Anniversary Edition (Maryknoll: Orbis, 2010); originally published by (Philadelphia: J.B. Lippincott, 1970).

[31] Ada-María Isasi-Díaz, *Mujerista Theology: A Theology for the Twenty-first Century* (Maryknoll: Orbis, 1996).

Tillich's Influence on Pastoral and Practical Theological Methodology

This leads to the final arena of Tillich's influence, his influence on pastoral and practical theological methodology. Tillich, like all existentialist thinkers, emphasized the importance of context in theology at a time when "systematic" theology was very often so abstract as to be unintelligible to all but an elite few scholars in the ivory tower (or steeple). At roughly the same time, psychology—at first through field theory and family systems theories—was breaking down the one-on-one medical model of psychotherapy established during the heyday of a particular type of classical psychoanalysis in the US in the 1940s through the 70s. The notion that the most symptomatic member of a family, or the "identified patient" (the "IP") might be carrying the dysfunction and distress of the whole family contradicted notions of mental or emotional illness as something purely intrapsychic, a result of internal unconscious conflicts within isolated individuals. Pastoral counseling, with a few exceptions, pretty much left psychoanalysis cold after the 1960s—regrettably, from my point of view, but that's a matter for another day!—because a theological method of correlation between theology and the world, or between the human person and the divine, was much better "correlated" with either a Rogerian human potential approach, or with the then more contextual family systems approach.

In pastoral theology, and in practical theology more generally (as that umbrella term has come more recently to take on a life of its own as an academic discipline), Tillich's method of correlation has been probably the most significant framework for all our work. The method has been used most in recent times through the further critique and elaboration by David Tracy,[32] as a "mutual critical correlation" in which both theology and the world pose questions, and both give answers—and the methods of social science and hermeneutical analysis can be applied to both. Mark Kline Taylor's liberation-oriented work in *Remembering Esperanza*[33] has given further impetus in pastoral theology to viewing experience and theory or theology as a false dichotomy, and there is now a growing number of methodological texts in practical theology in which some form of generative spiral is used to theorize the interplay of both, as in Don Browning's "practice-theory-practice" model,[34] and

---

[32] Tracy, *Blessed Rage for Order*. See also David Tracy, *The Analogical Imagination: Christian Theology and the Culture of Pluralism* (New York: Crossroad, 1981).

[33] Mark Lewis Taylor, *Remembering Esperanza: A Cultural-Political Theology for North American Praxis* (Maryknoll: Orbis, 1990).

[34] Don S. Browning, *A Fundamental Practical Theology: Descriptive and Strategic Proposals* (Minneapolis: Fortress Press, 1991)

Emmanuel Lartey's "Learning Cycle for Liberative Pastoral Praxis."[35] Even as systematic theology as a discipline has moved increasingly to embrace human experience and the relevance of theology for practice,[36] as of the late twentieth century, concern with extremes of human suffering, evil, and the question of theodicy have perhaps eclipsed the theme of existential anxiety per se, although they are related. But theologians, both systematic and pastoral, continue to walk through the door Tillich threw open, correlating human experience with theological insight—in the words of Jürgen Moltmann, theology now must address "the open wound of life in this world."[37]

---

[35] Lartey, *In Living Colour*, 132. See also Dorothy C. Bass and Craig R. Dykstra, *For Life Abundant: Practical Theology, Theological Education, and Christian Ministry* (Grand Rapids: Eerdmans, 2008); Pamela and Michael Cooper-White, *Exploring Practices of Ministry* (Minneapolis: Fortress Press, 2015); Thomas Groome, *Sharing Faith: A Comprehensive Approach to Religious Education and Pastoral Ministry* (San Francisco: HarperSanFrancisco, 1990); and Richard Osmer, *Practical Theology: An Introduction* (Grand Rapids: Eerdmans, 2008).

[36]E.g., Edward Farley, *Good and Evil: Interpreting a Human Condition* (Minneapolis: Fortress, 1990); and Wendy Farley, *Tragic Vision and Divine Compassion* (Louisville: Westminster John Knox Press, 1990); Jürgen Moltmann, *The Trinity and the Kingdom: The Doctrine of God*, trans. Margaret Kohl (Minneapolis: Fortress Press, 1993); Dorothee Soelle, *Suffering* (Philadelphia: Fortress Press, 1975); see also Pamela Cooper-White, "Suffering," in *The Wiley-Blackwell Companion to Practical Theology*, ed. Bonnie J. Miller-McLemore (Malden/Oxford: Wiley-Blackwell, 2012), 23-31.

[37]Jürgen Moltmann, *The Trinity and the Kingdom*, 49.

The Need for Paul Tillich's Method in Theological Bioethics

Devan Stahl

A funny thing happened on the road to bioethics. As thinkers began to ask how new forms of medicine challenged our age-old conceptions of human nature, morality, and dignity, religious thinkers—those perhaps most prepared and most well-suited to answer such questions—were quickly pushed to the margins of the conversation. Those who tell the birth story of bioethics cannot help but mention the early input by theologians; however, within a generation, philosophers, sociologists, and lawyers began to question the suitability of theologians to speak to America's progressively pluralistic society.[1] This seems odd considering the fact that theologians have been grappling with how to do theology in a secular world for at least two centuries prior to the formation of bioethics as a discipline. More recently, many have begun to see the deficiencies of relying upon a purely secular-based philosophy to bring content-full resolutions to the continuing disputes in bioethics. Perhaps the time is once again right to call upon theologians whose rich traditions might add a thick moral vision to bioethics.

In response to the more recent calls for theological reflection in bioethics, theologians have taken a few different tactics. Roman Catholics have maintained medical institutions where their theology can be practiced. Others, particularly those from more conservative and neo-orthodox traditions have eschewed the secular bioethics altogether in favor of talking exclusively to the faithful. The common caricature of liberal theologians, on the other hand, is that they are quick to abandon their religious language and tradition in favor of a rationalistic ethic that can serve as an apology for any and every medical technology created. While more conservative theologians have been deemed too "irrational" to make their viewpoints relevant in the public arena, liberal theologians have made their particular views irrelevant by refusing to distinguish their rationality from that of secular philosophy. The question, then, for liberal theologians is: What can a theologian offer to bioethics that an ethically minded philosopher cannot?

---

[1] Albert R. Jonsen, *The Birth of Bioethics* (New York: Oxford University Press, 1998).

In a 2014 issue of *Christian Bioethics*, the journal's founder and Editor-in-Chief, H. Tristram Engelhardt, Jr. accuses Paul Tillich of being a post-theistic, anti-supernaturalist, Heideggerian philosopher masquerading as a theologian.[2] In his article, Engelhardt blames liberal theologians like Paul Tillich for the current anemic nature of theological bioethics.[3] He argues Christian bioethics has collapsed into a secular rationalistic ethic and, more often than not, fails to be authentically Christian. Such charges are often leveled against liberal theologians in the bioethics field. Tillich scholars, however, will likely find Engelhardt's critique to be an inaccurate appraisal of Tillich's project and his influence on theological ethics. In opposition to Engelhardt's assessment, Tillich's theological method may actually invigorate liberal theological bioethics and help liberal theologians create the very distinctively Christian voice in bioethics that Engelhardt seeks.

In opposition to those who believe liberal theology is inadequate to address pressing issues in bioethics, Paul Tillich presents an ideal method for engaging the medical sciences through his particular account of metaphysics. Tillich's metaphysical commitments allowed him to both affirm and critique aspects of the medical culture he encountered in the twentieth century. In what follows, I briefly describe how Tillich's metaphysics transitions into his "theology of culture," which he uses to discern how the Spirit moves in cultural practices. Next, I explain how Tillich's metaphysical claims inform his understanding of the relationship between God and the natural world. Finally, I explore how Tillich understood health and how he deployed his theology of culture to dialogue with the rising field of depth psychology. Ultimately, I hope to show how Tillich's method allows liberal theologians to make distinctive theological claims in dialogue with the medical sciences. To remain distinct in the field of bioethics, liberal theologians need to reconnect with the vision of the world that made them unique in the first place, and in so doing we will see the difference that liberal theologies can make within the field of bioethics.

The Need for Metaphysics and Tillich's Theology of Culture

Unlike early Protestant bioethicists such as Joseph Fletcher, who sought to avoid metaphysics and reduce the essence of being to a rationalistic ethic,[4] Tillich grounded his dogmatic ethics in a metaphysical ontology. As A. James

---

[2] H. Tristram Engelhardt, Jr., "The Recent History of Christian Bioethics Critically Reassessed," *Christian Bioethics* 20, no. 2 (2014): 146-67.

[3] Engelhardt, 147-48.

[4] See, for example, Joseph F. Fletcher, *Situation Ethics: The New Morality* (Louisville: Westminster John Knox Press, 1997).

Reimer describes it, "Tillich's dogmatics is grounded in a metaphysics of Being. ...His is...an ontological foundationalism premised on a very distinct understanding of the Unconditioned as the a priori of all that is conditioned."[5] For Tillich, the Unconditioned God sustains the essentiality of all being while shattering and transforming being. Metaphysics is "the question of the essence of being."[6] Tillich's insistence that God conditions and unites all essential reality allows him to deploy a correlative method that looks for the latent spiritual dimension present within secular cultural formations.

Tillich understood his metaphysical task as studying and tracing the movements of the Unconditional within culture. The theologian as meta-physician is tasked with tracing our "meaning-giving orientation" through both the theoretical and practical spheres. For this reason, Tillich could not completely separate his metaphysics from his ethics. Tillich states: "Every proposition of a creative metaphysics is an expression of an ethos; every ethos expresses a metaphysics."[7] Tillich's metaphysics is thus defined from "both the ontological and the social-ethical side."[8] Ethics and metaphysics share, for Tillich, a concern with the Unconditional, or human being's meaningful reach toward that which seems beyond all conditions.[9] From the perspective of the primal connectedness of all human and nonhuman nature, Tillich offered a social-ethical critique of culture that exists within an understanding of the uniting ground of all being. In other words, before we know how we should interact with the other, we must first know how everything is essentially connected. To distance himself from a classical metaphysics, which tended to refer to God as the totality of being, Tillich later referred to his metaphysical ethics as a "theology of culture."[10]

Tillich's theological task may be seen in two interrelated moves: analyzing and expressing the latent spiritual depth present in contemporary cultural formations and adapting the Christian message to dilemmas facing society. For Tillich, these two moves are actually one, because it is the one God who creates and redeems the world. Tillich believed we might actually heighten our awareness of the radical dissimilarity between the Christian message and

---

[5] A. James Reimer, *Paul Tillich: Theologian of Nature, Culture and Politics* (New Brunswick: Transaction, 2004), 181.

[6] Reimer, 186.

[7] Paul Tillich, *The System of the Sciences According to Objects and Methods*, trans. Paul Wiebe (Lewisburg: Bucknell University, 1981), 201.

[8] Reimer, *Paul Tillich*, 186.

[9] Mark Kline Taylor, "The Theological Development and Contribution of Paul Tillich" in *Paul Tillich: Theologian of the Boundaries*, ed. Mark Kline Taylor (Minneapolis: Fortress Press, 1991), 195.

[10] Tillich, *The System of the Sciences*, 210.

human situation by being open to finding God's Spirit moving in secular culture.[11] Likewise, a Christian bioethics that engages secular culture might help people see the difference between common arguments within bioethics, such as principlism or utilitarianism, and the Christian message. The church must understand how it has divided itself against culture in order to, once again, become relevant within culture. Insofar as theology and religion have been expelled from contemporary bioethics, liberal theologians must understand why their contributions have been ignored before they can begin to speak out against particular medical or bioethical projects.

God, the Natural World, and Science

Tillich speaks to the natural sciences from his metaphysical grounding as it is worked out in his theology of culture. The need to understand the proper place of God in the natural world is just as pressing in Tillich's time as it is in ours. We must understand how God interacts with and graces the material world if we are to understand the appropriate role of medicine in our lives. If God created the world to be left to its own devices (as in deism), then scientific progress might direct the path toward salvation. On the other hand, if God is utterly indistinguishable from the finite world (as in pantheism), the ends of medicine and the ends of God cannot be found to contradict in any meaningful way. If God both grounds the world and transcends the world, however, then medicine may become a potential mediated form of God's grace or a destructive force of idolatry. Tillich preached: "The greatest triumph of science was the power it gave to man to annihilate himself and his world."[12] Theology must give voice to both the constructive and destructive potentialities inherent in scientific progress, particularly in the power of medicine to annihilate humankind. We must first understand how God interacts with the world if we are to understand our proper orientation toward the medical sciences.

Tillich understood the historical conflicts between science and religion as evidence of ontological and epistemological confusion. Theology, according to Tillich, must equally reject naturalism and supranaturalism, because both mistake God for a being amongst beings. Against naturalism, Tillich writes: "The main arguments against naturalism, in whatever form, is that it denies the infinite distance between the whole of finite things and their

[11] Taylor, "The Theological Development," 22.

[12] Paul Tillich, "The Shaking of the Foundations," in *The Shaking of the Foundations*, ed. Paul Tillich (New York: Charles Scribner's Sons, 1955). Tillich here is speaking about nuclear weapons, but the medical sciences have engineered superviruses that could have devastating consequences on the human population.

ground with the consequence that the term 'God' becomes interchangeable with the universe and is therefore semantically superfluous."[13] Anyone who believes that natural science can disprove the existence of God is speaking from a perspective of naturalistic faith that confuses nature with the ground of being. Nature, unlike Christ, cannot conquer the threat of nonbeing. Moreover, naturalism does not allow sufficient room in its metaphysics for God's (supra)personal reality.

Supranaturalism on the other hand, "separates God as a being, the highest being, from all other beings, alongside and above which he has his existence."[14] In this scheme, God stands in a separate space above nature and acts as a cause alongside other causes. Such a God could only be an extension of the categories of finitude. Supranaturalism ends up naturalizing God. Tillich understood God as neither alongside things nor above them, but "he is nearer to them than they are to themselves. He is their creative ground, here and now, always and everywhere."[15] Unlike a pantheistic God, however, Tillich's God is 'self-transcendent,' meaning God transcends that of which he is the ground. Here God has freedom from, and for, the other. Tillich took our modern obsession over understanding how God acts in nature as rooted in our existential anxiety over non-being. It reveals our quest for a rational explanation of causation. In opposition to the gods of naturalism, supranaturalism, evolutionary materialism, and intelligent design, only Christ can conquer the threat of nonbeing.

Tillich cautioned theologians not to succumb to existential anxiety and allow scientific discovery to confirm or unsettle the truth of their faith. Unfortunately, this is all too common in supposed religion-science dialogues today. Contemporary scientists are almost never persuaded to change their theories based on Christian dogma, but some Christian theologians are all too eager to question their own doctrine based on scientific discovery.[16] Tillich warns us, however, that the truth of revelation cannot be confused for the truth of scientific discovery. Science understands reality in terms of objectified

[13] Paul Tillich, *Systematic Theology*, vol. 2 (Chicago: University of Chicago, 1957), 7.

[14] Tillich, 6.

[15] Tillich, 7.

[16] For example, in 1992, the General Board of Church and Society of the United Methodist Church went so far as to assert "developments in genetic science compel our reevaluation of accepted theological/ethical issues including determinism versus free will, the nature of sin, just distribution of resources, the status of human beings in relation to other forms of life, and the meaning of personhood." See United Methodist Church, *The Book of Resolutions* (Nashville: The United Methodist Publishing House, 1992), 332.

materiality. Revelation, on the other hand, rejects the idea of God as an object among others in the world. We must objectify the world scientifically in order to know it. We must be grasped by something we cannot contain in order to know God. Any attempt to know God through scientific modes of understanding, therefore, immediately becomes idolatrous.

Theological bioethicists ought to carry this logic into their understanding of the human person. It is increasingly common in the biological sciences to speak of the human person as if she were the sum of her biological processes. Through medico-scientific projects such as sequencing the human genome and mapping the human brain, it is becoming more routine in medical discourse to reduce persons to their bodily functioning.[17] Science must objectify the human person in order to know it (and yes, the human person will always be an *it* to the scientist), but theologians recognize that persons are never merely the sum of their parts because God is the ground of all being. For Tillich, the question of being is ultimately a theological question, and that can never be answered adequately by the natural or practical sciences. Any attempt to understand the totality of human life solely through the medical sciences, therefore, will also become idolatrous.

Health, Disease, and Depth Psychology

Medicine can still function as an element of God's grace despite the tendency of the medical sciences toward reductionism. Health, in its deepest sense, is fundamental to our salvation. The human situation is such that disease is a constant threat. As Tillich said, "The gift of freedom implies the danger of servitude; and the abundance of life implies the danger of sickness."[18] Health, for Tillich, is the unity of the many divergent trends in our life. When Jesus commanded his disciples to heal, he did not distinguish between bodily, mental, or spiritual diseases. Our health requires that all dimensions of our life—physical, chemical, biological, psychological, mental, cultural, and historical dimensions—be in unity.

Tillich believed that the healing of disease is the power of God at work in the world as exhibited in the life of Jesus. Jesus is the savior whose healing power indicates the coming of the new eon, because in him, there is no conflict between the religious and medical.[19] After describing the power Jesus gave his

---

[17] Some scientists have gone so far as to assert that religious faith is encoded in our genes. See Dean H. Hamer, *The God Gene: How Faith is Hardwired into our Genes*, 1st ed. (New York: Doubleday, 2004).

[18] Paul Tillich, "Heal the Sick; Cast out the Demons," in *The Eternal Now*, ed. Paul Tillich (New York: Charles Scribner's Sons, 1963), 24.

[19] Tillich, 352.

disciples to heal all manner of disease and sickness, Tillich declares, "the identity of healing, bodily and mental, and the presence of salvation can not be expressed more clearly."[20] Since Jesus handed this healing power over to the disciples, Tillich believed that announcing salvation is at hand and the ability to heal are one and the same act.[21] Our hope resides in Christ, who has demonstrated the healing of disease in all its dimensions even though we live in a diseased and disintegrated world.

Disease remains an unambiguous indicator of all humanity's separation from the divine in Tillich's theology. Medicine, which has the potential to cure biological and mental diseases, is capable of participating in the unity of the human with the divine. For this reason, we can say that medicine has the potential to mediate God's grace. When we are ill, medicine often offers us our first chance of healing. Tillich believed that "Jesus was called a physician, and it is the physician for whom we ask first when we are looking for health. And this is good. For, as all generations knew, there is healing power in nature. And much healing is possible if this power is wisely used and skillfully aided."[22] The physician using her skills helps us tremendously, even if she cannot cure all the disintegrated or diseased dimensions of our lives. Of course, medicine, by itself, cannot make people healthy. In his own time, Tillich observed:

> We have discovered drugs with an almost miraculous power. The average length of our lives has been stretched beyond any former expectation. But many in our nation cannot stand this health. They want sickness as a refuge into which they can escape from the harshness of an insecure life. And since the medical care has made it more difficult to escape into bodily illness, they choose *mental* illness.[23]

Health, for Tillich, can never be reduced to the proper functioning of one dimension of our lives, nor can it be seen as an individual endeavor.

> None of us is isolated. We belong to our past, to our families, classes, groups, nations, cultures. And in all of them health and illness are fighting with each other. How can we be whole if the culture is split

---

[20] Paul Tillich, "The Relation of Religion and Health: Historical Considerations and Theoretical Questions," in *The Meaning of Health*, ed. Peter LeFevre (Chicago: Exploration Press, 1984), 19.

[21] Tillich, 19.

[22] Paul Tillich, "On Healing (I and II)," in *The New Being*, ed. Paul Tillich (Lincoln: University of Nebraska, 1955), 39.

[23] Tillich, 36.

within itself, if every value is denied by another one, if every truth is questioned, if every decision is good and bad at the same time?[24]

Tillich believed that cultures often help create disease. Individual sickness must be understood as set within the context of a society that values certain aesthetics and activities of persons. Tillich states that "there may be something in the structure of our institutions which produces illness in more and more people."[25] We ought to expect to find our bodies, minds, spirits and even our institutional structures susceptible to disintegration and illness in a broken world. Tillich advocated that a plethora of healers must collaborate to mend persons in all dimensions of their lives, because there are so many ways that a person might become diseased. The physician, psychologist, priest, and social healer need to come together to drive away the demonic forces of illness. The question remains, however, if this vision of collaboration is truly being achieved in the current "bio-psycho-social-spiritual" practice of medicine. Is our contemporary medical world capable of facilitating true, equal cooperation amongst healers?[26]

What would cooperation and mutuality look like in the medical sciences? Tillich modeled his understanding of the proper relationship between the medical sciences and theology in his engagement with depth psychology. Tillich engaged psychology in response to the great need he saw to help heal the mental illnesses that plagued Americans in the mid-twentieth century. All the aspects of Tillich's theology described above come together in a positive project. Tillich shows why psychology cannot function without a metaphysical ontology that theologians are able to provide. He describes how psychological questions require and condition theological answers and even how psychology may prompt theologians to reevaluate their own latent ideologies.

In dialogue with psychology, Tillich employs his theology of culture to announce the necessary involvement of theology in the psychological pursuit. Tillich believed psychoanalysis confirmed many elements of the Christian tradition. Tillich elaborated on how the truth claims represented in the Bible could be compatible with the deepest insights of psychology, even though many psychologists, including Freud, insisted that they had discredited religion.

---

[24] Tillich, 40.

[25] Tillich, 35.

[26] For more on the biopsychosocialspiritual model of medicine see Jeffery Bishop, "Biopsychosocialspiritual Medicine and Other Political Schemes," *The Journal of Christian Bioethics* 12, no. 3 (2009): 254-76.

> If we enter the levels of personal existence which have been rediscovered by depth psychology, we encounter the past, the ancestors, the collective unconscious, the living substance in which all living beings participate. In our search for the "really real" we are driven from one level to another to a point where we cannot speak of level any more, where we must ask for that which is the ground of all levels, giving them their structure and their power of being.[27]

Tillich did not look to psychology to prove the truth of Scripture. Instead, he found within psychology an often unacknowledged drive toward the spiritual dimension through the ground of being. Tillich shows how psychological questions require and condition theological answers.

Tillich was able to advocate for an understanding of God's interaction with the world that conditioned psychological healing by incorporating his metaphysics into the discipline of psychology. Psychology must resist supranaturalism and pure naturalism in order to reach the essential person and relieve her anxiety. The assumption that healing is solely affected by an outside power would be a form of dehumanizing heteronomy. This could not promote health. On the other hand, psychology must avoid a pure naturalism, which denies the human's relation to the divine as "humanity's ultimate healing resource."[28] For Tillich, psychology functions appropriately when it is able to mediate the depth dimension of humanity with divine healing.

Tillich also attempted to answer questions he saw inherent or latent within depth psychology with the Gospel message. Tillich found that many of the questions posed by depth psychology demand a theological response. For example, Tillich believed his description of the human spirit being grasped by the divine Spirit "through a power working from within the human"[29] resonated with major themes from within depth psychology. Tillich refused to reduce this encounter with the divine to a purely psychological event, but he admits that within the revelatory event, the psychological and spiritual cannot be clearly distinguished by the human being. Tillich believed that neither medicine nor psychology should attempt to discount or subsume the religious into their schemes. Ultimately, Tillich saw the psychologist as a natural partner of the priest, each functioning independently but with shared goals. All relevant faculties must be involved, including the theologian whose

---

[27] Paul Tillich, *Biblical Religion and the Search for Ultimate Realty* (Chicago: University of Chicago, 1955), 13.

[28] John Dourley, "Tillich in Dialogue with Psychology," in *The Cambridge Companion to Paul Tillich*, ed. Russell Re Manning (New York: Cambridge University Press, 2009), 248.

[29] Dourley, 241.

work addresses the question of being and points toward the ultimate source of healing in order to truly conquer disease.

Conclusion

The liberal theologian who becomes a mere apologist for medicine or secular bioethics has failed to take seriously the correlative project Tillich presents. The question of being demands a theological answer. If she believes the Christian message is of ultimate concern, the theologian cannot simply accept the answers to the questions of life offered by the bioethicist, physician, geneticist, or neuroscientist. The theologian must also reject any formulation of the ontological question that contradicts the theological answer. Tillich would likely have much to say to contemporary medical practices, which tend to radically fragment and objectify the human person. Modern medicine can extend human life, but it can never explain finitude and it cannot conquer the threat of non-being.

Liberal theologians, who hold particular metaphysical claims, are uniquely equipped to critique medicine's metaphysics in the public arena. The theologian cannot simply affirm Western medicine's quest for human normalcy, nor can she approach bioethics believing she will be unable to make a practical difference in public discourse. The presumption that we are all able to begin a conversation about morality without sharing a common understanding of the purposes of humankind is not merely the result of bad theology, but is also a product of the domination of the physical sciences (medicine included) in the Western world. Philosopher E.A. Burtt notes that with the advent of the modern natural sciences humankind's "purposes, feelings, and secondary qualities was shoved apart as an unimportant spectator and semi-real effect [of the great mechanical drama]."[30] In other words, the sciences have helped create a world in which human beings see themselves as swept up in the great march of the world without the ability to make any real impact on its course. H. Tristram Engelhardt, Jr. is right to criticize Christian theologians for allowing themselves to be coopted in modernity's march toward the flattening out of moral debate.

Theologians have the opportunity to be deeply and profoundly prophetic by marching against the tide of the medical machinery. Not only can liberal theologians call the health care system to account for failing to provide medicine to our society's most vulnerable, they can also show how medicine has already altered our culture's perception of what the human is owed by virtue

[30] E.A. Burtt, *Metaphysical Foundations of Modern Physical Science* (Amherst: Humanity Books, 1999), 104.

of her existence. If we agree with Tillich that the "question of being" is a religious question, then we are free to challenge the very ground upon which medicine stands. Rather than providing answers to the problems already given, theologies that deploy a robust metaphysics will be able to broaden the debate and question all medical practices and categories. In a future yet be to be seen, we may find vast possibilities.

TILLICH & SOCIETY

Tillich's Influence on Pastoral Social Work

William G. Ressl

Pastoral social workers are equipped with both a graduate degree in divinity and in social work, often in the form of a dual Master of Divinity (MDiv) and Master of Social Work (MSW) degree. The period of preparation can be daunting. The journey takes several years through two master's degrees, ordination, and licensure as a clinical social worker. The dual degree requires development as an interdisciplinary professional integrating principles and practical methods from pastoral theology and social work. Yet there is no integrative framework for interdisciplinary professional development or practice. Dual degree programs lack "theoretical and practical integration, dual identity formation, site development, supervisory qualifications, spiritual formation, and evaluative criteria."[1] Students must attempt to put "the puzzle pieces together to form an integrated worldview."[2]

Tillich's life experience and theological system provides a professional and theological frame of reference for the pastoral social worker functioning between the worldviews of pastoral theology and social work. His legacy as a theologian doing social work serves as the starting point as it lifts up the importance of self-autobiography, and then guides the pastoral social worker to use important principles from Tillich's thought as a reflective frame for interdisciplinary professional identity and practice.

Tillich viewed his emigration from Germany to New York City in 1933 at age forty-seven as "a good destiny."[3] This good destiny led him to combine philosophical creativity with social relevance. A good destiny can emerge from a stress-filled reality and lead to dynamic new forms of functioning. Tillich's example offers pastoral social workers encouragement as they accept the freedom to transcend individual disciplines into a new functionality. The destiny of emigration meant that Tillich came to "New York, the largest of all large

---

[1] Daniel Lee, "Conclusion: Current State of Social Work and Divinity Dual Degree Programs," in *Social Work and Divinity,* eds. Daniel Lee and Robert O'Gorman (Binghamton: The Haworth Social Work Practice Press, 2005), 143.

[2] Beth Muehlhausen, "Dual Degree Programs in Social Work and Divinity: Graduates' Experiences of 'Journey Companions'" (PhD diss., Indiana University School of Social Work, 2010), 57.

[3] Paul Tillich, *My Search for Absolutes* (New York: Simon and Schuster, 1967), 30.

cities."[4] He now belonged to "two worlds: to the Old as well as to the New into which one has been fully received."[5] Unfamiliar with local customs and unable to speak English, Tillich and his family required the support of others to adapt in the new world. With Reinhold Niebuhr's support, Tillich joined the faculty of Union Theological Seminary in New York City. Within seven years "he had seen the entire country...Chicago and the Midwest, the Southeast, New England, and finally the west coast, traveling as far northwest as Lake Louise in Canada.... He traveled by bus, train, and car.... He came in contact with people in almost every walk of life; he asked questions, and he listened."[6] From his students at Union, "he learned about the American mind and its uniqueness: namely, that it joined action to thought, tested theory by means of assessing its practical consequences, and regarded the Christian church as a social agent."[7]

Tillich recognized the need for a social support system for immigrants arriving from Nazi Germany. He co-founded "Self-help for Emigres from Central Europe"[8] in New York City on November 25, 1936. It was "an organization of refugees for refugees, giving advice and help to thousands of newcomers each year, most of them Jews."[9] He became a theologian doing social work providing basic social work services including job referrals and connecting individuals within community. It also helped him sustain contact with the Old World. Tillich's office at Union was an open door to many travelers as they got off the boats from Europe. "Tillich's generosity was soon made apparent to his colleagues at Union, who witnessed a steady procession of visitors to his office."[10] As a theologian doing social work, refugees found in Tillich a pastor who listened, a counselor who helped them belong, and an administrator who could link them with needed resources and opportunities. Tillich notes that "this activity brought me into contact with many people from the Old World whom I never would have met otherwise, and it opened

---

[4] Tillich, 30.

[5] Tillich, 50.

[6] William Pauck and Marion Pauck, *Paul Tillich: His Life and Thought* (New York: Harper & Row, 1989), 180.

[7] Pauck and Pauck, 177.

[8] Tillich, *My Search for Absolutes*, 51. Today it is known as Selfhelp Community Services, Inc., and it "is one of the largest health & human service organizations in the NYC area, serving 20,000 vulnerable New Yorkers, of which 4,500 are Holocaust survivors." Selfhelp Community Services, Inc., "About," Facebook, July 29, 2019, https://www.facebook.com/pg/SelfhelpCommunityServices/about/?ref=page_internal.

[9] Tillich, *My Search for Absolutes*, 51.

[10] Pauck and Pauck, *Paul Tillich*, 157.

to view depths of human anxiety and misery and heights of human courage and devotion which are ordinarily hidden from us. At the same time, it revealed to me aspects of the average existence in this country from which I was far removed by my academic experience."[11]

The Autobiographical Sketch

Self-disclosure in the form of an autobiographical sketch can be valuable to understand the personal assumptions informing the actions of professionals who serve others. This requires more than a few reflection papers written as part of a graduate degree. Autobiographical self-disclosure makes visible the underlying beliefs, values and principles, objectivity, self-care techniques, as well as standards of competence, and perspectives on social justice, personal integrity, and the dignity and worth of the person that informs one's use of theory, theology, and practice models. A rich heritage of autobiographical sketch rises from both social work and divinity.[12] Delores Williams, Paul Tillich Professor Emerita of Theology and Culture at Union Theological Seminary in New York, notes "that theologians, in their attempt to talk to and about religious communities, ought to give readers some sense of their autobiographies"[13] to help their audience discern the type of theology that is being presented, theorized, theologized, and practiced.

Paul Tillich painted a picture of the factors that influenced his intellectual thought and practice through three autobiographical sketches: *On the Boundary*;[14] *My Search for Absolutes*;[15] and, posthumously, *My Travel Diary*.[16] Each unfolds the reality of being a theologian on the boundaries of life prac-

---

[11] Tillich, *My Search for Absolutes*, 51.

[12] Autobiographical sketches from social work and divinity include: Jane Addams, a mother of social work, see Jane Addams, *Twenty Years at Hull-House with Autobiographical Notes* (New York: The MacMillan Company, 1911); Anton Boisen, founder of Clinical Pastoral Education (CPE) and foundational voice in the study of pastoral theology, see Anton Boisen, *Out of the Depths* (New York: Harper & Brothers, 1960); and, William G. Ressl, theologian doing social work and foundational voice in pastoral social work, see William G. Ressl, "On Giant Shoulders: Teaching through Paul Tillich's Legacy of Being a Theologian Doing Social Work," *The North American Paul Tillich Society Bulletin* 42, no. 2, (Spring 2016): 17.

[13] Delores Williams, *Sisters in the Wilderness* (Maryknoll: Orbis Books, 1998), ix.

[14] Paul Tillich, *On the Boundary* (New York: Charles Scribner's Sons, 1966).

[15] Tillich, *My Search for Absolutes*.

[16] Paul Tillich, *My Travel Diary: 1936, Between Two Worlds*, ed. Jerald C. Brauer and trans. Maria Pelikan (New York: Harper & Row, 1970).

ticing as pastor, teacher, and theologian doing social work. The reality of Tillich's lived experience offers pastoral social workers insight into the courage that is required within the boundary situations of life, specifically when one is caught between two worldviews. The various contextual situations informing Tillich's development can help pastoral social workers understand their individual journeys of self-growth as an interdisciplinary professional. The dynamic process of professional development includes the interplay between biological, psychological, social, and spiritual factors that shape self-image as well as professional identity.

In *On the Boundary*, Tillich reflected on early life boundary situations that provided symbolism for his theological foundations. He noted, "I was about eight when I first wrestled with the idea of the Infinite."[17] On his annual visits to the Baltic Sea he experienced the power of creation and the presence of the infinite unfolding. In the contemplation of the turbulent sea a boundary situation became visible forming the foundation for his theological development. It set in motion symbolism that provided substance for understanding the human boundary situation, the theory of dynamic mass, the doctrines of the Absolute, and the substance of religion.[18] Similarly, pastoral social workers are encouraged to reflect on the early life experiences that provide symbolism for the meaning making structures which inform their professional development and practice.

Tillich defined a "period of preparation" grounded in specific contextual situations that provided the foundation for his self-image and professional identity as pastor, academician, and theologian doing social work.[20] Tillich's early life was informed by the realities of his father's ministry and privileged social position. Completing university in 1911, he was ordained in 1912 into the Evangelical Lutheran Church of the province of Bradenburg, following in his father's footsteps. His practical ministerial experiences included "two years of parish work and four years as a field chaplain on the Western front"[21] as well as "a brief period in church administrative work"[22] after the war. One can imagine parish work involved the traditional duties of an ordained minister offering pastoral care and leadership as well as leading sacramental worship. As a field chaplain during World War One, he witnessed the horror of war that contributed to emotional crises. The brief period of administrative church

[17] Tillich, *On the Boundary*, 30.

[18] Tillich, 18.

[20] Tillich, *My Search for Absolutes*, 38.

[21] Tillich, *On the Boundary*, 32.

[22] Tillich, 32.

work after the war provided a time to develop a philosophical and theological framework for practical ministry.

Tillich claimed, "The First World War was the end of my period of preparation."[23] He noted that "it required a world war and a political catastrophe before I was able to break through this system of authorities and to affirm belief in democratic ideals and the social revolution."[24] Tillich left pastoral ministry to explore the philosophical realities of life. From 1919 to 1924 he lectured on a number of subjects such as art, depth psychology, philosophy, politics, and sociology. His theological development articulated cultural issues that had been excluded from previous theological discourse.

Tillich's exploration of boundary situations contributed to the method of correlation. This method links Christian answers to questions that are asked about human existence, destiny, and the meaning of salvation. The method of correlation "seeks to satisfy two basic needs: the explication of the truth contained in the Christian message and the interpretation of this truth for every new generation."[25] Living the method requires an examination of the spiritual foundations of life and naming that which grounds one's faith. For Tillich, living the method informed by faith meant first and foremost being a theologian. He wrote: "Nevertheless I was a theologian, because the existential question of our ultimate concern and the existential answer of the Christian message are and always have been predominant in my spiritual life."[26] Like Tillich, pastoral social workers need to name what grounds their existence. Does their faith focus toward the ultimate concern or is it set on some other secondary concern? What are they first and foremost—theologian or social worker?

Tillich's experience set in motion an understanding of the power of being. Dynamic mass opposes social powers with prophetic movements of liberation as concrete expressions of the New Being. "Dynamic mass is pointing to a new theonomous situation, where culture recovers its religious, living, and creative substance, without losing the autonomy of its rational forms."[27] The expectation of a transformed reality from the structures of destruction and non-being invites conversation about individual transformation and social reform.

---

[23] Tillich, *My Search for Absolutes*, 38.

[24] Tillich, 31.

[25] John Newport, *Paul Tillich: Makers of the Modern Theological Mind*, ed. Bob E. Patterson (Peabody: Hendrickson Publishers, 1984), 86.

[26] Tillich, *My Search for Absolutes*, 36.

[27] Jean Richard, "The Hidden Community of the Kairos and the Spiritual Community: Toward a New Understanding of the Correlation in the Work of Paul Tillich," in *Paul Tillich's Theological Legacy: Spirit and Community*, ed. Frederick J. Parrella (New York: Walter de Gruyter, 1995), 54.

Tillich's examination of church and society led to the recognition that the gospel needed to be communicated with non-ecclesiastical language. New terminology for scripture and liturgy was needed for the contemporary situation. This resulted in new symbols replacing traditional terminology: ultimate concern for God, New Being for Jesus the Christ, and Spiritual Presence for Holy Spirit. His experiences at the boundary of religion and culture led to a history of culture from a religious viewpoint, recognizing that artistic expression is an experience of cultural forms with religious substance. It also contributed to a philosophy of freedom recognizing the prophetic elements in Freud and Marx.

Pastoral social workers can voice the prophetic elements for a new theonomy that bursts forth through current events and movements. For instance, the authentic "homeland"[28] of humankind is the Kingdom of God in which there are no aliens, and "the boundary between native and alien land ceases to exist."[29] This encourages pastoral social workers to honor the uniqueness of each individual's social position and cultural location while recognizing the connectedness of humanity's common "homeland" made visible in the transcendent reality of the Kingdom of God in the here and now of the present. Awareness of the infinite that transcends all human possibility reveals that even our highest levels of accomplishment are only fragmentary. Nevertheless, we need not fall into despair. Pastoral social workers can accept the fragmentary expressions of the ultimate in the awareness that these still link us intimately with past, present, and future realities.

Tillich's lived legacy as a self-reflective interdisciplinary professional is a model for a pastoral social work method informed by faith. The academic foundation for the pastoral social worker is rooted in the Master of Divinity (MDiv) and Master of Social Work (MSW) degrees. However, the duality creates its own ambiguities. There are biases within both disciplines. Pastoral social workers regularly cope with boundary situations requiring the integration of two worldviews in their professional identity. At times, they may feel like outsiders to the mainstream views that inform both disciplines. They are social workers thinking as theologians, and theologians acting as social workers.

---

[28] Tillich, *On the Boundary*, 92-96.

[29] Tillich, 96.

Integrative Principles

Tillich's fifteen years of service as the first chairman of Selfhelp provided a unique contextual opportunity. He recognized the importance of building and maintaining relationships. He was aware of the roles and responsibilities between himself, the client, the larger client systems, and the transparency of dynamic interactions. He understood the role of empathy, power, and issues of diversity related to assessing needs, communication, possible interventions, and the realities of violence within the immigrant experience. Tillich defined his philosophy of social work in 1961 on the twenty-fifth anniversary of Selfhelp's founding. He affirmed the need for social work to address and reform every social structure and social mechanism that disempowers and disenfranchises. Humanity never functions in an ideal state for prolonged periods. Legalisms are estranged potentialities that forever create deficiencies, suffering, and oppression for some. The pastoral social worker must address these oppressive deficiencies in every social mechanism, in every organization, and in every community. Tillich names two important ideas for doing social work, "listening love"[30] and the aims of social work defined through "several degrees."[31]

In *The Philosophy of Social Work,* Tillich named "listening love"[32] as a "fundamental principle"[33] for social work. It is "one of the decisive characteristics of love that it listens sensitively and reacts spontaneously."[34] Love that listens is more than gathering assessment information or diagnosing individuals through empirical knowledge with predefined psychological constructs. Listening in love strives to know the other, not just as an object, but as a person. It "is the first step to justice in person-to-person encounters."[35]

Listening sensitively begins by addressing the concrete situation in which individuals find themselves with "the help of psychological and sociological insights into the internal as well as external conditions of an individual's predicament."[36] It strives to penetrate sensitively into the dark spaces of existence to make one aware of inhibitions and motives that do not point towards the

---

[30] Paul Tillich, "The Philosophy of Social Work," in *The Meaning of Health: Essays in Existentialism, Psychoanalysis, and Religion*, ed. Perry LeFevre (Chicago: Exploration Press, 1984), 180.

[31] Tillich, 182.

[32] Tillich, 180.

[33] Tillich, 180.

[34] Tillich, 180.

[35] Paul Tillich, *Love, Power, and Justice: Ontological Analyses and Ethical Applications* (London: Oxford University Press, 1954), 85.

[36] Tillich, *My Search for Absolutes*, 109.

ultimate. For instance, individuals may "seem to be aggressive, but what they express may be love, inhibited by shyness. They may seem to be sweet and submissive and they are actually symptoms of hostility. Words, well meant, but uttered improperly, may produce in reaction complete injustice."[37]

Love accepts the other for who they are, where they are, and what they are. It provides a pathway for transformation that fulfills basic needs and reforms relationships. Love allows genuine moral decisions to be made within concrete relationships. It actualizes hidden possibilities of the spiritual life creatively shaping future ethical consciousness through "the creative excitement of moral life."[38] This form of relationship requires a "critical love, which at the same time accepts and transforms."[39] It appears "as the prophetic spirit which lists where it will, without ecclesiastical conditions, organization, and traditions."[40] It unites the ecstatic and rational elements offering an understanding of how participatory relationships can function transcending the limits of social work techniques while contributing "to the ultimate aim of being itself."[41]

Ultimate concern addresses individual as well as social realities. The human condition includes both a search for ultimate concern and a focus on more concrete concerns. Ultimate concern defies definition and is only described by symbols like God, Logos, New Being, and Spirit. Tillich noted that "in his name the great commandment is given: 'You shall love the Lord your God with all your heart, and with all your soul, and with all your might' (Deut. 6:5). This is what ultimate concern means and from these words the term 'ultimate concern' is derived. They state unambiguously the character of genuine faith, the demand of total surrender to the subject of ultimate concern."[42] The experiences of life can focus symbols of ultimate concern, New Being, and eternal life toward new realities.

At the time same, more concrete concerns rise from and often confine individuals within existential estrangement. They are known through all the daily experiences of life. Humanity struggles with secondary concerns that are less than ultimate. This results in an empty, self-centered search for healing in the wrong places resulting in acute or chronic anxiety. Making secondary concerns ultimate can result in abuse, oppression, addictions, environmental

---

[37] Tillich, *Love, Power, and Justice*, 85.

[38] Tillich, *My Search for Absolutes*, 111.

[39] Tillich, "The Philosophy of Social Work," 181.

[40] Paul Tillich, *The Protestant Era* (Chicago: The University of Chicago Press, 1948), 232.

[41] Tillich, "The Philosophy of Social Work," 183.

[42] Paul Tillich, *Dynamics of Faith* (New York: Harper Colophon Books, 1958), 2.

waste, and a general combative nature. In short, it draws the individual toward non-being.

Non-being can occur as secondary concerns claim ultimacy. Non-being is manifest through existential anxieties of finitude, despair, doubt, condemnation, guilt, and meaninglessness. Yet ever present in these anxieties is New Being, because within the power of being both non-being and New Being are ever present. "Being a creature includes both the heritage of nonbeing (anxiety) and the heritage of being (courage)."[43] All forms of non-being can be transformed through courage that rises from the promise of New Being. Such courage recognizes "the ecstatic manifestation of the Ground of Being in events, persons, and things. Such manifestations have shaking, transforming, and healing power"[44] within all creation as they break through all the struggles and tensions of estranged existence. New Being is a manifestation of grace that makes visible reformative possibilities. Grounded in ultimate concern, it allows full participation in the multi-dimensional communion of life known as the Spiritual Community. "He who participates in the Spiritual Community is united with God in faith and love. He is a creation of the divine Spirit" and a manifestation of the New Being.[46]

Awareness of human functioning is vital for learning about the manifestation of the Spiritual Presence within life. "Without knowing what spirit is, one cannot know what Spirit is."[47] Tillich noted that the aim of social work has "several degrees."[48] Each provides insights to understand human functioning within a therapeutic relationship.

First, social work must address the immediate need in a timely fashion.[49] This ensures that the person needing help feels accepted and affirms their willingness to face the consequences of that help. The pastoral social worker must be willing to participate in a shared journey that manifests itself in a communion of healing with the Spiritual Presence.

---

[43] Paul Tillich, *Systematic Theology*, vol. 1 (Chicago: The University of Chicago Press, 1951), 253.

[44] Paul Tillich, *Systematic Theology:* vol. 2 (Chicago: The University of Chicago Press, 1957), 166.

[46] Paul Tillich, *Systematic Theology*, vol. 3 (Chicago: The University of Chicago Press, 1963), 217.

[47] Tillich, 22.

[48] Tillich, "The Philosophy of Social Work," 182.

[49] Tillich, 182.

The principle of "increasing awareness"[50] within the process of New Being illuminates the challenge for both the client and the professional. Awareness of the "circular movement"[51] for centeredness makes visible the processes of self-integration and disintegration, the struggle with finitude, non-being and being, separation and unity, as well as the factors defined through the individual ontological polarities of individualization and participation. Ontological anxiety is ever present and fuels loneliness and withdrawal. The pastoral social worker helps the individual find the courage to transcend loneliness into personhood, and estrangement into multi-dimensional communion. Of course, this is never permanent. Anxiety manifesting as loneliness and estrangement returns. The threat of non-being can never be finally alleviated, but courage from the Ground of Being helps turn separation into participation with ultimate concern.[52]

Second, social work must guide the individual toward independence within the limitations of specific situations.[53] The pastoral social worker must be prepared to help a client become free of those things that bind and oppress in concrete situations of life.

Tillich might describe social limitations as forms of demonic repression of an individual by society. Demonic repression suppresses creativity that might otherwise empower independence. The process of transformation is one of "increasing freedom"[54] that emphasizes the potentiality of individual and societal spiritual growth. Hope lies in a recreation of humanity, albeit transient and fragmentary, through personal relations that minimize objectification and pursue multi-dimensional communion. Old laws make way for new realities. Within freedom there is courage to resist pressure by the norms of society and take risks. New dimensions of reality open, encouraging reformation and transformation.[55]

These two principles address what might be called the "horizontal direction"[56] of human functioning. The horizontal quest for spiritual growth and self-alteration makes freedom visible within the ontological polarities of dynamics and form. Self-creativity is actualized as the individual struggles with doubt and meaninglessness. It is driven into meaninglessness as doubts rise

---

[50] Tillich, *Systematic Theology*, vol. 3, 231.

[51] Tillich, 30.

[52] For more on "estrangement, suffering, and loneliness," see Tillich, *Systematic Theology*, vol. 2, 70.

[53] Tillich, "The Philosophy of Social Work," 182.

[54] Tillich, *Systematic Theology*, vol. 3, 231.

[55] For more on "increasing freedom," see Tillich, 232.

[56] Tillich, 31.

about the reason for one's existence and one's relationship with the Divine.[57] Estranged existence known as despair manifests itself as a chaotic formlessness—empty, lacking vitality, and filled with formless urges. Transformation is possible through an essential vitality that fuels growth and transforms chaotic formlessness into a new form that reshapes life in participation with the ultimate.[58]

Third, social work must ensure that the one being helped knows their significance as a human being.[59] The pastoral social worker must take time and show genuine interest in the person and not simply objectify them as another client or case. Take time to help the individual discover their significance as unique and incomparable beings.

The principle of "increasing relatedness"[60] connects new self-awareness with improved social relationships. It includes a vertical quest, "driving toward the sublime,"[61] that links power and justice with the polarities of freedom and destiny. Love informs and reshapes the dynamics of power and justice in all relationships. However, this self-transcendence is constantly threatened by anxieties over guilt and condemnation. Tillich might describe this as a form of profanization. This occurs when social norms are given absolute validity and become heteronomously oppressive over an entire group. Society elevates doctrines, rules, and laws to absolute validity that can never be realized by the individual. These are non-actualized potentials over which individuals feel chronic guilt and fear inevitable condemnation. Yet heteronomy can become receptive to Spirit through acts of courage. Courage transforms guilt and condemnation into an essential belongingness. It replaces anxiety as individual, and relational identities transform to become open to communion with others and in ultimate relationship with the Divine.[62] This in turn can lead to the development of Spirit-filled affirming groups behaving in new ways as a Spiritual Community resulting in larger cultural impact. Tillich noted that "theonomous culture is Spirit-determined and Spirit-directed culture, and Spirit fulfils spirit instead of breaking it."[63] This healing comes not from human ac-

[57] For more on "estrangement, doubt, and meaninglessness," see Tillich, *Systematic Theology*, vol. 2, 72.

[58] For more on the impact of finitude on "dynamics and form," see Tillich, *Systematic Theology*, vol. 1, 199.

[59] Tillich, "The Philosophy of Social Work," 182.

[60] Tillich, *Systematic Theology*, vol. 3, 231.

[61] Tillich, 31.

[62] For more on "guilt and condemnation," see Paul Tillich, *The Courage to Be*, 2nd ed. (New Haven: Yale University Press, 2000), 51.

[63] Tillich, *Systematic Theology*, vol. 3, 250.

tions but from the power that transcends all, a dimension of the Divine. However, it "is always fragmentary because of the existential estrangement underlying human history, and its defeat is always limited by the fact that human nature is essentially theonomous."[64]

The final aim of social work is to help every individual feel significant and empowering them to fulfill their ultimate goals.[65] Pastoral social workers can model and communicate grace that opens pathways toward essential realities. Clients can be freed to recognize how their humanity can be reunited with the ultimate, rather than compulsively focused on secondary concerns.

"Increasing transcendence"[66] manifesting itself under the impact of the Spiritual Presence unites self-awareness, freedom, and destiny. Glimpses of theonomy break through heteronomous structures. Essence breaks through estrangement; the Divine fuels vitality in all relationships. In every moment, the conditions of life balance the conditions of death. New Being is present minimizing an ultimate focus on secondary concerns. Tiredness, sickness, intoxication, neurotic compulsions, and psychotic splits are answered by the quest for centeredness on the ultimate concern. Hope is grounded in the potential of an ultimate relationship with God, and the responsibility of individual decision-making that is ever present in the human spirit. The result is not necessarily a *religious* community but the anticipation of a new theonomous reality in which the autonomous human being and heteronomous society transcend this tension "horizontally" in universal inclusiveness and "vertically" in Spiritual Presence. "Theonomy saves humanity in every human encounter."[67]

In essence, social work helps the individual connect with "the universal community of all beings in which any individual aim is taken into the universal aim of being itself."[68] This does not imply evangelizing or proselytizing. Rather, listening sensitively in love responds to human needs, de-objectifying relationships, and creating spirit-filled moments. The larger vision of social work is that the essential possibilities for all humanity and transient reality be

---

[64] Tillich, 250.
[65] Tillich, "The Philosophy of Social Work," 182.
[66] Tillich, *Systematic Theology*, vol. 3, 231.
[67] Tillich, 262.
[68] Tillich, "The Philosophy of Social Work," 182.

realized. Social work, as an action grounded in Spirit, is a transformative process within a therapeutic relationship. It is "New Being as process"[69] illustrating a theologically grounded path toward transformation and the "process of life"[70] made visible through the horizontal movement for growth as well as the vertical drive for the sublime. Together, these processes form a reflective frame addressing autonomy, heteronomy, and theonomy in life and practice. It all begins in the simple act of being reflective of one's own reality and then being present in relationship with others, so that ultimate healing may occur for self and others. Each pastoral social worker contributes "to the ultimate aim of being itself in our small way—and every individual's way is small. To give such inspiration may be a function of an hour of memory such as the present one."[71]

The interdisciplinary practice of pastoral social work is an act of dedication to the potentiality of theonomy here and now. As professionals, our function is to listen in love to our clients in more than mechanical ways. Clients can be freed to recognize how their humanity can be reunited with the ultimate, rather than compulsively focused only on secondary concerns. Tillich's life and thought can serve as the foundation for an integrative framework for interdisciplinary professional development and practice.

---

[69] "New Being as process" (Tillich, *Systematic Theology*, vol. 3, 231) brings to light the complexities, struggles, and tensions associated with secondary concerns and striving toward a New Being focused on the ultimate concern. Four principles define the impact of New Being on human existence, namely: "first, increasing awareness; second, increasing freedom; third, increasing relatedness; fourth, increasing transcendence. How these principles will unite in a new type of life under the Spiritual Presence cannot be described before it happens, but elements of such a life can be seen in individuals and groups who anticipated what may possibly lie in the future." These principles unite religious and secular traditions as well as inform an image of life as a Christian.

[70] The "process of life" (Tillich, *Systematic Theology*, vol. 3, 30) occurs when "potentiality becomes actuality" through the three elements of "self-integration, self-alteration, and return to one's self." This process is visible through the circular movement for centeredness, the horizontal movement for growth, and the vertical drive toward the sublime (Tillich, 30-32). Each movement is linked to corresponding individual and social community-based meaning making ontological polarities that offer clarity on the challenges of essential New Being and estranged non-being as well as the constant struggle between an essentially grounded search for meaning in one's ultimate concern and an existentially focused experience on secondary concerns. For instance, individualization and participation (individual polarities) correspond with verity and adaptation (social community-based polarities). Dynamics and form correspond with transcendence and form affirmation. Freedom and destiny correspond with tradition and reformation. Each set of polarities help to define how meaning is actualized, spanning the existential realities of being estranged, in non-being, to essence filled New Being (Tillich, *Systematic Theology*, vol. 3, 182-220).

[71] Tillich, "The Philosophy of Social Work," 183.

Feminist Theologies in Conversation with Paul Tillich

Rachel Sophia Baard[1]

This essay aims to place the theology of Paul Tillich in conversation with feminist theology. Feminist theology, defined by Maria José Rosado-Nunes as the "radical critique of patriarchal reasoning in the field of theology," is a form of theology focused on the wellbeing of women.[2] To that end, feminist theology sets itself several tasks: to challenge religious teachings that denigrate or otherwise harm women; to retrieve forgotten female voices in the history of the church; and to address concrete social issues that are of particular significance to women, such as gender violence. The field of feminist theology is characterized by ideological, theological, ethnic, cultural, religious, and contextual diversity, so much so that it might be better to speak of "feminist theologies." Any conversation between feminist theologies and the theology of Paul Tillich will be marked by several difficulties, one of which is the fact that Tillich, for the most part, did not address feminist concerns. Furthermore, there is some suspicion about Tillich when it comes to his relationship with women. Nevertheless, there is also room for conversation between Tillich and feminist theologies, not only on doctrinal and thematic issues, but most significantly on theological method. In what follows, I will briefly introduce both conversation partners, examine thematic overlaps between them, and then, in conclusion, focus on theological method as the main point of contact between Tillich and feminist theologies.

The Conversation Partners

Feminist theology starts with women's experience, a methodological approach that has invited further conversation about whose experiences and what kinds of experiences are taken into account in the formulation of feminist theology.

---

[1] Part of the content, in particular the doctrinal discussion, is re-used (with some modification) from the essay, "Tillich and Feminism" by Rachel Sophia Baard in the *Cambridge Companion to Paul Tillich*, ed. Russell Re Manning (New York: Cambridge University Press 2009), with the permission of Cambridge University Press.

[2] Maria José Rosado-Nunes, "New Paradigms in Feminist Theological Thought: The Longing for a Just World," in *Feminist Intercultural Theology: Latina Explorations for a Just World*, eds. María Pilar Aquino and Maria José Rosado-Nunes (Maryknoll: Orbis, 2007), 1.

This conversation has given rise to a call to include more voices in the feminist conversation, and to avoid assumptions about the typical experiences of various groups of women. After all, nationality, race, class, sexual identity, etc., all intersect with gender to shape our experiences. As a result, feminist theologies might be best understood in terms of multiple different conversations about women's flourishing, and inclusive of the perspectives of womanist and *mujerista* theologians—i.e., women theologians who work on the intersection of race and gender in African American and US Latinx communities, respectively. Furthermore, feminist theologies are global, including not only the work of Western feminists, but also the work of African, Latin American, and Asian women theologians, who may or may not choose to use the term "feminist" but whose scholarship is focused on women's flourishing. Feminist theologies are also often ecumenical and interreligious, transcending the boundaries of denominational and even religious traditions.

In analyzing women's experiences, feminist theologians, for the most part, lean towards concrete human experiences and concrete social issues, such as gender violence. The focus on women's experiences reflects feminist suspicion of starting theological inquiry with classical religious traditions, since the latter have been largely male dominated. Instead, feminist theologies interrogate classical traditions from the vantage point of women's experiences. However, feminist theologians take several different stances on religious traditions, sometimes rejecting it outright ("radical" feminism), sometimes merely suggesting more inclusion of women ("conservative" feminism), and sometimes operating with a combination of serious critique and deep retrieval of "classical" traditions ("reconstructionist" feminism). Overall, one can say that feminist theologies are vibrant, ongoing, diverse, and ever-evolving expressions of theology that are often critical of traditional religion even as they strive to retrieve elements from it that are beneficial to women.

What do these theologies have in common with Paul Tillich, a male theologian whose work is known for its abstractions rather than its concrete focus, and a man who, moreover, had a reputation for being a womanizer who at times objectified women? Paul Tillich (1886-1965) was undoubtedly one of the giants of twentieth century Protestant theology. In the United States he is primarily known for the philosophical bent of his theology and for the theological method of correlation, which offered a theological engagement of existentialist questions, and thereby provided an alternative to the neo-orthodox theology of Karl Barth, that other giant of twentieth century Protestantism. But Tillich was also a theologian whose consciousness had been shaped by his traumatic experiences as army chaplain during the First World War, his conversations with socialist thinkers in the Kairos Circle in Berlin in the 1920s, and his loathing of the Nazis. His writings against Nazism, his actions against Nazi students as dean at the University of Frankfurt, and his support of Jews, soon earned him the ire of the Nazi regime and dismissal from his post at the University of Frankfurt. Escaping arrest, Tillich arrived in the United States in November 1933, having been invited to join the faculty of Union Theological Seminary in New York City, where he would teach until 1955 (after that, he taught at Harvard until 1962, and subsequently at the University of Chicago until his death in 1965). Here, Tillich had to learn English and reshape his theology for a new context, shifting to primarily existential matters in his theology, expressed in texts such as *The Courage to Be*, and to the completion of his three-volume *Systematic Theology*.[3]

Tillich's admirable rejection of Nazism (and his early diagnosis of the problem) surely earns him some respect from the perspective of intersectional feminism. Apart from his friendship with Jews, the religion of Judaism and the Jewish roots of Christianity were central to Tillich's understanding of Christianity (in contrast to the Nazi effort to "de-Judaize" Christianity), especially because of the Jewish prophetic tradition, a tradition known for its criticism of social injustices. From this he derived one of his theological guiding principles, the Protestant Principle, "that element of perpetual critique that stands against the ever-present threats of idolatry and utopianism," which has been of particular significance to at least one prominent feminist interpreter of Tillich, Mary Ann Stenger.[4] In fact, I would argue that the centrality of the prophetic element is one of the things that Tillich shares with feminist theologians.

But other than that, there initially seems to be no reason to place Tillich and feminist theologies in conversation with each other, since they appear to have little in common other than a general prophetic aim at issues of social justice. Valerie Saiving's 1960 essay, *The Human Situation: A Feminine View*, is usually seen as the start of modern feminist theology, but the field did not

---

[3] Paul Tillich, *The Courage to Be* (New Haven: Yale University Press, 1952); *Systematic Theology*, three volumes (Chicago: The University of Chicago Press, 1951, 1957, 1963 respectively).

[4] The definition is from Ronald H. Stone, "The Aims of World War II," in *Dialogues of Paul Tillich*, eds. Mary Ann Stenger and Ronald H. Stone (Macon: Mercer University Press, 2002), 230. For Stenger's discussion of the Protestant Principle in relation to feminist theology, see *Dialogues of Paul Tillich*, 113-21. For Tillich's own explanation, see Paul Tillich, "The Protestant Principle and the Proletarian Situation," in *The Protestant Era* (Chicago: University of Chicago Press, 1948), 161-81.

really take off until the 1970s.[5] Tillich died in 1965, so his era did not overlap much with that of feminist theology, and as a result there was relatively little engagement of feminist concerns in his thought, and therefore apparently little incentive for feminist theologians to engage him. Moreover, feminist theologians have reason to be suspicious of Tillich, primarily due to revelations of Tillich's extramarital affairs and pornographic habits in his wife Hannah Tillich's memoirs.[6] The feminist icon Mary Daly, who was initially quite appreciative of Tillich, turned away from his theology after the publication of these memoirs, since she saw his sexual exploits as reflections of patriarchal constructions of sexuality in terms of domination.[7] Feminist theologians might also agree with Alexander Irwin, who accused Tillich of an inability to live up to the demands of justice in his personal relationships.[8]

Numerous Tillich scholars have defended him on the grounds that Hannah herself had affairs and that their marriage, contracted in the bohemian atmosphere of Berlin during the Weimar years, was always understood to be an open one. These defenders have pointed to the trauma that Tillich suffered during the First World War, causing him to rebel against old norms and experiment with new ones. Others have offered arguments against bourgeois marriage, feminist retrievals of sadomasochism, and arguments that Tillich's erotic misconduct should be seen as the other side of an erotic virtue.[9] However, none of these defenses are guaranteed to lift the suspicion with which feminist theologians approach Tillich.

However, seeking absolution for Tillich might not be necessary. It might be best to simply start with a recognition that, when it comes to sexuality and treatment of women, Tillich was deeply flawed. Tillich himself wondered: "Was my erotic life a failure, or was it a daring way of opening up new human

---

[5] Valerie Saiving, "The Human Situation: A Feminine View," in *Womanspirit Rising: A Feminist Reader in Religion*, eds. Carol Christ and Judith Plaskow (San Francisco: Harper & Row, 1979), 25-42. The essay was originally published in the *Journal of Religion* 40, no. 2 (April 1960): 100-112.

[6] Hannah Tillich, *From Time to Time* (New York: Stein & Day, 1973).

[7] Mary Daly, *Gyn/Ecology: The Metaethics of Radical Feminism* (Boston: Beacon Press, 1988), 94-95.

[8] Alexander C. Irwin, *Eros Towards the World: Paul Tillich and the Theology of the Erotic* (Minneapolis: Fortress Press, 1991), 117.

[9] See, e.g., Rollo May, *Paulus: Reminiscences of a Friendship* (New York: Harper & Row, 1973); Marcella Althaus-Reed, *Indecent Theology: Theological Perversions in Sex, Gender and Politics* (New York: Routledge, 2000); Carter Heyward, *Touching Our Strength: The Erotic as Power and the Love of God* (San Francisco: Harper & Row, 1989).

possibilities?"[10] It seems fair to suggest that, despite Tillich's warm friendships and rich relationships with women (most of which were indeed just friendships and not necessarily sexual relationships), he was not quite able to escape patriarchal objectifications of women.

At the same time, one might keep in mind what those who knew him personally said of him. Tillich's biographers repeatedly refer to his magnetic and warm personality and the positive impact that he had on people.[11] His former student Ann Belford Ulanov writes that Tillich always "saw the specific person before him," and saw women as "individual persons, complete in their own right," calling them to "affirm their own being." In her view, Tillich "was much more than the recent gossip about his problems with women suggests."[12]

The reality is that few male theologians in the church's history can pass the feminist litmus test. Tillich is no exception here, but he is not necessarily worse than other significant male theologians of the twentieth century (nor of other centuries). Not unlike feminist theologies, which start with human experiences, Tillich's theology risked "being in touch with the unrepeatable tensions of his present."[13] That risk taking sometimes led him down problematic paths, but it is also what makes him compelling in many ways.

In fact, this methodological starting point in the "unrepeatable tensions of the present" is the most significant meeting point between feminist theologies and Tillich. However, feminist theologians have also engaged Tillich on doctrinal issues, such as the doctrines of sin, justification, and God, and Tillich in turn addressed some issues in his theology that later became discussion points in feminist theologies. In the following sections, we first look at doctrinal areas where feminist theologians engaged Tillich, then the occasions where he mentioned issues that were of later concern to feminist theologians, and then finally the most important commonality between Tillich and feminist theologies, that of theological method.

---

[10] May, *Paulus*, 65.

[11] Wilhelm and Marion Pauck, *Paul Tillich: His Life and Thought* (New York: Harper & Row, 1976).

[12] Ann Belford Ulanov, "The Anxiety of Being," in *The Thought of Paul Tillich*, eds. James Luther Adams, Wilhelm Pauck, Roger Lincoln Shinn (San Francisco: Harper & Row, 1985), 120.

[13] Mark Kline Taylor, ed., *Paul Tillich: Theologian of the Boundaries* (Minneapolis: Fortress Press, 1991), 11.

Feminist Engagement with Tillich

One of the first feminist theologians who made use of aspects of Tillich's thought was Mary Daly. Although Daly accused Tillich of being unaware of gender issues, she recognizes in one of her earlier works, *Beyond God the Father*, that "his manner of speaking about the ground and power of being would be difficult to use for the legitimation of any sort of oppression," and that it is "potentially liberating in a very radical sense."[14] In that book she furthermore makes use of Tillich's ontological categories to analyze patriarchy as that which destroys women's participation in Being, and describes feminist consciousness as participation in New Being. The later Daly was far more critical of Tillich (especially of his personal life), yet even in the book where she lodges her central critiques of Tillich, *Gyn/Ecology*, traces of Tillich's ontological language can still be seen (e.g., when she speaks of the self-affirming being of women's participation in the divine).[15]

Tillich's ontological perspectives also play a potential role in what is perhaps the most important existing doctrinal conversation about Tillich in feminist theologies, which is centered on the themes of sin and grace. In classical Christian perspectives on sin, which go back to the theology of Augustine of Hippo in the fourth century, sin is seen as being rooted in pride or "self-centeredness" (also sometimes described as *hubris* or self-elevation), which is seen as the opposite of a God-centered life. Augustine's analysis is persuasive and thoughtful, but the way the emphasis on pride is often translated in common church language makes it sound as if a sense of personal self-worth is sinful and as if the true Christian virtue is to think nothing of oneself. Feminist theologians have pointed out that women have been subjected to narratives of humility, self-sacrifice, and submission more than men have been, and that women will therefore hear the emphasis on the sinfulness of pride and the importance of humility differently than men generally would. In fact, they have suggested that women are generally prone to sins that are the very opposite of pride, variously described as lack of ambition, self-loss, or "passivity." As a result, one might even argue that the focus on pride not only fails to address women's typical sins, but aggravates the female tendency to negate the self.[16] Here it might be helpful to remember the classical understanding of sin

[14] Mary Daly, *Beyond God the Father: Toward a Philosophy of Women's Liberation* (Boston: Beacon, 1973), 20.

[15] Daly, *Gyn/Ecology*, 94-95, 435-36n40, and 111.

[16] See Saiving, "The Human Situation," 100-112; Susan Nelson Dunfee, "The Sin of Hiding: A Feminist Critique of Reinhold Niebuhr's Account of the Sin of Pride," *Soundings* 65 (Fall 1982): 316-27; and Mary Potter Engel, "Evil, Sin, and Vi-

in terms of the Greek term *hamartia*, i.e., "to miss the mark." It is plausible to suggest that both the self-centered life and the self-negating life are expressions of a life that is "missing the mark."

Tillich's theology expresses something of this dual nature of sin when he recognizes not only the sins of the powerful, but also the "sins of weakness."[17] To be sure, he places other forms of sin second to pride in his discussions of sin in volume two of the *Systematic Theology*, thereby suggesting a male-centered perspective, as Judith Plaskow has pointed out.[18] Nevertheless, some other feminist theologians see potential in Tillich's analysis of the human condition for thinking about the concept of sin, especially his concept of "estrangement" from our essential selves. In the existential state of estrangement, the polar ontological elements of individualization and participation risk breaking down into either loneliness, "in which world and communion are lost," or collectivization, "a loss of individuality and subjectivity whereby the self loses its self-relatedness and is transformed into a mere part of an embracing whole."[19] On both sides of these polar opposites we move towards "not being what we essentially are."[20] This phrase evokes the emphasis on "missing the mark" in the classical *hamartia* concept, indicating ways in which people suffer from distortions in their humanity, and Tillich's analysis suggests that this can include both extreme individualization (pride), and extreme participation in the realities of others (self-loss). This corresponds with feminist theologian Susan Lichtman's statement that "both the prideful person, and the passively dependent one, portray a person alienated from his/her own true nature."[21] In this manner, Tillich's ontological analysis, more than his discussion of the moral category of sin, offers potential for the feminist restatement of sin in terms of either pride or self-loss.

Moreover, the concept of estrangement helps to highlight the emphasis on a less moralistic perspective on sin that is found in the classical doctrine of original sin. One should note that feminist theologians are very critical of the

---

olation of the Vulnerable," in *Lift Every Voice: Constructing Theologies From the Underside*, eds. Susan Brooks Thistlethwaite and Mary Potter Engel (San Francisco: Harper & Row, 1998), 159-71.

[17] Paul Tillich, *The Interpretation of History* (New York: Charles Scribner's Sons, 1936), 93.

[18] Tillich, *Systematic Theology*, vol. 2, 47-55; Judith Plaskow, *Sex, Sin and Grace: Women's Experience and the Theologies of Reinhold Niebuhr and Paul Tillich* (New York: University Press of America, 1980).

[19] Tillich, *Systematic Theology*, vol. 1, 174-86.

[20] Tillich, 199.

[21] Susan Lichtman, "The Concept of Sin in the Theology of Paul Tillich: A Break from Patriarchy?" *The Journal of Women and Religion* 8 (Winter 1989): 49-55.

doctrine of original sin, not only because of the classical emphasis on pride that is part of it, but also because it has often been used to blame women for sin. The latter is due to the association of the doctrine with the story of Adam and Eve, and the theme of Eve's guilt which has been prevalent throughout Christian history. In contrast to the tendency to turn the concept of sin into a blame game, feminist proposals for understanding sin center on a sense of inner disintegration, or what Rita Nakashima Brock calls "brokenheartedness…something to be healed."[22] Ironically, this is not far removed from the central metaphors of the doctrine of original sin, which depict sin in terms that evoke a sense of brokenness, the presence in our lives of distortions in need of healing.[23] In the classical doctrine of original sin, theologians like Augustine insisted that individual wrongful acts are not the real problem, but are rather the manifestations of a more fundamental problem, a brokenness within the self, and a chasm between humanity and the divine. This general sensibility is also captured to some extent in Tillich's concept of estrangement (although Tillich does not necessarily understand estrangement in moral terms). As such, Tillich's notion of estrangement provides a helpful way of expressing the valuable classical insight that sin is not simply a matter of individual acts in a manner that is compatible with feminist concerns.

The feminist conversation on Tillich's perspective on grace, which flows from the conversation on sin, needs further attention. Influenced by his teacher Martin Kähler, Tillich placed great emphasis on the doctrine of justification by grace alone, extending its implications beyond the idea of being justified despite our sin, to include the idea of us being justified despite our doubts. Tillich expresses his emphasis on pre-emptive grace in a passage from his most famous sermon, "You are Accepted:"

> Grace strikes us…when we are in great pain and restlessness…when we walk through the dark valley of a meaningless and empty life…when despair destroys all joy and courage. Sometimes at that moment a wave of light breaks into our darkness, and it is as though a voice were saying: "You are accepted. *You are accepted*, accepted by that which is greater than you, and the name of which you do not know. Do not try to do anything now; perhaps later you will do

[22] Rita Nakashima Brock, *Journeys by Heart: A Christology of Erotic Power* (New York: Crossroad, 2000), 7.

[23] For a lengthier discussion of feminist conversations on sin and of the structural similarities between feminist and classical expressions of sin, see Rachel Sophia Baard, *Sexism and Sin-Talk: Feminist Conversations on the Human Condition* (Louisville: Westminster John Knox Press, 2019).

much. Do not seek for anything; do not perform anything; do not intend anything! *Simply accept the fact that you are accepted!*[24]

However, the emphasis on the passive receiving of grace found in this doctrine (both in its classical expression and as appropriated by Tillich) has been scrutinized by some feminist theologians such as Judith Plaskow, who argues that this emphasis aggravates "women's sin" of "passivity."[25] Mary Daly also had some concern about this emphasis: she describes Tillich's doctrine of acceptance as a masochistic torture chamber in which the female victim is condemned to live with the "knowledge" that she is really guilty and deserving of condemnation, despite the belief that a loving God forgives her.[26] Serene Jones, although not focusing on Tillich's version, levels similar criticisms against the Protestant doctrine of justification, particularly its classical emphasis on the shattering of the self.[27] In slight contrast, Elisabeth Moltmann-Wendel suggests that the doctrine has liberating possibilities, but she also says that it "has never been applied to women and worked out in terms of their own selves."[28]

There are elements of truth in these critiques. The emphasis on passive receiving of grace in the Protestant doctrine of justification, when tied to a view of pride as the quintessential sin, often leads to the presupposition that the prideful self must be shattered in order to be able to properly receive grace. This presupposition is rooted in the idea that the idea of humans contributing to their salvation is rooted in pride, and that this pride (and therefore the centered self) should be shattered if the person is to be ready to receive free grace. How offensive this perspective can be from a feminist perspective can be seen in the work of Karl Barth, who depicts the recipient of divine grace as a "non-willing, non-achieving, non-creative, non-sovereign," female figure, who passively awaits and receives the "grace" coming from above, from the male Christ (and elsewhere Barth is quite insistent on the masculinity of Christ).[29] In this

[24] Paul Tillich, "You Are Accepted," in *The Shaking of the Foundations* (New York: Charles Scribner's Sons, 1948), 161-62.

[25] Tillich, 157.

[26] Daly, *Gyn/Ecology*, 377.

[27] Serene Jones, *Feminist Theory and Christian Theology: Cartographies of Grace* (Minneapolis: Fortress Press, 2000), 49-68.

[28] Elisabeth Moltmann-Wendel, *A Land Flowing with Milk and Honey: Perspectives on Feminist Theology* (New York: Crossroad, 1988), 157.

[29] Karl Barth, *Church Dogmatics*, vol. 1/2, eds. G.W. Bromiley and T.F. Torrance, trans. G.T. Thomson and Harold Knight (Edinburgh: T&T Clark, 1956), 188ff. See also Karl Barth, *Church Dogmatics,* vol. 3/4, eds. G.N. Bromiley and T.F.

way, the Protestant emphasis on passive receiving of grace takes on a gender element that in fact obscures the liberating potential of the doctrine.

In my own feminist engagement of this topic, I have argued that such a liberating potential exists in Tillich.[30] Not only is there in Tillich a strong sense of the possibility of sins other than pride as foundational within the human psyche (something that, in all fairness, is present in Barth's perspective on sin too), but Tillich operates with a very different perspective on God, which situates the doctrine of justification in a different spatial metaphor. In contrast to the traditional metaphor of God as the "Highest Being" or Karl Barth's "Totally Other," Tillich speaks of God not as a Being but as Being-itself or the Ground of Being. In short, for Tillich, God "transcends every being and also the totality of beings."[31] The feminist theologian Rosemary Radford Ruether uses similar language when she speaks of God as "primal Matrix, the ground of being-new being, [who] is neither stifling immanence nor rootless transcendence."[32]

In Tillich's perspective on God, divine transcendence is therefore not understood in the classical spatial metaphor of "high above" (a metaphor that really belongs more to the geocentric universe of medieval theology than to modern cosmology), but rather in terms of transcending the concept of God as a Being above other beings, insisting instead that God is best understood as Being Itself and as the Ground of all Being. As such, it is less personal than traditional theistic images for God, but at the same time this perspective opens up the possibility of a more intimate yet transcending divine presence. Within this schema the Protestant insistence on free grace is not understood in terms of the Totally Other who comes from above to shatter the recipient of grace in order to make them able to receive it in humility, but is instead imagined in terms similar to what feminist theologian Rita Nakashima Brock calls a "primal interrelatedness."[33] Therefore, the free grace that is offered in the Protestant doctrine of justification can here be viewed not as a shattering reality but as a grounding reality that frees the recipient of grace from sin, whether the sins of self-centeredness or the sins of self-loss, and frees up the

Torrance, various translators (Edinburgh: T&T Clark, 1961), 161, for his argument against the "feminization" of Christ.

[30] Rachel Sophia Baard, "Original Grace, Not Destructive Grace: A Feminist Appropriation of Paul Tillich's Notion of Acceptance," *Journal of Religion* 87 (July 2007): 411-34.

[31] Tillich, *Systematic Theology*, vol. 1, 237.

[32] Rosemary Radford Ruether, *Sexism and God-Talk: Toward a Feminist Theology* (Boston: Beacon, 1993), 85.

[33] Brock, *Journeys by Heart*, 8.

actions of the recipient of sin to come from a place of freedom instead of compulsion. This theme needs to be worked out at greater length, but my basic contention here is that Tillich's spatial metaphor for God as Ground of Being offers the possibility of a different and far more liberating view of the Protestant doctrine of justification, which addresses feminist concerns with this doctrine.

A related theme that deserves further feminist reflection is Tillich's concept of Christ as New Being, "the one in whom the conflict between the essential unity of God and man and man's existential estrangement is overcome."[34] The internal disintegration suggested in Tillich's concept of estrangement, which can take the form of the self-loss described by feminists in their analysis of the human condition, is overcome in the New Being in whom one finds the courage to be the self that both belongs to the world and transcends it.[35] In the New Being "the eternal unity of God and man becomes actual under the conditions of existence without being conquered by them."[36] By implication, the New Being enables self-integration, the holding together of the ontological elements of individualization and participation, i.e., estrangement from our true being and from the Ground of Being is overcome in New Being.

Tillich's perspective on the Christ event as a communal phenomenon that transcends the historically male figure of Jesus of Nazareth has the potential to address feminist concerns about the harmful ways in which the maleness of Jesus has been used against women (see, for example, Rosemary Radford Ruether's question whether a male Savior can save women).[37] Indeed, one sees similar moves being made by some feminist theologians. For example, Rita Nakashima Brock suggests a Christology "not centered in Jesus, but in relationality and community as the whole-making, healing center of Christianity" (Christa/Community).[38] Similar emphases can be found in *mujerista* and womanist Christological perspectives.[39]

---

[34] Tillich, *Systematic Theology*, vol. 2, 125.

[35] Tillich, *Systematic Theology*, vol. 1, 169-70.

[36] Paul Tillich, *Systematic Theology*, vol. 3, 270. See also pp. 32-34, 38, 41-44, 268-71.

[37] Tillich, *Systematic Theology*, vol. 2, 97-99. On a basic statement of the problems inherent in a masculinist Christology, see Rosemary Radford Ruether, "Can a Male Savior Save Women?," in *Sexism and God-Talk: Toward a Feminist Theology* (Boston: Beacon, 1993), 116-38.

[38] Brock, *Journeys by Heart*, 52.

[39] Ada María Isasi-Díaz, in *La Lucha Continues: Mujerista Theology* (Maryknoll: Orbis), 251-57, specifically utilizes a Christology of community in her work. For a womanist Christology that is rooted in the specific experiences of African American

Feminist Themes in Tillich

Tillich himself did not engage feminist concerns much, largely because most of his theological work was done before modern feminist theology was developed, but there are elements in his thought that point to an underlying awareness of the significance of gender as an interpretative lens in theology. Foremost among these is his discussion of the traditionally male language for God, which feminist theologians have presented as a problem. For example, in one of the best treatments of this topic, Elizabeth A. Johnson points out that the symbol of an exclusively male God "functions to support an imaginative and structural world that excludes or subordinates women."[40] In the third volume of his *Systematic Theology*, Tillich associates God as the Ground of Being with "the mother-quality of giving birth, carrying, and embracing," in contrast to the "demanding father-image of…God."[41] Tillich does seem to be somewhat anxious about the maternal Ground of Being which he describes as "calling back, resisting independence of the created, swallowing it."[42] This anxiety is amplified by earlier references in the first volume of the *Systematic Theology* to the Ground of Being as the Abyss, "the abysmal character of the divine life."[43] Nevertheless, the ecofeminist theologian Sigridur Gudmarsdottir has appropriated the concept of the Abyss as ground for feminist praxis in her book, *Tillich and the Abyss*.[44]

Tillich's sensitivity to issues of gender can also be seen in his perspective on the Spirit, in particular his idea that "ecstatic character of the Spiritual Presence … transcends the alternative of male and female symbolism."[45] The male and female symbolism he is referring to here is that of the traditional association of men with reason and women with emotion: his awareness of this problematic dualism invites further feminist engagement. Feminist engagement of Tillich on the issue of dualism, however, should also include critique of his lament about female participation in fascist ideology in *The Socialist Decision*. Tillich links political romanticism (such as that of the Nazis)

---

women, see Jacquelyn Grant, *White Women's Christ and Black Women's Jesus: Feminist Christology and Womanist Response* (Atlanta: Scholars Press, 1989).

[40] Elizabeth A. Johnson, *She Who Is: The Mystery of God in Feminist Theological Discourse* (New York: Crossroad, 1995), 4-5. See also Sallie McFague, *Metaphorical Theology: Models of God in Religious Language* (Philadelphia: Fortress Press, 1982).

[41] Tillich, *Systematic Theology*, vol. 3, 294.

[42] Tillich, 294.

[43] Tillich, *Systematic Theology*, vol. 1, 156.

[44] Sigridur Gudmarsdottir, *Tillich and the Abyss: Foundations, Feminism, and Theology of Praxis* (London: Palgrave Macmillan, 2016).

[45] Tillich, *Systematic Theology*, vol. 3, 294.

to the myth of origin, and says that women are sometime prone to reject the rationalistic ideologies that have worked for women's emancipation in favor of romanticism due to the "powers of origin possessed by woman by virtue of her resonance with eros and motherhood."[46] His association of women with the romantic myth of origin that needs to be broken "by the unconditional demand [that] is the root of liberal democratic, and socialist thought in politics," is deeply problematic (in fact, it evokes a more violent metaphor than the one previously noticed in Karl Barth's doctrine of justification!).[47] In Tillich's thought it is the prophetic principle that breaks through the myth of origin to open the possibility of religious socialism, which is the goal of his political analysis. His analysis is persuasive in itself, but the inclusion of dualistic presuppositions that associate women with the myths of origin and men with the rational principle, is deeply problematic. Given the fact that men are often more conservative than women and that later feminism often rested on liberal and even socialist thought, his analysis appears to be flawed here. Further feminist analysis is warranted, but as a preliminary conclusion, one might say that despite these traces of traditional patriarchal dualism in his thought, it is also true that he concluded that "socialism cannot possibly tolerate the restoration of male patriarchalism."[48]

The Main Meeting Point: Theological Method

The most significant point of contact between Tillich and feminist theologies has to do with theological method. In contrast to many other theologies, Tillich's method of correlation does not start with an authoritative religious tradition but posits the human situation as the starting point of theological reflection. Given the feminist starting point in women's experience, it is not surprising that feminists like Mary Daly found Tillich's method "less inadequate" than that of other twentieth-century theologians.[49]

Tillich distinguishes between two types of theology: kerygmatic theology, in which "the kerygma—the message—is reproduced, interpreted, and organized either in predominantly biblical terms or in terms taken from the classical tradition;" and apologetic theology, in which theology answers "the questions asked of, and the criticisms directed against, a concrete religion."[50]

---

[46] Paul Tillich, *The Socialist Decision*, trans. Franklin Sherman (New York: Harper & Row, 1977), 152-53.

[47] Tillich, 5.

[48] Tillich, 152-53.

[49] E.g., Daly, *Beyond God the Father*, 200n10.

[50] Paul Tillich, "The Problem of Theological Method," *Journal of Religion* 27, no. 1 (January 1947): 25.

His own method of correlation is a form of apologetic theology in which question and answer is "correlated in such a way that the religious symbol is interpreted as the adequate answer to a question, implied in man's existence, and asked in primitive, pre-philosophical, or elaborated philosophical terms." In this method "the form of the questions...is decisive for the theological form in which the answer is given" and "the substance of the question is determined by the substance of the answer."[51]

The important twentieth century theologian, Karl Barth, whose theology might be described as a kerygmatic form of theology, opposed apologetic theologies, fearing that they would make theological reflection dependent on the cultural fashions of the day. (Given the way in which the Nazis appropriated Christian theology for their own ends, Barth had reason to fear this kind of cultural accommodation.) Tillich responded to this fear by recognizing that there is indeed a "danger that in this way (the method of relating theology to culture) the substance of the Christian message may be lost," but added that dangers "are not a reason for avoiding a serious demand.[52] Indeed, correlation does not have to mean that theology simply echoes culture. Instead, "it does mean that the objective and the subjective side of faith are interrelated, for faith is the expression of the impact of an ultimate concern on the human personality."[53] Indeed, while Barth may have feared that correlation runs the risk of having the answer be determined by the question, Tillich's fear was that Barth's kerygmatic approach might give answers to questions modern humans are not asking. In contrast, Tillich's method is, in the words of Mark Taylor, "an interpretive art requiring sensitive readings of both human situations and also of Christian symbols in the tradition."[54]

This approach constitutes a more intelligible theology, since, as Roger Haight notes, "understanding in theology must correlate with our knowledge and understanding of our situation in the world."[55] Haight argues that some kind of correlation between contemporary human experience and history "has characterized all of the creative theology of the modern period," adding that "even the theology of Karl Barth is a response to human culture, albeit a negative one, which contains far more borrowing from his contemporary world

---

[51] Tillich, 24, 25.

[52] Tillich, *Systematic Theology*, vol. 3, 4.

[53] Tillich, "The Problem of Theological Method," 25.

[54] Mark Kline Taylor, *Paul Tillich*, 126-27.

[55] Roger Haight, *An Alternative Vision: An Interpretation of Liberation Theology* (Mahwah: Paulist Press, 1985), 7.

than his principles admit."[56] He cautions against seeing the method of correlation as a mechanical, step-by-step process. Rather, he says, "correlation is simply descriptive of the structure of theology and theological statement."[57] It is worth including a lengthier statement by Haight on the method of correlation:

> It is a basic hermeneutical structure, a method of interpretation and reinterpretation that requires fidelity to Christian sources and adequacy to human existence as it is experienced today. In all of this, there may be a general fear that beginning with our own contemporary experience and allowing our questions to be the interpreting factor of the meaning of the Christian message may intrinsically distort that message, since in general questions determine the response or interpretation that is given. This is indeed a danger, but it is also the price that must be paid, the risk that must be taken, to have an intelligible theology in our time. At the same time this caution is also a reminder that the Christian message from out of the past can confront and call into question our contemporary human experience. This is a theme from a theology of the Word such as Karl Barth's that has perennial value even within a method of correlation.[58]

David Tracy's modern adaptation of Tillich's approach in terms of "mutually critical correlation" emphasizes that personal perspectives shape theological insights. This recognition would support the feminist contention that classical theologies are largely androcentric (premised on the experiences of ruling males), that kerygmatic theologies often serve to baptize male perspectives as revelatory, and that a correlational type of approach is better suited to express feminist contention that women's experiences matter in formulating theological insights.

The emphasis on women's experience as a methodological starting point for feminist theology means that the latter recognizes the importance and inevitability of doing theology from a particular social location. This particular emphasis differs in some respects from Tillich's method, which correlates answers derived from Christian texts with questions raised by analysis of the "universal" human situation. Feminist scholars argue that the assumption of a universal human situation tends to universalize the experience of Western

---

[56] Haight, 48.
[57] Haight, 49.
[58] Haight, 49.

males—it thus hides patriarchal interests and exhibits androcentric tendencies. Nevertheless, it is his openness to the "human situation" that makes Tillich more appealing to the feminist theological project than many other male theologians. In fact, his centrality in advocating for a correlational approach makes him an important ally for feminist theologians against the conservatism on gender issues and the authoritarian tendencies of kerygmatic theologies.

To be sure, Tillich's description of the "situation" in terms of philosophical concerns is quite different from the feminist emphasis on concrete, rather than philosophical, situations. Thus the feminist approach is not identical to Tillich's more abstract, existential project. However, feminist theological method finds a point of contact with Tillich's emphasis on the prophetic principle. Furthermore, in its openness to human situation as theological starting point, it is in line with his "genuine pragmatism which refuses to close any door."[59]

In this emphasis to "human situations" as starting point for theology, feminist theologies not only share a basic theological approach with Tillich which is in contrast with the other main theological trajectory of the twentieth century, that of kerygmatic theology, but are also open to the same criticism from the side of kerygmatic theologians. The accusation frequently lodged against feminist theologies that they are absolutizing women's experience as a separate source for theology alongside revelation, is little more than a version of the Barthian fear that the "situation" or "culture" will overshadow theology. However, feminist theologians, much like Tillich, would suggest that risk is no reason not to heed serious demand.

An engagement with Tillich might also help feminist theologies express feminist theological method better in order to address these concerns. For example, Mary Ann Stenger suggests that Tillich's critique of idolatry might serve as an important warning against any tendencies to view women's experience as normative and absolute.[60]

Moreover, there are insights expressed in Tillich's method of correlation that might be useful in refining feminist theological method. Of particular importance is the fact that Tillich emphasizes that human experience is not in itself a positive source or norm of systematic theology. Our experience is changing and fragmentary, and as such, it is not the source of truth—yet, without it, no truth can become our truth.[61] Indeed, there "is no meaningful

---

[59] Tillich, "The Problem of Theological Method," 17.

[60] Stenger, *Dialogues of Paul Tillich*, 117, 129-39.

[61] Tillich, "The Problem of Theological Method," 22.

speaking of God except in an existential attitude or in the situation of revelation."[62] The concept of *kairos*, which points to revelation in specific times and contexts, might be particularly helpful here. Tillich made extensive use of this concept, describing the *kairos* as that "moment rich in content and significance," when "the eternal breaks into the temporal, and the temporal is prepared to receive it."[63] This concept helps to express the idea that the issue is not one of experience plus revelation as double norm for theology, but, instead, that "not experience, but revelation received in experience, gives the content of every theology."[64] This would imply that the feminist methodological starting point is not positing women's experience as revelatory in itself, but is simply a recognition that divine revelation happens in human experience, including women's experiences. Emphasizing female experience as the methodological starting point for feminist theology has the merit of retrieving silenced voices and showing that revelation is received also in female experience. When understood with reference to the *kairos* concept, this is not a matter of putting the finite and the infinite on the same level—i.e., it is not idolatry—but of pointing to those moments of revelation, i.e., moments in which the finite and the infinite meet, which have been ignored by "official" tradition. In short, feminist method might be best understood as seeing revelation as happening in the midst of women's experience.

Provided we do not reduce Tillich's method to a formal question-and-answer schema, but rather see it as a dynamic mutually critical correlation, and avoid an overly abstract perspective on the situation, Tillich's method remains relevant for feminist theology. In his method of correlation, Tillich expresses the implicit or explicit method of any theology that would transcend either Protestant fundamentalism or Catholic authoritarianism (in other words, various forms of top-down use of Scripture or Tradition that have the effects of silencing feminist or other liberationist voices). At best, his approach can be seen as a hermeneutical approach in which situation and historical kerygma engage each other in a mutually critical endeavor. Tillich's method is not only still relevant, but is indeed at the heart of any contextual theology, and hence of any theology, since all theologies ought to be recognized as to some extent contextual.

In short, in his method of correlation, Tillich helped to develop an approach to theology that does not see its task as one of "speaking into" human situations from the vantage point of the Bible or the "official" (male) tradition, but as one of taking human experiences seriously in doing theology. It is a

[62] Tillich, 24

[63] Tillich, *The Protestant Era*, 33, and xix.

[64] Tillich, "The Problem of Theological Method," 23.

recognition that the content of theology is revelation received in experience, both the revelatory experiences of the classical traditions, and those of long-ignored voices and "new" situations such as those brought forward by women.[65] While there are indeed significant differences between Tillich and feminist theologians (and among different feminist theologians) with regard to theological method, it is at this point where our two conversation partners have the potential for a true alliance.

[65] Tillich, 23.

Cultural Transformation as Ultimate Concern: Tillich in Conversation with the Black Liberation Theology of James Cone

Zachary Royal

The cultural embeddedness of religion enables theologians to examine and critique both the *cultural* theology of Paul Tillich and the *contextual* theology of James Cone. When *cultural* theology is placed side by side with *contextual* theology through the theological lens of the cultural embeddedness of religion, the notion of the transformation of culture as ultimate concern comes to the forefront. The notion of cultural embeddedness does not merely illumine cultural and contextual theology. It unites the two as well, revealing the critical social factors that drove Paul Tillich and James Cone to wed Christianity to the social movements of their day.

The union of cultural and contextual theology through the theological lens of cultural embeddedness shows that, although their historical periods were different, their theological goals were the same. For both, the "freedom movement," that Tillich defined as the "prophetic– political demands for social justice"[1] became the theological blueprint for the construction of a new humanity, and the "ultimate concern," regarding cultural transformation. Tillich and Cone both demand reformation of the church and transformation of society. This places Tillich and Cone in conversation. It brings them together on the one goal of theology that is common to both: transformation of culture that resides at the core of any serious theology of mediation.

In the following pages I trace Tillich's notion of cultural synthesis from its origins in Troeltsch's synthetic proposal for twentieth century theology to its high point in conversation with Schleiermacher's attempt to construct a mediating theology of culture, to Tillich's appropriation of this synthesis in his famous essay "On the Idea of a Theology of Culture." I then show how Cone appropriated Tillich's cultural theology, theological method, and systematic proposal for the cultural embeddedness of Christianity in his principle

---

[1] Paul Tillich, Theology of Culture (New York: Oxford University Press, 1959), 28.

works, *Black Theology and Black Power*, *A Black Theology of Liberation*, and *God of the Oppressed.*

My goal is threefold. First, to reveal how their revolutionary theological method (a method of mediation that can be traced from Augustine to Schleiermacher and Troeltsch) enabled both to conclude that Christian revelation must be correlated with the human situation. Second, to show how the experience of revelation within the human predicament provides humanity with the fundamental criteria for being prophetically self-critical. Finally, to argue that this critical prophetic perspective can help theology and the church redefine mass movements for justice, dignity, and freedom occurring within secular culture.

Troeltsch, Tillich, and the Quest for a Public Political Theology

Tillich's proposal owes its greatest debt to the cultural theologian Ernst Troeltsch, the much-maligned giant of late nineteenth and early twentieth century theology. Troeltsch not only crafted the notion of cultural embeddedness, but also stands behind Tillich's pioneering synthetic proposal for a mediating theology in his famous essay, "On the Idea of a Theology of Culture." Moreover, I assert, with Russell Re Manning, that, "Tillich's project is in many ways a development of the central themes of Troeltsch's life's work as the systematician of the history of religions school."[2]

Most importantly, Troeltsch taught Tillich how the construction of a culturally embedded theology that brings Christianity into dialogue with contemporary culture requires a revolution in theological method. In his groundbreaking work, *Religion in History*, Troeltsch sketched the outlines of a radically new approach to theological method.[3]

According to Troeltsch, the rise of the historical critical method has destroyed or exploded the theological method of nineteenth century theology. Another theological method was necessary. This new method for constructing theology, the critical historical method, is like "leaven," he claims. It not only changes the old method, it explodes every theological method that came before it. Thus, the radical, transformative power of the new historical method in theology makes it impossible for theology to lean upon its dogmatic (neo-orthodox) assumptions, assumptions that forced such theology to divorce Christianity from contemporary culture. For Troeltsch, a new theological method is necessary, a method that takes its theological cue from history.

---

[2] Russell Re Manning, *Theology at the End of Culture: Paul Tillich's Theology of Culture and Art* (Leuven: Peeters Publishers, 2005), 9.

[3] Ernst Troeltsch, "Historical and Dogmatic Method in Theology," in *Religion in History* (Minneapolis: Fortress Press, 1991), 23.

Tillich surpasses Troeltsch by revising his "method" (as John R. Stumme keenly observes)[4] to be not just "methodological." It was sociopolitical and theological. By 1919, war and revolution had forced Tillich to take a theological stance more radical than his famous teacher Ernst Troeltsch. Germany was divided theologically between radical religious socialists and the authorities of the conservative church. Between these extremes stood the liberal Evangelical Social Congress, to which belonged the theological "superstars" of the early twentieth century: William Bousset, Otto Dibelius, Karl Heim, Rudolf Otto, Martin Rade and Ernst Troeltsch. They were the most progressive and radical Christian thinkers of the day, and Tillich broke with them! Moreover, Tillich even broke with the most important theologian of the History of Religions School, Ernst Troeltsch!

Tillich parted company with the most radical theologians of his day. The earth had begun to shake. Liberal reform could not do justice to the theological revolution that was underway. As A. James Reimer points out, Troeltsch's method failed because it judged history from within history.[5] This was the reason, Tillich felt, that the student must now surpass the teacher. For Tillich, the paradoxical breakthrough of the unconditioned—a breakthrough that was causing the earth to shake—was more radical and revolutionary than the liberal reformist spirit of the Evangelical Social Congress. For him, reformism, i.e., progressive liberal Christianity, did not take the present period—the revolutionary significance of that historical moment—seriously. Tillich's religious socialism described a breakthrough of the unconditioned that Troeltsch's theology (and method) never did. Tillich said that Troeltsch's method could only serve as the "negative presupposition for every future construction."[6]

For Tillich, Troeltsch's theology failed for two reasons. He was unable to see what was happening in the trenches of the First World War and the streets of Berlin. In the trenches of the First World War, Tillich had come face to face, as Stumme said, with the "everyday people" the Kaiser seemed to have forgotten—the Proletariat.[7] Tillich came into personal contact with them and experienced their bitterness about having to fight and die in a meaningless war. He found out how the proletariat considered the church nothing

---

[4] John R. Stumme, *Socialism in Theological Perspective: A Study of Paul Tillich 1918-1933* (Montana: Scholars Press, 1978), 28-29.

[5] A. James Reimer, *Paul Tillich: Theologian of Nature, Culture and Politics* (Piscataway: Transaction Publishers, 2004), 161.

[6] Stumme, *Socialism in Theological Perspective*, 28.

[831] Stumme, 21.

but a pawn of the ruling class. It was here that Tillich became alive to the political situation, and it was here that he affirmed the revolution.

Tillich, Schleiermacher, and the Crisis of Cultural Embeddedness

Tillich's project for the cultural embeddedness of theology is indebted to one man, the father of modern theology, Friedrich Schleiermacher. Russell Re Manning writes: "If it is Kant who set the framework within which the questions for 'modern theology' were posed, it was largely Schleiermacher who determined the form of the answers."[8] Russell then cites Ninian Smart's evaluation of Schleiermacher as "arguably the greatest theologian of the nineteenth century, if not the entire modern age," because in him, "the nineteenth century found…for at least a while, its most effective answer to the strictures of religious thought imposed by Kant's Critique of Pure Reason."[9]

Ironically, for Tillich, it was Schleiermacher's theological answers to Kant's devastating *Critique of Pure Reason* that formulated the real crisis for mediating theology both in the nineteenth and twentieth centuries. This motif became the foundation for Schleiermacher's address to Jacobi, the core of Tillich's struggle with Barth's neo-orthodox theology, and the substance of Tillich's feud with his good friend Emanuel Hirsch. Most importantly, it framed the structure of the modern debate regarding the relationship of philosophy and religion. Schleiermacher stands at the forefront of a theological tradition to which Tillich belongs—the Schleiermacher-Troeltsch line of mediating theology—that is dedicated to the notion of cultural embeddedness. Moreover, it is interesting to see how Tillich used one (Schleiermacher), to transcend the other (Troeltsch), and, by doing so, Tillich surpassed his own teacher, overcame the crisis in his own theological method, and succeeded in embedding the Christian religion in the new sociopolitical cultural setting of the twentieth century.

John Clayton explores how Schleiermacher framed the dilemma regarding modern theologies of mediation. "Is it possible," Schleiermacher asks, "to conceive, let alone establish a relationship between Christianity and culture in which there is a genuine and thorough-going reciprocity that threatens the autonomy neither of religion nor of culture?"[10] In his previously unpublished

---

[8] Russell Re Manning, *Theology at the End of Culture*, 5.

[9] John Powell Clayton, *The Concept of Correlation: Paul Tillich and the Possibility of Mediating Theology* (Berlin: Walter de Gruyter, 1980), 42.

[10] John Powell Clayton, The Concept of Correlation: Paul Tillich and the Possibility of a Mediating Theology (Berlin: Walter de Gruyter, 1980), 42.

work from 1923 or 1924, entitled, *Schleiermacher und die Erfassung des Gottlichen im Gefühl*, Tillich reveals how his theology of culture is his attempt to surpass Troeltsch and resolve "Schleiermacher's dilemma."[12] The text, Tillich's earliest and most systematic treatment of Schleiermacher's thought, has three sections, but it was Tillich's interpretation, in the third section, of Schleiermacher's classic text, *On Religion: Speeches to Its Cultured Despisers,* that reveals the true reason Tillich ultimately rejected even Schleiermacher's attempt to wed religion and culture. A. James Reimer shows us why. Tillich, Reimer suggests, rejected Schleiermacher's *Kulturprotestantismus* for the same reason he rejected Troeltsch's. For Tillich, Troeltsch and Schleiermacher failed because both sought to correlate Christianity with German bourgeois culture. For Tillich, war and revolution, and the democratic movement for social change in Germany demanded that Christianity be correlated neither with the German bourgeoisie nor the cultural elite, but with the proletariat!

This was why Tillich's project for cultural embeddedness was so shocking and revolutionary. It anticipated James Cone forty years later, who would demand that theology in the twentieth century be constructed with the common person in mind! When constructing theology for common, everyday people, cultural theology must never be separated from contextual theology. This was at the heart of the battle for the future of theology waged between Barth, Hirsch, and Tillich in the 1920s and 1930s in Germany. Tillich knew that when cultural theology was wedded with contextual theology, modern theology had the potential to address the needs of those who suffer—the victims of both liberal and conservative Christianity. As Stumme notes: "The self-assured period of 'scientific theology' was over, and the profession of theology was in a concrete identity crisis."[13] The question asked by the dialectal theologians in the 1920s ("How can we speak of God if we are human?") was not enough for Tillich. He went even further and dared to ask how human beings might relate religious speech about God to the proletariat.

The Culmination of the Notion of Cultural Embeddedness

There are stunning parallels between Tillich and Cone. They chose to become professional theologians that revolutionized the practice of theology. They constructed their respective theologies in similar ways, culminating in similar notions of the cultural embeddedness of Christianity. The first similarity in-

---

[12] Paul Tillich, in English translation, *Schleiermacher and the Inclusion of the Divine within Feeling*, in *Theology At the End of Culture: Paul Tillich's Theology of Culture and Art*, Russell Re Manning (Leuven, Belgium 2005), 41-49.

[13] Stumme, *Socialism in Sociological Perspective*, 15, 19-29.

volves a little-known irony about Tillich and Cone as both began their respective quests for a culturally embedded theology of mediation. Ronald H. Stone reveals the heart of the irony regarding Niebuhr and Tillich, namely that "the theories of their respective dissertations and theses were neither immediately relevant to the war they found themselves in nor to their developed practical work."[14] Incredibly, neither of Tillich's two dissertations, *Mysticism and Guilt Consciousness in Schelling's Philosophical Development* (1910),[15] nor *The construction of the History of Religion in Schelling's Positive Philosophy* (1912), nor Cone's PhD dissertation on Karl Barth's theological anthropology entitled, *The Doctrine of Man in the Theology of Karl Barth*, prepared them for their future theological vocation. Tillich's two dissertations prove that, regarding the practice of theology, he was grossly ill prepared to do the very thing he had been trained to do. Most importantly, his lack of theological preparation prevented Tillich from resonating with the deepest levels of the thought of the philosophical theologian whose work forms the deep structure of Tillich's theology of culture.

Although the two dissertations form the bedrock of his theological project, and Schelling's ontology is the touchstone of Tillich's political philosophy as well as his theology of culture, the political implications of Schelling's theological writings in Tillich's pre-war theological training were never explored. Ronald H. Stone's provocative book, *Paul Tillich's Radical Social Thought* explains this irony.[16] Tillich's theological naiveté, or as Stone describes it, his political innocence, blinded the promising young theologian to the very theme that, almost half a century later, would form the centerpiece of Cone's contextual theology—the notion of freedom or liberation. It seems as if Tillich's early metaphysical training led him to contradict the very theological tradition that he would later use to revolutionize the field of theology. Tillich's failure to explore the political implications of Schelling's thought seemed to make him more dedicated to the Kierkegaard-Barth line, at least with regard to his theological method, than the Schleiermacher-Troeltsch tradition. It was only after his lecture to the Kant Society, "On the Idea of a Theology of Culture," that Tillich was able to take a political stance on the boundary between theological liberalism and the emerging dialectical theology. War and revolution forced Tillich to abandon any dialectical approach to theology that stressed

[14] Ronald H. Stone, *Politics and Faith* (Macon: Mercer University Press, 2012), 28.

[15] Paul Tillich, *Mysticism and Guilt-Consciousness in Schelling's Philosophical Development*, trans. Victor Nuovo (Lewisburg: Bucknell University Press, 1974).

[16] Ronald H. Stone, *Paul Tillich's Radical Social Thought* (Atlanta: John Knox Press, 1980), 25.

any metaphysical communion with God which ends in political impartiality, and the preoccupation with the individual over a sociopolitical commitment to Christ that is rooted in social responsibility and takes the needs of the proletariat, ordinary people, with absolute seriousness.

In the same way, James Cone's theological training left him unprepared for the social revolutions of the 1960s. Cone awakened to the shortcomings of his training after he earned his PhD at Northwestern University.

If Tillich's early theological training left him ill prepared to formulate a constructive theology of cultural embeddedness, then what person or event enabled him to break out of his theological lethargy and apply his learning to construct his proposal for a radically new interpretation of modern theology as a theology of culture? Tillich's use of Marxism enabled him to transcend his political innocence and appropriate the theological training he learned in seminary. Tillich's use of Marx allowed him to apply Schelling to his sociopolitical cultural setting, rescued his theological method from the Kierkegaard-Barth tradition, and placed him squarely within the Schleiermacher-Troeltsch tradition, allowing him to take his stand firmly along the boundary between theological liberalism and dialectical conservatism. Here is how.

James Luther Adams shows just how important Marx's thought was in the construction of his theology of culture.[17] Adams claims that, for Tillich, existential philosophy was just as important as theology in the construction of his project. Adams held that Tillich distinguished between two traditions of existentialism, one which stemmed from Kierkegaard and proceeded to Heidegger, Sartre, Bultmann, and even Barth. Adams believed Tillich would name Schelling as the originator of this tradition, identifying his own affinities with this line. Tillich, however, saw himself related to a second tradition, a prophetic philosophical line that came from Marx and Nietzsche but stretched back to the prophets of the Old Testament, and included religious as well as anti-religious personalities . In an article entitled, "Ideen zur Geisteslage der Gegenwart," Tillich relates himself to the second philosophic tradition.[18]

In choosing what I have named the "Marx-Schelling" tradition over the "Kierkegaard-Heidegger" tradition, Tillich wedded Marx and Schelling not just to unite cultural theology with contextual theology, but because Tillich believed that the notion of the cultural embeddedness of Christianity within culture must be placed side by side with the notion of the sociopolitical transformation of culture. Tillich, like Cone half a century later, shared with persons within the ivory tower of academia, the Kant Society, what constructive

[17] James Luther Adams, introduction to *Political Expectation*, by Paul Tillich (New York: Harper & Row, 1971), ix.

[18] Adams, x.

theology might look like for ordinary, everyday people who lived beyond those ivory towers—the proletariat. Tillich, like the later Cone, sought to theologize to both the church and the academy. He submitted his constructive proposal for cultural embeddedness to both religion as well as culture.

While Tillich's 1919 essay "On the Idea of a Theology of Culture" forms the heart of this presentation, ironically, the problem Tillich faced then is not as clearly explained in, "On the Idea," as it is in chapter four of his seminal text, *The Protestant Era*.

Caught between "orthodox-exclusive" and "secular-rejective" approaches to the cultural movement to reconstruct society, Tillich rejected both and formulated a different theological approach to rebuilding German society that would include both religious conservatives and secular radicals. Tillich formulated this religiously inclusive approach because, as he mentioned in his words quoted above, he had spiritual ties with both sides. He explains it eloquently in volume three of his *Systematic Theology*: "Since a split between a faith unacceptable to culture and a culture unacceptable to faith was not possible for me, the only alternative was to attempt to interpret the symbols of faith through the expressions of our own culture."[19]

It seems that, for Tillich, cultural embeddedness has one goal: the transformation of culture. And if the transformation of culture is culturally embedded as theology's most important project, then for Tillich, and Cone some fifty years later, cultural transformation is of ultimate concern because the Proletariat—the domain of the oppressed—becomes the theatre for the contemporary revelation of God. When the church "loses its mind" (as my theological advisor, Stephen G. Ray once said) and closes the mouths of its prophets within its walls, it is then that God raises up prophets for the church who don't even belong to the church, to attack and free the church from the grip of a theology that identifies God with bourgeois society—the most wealthy and powerful persons within culture that belong to the church!

New Horizons in the Theology of Tillich and Cone

A careful analysis of Tillich's notion of cultural embeddedness leads us to the heart of this paper. Tillich has shown how he seemed to be the only theologian at the dawn of the twentieth century who was willing and able to wed theology and philosophy, Christianity and cultural movements for social change, and cultural embeddedness and the notion of cultural transformation for the sake of the poor and the downtrodden. In the latter part of the twentieth century, only one theologian attempted to culturally embed Christianity and to wed it

[19] Paul Tillich, *Systematic Theology*, vol. 3 (Chicago: University of Chicago Press, 1963), 5.

with the notion of cultural transformation: James Cone. When Cone's black theology is placed in dialogue with Tillich's cultural theology, then the magnitude of Cone's theological achievement can be seen. Most importantly, we see how, theologically, both theologians developed the same theological project; they merely started from opposite sides of the theological spectrum—Tillich from the cultural theology side and Cone from the contextual side. When Tillich's cultural project is placed side-by-side with Cone's project, the contours of Cone's project match Tillich's at almost every historical turn. His black liberation theology was a contextual theological project that wedded North American Protestant Christianity with the freedom movement of the 1960s—the Civil Rights Movement.

For Tillich, it was Marx and Nietzsche's voice that shook him out of his theological lethargy during the war and the start of the revolution. For Cone, it was Martin King and Malcolm X's voice, and Malcolm's devastating critique of North American Christianity, that shook Cone from his theological complacency and forced him to an unprecedented theological conclusion: "Christianity...is Black Power."[20] It was an unprecedented theological move that correlated Malcolm X and Martin King, and North American Protestant Christianity with the Freedom Movement—the Civil Rights and Black Power movements of the 1960s. This was the genius of Cone's first book, a theological masterwork entitled *Black Theology and Black Power*. The stunning theological irony at the heart of the book was how, when Cone wedded Martin King and Malcolm X, he was often severely criticized of "reverse racism." However, Cone had simply done the same thing Tillich had done half a century earlier; Cone correlated Christianity with the Freedom Movement. Black Theology and Black Power is Cone's plea for the cultural embeddedness of Christianity. Most importantly, Cone's work was the first attempt since Tillich to wed cultural theology to contextual theology for the sake of the poor and oppressed.

In order to correlate Christianity with the Civil Rights and Black Power movements, Cone had to revise his theological method. His methodological revision called for the ultimate rejection of the "Kierkegaard-Barth" tradition, the very method Cone had been trained in, and forced him to embrace the "Schleiermacher-Troeltsch" tradition, just as Tillich had done at the dawn of the twentieth century. Cone's next book, *A Black Theology of Liberation*, reveals why, even though Cone is unaware of it, his theological project had reached critical mass; in order to construct a black theology of liberation, Cone would

[20] James Cone, *Black Theology and Black Power* (Maryknoll: Orbis Book, 1969), 3.

have to break with Kierkegaard and Barth and embrace Schleiermacher and Troeltsch by revising his theological method.

In *A Black Theology of Liberation*, Cone reveals his theological method of correlation. Cone borrows Tillich's method of correlation when he weds Malcolm and Martin and theology with the Civil Rights Movement. It is here that Cone revises his method, breaking with the Kierkegaard-Barth tradition.[21] Cone revised his theological method, moving to Schleiermacher-Troeltsch, the theological tradition to which Tillich belonged. Cone united theology and the Civil Rights Movement because, "Black people need to see some correlations between divine salvation and black culture."[22] The sheer, unmitigated suffering of the poor made black life a battlefield, the place where the threat and reality of not being was forever in play. For Cone, only a divine "answer" could address the existential "question" of oppression, suffering, and death. Only "divine salvation" could offer a meaningful answer to the plight of oppressed persons in black culture. A kerygmatic theological method that divorced theology from culture was inimical to Cone's theological project. His project, like Tillich's, demanded the cultural embeddedness of Christianity, a Christian theology that was linked to culture. This is the reason Cone revised his theological method.

For African Americans like me, Tillich's theology can enrich black theology in at least three ways.

First, the correlation of Cone and Tillich will enable black theology to revise its notion of theodicy. This is where black theology's method breaks down. The problem is clearly expressed in William R. Jones' classic, entitled, *Is God a White Racist?*.[23] Jones writes that problems with black theology's method arise when, addressing the notion of theodicy, one comes face to face with the issue of divine racism. Jones states: "The problem of theodicy is further underscored when we consider ... that every alleged act of God's benevolence can easily be interpreted as an instance of his malevolence."[24] Jones is keenly aware that the central affirmation of black theology—that the God of Jesus Christ is a Liberator—can be interpreted malevolently; God might *not* be a Liberator, in fact, God might be a divine racist! Black theology's method

---

[21] James Cone, *Black Theology and Black Power* (Maryknoll, NY: Orbis Book, 1969), P.3

[22] Cone, *A Black Theology of Liberation*, 25.

[23] William R. Jones, *Is God A White Racist? A Preamble to Black Theology* (Boston: Beacon Press, 1973).

[24] Jones, xxv.

breaks down because, although using Tillich's analogy, the criteria of the "existential question" regarding black life—to "be or not be be,"—is present, the "Revelatory Answer" regarding divine salvation is nonexistent because, despite black suffering, there is no point in history where that suffering is addressed by God. As such, a correlation between God and black suffering is impossible to achieve and, for lack of a genuine theological method, black theology implodes, collapsing from within.

Ironically, it is Tillich's pre-war dissertations that can transform black theology's preoccupation with theodicy. Cone scholars, using Tillich's first dissertation, *The Construction of the History of Religion in Schelling's Positive Philosophy*, can use the political implications of Tillich's Schelling studies to revise theodicy. Most importantly, black theology can use the most important work that undergirds Tillich's first dissertation, Schelling's *On Human Freedom*. Schelling's theodicy project is a critical lens that Black liberation theologians can use to revise theodicy. It makes freedom and liberation the key paradigm for theology and the notion of struggle (within the God of Jesus Christ) as the source and wellspring of divine life as well as the foundation, ground, and aim of all that is created and oppressed. The reconciliation of this crisis, tension, or struggle within the Triune God would be the ground, aim, and goal of creation's new future, a future created by an eternally free and liberated God who has created an eternally free and liberated future.

Second, wedding Tillich and Cone enables black theology to construct a liberation theology that takes the plight of the oppressed seriously. By focusing on Tillich's first dissertation as well as his constructive theological statement, "On the Idea of a Theology of Culture," black theology can not just break with the Kierkegaard-Heidegger tradition, it can embrace the Schelling-Marx philosophical tradition, appropriating Marx and Schelling to construct a philosophically sophisticated black theology of process.

Tillich's dissertations provide the theological lens black theologians need to correlate philosophy and theology in the twenty-first century. Black theologians can wed Schelling and Marx, as Tillich did, to construct a black theology that addresses the poor and oppressed. Tillich's dissertations and programmatic constructive statements of 1919 lay the groundwork for a metaphysical, process black theology that explores the *history* of the oppressed. When Cone scholars appropriate the political implications of Tillich's first dissertation, in tandem with Schelling's works, *On Human Freedom* and *Ages of the World*, they can, once again, make the case for Cone's revelatory insight about how historical context and modern history become the contemporary theater in which the liberation struggle for freedom and human dignity takes center stage. God struggles to free God's self from the chaotic abyss to create and "be" for the world. And because God is eternally free from chaos, oppression, and darkness, oppressed humanity, through Christ, can also extricate itself from the abyss of colonialism, slavery, and oppression to become free for God *within* the world. History, for the Cone scholar, becomes the theatre where both divinity and humanity extricate themselves from hell or abyss of oppression to become free for one another! The union of Tillich and Cone produces a theology that is at once anthropological and metaphysical. The divine struggles *for* change and humanity's struggles *to* change, and the notion of cultural embeddedness, may now be placed side by side in the twenty-first century.

Finally, correlating Tillich and Cone in a twenty-first century black theology will allow black theologians to revisit the notion of the Trinity, constructing a triune metaphysics that provides a philosophical foundation for contextual theology, something James Cone never achieved. By embracing Tillich's dissertations as well as his 1919 *Kulturvortrag*, twenty-first century Cone scholars can use the Marx-Schelling philosophical tradition to construct a triune, process philosophy of freedom that focuses on the mutual movement of humanity and divinity from chaos to communion, and from communion to community. The threefold movement from God to humanity and into community not only places black theology on a firm philosophical foundation, it aids in the creation of a phenomenology of social change. A phenomenology of social change with ties to prophetic, North American Protestantism is needed because it reveals the third most important truth about the notion of cultural embeddedness in Tillich and Cone. A social phenomenology with theological insights can enable theology and the church to redefine the various movements for justice, dignity, freedom, and democracy occurring within contemporary secular culture. The freedom movement becomes the theological blueprint for the construction of a new humanity, and the "ultimate concern" regarding cultural transformation, for twenty-first century scholars of Tillich and Cone demand the reformation of the church and the transformation of society.

TILLICH & POLITICS

The "Boundary" in Paul Tillich's Sociopolitical Thought

Matthew Lon Weaver

In 1930, Paul Tillich declared: "The boundary is the most fruitful place for [gaining] knowledge."[1] Tillich later began the autobiography that initially introduced him to the English-speaking world with an explanation of that statement: "When I was asked to give an account of the way my ideas have developed from my life, I thought that the concept of the boundary might be the fitting symbol for the whole of my personal and intellectual development," a place "fruitful for thought" but "dangerous in life."[2] After describing twelve boundaries that characterized his life and work up to that time (1936), Tillich closed with the observation that one "who stands on many boundaries experiences the unrest, insecurity and inner limitation of existence ...[and] the impossibility of attaining serenity, security and perfection," culminating in the Eternal, that which limits all of finite reality, before which "even the very center of our being is only a boundary and our highest level of accomplishment is fragmentary."[3] The "boundary" is a theological metaphor expressing humility, implying pessimism, and conveying openness.

The boundary idea is evident in a range of cross-disciplinary partnerships including social and political commitments in both his German and American periods. In Germany, he expressed this through his advocacy of revolution against the empire following World War I and a range of social and political treatises on socialism, religion and culture, Christianity and socialism, Protestant critique of culture, philosophy of history, and philosophy of power. In the United States, he was active in projects seeking the well-being of European expatriates and immigrants with the rise of Nazism and war, articles about religion's connection to dictatorship and democracy, reflections on international government, radio speeches, advocacy for a just peace and a resurrected Germany following the war, and intermittent projects directed at a range of causes during the subsequent cold war period.

---

[1] Paul Tillich, *Religiöse Verwirklichung* (Berlin: Furche-Verlag, 1930), 11. All German translations mine.

[2] Paul Tillich, *On the Boundary: An Autobiographical Sketch* (New York: Charles Scribner's Sons, 1966), 13.

[3] Tillich, 97, 98.

The boundary idea is present in two extensive writings from the American period: his fragment on international organization, "Religion and World Politics," completed on the brink of World War II; and the first speeches broadcast over the Voice of America, beginning just months after the entry of the United States into the war. Tillich modeled a practice of existence and political analysis on the boundary in the mid-twentieth century that can help us approach issues of political significance in the first half of the twenty-first century.

The Idea of World

In 1939 Tillich wrote the fragment, "Religion and World Politics." This work was the fruit of Tillich's repugnance toward nationalism. The key message of the book was that religion "demands that world politics be *world*-politics;" therefore, any "national politics should turn itself into the instrument of world politics because the political goal is not 'nation' but, rather, 'world'."[4] He organized the book in three sections. Part one concerned basic problems in the relationship of religion to politics. Part two concerned the dynamics at work in that relationship. Part three concerned world politics and the prophetic spirit.[5]

Tillich defined politics as the process of "organizing humanity's collective life" and world politics as the organization of "the collective life of humankind as a whole."[6] He observed this distinction in the history of religion and culture. In ancient Greece and Rome, he saw "the depoliticization of general consciousness."[7] Similarly, Pauline Christianity "devalued political citizenship in favor of citizenship in the Kingdom of Heaven," echoed later in Luther's writings where government had a "negative police function, not creative formation."[8] In Gregory VII and Innocence III, Tillich saw "the consciousness of the Christian church as representing the universal unity of the kingdom of God within history," rooted in the prophetic tradition, with imperialistic missions by nations as forerunners to a true, universal theocracy.[9] The subsequent collapse of secular and papal imperialisms of the Middle Ages led to an "anti-theocratic and anti-world-political meaning of politics" and

---

[4] Paul Tillich, "Religion und Weltpolitik," 1939, in *Die Religiöse Substanz der Kultur: Schriften zur Theologie der Kultur*, in *Gesammelte Werke*, vol. 9, ed. Renate Albrecht: 139-204 (Stuttgart: Evangelisches Verlagswerk, 1967), 139.

[5] Tillich, 139-49.

[6] Tillich, 140.

[7] Tillich, 140-41.

[8] Tillich, 141.

[9] Tillich, 141, 142.

the rise of city-states.[10] Religion became tolerated or bureaucratized according to the needs of governments. Their primary goal was an imperialistic, bourgeois, economic-political one, not a religious one. The religious impulse became an individualistic "eternal peace" rather than a world-forming one. Nonetheless, Tillich saw the world-political element continuing in proletarian, humanistic, pacifistic, world-government discussions.[11]

Tillich began the discussion of "world" with the idea of "world-having". He argued that this precedes the concept of "world." While crediting Heidegger for the basic idea, he criticized his nationalistic, pagan development of it. To "have world" means to define oneself as both separate from and part of a larger entity. One can stand apart from both the comprehensive unity of reality and one's individual self. This is different from merely living in an environment, a state of being in which one cannot stand apart from the self and the whole.[12]

"World-having" means three things. First, one "belongs to an all-inclusive unity." One is not merely a part of the world. A nationalist, for example, does not "have world."[13] "World-having" means that one exists within a world-self-correlation. Tillich believed that "the denial of world-having universality denies the self as self and, with it, the presupposition of humanity possessing value. It is the world-self-correlation on which the human as human rests."[14] Second, "world-having" means belonging to an integrated structure. This structure "sets self and world in one another and with one another," a structure without which both would cease to be.[15] Consequently, "the human is negated when the world-political is negated."[16] Third, "world-having" means to possess infinitude. This is the capacity to transcend the given and to conceptualize infinite possibilities in each moment. Tillich argued that this is unique to healthy members of the human species. The opposite of infinitude is fixated narrowness, unwilling or incapable of transcending.[17] Tillich drew out the implications of "world-having" for different concepts of world, beginning with the technical concept of world.

With Heidegger, Tillich saw the technical world concept as the most primal. It is the "tool-having quality of the world" that embodies infinitude's

[10] Tillich, 142-43.
[11] Tillich, 144, 145.
[12] Tillich, 145.
[13] Tillich, 145-46.
[14] Tillich, 146.
[15] Tillich, 146, 147.
[16] Tillich, 147.
[17] Tillich, 147, 148.

transcendent capacity for free creation.[18] Freedom for creation develops the courage required for an awareness of being in the world. While Nietzsche called humanity "the most courageous *animal*," overlooking the free creativity that distinguishes human beings from animals, Tillich called humanity "the most courageous *being*," able to mature into "world political thinking."[19] The idea of a technical world is the ability to create a shelter from the overwhelming expanse of world. There, one gains courage to embrace or reenter world. This parallels the self-world-correlation.

A physical house symbolized the human possibility of making "world" the house of humanity, that adapts to "the needs and ends of human existence, to include the enemy, the one standing in opposition, into the being-sphere of the self, to actually bridge the distance between world and self, a distance which is structurally infinite."[20] The house represents the finite consequences of creative action. It is never a final stopping point that enslaves humanity, but a starting point that empowers humanity's freedom. Similarly, the idea of a technical world contains both infinite possibility and risk of finite fixation.[21] The idea of progress might be innate to the technical world, but Tillich claimed that questions of meaning go beyond technological progress. In philosophy and art, there is "a freer grasp of meaning in the interplay of world and self," expressing transcendent infinitude. There, progress is a subordinate tool.[22] In moral thought, to assume the progressive, ethical "formation" of a human being is to dehumanize them and turn them into tools. Such an assumption severs them from the world-having infinitude of freedom and denies humanity's identity, combining freedom and fate. Finally, in both politics and religion, "the grasp and realization of infinite meaning and not a means-end-relationship" puts these well beyond the reach of progress.[23]

Tillich wrote that technical capacity implies having theoretical capacity. The technical world implies theoretical world. One shapes material one understands. The theoretical world concept possesses three characteristics that are consistent with "world-having." It understands the world as a unity; has a structure that is both scientific and ontological (the former dealing with the structure of beings, the latter asking what it means to be in the first place); and possesses infinitude. The theoretical world corrects the temptation to focus on the finite quality of the physical world by seeing "within the process of

---

[18] Tillich, 149.

[19] Tillich, 149-50. My emphasis.

[20] Tillich, 150.

[21] Tillich, 150.

[22] Tillich, 150-52.

[23] Tillich, 152-54.

knowledge itself the infinitude of the question, the pressure to transcend every achieved outcome."[24]

Political ideology arises out of the failure of the theoretical world concept to transcend the "being-structure" of specific individuals or groups in order to reach the world-structure when building the theoretical world. Despite the efforts of philosophers throughout time to reach objectivity, Tillich asserted that reality is "always a subject-object structure."[25] The self is irremovable from the theoretical process. The world-self-correlation remains in the political situation. Tillich saw the extremes within the theoretical world that crushed the correlation. In logical positivism, the objective self overwhelms the subjective self. In Nazism, subjectivity destroys objectivity. In objectivity, the self disappears. In subjectivity, the objective limits freedom exercised in the face of fate. The necessity of decision-making "compels the knowing self to reflect on itself, to continuously foster the ideology-suspicion toward itself and to place decision into the relationship of analysis of the concrete situation, in which a spiritual-intellectual creation shall emerge."[26]

Both the technical and theoretical world concepts were threats to the self-world correlation. The self's expansion into the world (technology) too easily blended with the self's hiding from the world (theory). A glimmer of the self's restraint exists in the technical world concept through the requirement that it function within the world's given structure. A spark of the self's power over against world remains in the theoretical concept through the self's perpetual questioning, manifesting its infinitude. For Tillich, it is the moral element in a human being that is essential to prevent the blending of self and world, preserving the self-world-correlation that enables world-having to exist.[27]

The moral dimension is primarily an expression of limit in which the individual self experiences another individual self. "The other self demands to be acknowledged as such, namely as the bearer of a self-world relation," and therefore it is there "in the moment when one encounters another as another, when he appears to the 'I' as a 'you,' and … circumscribes the human claim, 'I.'"[28] This maintains the integrity of the self, refusing to be a means to a technological end while avoiding being reduced to a general self that is the object of theorizing.[29]

---

[24] Tillich, 154-56.
[25] Tillich, 156.
[26] Tillich, 156-58.
[27] Tillich, 159-60.
[28] Tillich, 160.
[29] Tillich, 161.

Tillich wrote that "The discovery of the 'you,' or the experience of the boundary of the self, drawn by the other self, has unconditional character," the boundary being the unconditional demand for justice.[30] Ongoing decision-making forms the fabric of social humanity and leads to the moral world and systems of justice, that is, "the acknowledgement of the encountering self as self and, in that, as equal." Furthermore, the boundary situation—as the locus of justice-bearing encounters of the self and world—"can only occur generally when freedom is realized."[31] In addition to equality and freedom, justice requires the "world-having" self's fulfillment or *eudaimonia.* A risk peculiar to the technical world concept is that the self-as-part-of-world is unresponsive to the demands of the self-set-against-world. Immorality results. A risk peculiar to the theoretical world concept is that the self-set-against-world never enters world. Dehumanization occurs. In the moral world concept, justice enables each human being to unite itself as *part* of the world with itself as *set against* the world.[32]

A fourth world idea is required to bring the other three non-religious concepts together to support "world-having:" the political world concept. It contains both the power to be and the ethical limits to being (justice). Power is expressed in both the ability to exist in relationships and the concrete expression of justice through the combination of "custom, right/authority, and ethos."[33] Tillich understood the political metaphor of the Kingdom of God to imply the central importance of the political world concept. By including elements of the other world concepts, it neither shattered the world-self-correlation (as in the technical and theoretical world concepts) nor brought an inadequate power of being to "world-having" (as in the ethical world concept). The political concept assumes that each self has a power of being. This is the self's potential to exist, both in relation to the world and within itself. This gives it "the infinitude and inexhaustibility of being, the infinitude of resistance against annihilation."[34] According to Tillich, beliefs in an afterlife, the immortality of the soul, and the resurrection symbolize the self's power "to offer resistance against every disintegrating force, to actualize itself unconditionally."[35]

Tillich argued that political community drew on the powers of self and world but required "a third form of power," through which the existing self

[30] Tillich, 161, 162.
[31] Tillich, 163-64.
[32] Tillich, 164-66.
[33] Tillich, 166-67.
[34] Tillich, 168-69.
[35] Tillich, 169.

"realizes itself as part of the world" through interaction with other parts of existence. Individuals become part of a system that has "the ability to force a manner of conduct."[36] Reduced to a mechanical process of endless interchanges, this system could lose the ethical concept of world. Thus, justice is a crucial part of these interactions. Tillich wrote: "The force which the political community exercises operates 'ethically' when it is acknowledged as [a] just force....If there were then only force, it would come to a struggle of natural forces, not to a struggle over justice. If there were only justice, then there would be no history."[37] For him, outcomes trumped forms of government, whether they were democracies or dictatorships. What mattered was a government's success in bringing about justice: the more demands for justice it answered affirmatively, the more just its power was.[38] The cognitive infinitude from the theoretical-world concept can produce the principles required "for [political] systems to make good on the demand for justice without toppling over into injustice as a result of powerlessness."[39]

The weakness of political power is that it is built on particularity: a particular communal "self." This is a barrier to "world-having." The self (even if collective) breaks the self-world correlation, giving "unconditional character to the particular... [and] denying any possible community with [a] superior power shared by sovereign states. With that, it destroys the political and the ethical world and, thus, world in general."[40] Tillich's experience in World War I and under Nazism undoubtedly informed his thought here. The behavior of sovereign nations was a dangerous threat to the world. Such situations questioned "the presuppositions of human being and world-having as such."[41] Tillich argued that the "salvation of the political world-concept and, with that, of world in general is dependent upon the conquest of sovereignty."[42] He called for "world" to become political reality, rejecting both the imperialist model and the partial-sovereignty model of the League of Nations. Instead, he proposed "the erosion of individual state sovereignty from within through the formation of overlapping communities as future bearers of a united world-power. It is the horizontal solution in contrast to the vertical one of imperialism and the ineffectual mixed one of the League."[43] He proposed constructing

[36] Tillich, 168, 170.
[37] Tillich, 170-71.
[38] Tillich, 171-72.
[39] Tillich, 173.
[40] Tillich, 173.
[41] Tillich, 173-74.
[42] Tillich, 174.
[43] Tillich, 174-75.

the political world, first, on direct encounters of neighbors; next, on "indirect encounter, memory and anticipation, past and future of the [direct] encounter;" and, finally, on a commitment to justice that arises to create a legal system answering the countless claims for justice posed by selves.[44] Rigidly hierarchical societies would undermine this process, thus, undermining universal world-having and preventing the emergence of justice.[45]

Tillich believed the political is part of personhood. Deference to the technical world concept comes at the cost of self—"the lower limit of the political." Deference to the theoretical world concept embraces self and transcendence, but leads to a dehumanized "angel-world."[46] Tillich insisted that "the theoretical world itself is dependent on the completing-itself-within-the-political structure of world-having."[47] In the end, Tillich described his treatment of the non-religious concepts of world and "world-having" as a "permanent square [containing] the perimeter of the ideas" expressive of world-having.[48] Tillich's understanding of world politics establishes the context for his views on religion's relation to "world-having."

Religion and the World

Tillich argued that it was necessary to go beyond the self-world-correlation to seek the source of correlation itself, in order to reveal how this source relates to being human. He sought "the place where the religious breaks into the human, the boundary of the self-world-correlation which points to a *beyond the boundary* [my emphasis]." The source of world and self is something beyond both, even as it is the "ground" of both. This source is beyond their control. It is "the religious concept of revelation."[49] The religious "qualifies the other world concepts but adds nothing new." First, the religious that is "beyond world and self" created the self-world-correlation. Second, the self-world-correlation exists in reality in a "rebellious/fallen" condition in ways contrary to the intent of the religious that is "beyond world and self."[50] He saw the fallenness of world and self as both universal and inevitable. It was universal in its independence of the decisions of individuals and inevitable as a consequence of freedom and fate.

[44] Tillich, 175.
[45] Tillich, 176.
[46] Tillich, 176-77.
[47] Tillich, 177.
[48] Tillich, 177.
[49] Tillich, 178-79.
[50] Tillich, 180-81.

Tillich affirmed the technical world's expansion of knowledge as "progress" yet also affirmed religion's "rejection of progress as hubris." While humanity cannot save itself, religion establishes the "supra-worldly unity of everything existing."[51] The theoretical objectifies things, while the mythical sees things not "in their power to be, but rather in their 'primordial-state,' their standing in the power of the 'beyond self and world.'"[52] The theoretical world can only understand the truth of this revelatory logos "metaphorically and fragmentarily," which would be sufficient to "preserve the theoretical world from destruction."[53] The individual is "grasped as the locus of truth."

Tillich believed the doctrine of the Kingdom of God bridged the gap between the world-self-correlation and the beyond-self-and-world. As political symbol (*Kingdom* of God), "it confirms the elements available in" the world's political phenomena. As religious symbol (Kingdom *of God*), individualization and separation are dissolved into the "supra-worldly unity of love." The "supra-worldly is not only the transcendence, but also the fulfillment, of world." This is the exclusive domain and the radical nature of prophetic religion. "It is radical because it goes to the root of every ideology, the tragic estrangement of the individual self from the world and, with that, its separation from the beyond self and world."[54] In Tillich's thought, the prophetic is suspicious of any individual or political ideology. In the end, "the religious spirit alone is capable of resolving ideologies, individual and political, without driving into skepticism and inaction."[55]

Tillich wrote on the boundary between the land of his birth and the land that saved him and his family, a period between national identities and perhaps the most existentially charged period of his disdain for national sovereignty. It makes sense that Tillich would give serious thought to the structure of reality that could overcome the significant weaknesses of the nation-state. He embraced the ancient Greek truth that to be human is to be political. He knew the history of Christianity's debate over the relationship of religion to politics as the ongoing cycle of the church between escape from the political and embrace of the political. He appreciated the impact of the technological mindset, always aware of its risks of self-satisfaction in the face of our creations and of a superficial ignorance avoidance of questions about their meaning. He acknowledged humanity's significant cognitive capacity for understanding reality, our continuous ability to conceptualize and to question, to

[51] Tillich, 184-85.

[52] Tillich, 186-87.

[53] Tillich, 189.

[54] Tillich, 191.

[55] Tillich, 192.

criticize the past and conceive the new. He identified the qualities of infinitude and dynamism and invited us to engage the totality of existence.

The moral realm was the element that measured the achievements of theory and technology by the standard of justice, and that guided humanity to navigate the boundaries of being against being. In the end, the religious dimension provides the meaning-giving depth of reality. It supplies the visionary, prophetic conscience and critique of the political process. It rightly values the strengths and weaknesses of all other conceptions of world, insisting on providing the incessant, mantric *om* of justice.

The Voice of America

Tillich began to write speeches for the Voice of America in 1942, about two years after he became a citizen of the United States.[56] He called his German listeners to muster courage to use the freedom innate to their humanity to resist Nazism, facing the consequences of this resistance and taking responsibility for Germany's fate. He expressed his deep concern about the presence of terror within German society and its descent into desperation. As remedy for this, he encouraged Germans to adopt a longer-term view on their situation, that is, to face the short-term suffering of confronting Nazism as the basis for building a just society that could endure long into the future. He called his listeners to take actions that challenged the indignities and dehumanizing consequences of Nazi policy. This meant rejecting hatred and forging paths that constantly affirmed the inestimable depth of human dignity and pursued a political life free of idolatrous deference to leadership. This involved a strategy of fully embracing creative action guided by justice, fully embracing truth in its most profound and liberating dimensions, rejecting the falsehoods of propaganda, and conducting science in a meaning-filled way. He described what it meant to live on the boundary between a new homeland and the terror state of Nazi Germany. His two themes were *orientation* and *action*.

---

[56] Tillich wrote weekly speeches for the Voice of America from late March 1942 through early May 1944. The discussion here focuses on the 1942 speeches. There are three sources for the speeches by Tillich cited here: (1) *An meine deutschen Freunde: Die politischen Reden Paul Tillichs während des Zweiten Weltkriegs über die Stimme Amerikas, Ergänzungs- und Nachlassbände zu den Gesammelten Werken von Paul Tillich Band III* (Stuttgart: Evangelisches Verlagswerk, 1973), hereafter cited as EW III; (2) *Against the Third Reich*, trans., Matthew Lon Weaver (Louisville: Westminster John Knox Press, 1998), hereafter cited as *ATR*; and the (3) Paul Tillich Archive at Harvard Divinity School, hereafter cited as *PTAH*. The citations for the speeches will begin with VOA followed by the details of the specific sources.

Tillich addressed three general areas—freedom, fear, and future—to orient people in the face of a brutal terror state. He saw humanity as a combination of freedom and fate. Tillich argued that fate shapes culture in concrete ways: "On the battlefields, in the military hospitals, in the cellars of smashed houses, through the reading of death reports from the front into the homeland and from the homeland to the front, under the hate-filled glances of the conquered peoples, in the shortage of everything, ...in the hopeless reflections about the end, ...in all of this the educator is operating whose name is fate."[57] He saw a connection between a nation's character and its fate, and observed that it takes courage to face one's fate. Resistance to Nazism—the exercise of freedom—could change a nation's fate.[58]

Unfortunately, German idealists of the late eighteenth and early nineteenth centuries tended to limit their understanding of freedom to personal rather than political freedom, planting the seeds of hatred.[59] In contrast, Tillich pointed to the Atlantic Charter's commitment to a "freedom from fear for all nations." Economic security and freedom were foundational for democracy. True international community was based on free and creative unity rather than Nazism's false, enslaving, and destructive "unity."[60] Nazism brought deep national guilt. Among those who maintained their humanity, guilt led to despair, then to despairing courage...ending in collapse, yet awakening the fear of losing their soul. Yet for some it gave rise to the courage to resist. Tillich observed the fear of lost meaning present in Germany which he defined as "the fear of losing oneself and one's divinely-determined destiny... [and] one's own eternal meaning in life."[61] Tillich exhorted his audience to face despair with courage.

Reflecting on the future with his listeners, Tillich warned that Nazism meant a future of "evil and destruction."[62] The fight against Nazism meant "the creative rebirth of Germany and Europe," cured of its "all-destroying

---

[57] VOA #6, 5/1942, *EW III*, 35 & 36; VOA #19, 8/1/1942, *EW III*, 78; VOA #31, 10/27/1942, *EW III*, 123; VOA #31, 10/27/1942, *EW III*, 123-24.

[58] VOA #32, 11/3/1942, *ATR*, 81; VOA #35, 12/42, *ATR*, 86; VOA #19, 8/1/1942, *EW III*, 81; VOA #10, 5-6/1942, *PTAH*, bMS 649/111 (11), 1-2.

[59] VOA #4, 4/20/42, *ATR*, 21; VOA #23, 8/28/42, *ATR*, 54 & 55; VOA #4, 4/20/42, *ATR*, 22; VOA #9, 5-6/1942, *PTAH*, bMS 649/111 (10), 2.

[60] VOA #28, 10/6/42, *ATR*, 69; VOA #28, 10/6/42, *ATR*, 69; VOA #26, 9/1942, *PTAH*, bMS 649/111 (27), 3; VOA #26, 9/1942, *PTAH*, bMS 649/111 (27), 3; VOA #27, 9/29/1942, *EW III*, 106.

[61] VOA #4, 4/20/42, *ATR*, 24; VOA #12, 6/15/1942, *EW III*, 48, 50, 52.

[62] VOA #36, 12/8/1942, *ATR*, 93.

sickness."[63] He urged the Allied nations to reject a bad, retributive peace rooted in fear at war's end. Rather, they must seek a postwar internationalism despite the tug of postwar nationalism in various parts of the world.[64] During Advent of 1942, he reminded Germans of the Advent hope of purification: "Nothing is more difficult and more painful than such catastrophes of hope. But, at the same time: nothing is more purifying!"[65] Christianity, democracy, and socialism all maintained hope for humanity as a whole that transcends all limited, exclusionary identities.

The second theme in his Voice of America speeches focused on action. He pointed to four different matters: human dignity, the prophetic spirit, truth, and resistance. Tillich saw Nazism as a descent into utter dehumanization. It was a symptom of a people that had lost a unifying center of meaning. It used hatred as its central tool for eroding human dignity.[66] It confused the unity of a machine with free and creative community. It taught disdain for the other in contrast to Goethe's teaching of reverence for others.[67] It put before the world a fundamental choice: "Shall that which is bestial or that which is divine in humanity triumph?"[68] Tillich's rejection of hatred was not a rejection of passion: "*We do not want to take your passion when we take your hatred*.... But hatred is no great passion, and it can create nothing great: it can only destroy."[69] Germans needed to acknowledge that hatred leads to the idolatry of nationalism. Tillich argued that, in failing to reject Nazism, Germans had surrendered their dignity and their basic human rights.[70] This was tied to justice, including a just, stable economic system and freedom within a democracy. Nazism's arrogant declaration of a superior race denied the Christian notion of the humanity shared by all people.[71] Thus, Tillich called Germany to liberate itself "from the chains of the man-beast... [from] the tyranny of the inhuman within the human being."[72] To do so required the impetus of the prophetic spirit.

---

[63] VOA #34, 11/1942, *PTAH*, bMS 649/112 (4), 4; VOA #36, 12/8/1942, *ATR*, 94.

[64] VOA #15, 7/3/1942, *EW III*, 62; VOA #16, 7/10/1942, *EW III*, 67.

[65] VOA #36, 12/8/1942, *ATR*, 91, 93 & 94.

[66] VOA #25, 9/12/42, *ATR*, 62.

[67] VOA #7a, 5/1942, *ATR*, 30.

[68] VOA #9, 5-6/1942, *PTAH*, bMS 649/111 (10), 3.

[69] VOA #25, 9/12/42, *ATR*, 64.

[70] VOA #26, 9/1942, *PTAH*, bMS 649/111 (27), 3; VOA #7, 5/11/42, *ATR*, 27-28.

[71] VOA #33, 11/1942, *PTAH*, bMS 649/112 (3), 3.

[72] VOA #9, 5-6/1942, *PTAH*, bMS 649/111 (10), 4.

Tillich believed that while national identity held substantial value, nationalist idolatry "ripped to pieces the religious, intellectual, and ethical oneness of the human race ... through a neo-pagan national power-worship" and, consequently, was "a powerful warning to all nations to free themselves from this poison."[73] Ultimately, by rejecting criticism of the state—rooted in the Jewish prophetic tradition—Nazism destroyed the rule of law.[74] Nazism's defiance of justice rejected human dignity at its depth, cloaking its terrorizing injustice beneath a veil of apparent justice. It failed to see that justice "tears apart enslavement beneath will-to-power and hatred and arbitrariness... seeking the universal which is greater than the individual person and the individual nation, that is, the human and divine which overcomes death."[75] Religious traditions, and especially Judaism, are guardians of justice. "God's holiness takes effect in his justice, and no one is more repugnant to him than the one who destroys justice."[76] Legitimate power is creative and life-giving. "Power should protect life by protecting the rights and being which every living thing has."[77]

One of the sources of the Nazi crisis was an existential conflict over truth. German propaganda had a primary role in it. It misrepresented Allied intentions to sow seeds of fear and hatred. It concealed the truth that Nazism was trying to preserve its power by "drawing an entire group of nations to their own destruction."[78] Tillich understood the logic of this. Truth is disruptive and revolutionary: "In a deep sense, every thought and writing and utterance and form must be revolutionary....It must be a bit prophetic, it must condemn and demand, it must give hope....[Otherwise,] it creates a diversion from the truth."[79] It expresses a basic quality of the spirit in its creative openness: "it looks out beyond the limits of life, it is truth which breaks through the chains of propaganda, falsehood and fanaticism."[80] The crisis of truth was also revealed in science and technology. Tillich knew that the scientific community sought to understand the mechanics of reality and technology. What was missing was a concern for the meaning of reality: "[It is] part of the German

---

[73] VOA #17, 7/17/1942, *EW III*, 72; VOA #20, 8/8/1942, *EW III*, 85; VOA #1, 3/31/1942, *ATR*, 14-15; VOA #16, 7/10/1942, *EW III*, 64-65.

[74] VOA #5, 4/27/1942, *EW III*, 33.

[75] VOA #7, 5/11/42, *ATR*, 25; VOA #7, 5/11/42, *ATR*, 26; VOA #2, 4/42, *ATR*, 19-20.

[76] VOA #7, 5/11/42, *ATR*, 27.

[77] VOA #29, 10/13/1942, *ATR*, 73 & 74.

[78] VOA #30, 10/20/1942, *ATR*, 76; VOA #18, 7/25/1942, *EW III*, 74-75; VOA #26, 9/1942, *PTAH*, bMS 649/111 (27), 3-4; VOA #12, 6/15/1942, *EW III*, 49-50.

[79] VOA #24, 9/4/42, *ATR*, 58-59.

[80] VOA #2, 4/42, *ATR*, 19.

tragedy that scientists and engineers could identify and control nature, to be sure, but never asked: to what end? For whom? What happens to the human being who is doing all of this?...[Thus,] when the hour had come, it became neutral and fell, to the power of destruction as welcome tools in its hand."[81] For Tillich's audience, facing the painful truth was key to Germany's salvation: "National Socialism must be disclosed in its wickedness, broken in its will, hindered in its conquest, and conquered in its power."[82] In the end, to reject propaganda and embrace truth required a deep inner strength that he sensed was growing in Germany.[83]

The Voice of Tillich Today

In the long run, the power-idolatry of any oppressive regime is no match for justice.[84] Tillich claimed that "the prophetic task of the church" was to bring a message of just self-restraint in the face of the vengeful temptations open to the victorious Allied nations.[85] He called US Vice President Henry Wallace's summons to pursue a just, revolutionary restructuring of the social order of the world the voice of the prophetic spirit.[86] This struggle requires that we face the truth—and act on the truth—with courage.

The central function of prophetic critique is significant. Tillich described the centrality of this function as "the power of criticizing and transforming each of Christianity's historical manifestations."[87] This is part of theology's ongoing task of mediation: "mediation between the eternal criterion of truth as it is manifest in the picture of Jesus as the Christ and the changing experiences of individuals and groups, their varying questions and their categories of perceiving reality."[88] The mediation process, what Tillich refers to as the process of correlation, occurs on the boundary.

---

[81] VOA #24, 9/4/42, *ATR*, 58 & 59.

[82] VOA #5, 4/27/1942, *EW III*, 30, 31; VOA #20, 8/8/1942, *EW III*, 83; VOA #29, 10/13/1942, *ATR*, 71 & 72; VOA #25, 9/12/42, *ATR*, 64.

[83] VOA #10, 5-6/1942, *PTAH*, bMS 649/111 (11), 4.

[84] VOA #29, 10/13/1942, *ATR*, 72-73.

[85] VOA #15, 7/3/1942, *EW III*, 63-64.

[86] VOA #15, 7/3/1942, *EW III*, 63-64.

[87] Paul Tillich, "Author's Introduction," in *The Protestant Era* (Chicago: University of Chicago Press, 1948), xxii.

[88] Tillich, xiii. The mediation process is what Tillich refers to as the process of correlation, most importantly in the *Systematic Theology*: it is his rendering of the classic dialectic approach to truth-seeking.

In 1939, it was mediation from the boundary perspective that led Tillich to develop his understanding of a world in which the technological, theoretical, moral, and political capacities of human beings could become rooted in humanity's religious dimension, chiefly through the prophetic spirit. His approach had continuing relevance as experiments in international organization were renewed following World War II, from the establishment of the United Nations in 1948 and the European Union in 1992. The ongoing difficulty of such efforts is manifest in the rise of Brexit in the United Kingdom, the revival of nationalisms across the world, and the tension between Trumpian nationalism and multicultural sentiments in the United States. Tillich claimed that "the prophetic task of the church" was to bring a message of just self-restraint in the face of the vengeful temptations open to the victorious Allied nations.[89]

In 1942 and the subsequent years of their writing, this boundary of mediation enabled Tillich to exhort his German audience to embrace the prophetic path of resistance to the terror of Nazi rule, facing the terrible truths about Nazi rule, indicting Nazism for its murderously dehumanizing policies, and defying its power by proceeding along paths that embraced and defended the dignity of all humanity. Tillich targeted its Machiavellian, *Realpolitik* approach to governance. His thoughts became a media project that competed with the propaganda overseen by the Nazi Minister Josef Goebbels. The seduction of power, and its consequence for ordinary people, remains in our current reality. Moreover, the use of communication media as an instrument of political discourse has grown to an unimaginable degree. Presently, social media has become a rhetorical free-for-all that is extremely difficult to manage. It competes with a plethora of strategies of civil discourse from the local to international levels. The continuing relevance of Tillich's work involves both content and media.

Paul Tillich described himself as one who combined an old world and a new world identity. He described his new home city—New York—as "a bridge between the continents;" and his new place of work—Union Theological Seminary—as "the lane on that bridge on which the churches of the world move."[90] Such metaphors speak to the boundary situations in which today's refugees, immigrants, and citizens experience today. Tillich knew that humanity experiences truth in a fragmentary way, that idolatrous insularity would remain tempting, and that the suspicion of ideology would remain necessary for the future. Tillich's new home offered opportunities for creative

[89] VOA #15, 7/3/1942, *EW III*, 63-64.

[90] Paul Tillich, "Autobiographical Reflections," in *The Theology of Paul Tillich*, eds., Charles W. Kegley and Robert W. Bretall (New York: Macmillan, 1952), 17, 19.

outcomes that can arise from life on the boundary, both theoretically and concretely.

Stanislaw Tillich, the Minister-President of the German state of Saxony from 2008-2017, directly referred to Paul Tillich at the 2016 Christmas Vespers at the Frauenkirche of Dresden. The reference was to one of Paul Tillich's last significant speeches on boundaries that was delivered on the occasion of receiving the Peace Prize from the Marketing Association of the German Book Trade in 1962. Paraphrasing Paul Tillich's message, Stanislaw Tillich wrote: "Only when we cross personal boundaries, when we approach other people, when we open ourselves to other cultures, only then do we unfold our full human potential."[91] Thus, to build and maintain societies guided by justice and open to prophetic critique, people of every age must heed the call to become people of the boundary.

[91] Stanislaw Tillich. "Rede Von Ministerpräsident Zur 24. Weihnachtlichen Vesper an Der Frauenkirche Am 23. Dezember 2016," Der Freistaat Sachsen, December 23, 2016, www.ministerpraesident.sachsen.de/rede-von-ministerpraesident-stanislaw-tillich-zur-24-weihnachtlichen-vesper-an-der-frauenkirche-am-23-dezember-2016-4946.html.

Tillich's Kairos and Its Trajectory[1]

Ronald H. Stone

Paul Tillich's *Systematic Theology*, vol. 3, published in 1963, should be taken as his definitive word on the concept of *kairos*.[2] He asserts that since he used the term in his socialist writings the term has taken on a life of its own. It has been used and misused. It has been used demonically as well as creatively. Noting that it is more dependent on vision than science, in his own use he wants to subject possible uses of *kairos* to the "great" *kairos* of the revelation of eternity meeting time in its New Testament context. Other claims for the right time can be judged by the meaning of the coming of Christ. In the *Systematic Theology* it is the break- through of the Kingdom of God. Long before the system was organized the term had become decisive for Tillich's presentation of religious socialism.[3]

Paul Tillich's intimate discussion group in Berlin after World War I came to bear the name of the Kairos Circle. The term has continued through history to be affirmed by circles of Christian believers and their allies who have wanted to radically change societies. Within the Kairos circle it was a resolution to the debate between activists and determinists who insisted that history would carry its own solutions forward. Action was needed, but it had to be in tune with the properties of the contemporary history which were open to radical change. Theologically, Tillich meant the term to bear the weight of the intersection of eternity and historical action. For him, history was ripe for the

---

[1] This article was first published in *The Bulletin of the North American Paul Tillich Society* (Summer 2011) and republished with my permission in *Paul Tillich-interprete de l'histoire*, Marc Dumas, Martin Leiner, Jean Richard, eds. (Berlin: Verlag Dr. W. Hopf, 2013). It is revised and edited for this volume. It is also published simultaneously in Ronald H. Stone, *The Ethics of Paul Tillich* (Macon: Mercer University Press, 2021).

[2]Paul Tillich, *Systematic Theology,* vol. 3 (Chicago: The University of Chicago Press, 1963) 369.

[3] See Ronald H. Stone, *Paul Tillich's Radical Social Thought* (Atlanta: John Knox Press, 1980) 49-53 for a fuller discussion of socialism and *kairos*. Marc Boss, "Tillich, Heidegger et la question du kairos," *Etudes Theologiques et Religieuses, 20001/1* suggests Tillich uses the word first in 1920.

fulfillment of the ideas of the religious socialists. By 1932, he understood religion would have to radically change to be open to socialism, and socialism would have to radically change to be open to the ultimate claims of religion.

In Berlin in 1951, he would say that the religious socialist ideas of the interwar period were basically correct. He expressed the *kairos* as the Kingdom of God which was both transcendent and historical. In history, the Kingdom of God was only fragmentarily present. He thought the Kingdom of God concept pointed to fulfillment only in its vertical dimension. Still it encouraged historical action in its immanent dimensions. In his personal opinion, the *kairos* lay ahead only in the distant future. He was speaking in Germany under Allied and Russian occupation. But in decolonization and the civil rights movement elsewhere in world, moments of *kairos* were producing significant breakthroughs in mixtures of social revolution, religion, and liberalism. Maybe the 1922 statement was more utopian than he admitted. The 1951 statement was unnecessarily confined to the context of the cold war, but as he said in the *Systematic Theology*, the concept had its own trajectory. The term was partly, and only partly, confirmed in the period of its own emergence. His definition was: "It's original meaning—the right time, the time in which something can be done—must be contrasted with *chronos*, measured or clock time. The former is qualitative, the latter quantitative."[4] He argues that its use in the New Testament shows it to reveal the maturity of time in which the Kingdom of God may manifest itself. But he notes the power to resist the Kingdom can also be magnified at the same time. He correctly notes the Biblical attribution of the term to both Jesus and Paul and mistakenly to John the Baptist.[5]

He noted the term had other Greek uses than the New Testament use, and he did not enter into any particular exegesis of the term. Lon Weaver has investigated different connotations to the term in the New Testament and noted its rare uses in the Septuagint.[6] Weaver noted how Tillich was partially wrong in his expectations of *kairos,* and he believed Tillich attached positive moral meaning to the term which it did not deserve. Tillich was careful in the

[4] Tillich, *Systematic Theology,* vol. 3, 369.

[5] Tillich, 369.

[6] He categorizes eighty-eight uses of the term in the New Testament and finds fifty-five illustrations relevant to Tillich's use of the term. Matthew Lon Weaver, *Religious Internationalism: War and Peace in the Thought of Paul Tillich* (Macon: Mercer University Press, 2010), 289. I think he misjudges Tillich when he criticizes Tillich for attaching a moral approval on the occasion of its use (292). Tillich is aware of its moral ambiguity and says so clearly in *Systematic Theology*, vol. 3, 371.

Systematic Theology to note the concept was used destructively, and in sentences reminiscent of his quarrel with Emmanuel Hirsch he mentioned the demonic distortion of the idea by the Nazis. The apprehension of *kairos* is in vision and involves risk, as one or a group may be mistaken. An examination of the trajectory of the concept risks judgments on whether a group was correct in perceiving the *kairos* or not. For Tillich a correct perception required correlation to the reality of Christ in Jesus, including the willingness to sacrifice the self for the cause. Prideful, self-serving movements could not be expressing an authentic *kairos*. Finally he said the true *kairos* is unique and the *kairoi*, or lesser expressions of historical fulfillment, are rare. History usually proceeds with only glimpses of *kairos*.

Contemporary use of the term are different from Tillich's meaning. *Kairos* is used in reference to the consort of the singers from The Holy Cross Monastery, a young adult, retreat center, many different prison ministries, a publishing house, a Canadian relief agency of the churches, a technical agency, and studies in rhetoric which find the term being used by various Greek authorities including Protagoras and Hippocrates. An alternative connotation of the term is associated with Kairos, the youngest of Zeus' offspring and the god of opportunity. This apparently led to financial firms taking the title. The inquiry of these reflections focuses on eight theological groups encouraging social/political action more accurately reflect Tillich's meaning to fit our times. Several organizations engaged in various excellent social service ministries are therefore not reported on in this confining of the term to groups seeking fundamental social change.

Kairos and Peacemaking

The Presbyterian General Assembly may have been the earliest Church body to pick up the symbol and make it part of its official teaching. In 1980, in a period of national discouragement over the retreat from Vietnam, Russian assertiveness, the revolution in Iran, and economic stagnation, this church saw an opportunity for a new emphasis on peacemaking. it launched a program of peacemaking sponsored an all church special offering to support it, hired several staff to work on the issues to change the consciousness of the church, to equip its members to engage in peacemaking, and to witness for peace to the nation. Its founding policy, *Peacemaking: The Believer's Calling*, requested Presbyterians to claim their vocation as peacemakers, and declared peacemaking as a priority for the church.[7] Significant votes in local churches chose to

[7] The United Presbyterian Church in the U.S.A., *Peacemaking: The Believer's Calling* (Louisville: Office of the General Assembly, United Presbyterian Church in the U.S.A., 1980).

support the program and the offering, and about one-third of approximately eleven thousand congregations chose to support the new effort. The language of *kairos* was used three times in the document to assert that this was the time for the church to act decisively with new thinking, a budget, and bold actions.

The nation thought otherwise, and it entered into a period of arms buildup and assertive militancy under the Reagan Administration. The Presbyterian Head of Chaplains resigned his military office believing the Administration was preparing to fight a nuclear war rather than deter one. The church opposed the Administration's wars in Central America. The church considered declaring itself a resistance community against militarism, but in 1988 it instead opted to encourage extraordinary efforts with ordinary means to practice peacemaking. Gradually, the peacemaking program declined, and it shared its financial resources with other aspects of the church's mission. Though *kairos* became an important symbol in the church's theology, the church probably misjudged the times in 1980, and neither the times nor the church tasted the proclaimed *kairos*. The failure of the Peacemaking Program to keep alive the spirit of peacemaking as a sign of the *kairos* accompanied the general decline and splintering of the Presbyterian Church (USA).

South African *Kairos*

Kairos is more central in the *Kairos Document* of South Africa than it was in the Presbyterian document.[8] In the 1986 edition it is defined as: "*Kairos* is the Greek word used in the Bible to designate a special moment of time when God visits his people to offer them a unique opportunity for repentance and conversion for change and decisive action."[9] The nation was in crisis and many were being killed in the movement to end apartheid. The document was drafted in a theological center, referred to many groups for amendment, published, criticized and then, in 1986, republished in a second edition. It recognized the divisions in the country and within the church. It criticized the theologies of state and church then dominant in the country and called for a prophetic theology that was very specific as to the social diagnosis of apartheid and then offered methods for Christian action against apartheid. Arguing that God sides with the oppressed and wants to liberate the people the document called for participating in the struggle, transforming regular church activities into social change, the initiation of special campaigns against the apartheid

[8] "The *Kairos Document*: Challenge to the Church" in,*Kairos: Three Prophetic Challenges to the Church*, ed. Robert McAfee Brown (Grand Rapids, Wm. B. Eerdmans, 1990), 26.

[9] Brown, 95

system in churches, activities of civil disobedience against tyrannical government, and the provision of moral guidance, including counseling the liberators against those who would act "thoughtlessly and wildly."

The prophetic theology was articulated in terms of classical reformed arguments against tyranny. A government which acts against the common good which it is to serve is no government and needs to be replaced with a just government. The document recognized that the majority of Christians in the country were oppressed by the apartheid ideology and government and had already chosen to replace it. It set itself against the theology of both the apartheid ideology and the temporizing opposition to apartheid of the English churches. In this case the church participation in the struggle deepened and within five years change came to South Africa and the theological contribution in this predominantly Christian nation was recognized. The document also helped Christians abroad think though the situation in South Africa and assist in supporting the struggle through divestment activities, boycotts, and civil disobedience.

Kairos Central America

The Kairos Central American document of 1988 evolved through a process in which hundreds reviewed the document in the midst of civil wars. It was a time of the height of liberation theology and the document expressed many of its themes. The sensitive reader picks up more Marxist themes than in the South African one, and, to that degree, it is closer to the language of Tillich's circle than its predecessors. The American empire is the enemy which allies with the church and the establishment to keep the poor in their exploited position. Jesus, the prophets, and Mary, who identify with the suffering of the poor are called into service as enemies of the empire. God's Kingdom, a utopia, is to be built on earth by the exploited masses of Central America, and the process is seen in the success of the Sandinista movement in Nicaragua. The exploitation began with the Spanish conquest and resistance against it has occurred for five hundred years. But now in the present, opposition to the evil of the establishment is rising and can succeed in restoring peace and justice to Central America. Readers of the document are asked to take sides in the struggle with the poor to overthrow the rulers. The hour is seen as decisive by the writers. More than two hundred thousand had been killed in the previous ten years of struggle and the writers believed history was coming to a climax. "This historic hour in Central America is a *kairos*, the passing of God incarnate in Jesus through the burning waste of Central America, calling us to fight for the Kingdom to the cross to unwavering hope, to invincible unity, to resurrection triumph."[10]

The appeals of the theologians assisting in the revolutions were heard abroad during the Cold War. In a peacemaking presentation in the University of Berlin I met theologians who were studying Spanish to better grasp liberation theology and who on the German-Poland border presented me with Nicaraguan coffee in 1983. But when I asked Bernard Häring in the Vatican how many were studying liberation theology there, he replied two, me and one of my students. The Vatican, with its campaign to free Poland, was not about to support any leftist revolutionaries against the United States in Central America. The Regan Administration thought it was fighting the Cold War there and not that it was aligning against a genuine long-standing revolution of the poor. The document dismissed the over-reaction from the United States, but it was real and, to a degree, as determinative as the opposition of the Catholic Church or the Latin American establishment. The fall of the USSR had negative consequences for the liberation movements in Latin America. As the Vatican encouraged the hardening of the hierarchy against liberation theology, the local authorities often responded to discredit the movement. Even within Peru, Father Gustavo Gutiérrez's movements were limited. I agree the revolutionaries found a moment of personal and communal *kairos*, but the progressives were up against fierce opposition which they named as anti-kingdom forces.

For the most part the establishment won the battles leaving a progressive remnant to work in more modest ways for the future, but hopes for radical change were defeated. Before the fall of the Soviet Union, decision makers in the US were pushed to extreme measures. Congress tried to shut down support for overthrowing the Sandinista government. President Reagan and his cohorts attempted to supply the Contras through the Iran-Contra deal discrediting their foreign policy and proving several of them guilty of illegal acts. The denial of the humanity of the poor continued. Later, the original revolutionaries would lose an election. Their return to power was very disappointing to the disaffected in Nicaragua by 2019. However the governments surrounding it failed to alleviate poverty also. Refugees fleeing Central America precipitated a crisis for the Trump Administration and would remain an election issue for the US in 2020. My colleague, the late Gonzalo Castillo-Cardenas and I toured Latin American liberation projects in 1990 from Nicaragua to Chile. A few years ago, reflecting on the Central American experience, he

[10] Brown, 95

suggested: "Our hopes for change were too high. There has been little improvement in the condition of the poor."[11]

While Robert MacAfee Brown saw similarities to the Barmen Declaration in these theologies, I see more cultural analysis characteristic of Tillich. The analysis is more from the church than Tillich's use of *kairos*, and the church is called to action in a way that Tillich could only have hoped for. However, the wider and more dramatic social critique is much more characteristic of Tillich than of Barth. The Barmen Declaration, for all of its power, was mostly confined to arguments for the freedom of the church to follow only Christ.[12] Brown began his story of *kairos* with Tillich, and then in an ending challenging the North American churches included the Barmen Declaration in the book.

Kairos and Church Struggle: Two Documents

Two church documents written in the last score of years take the struggle straight to the church while not neglecting the social and historical context. *The Road to Damascus, Kairos and Conversion* was published deliberately on the tenth anniversary of the Sandinista victory in Nicaragua, July 19, 1989. It represented the reflection of hundreds of people in Africa, Central America, and Asia. It is framed in terms of liberation theology, and thousands indicated by signing that it reflected their will. It focused on the conflict between the left wing and the right within the Christian community. That conflict, resulting in oppression and murder, is the *kairos* of which the document speaks. The theme of Paul's conversion from a persecutor to an apostle on the Damascus road carries the proclamation on into the conflict within the communities of the church. The church's absorption into the Empire is regarded as apostasy leading to idolatry, and right wing Christianity is denounced as heretical. "Those Christians who side with the imperialists, the oppressors and the exploiters of people are siding with the idolaters who worship power, money, privilege and pleasure."[13]

Kairos Europa flowed from the Ecumenical Assembly of European churches in Basel in 1989. It is a movement attempting to gather the churches in a *Status Confession* is against neoliberal economics and its consequences. Ulrich Duchrow models his remarks after the Barmen Confession and treats

[11] Gonzalo Castillo-Cardenas, phone conversation with the author, April 4, 2011.

[12] See Matthew Lon Weaver, "Theology of Resistance in Bonhoeffer and Barth," in *Resistance and Theological Ethics*, eds. Robert L. Stivers and Ronald H. Stone (Lanham: Rowman and Littlefield, 2004), 209-312.

[13] *The Road to Damascus: Kairos and Conversion* in Brown, 137.

neoliberal economic practice in national economics, the World Bank, and the International Monetary Fund as similar to Nazism and apartheid of the twentieth century even though its consequences of death and exclusion are more indirect.

The churches are called to redirect their investments and property to serve ecological and social welfare causes and away from banks and other institutions supporting capitalist globalization. A socially responsible economy is sought, which practices ecological responsibility. The movement calls for combating monetary policy, and privatization. The World Alliance of Reformed Churches, in its organization, has developed many studies around confession and economics and finds the means of confession palatable to many of its leaders. Resistance to the trend is high among Reformed Christians in the US who place more trust in the market mechanisms of the economy and its host of international institutions. The *Kairos Europa* tends toward the sharpness of *The Road to Damascus Document*, but with more of an emphasis upon economic theory. Earlier attempts to move toward a *Status Confessionis* against neoliberal economic trends have been led by Czech theologians more sympathetic to socialism than the reformed populations of the United States. Tillich's Kairos Circle concentrated less upon international economics, but the economic directions of that circle are distinctly echoed in this form of *Kairos* document. This author admits to less direct involvement with these two documents than the previous three and turns now toward the *Kairos Palestine* document *"A Moment of Truth."* The publication of the document and conversations with two of the authors inspired this paper.

Palestinian *Kairos*

The 2009 call to faith and action by the writers of *Kairos Palestine* honors the model of the South African document and study of Palestine. My visitations and study of Palestine since 1980 contribute to my support of their reading of the acts on the ground. They are occupied, subjected to apartheid like oppression, humiliated, and impoverished. Like the North American Native Americans, their land has been taken, their homes and crops destroyed, and they have been confined to reserves where they are dependent upon welfare from others for their survival. The writers of the document do not see signs of immediate or anticipated relief. They fear they may be close to losing hope for their own state despite the world's clamor that their rights be recognized. For them, the *kairos* is a moment to speak, to tell the truth, and as they say: "*Kairos* is the moment when we see God's gifts in the midst of our suffering."[14]

[14] *Kairos Palestine: A Moment of Truth,* 2010, https://www.kairospalestine.ps/index.php/about-kairos/kairos-palestine-document, 4.

The document is less on economics than on political theology. It lacks the socialist tendencies of the previous three documents. Rather, it is asking for the use of capitalist or mixed-economy means of boycott, divestment, and sanctions to dislodge Israel from its occupation. To this extent it is quite different from the political-economic theology of the original Kairos Circle, yet it continues the focus on time.

As Tillich became a supporter of Zionism, he shifted from the Time interpretation of Israel to the Space and Time interpretation, so this document is pushing for a Space-Time perspective. Jerusalem, or Al-Quds, is central to the document, and it is claimed as the future capital of Palestine. I read a paper on the pro-Zionism of Paul Tillich and Reinhold Niebuhr to a Christian audience including Arab scholars at Tantur between Jerusalem and Bethlehem in 1980. As the 2009 Christian document asserts, their perspective was that the sins of Europe should not have been repeated at the expense of the Arabs, as I was informed at the time. The issue is the land, and as an old Sioux chief in Iowa said in the previous century before he was murdered: "The white man wants all of the land."[15] To the Palestinian farmers, shepherds, and olive grove workers that I have visited, that is the issue here. In the United Nations only the United States of America supports Israel's expansion of its control of land and water of Palestine.

Beyond the facts of Israel's occupation and expansion on the ground, the document moves to its theology. It presents a Palestinian interpretation of faith, hope, and love as its foundation. Biblical criticism is utilized and fundamentalism rejected.

While theological themes are discussed, the idea that political policy could be read directly out of scripture is rejected. The Bible must be interpreted in a living way and in accordance with the rejection of repression, slavery, and the domination of one people over another. The document seems to me to be less utopian than some of the predecessor documents, and does not allow enthusiasm for political change to slip into romanticism. It is most Tillichian in its use of love, power, and justice, though it does not use Tillich's ontology at this point. Its tone is that of the mature Christian realist Tillich who demanded political change, perhaps in a tone like his denunciation of Hitler in 1933 or Senator Goldwater in 1964. It is most unlike Tillich in its rejection of Zionism and avoidance of socialist terminology.

The occupation is denounced as sin. Resistance to oppression is to be carried out under the ethic of love. Such an ethic based in an understanding of Jesus must reject fighting evil with evil, but hue to nonviolent resistance. The history of resistance includes defending their own land through Israel's

[15] This quote is a family memory from a pioneer great-grandfather.

courts. Political petitions are reissued. They endure beatings and rebuild their homes after they are destroyed. I have eaten in homes destroyed by Israel four times and in tents removed regularly and reestablished. To hold on to their land they have built caves when home rebuilding is forbidden. Then the caves are trashed by the occupiers. Their resistance includes civil disobedience, and I have joined with other Christians, Jews, and Moslem demonstrators in actions. Resistance has included violence as a response to violence, but the writers and signers of the document reject the evil of violence and call for nonviolent suffering. Their major call for solidarity from the world churches is a request that they come on pilgrimage to Palestine. The writers pledge to show them the reality of Palestine while they pray with them. Sabeel has developed its own liturgies for such pilgrimages but adjusts them to the needs of visiting groups. They also ask churches to join with Palestinian Christians in supporting boycotts, divestment, and sanctions against the occupation (BDS).

While rejecting the concepts of religiously based states, they pledge to work with their enemies and allies to build states for all based in justice and civil liberties. Within Sabeel, which is involved in the document, the debate between their policy of two-states and a one state solution continues. While there are articulate Palestinian voices for the one state solution as Israel's aggression with US support seems invincible, this would be a reluctant recognition of reality. The preferred outcome would be two states with Jerusalem divided or internationalized, refugees repatriated or compensated, and the 1967 boundaries restored. The language of reconciliation and forgiveness in the document seems consistent to the character of the writers I know who are listed in the document.

The statement is prophetic in its denunciations and strategies have been endorsed by heads of many of the churches in Palestine and for study by North American churches. It is part of the struggle within North American Protestantism to begin the divestment from American corporations that support the occupation, which is against international law. Israeli and Jewish denunciations of the *Kairos Palestine* are frequent, and they are available on the internet under *Kairos Palestine.* The support of this work by major Protestant denominations remains ambiguous with debates still going on within their ruling bodies. Some divestment has occurred, and resolutions critical of US foreign policy have been taken. In general the more fundamentalist/evangelical churches continue to support Israel's occupation, and the more mainline churches are critical of US economic policy regarding Palestine.

Kairos: Union Theological Seminary

The most recent institutional expression of *kairos* theological action has been at Union Theological Seminary.[16] The Seminary which provided a home for the political-refugee Tillich in 1932 launched the Kairos Center in 2013 drawing upon Union's Poverty Initiative Mission Project for its own major program. The Kairos Center threw itself into the Poor People's Campaign which renewed the heritage of the campaign planned by Martin Luther King, Jr. before his assassination in 1968. This current campaign, led by Dr. William Barber and Dr. Liz Theoharis of the Center, with Union's support, is organizing across the country to renew moral leadership in politics with a focus on poverty. The initiative involves the publication of research on removing poverty and training leadership to help the poor lead the campaign across the country resulting in arrests in Washington D.C. and state capitals. As a visitor to the Poor People's tent city in Washington D.C. in 1968, its sagging tents dripping in the rain were signs of the country's indifference to the poor after the murder of Martin Luther King, Jr. This revival promises the best of Dr. King and James Cone's liberation theology at Union and in the streets. The reports on the Center emphasize the joining of theological scholarship to action, embodying the best of the young Tillich who spoke at an Independent Socialist rally in the days of revolution in Berlin in 1918 (courting the Church-hierarchy's critique). From those actions and his ecumenical colleagues, Jewish and Christian, came the concept of kairos with its call for action in political-economic terms.

Conclusion

Tillich was correct in *Systematic Theology*, vol. 3, that the *kairos* theology has its own life. Political, economic, theological, and ideological elements are all involved in social change, as are nonviolent and violent means of change. The Palestinian document inspired these reflections, but as it recognized, its time is not immediate, and it differs from the more socialist documents in being less involved in economic analysis. On the other hand the *kairos* as eternal meaning intersecting the present is certainly evident in the Arab speaking world. Palestine may experience change in ways not previously perceived by the authors of the Palestinian document. Religion and socialism are reconciled in many places, and Tillich's early theology is relevant, but it must be remembered it was pre-New Deal. New developments of it may become more rele-

[16] Guthrie Graves-Fitzsimmons, "Igniting a Moral Revival," *Union Collective* (New York: Union Theological Seminary, Fall 2018), 8-13.

vant under social-welfare, mixed-market economies. Maybe the Union Seminary movement is a test of that possibility. Likewise, *The Road to Damascus: Kairos and Conversion* and *Kairos Europa* are recognized more as critical utopias than as immediate historical projects. *Kairos Central America* was defeated by state and church, but the poverty and suffering of Latin America still cry out for revolutionary change and may provoke misguided interventions from the US. The dream of countering American militarism has been eclipsed by militarism, economic interests, and ignorance regarding international affairs. The perceptions of *kairos* as glimpses of the Kingdom of God were real, but they have been buried under church bureaucratization and national security panics. The South African *Kairos Document* has approached the closest to fulfillment. Tillich saw his vision in the twentieth century as relevant to small groups, but it has grown and calls forth church response. Sometimes these come close to realization. When our movements fail or nearly fail, those still nurturing aspects of Tillich's thought are saved from cynicism by the same Spirit that prompted them in the first place.

Afterword
Hope for Our Times: Why Paul Tillich Remains Relevant

Echol Nix

We hope for good news especially during crises and difficult times. Some may ask: "Is there a word from the Lord?" Perhaps a fitting way to conclude *Why Tillich? Why Now?* is with his sermons. Erdmann Sturm divides Tillich's sermons into three historical periods, namely: (1) pre-World War I sermons between 1909 and 1914, (2) war sermons between 1914 and 1918, and (3) sermons in America between 1933 and 1965.[1] Tillich was convinced that theology must be done in correlation with the relevance of the Christian message for our time. Tillich wrote three sermon books, and selected sermons in *The Shaking of the Foundations* (1948), *The New Being* (1955), and *The Eternal Now* (1963) will show this correlation. Students and friends strongly encouraged him to publish his sermons so that they could better understand his thoughts. So, in the preface to *The Shaking of the Foundations*, he writes: "They believe that through my sermons the practical, or more exactly, the existential implications of my theology are more clearly manifest."[2] He further writes: "I should like to think that the sermons included have helped to show that the strictly systematic character of a theology does not prevent it from being practical—that is to say applicable to the personal and social problems of our religious life."[3] Similarly, Tillich writes in *The Eternal Now*: "It is my hope to show that the Christian message, be it expressed in abstract theology or concrete preaching is relevant for our time if it uses the language of our time."[4]

A survey of Tillich sermons reveals a theology of preaching understood not as a discipline completely separate and distinct from his systematic theology but one that seeks a language which expresses in other terms the human

---

1. Erdmann Sturm, "'First, read my sermons!' Tillich as Preacher," in *The Cambridge Companion to Paul Tillich*, ed. Russell Re Manning (Cambridge: Cambridge University Press, 2009), 109.

2. Paul Tillich, *The Shaking of the Foundations* (New York: Charles Scribner's Sons, 1948), iii.

3. Tillich, iii.

4. Paul Tillich, *The Eternal Now* (New York: Charles Scribner's Sons, 1963), 9.

experience to which biblical and ecclesiastical terminology point. Approximately one-third of the texts come from the Hebrew bible, including his sermon, "The Escape from God," based on Psalm 139: "O Lord, thou hast searched me and known me.... Thou knowest my downsitting and mine uprising." Also, about one-third of the texts come from the Gospels, including the sermon, "The Power of Love," based on Saint John 13:34-35: "A new commandment I give you, that you love one another, even as I have loved you." An example of a sermon from Paul's Epistles is "Do Not Conform" based on Romans 12:2a: "Do not be conformed to this eon but be transformed by the renewal of your mind."

Tillich uses biblical quotations from both the King James Version and the Revised Standard Version of the Bible to perhaps engage his readers in various and familiar ways. In each of the aforementioned selections, there are dialectical dimensions: downward and upward; love and hate; and non-conformity and conformity. The dialectic underscores Tillich's idea that the purpose of preaching is only possible by participating in, but not totally identifying with, the life situation of those to whom one preaches. For example, in his *Theology of Culture*, he writes: "We do not need to go into the problem of participation in respect to other groups. We in America know about that! We know about the bitter feeling or resentment of some of the groups among us, not because of lack of goodwill but because of our inability to participate. Think of groups like the Jews, the colored peoples, even sometimes Roman Catholics. Participation means participation in their existence, out of which we are supposed to give an answer."[5] Could the answer include supporting movements and campaigns that foster equity, racial justice, and job opportunities for the "least of these?" Tillich considers his preaching to be "apologetic." For him, this means a demonstration of Christianity's relevance to the contemporary world by showing that the answers to the questions of existence are found in the Christian message. Tillich regards the "answering to the questions" (used interchangeably with "apologetic") to be an "underlying element of theology" and, as a function of the church, should state and interpret the truth of the Christian message for every new generation.

Therefore, an apology is not only a defense of Christian faith against opposing viewpoints but also the answering of questions arising in a situation through the power of the Word of God. In Tillich's theology, human existence is the situation from which questions arise that are answered by the truth of the Christian message in terms relevant to human existence. The method used to accomplish this is a "method of correlation," as discussed in this vol-

[5] Paul Tillich, *Theology of Culture* (Oxford: Oxford University Press, 1964), 2.

ume. This method is evident in Tillich's *Systematic Theology* and in his sermons. It is a product of his own experiences as an ordained Lutheran minister; army military chaplain during World War I; and professor at Johann Goethe Universität Frankfurt, Union Theological Seminary, Harvard University, and The University of Chicago. Each experience marks a "boundary," and the concept of "boundary" is featured prominently in any discussion of his writings, including his sermons. As such, the "boundary" becomes a place of great conflict and risk, but it is also the place that offers the greatest possibilities for the divine intervention that can transform human existence. Tillich discusses this "dialectic of existence:" "The man who stands on many boundaries experiences the unrest, insecurity, and inner limitations of existence in many forms. He knows the impossibility of attaining serenity, security, and perfection. This holds true in life as well as thought and may explain why the experiences and ideas which I have recounted are fragmentary and tentative."[6]

Tillich's "dialectic of existence" coupled with thoughts for living on the boundaries point toward the Eternal. His sermon, "The New Being" shows this dialectic, and it connects his theology and apologetic preaching. Based on Galatians 5:16, the sermon includes themes in Tillich's *Systematic Theology* (specifically, in volume two), and it offers his Christological understanding: "Christianity is the message of the New Creation, the New Being, the new reality which has appeared with the appearance of Jesus who for this reason is called "the Christ." This understanding is reiterated throughout the sermon, specifically that we live in "the old state of things," but the "demand made upon us by Christianity is that we also participate in the New Creation."[7]

"The New Being" shows Tillich's staunch refusal to accept secularism's claim that reality is exclusively confined to the material universe, rendering religion to the realm of fantasy and magical thinking. Here, Tillich radically recasts the traditional terms and symbols of Christology in order to affirm the humanity of Jesus of Nazareth. According to him, if Jesus is understood as the Christ and if the Christ is to have any salvific significance for modern people, the entire terminology surrounding Jesus must be reframed so that the symbols of Christianity may be allowed to speak again. He rejects both the notion of Jesus as a supernatural person and the idea of Christ as a mere exemplar of ethical behavior. His vision of Jesus as the Christ or as the bearer of the New Being is not confined to the historical event of Jesus, but it is rooted in the

[6] Paul Tillich, "Retrospect: Boundary and Limitation," in *The Individual and His Religion: A Psychological Interpretation*, Gordon Allport (New York: Macmillan, 1950), 97-98.

[7] Paul Tillich, "The New Being," in *The New Being* (New York: Charles Scribner's Sons, 1955), 15.

nature of what it means to be human. The sermons in *The New Being* are not full-length sermons; in fact, some of them are as short as four or five pages. However, they are filled with the conviction that the event upon which Christianity is based has two sides, namely, the historic fact of the man—Jesus of Nazareth—and the reception of that fact by those who acknowledge him as the Christ.

As in *The New Being*, *The Shaking of the Foundations* and *The Eternal Now* employ ontological terms rather than the traditional terminology of the Bible or the early church. In *The Shaking of the Foundations*, Tillich sees the question of being as the fundamental question and in accordance with his method of correlation. The opening sentence in *The Shaking of the Foundations* says: "It is hard to speak after the prophets have spoken as they have in these pronouncements."[8] Consistent with his theological method, Tillich moves to the existential situation, saying that while in times past the prophetic words of the earth's destruction could be ignored, the world events of the recent past make that impossible. "The visions of the prophets have become an actual, physical possibility, and might become an historical reality."[9] Referring to the words of Second Peter concerning the vanishing of the heavens, the melting of the elements, and the burning up of the earth, Tillich makes clear reference to the threat of nuclear war. He writes: "This is no longer a vision; it has become physics."[10] Utilizing the image of an atom's power, he speaks of the divine action of creation in which the "fiery chaos of the beginning was transformed into the fertile soil of the earth."[11] While humanity is fashioned with the ability to discover the "key which can unlock the forces of the ground, those forces were bound when the foundations of the earth were laid."[12] Hence, humanity began to use this key and subjected it to human life, thought, and will. Here, Tillich thinks that modern scientists have become the prophets of our time, telling the present generation that the very existence of the earth is threatened unless humanity changes its ways. He also focuses his sermon, "Man and Earth," in *The Eternal Now* on the universal threat to human existence posed by the nuclear age. Using Psalm 8, he says that the representatives of the scientific community have "demanded a new line of research, a "science of survival."[13] Drawing upon the image of the "Great Flood," he continues, "The only difference between our situation and that of the Flood

[8] Tillich, *The Shaking of the Foundations*, 2.

[9] Tillich, 3.

[10] Tillich, 3.

[11] Tillich, 3.

[12] Tillich, 4.

[13] Tillich, *The Eternal Now*, 66.

is that in these stories, the God or gods bring about the destruction of life on earth because men have aroused divine anger. Today, the destruction and survival of life have been given in the hands of man."[14]

In "The Shaking of the Foundations," Tillich identifies the misuse of science as idolatrous, seducing people to "believe in our earth as the place for the establishment of the Kingdom of God, to believe in ourselves as those through whom this was achieved."[15] Tillich thinks it is idolatrous for humanity to believe that it can use this scientific knowledge creatively. "The human being is not God and whenever the human being has claimed to be God, and to rely on human systems of culture, technology, politics, or religion, the result has been disintegration."[16] For Tillich, the source of prophetic power is identified as residing in God, "who brings doom for the sake of eternal judgment and salvation."[17] God is the foundation of all foundations, the foundation that is "immovable, unchanging, unshakable, and eternal."[18] As such, God as the unshakable foundation becomes evident in the crumbling of earthly foundations, and in the face of this shaking of the foundations, "only two alternatives remain, namely, despair, which is the certainty of eternal destruction, or faith, which is the certainty of eternal salvation."[19] Therefore, the invitation is extended to choose faith, which enables one to see the manifestation of the Eternal in the "doom of the temporal" and thus to experience salvation. Similarly, in "Man and Earth," Tillich writes: "The questions of man and earth, this question that has plunged our time into such anxiety and conflict of feeling and thought cannot be answered without an awareness of the eternal presence."[20] The quote from the Psalmist: "Whither shall I go from thy Spirit? Or whither shall I flee from thy presence?" (Psalm 139), contributes to his conception of providence that is set within the context of history. For him, history possesses both an objective and subjective dimension. While the former represents factual occurrence, the latter identifies the necessary human element of reception and interpretation of these occurrences. Consequently, the human forms history as well as being formed by it. Thus, history is subject to the categories of existence, although time is its decisive category.

The movement of history and its ambiguities can be conceived of as a series of pulses involving conflict and crisis between growth and decay. Within

[14] Tillich, 66-67.
[15] Tillich, *The Shaking of the Foundations*, 5.
[16] Tillich, 5.
[17] Tillich, 5.
[18] Tillich, 5.
[19] Tillich, 10.
[20] Tillich, 77.

these periods, there are centers or moments that Tillich describes by the notion of *kairos*. These moments, even though they occur in history, and therefore under the fragmentary and ambiguous conditions of existence, represent the aim of history, which is the overcoming of the disruption between essence and existence as well as the resulting conflict, destruction, and meaninglessness which seem to characterize historical existence. However, Tillich claims that the central *kairos* is the appearance of the New Being in Jesus as the Christ expressed by the eschatological symbol of the Kingdom of God. The Kingdom of God is that state in which the disruption between essence and existence, between potential and the actual, is overcome completely and universally. While the Kingdom of God occurs in history, it also points beyond history to the transcendent reality of eternal life. The Kingdom of God cannot be fully grasped by the power of *kairos*, which gives meaning and direction to human existence in anticipation of the final goal of history as the Kingdom of God. This understanding of history can give humans faith and courage, specifically, the ability to be and to act "in spite of" the conflicts and ambiguities of existence.

In these sermons, Tillich suggests the "answer" to the ontological question of the human predicament or the manifestation of what concerns humanity "ultimately." The reception of the revelation is what he calls people to in these sermons so that "through the crumbling of the world, the rock of eternity and salvation which has no end, may be seen by people in faith."[21] Each of the three volumes seeks to communicate the Christian message so that contemporary men and women can discover and rediscover the relevance and ultimate significance of Jesus as the Christ. Jesus as the Christ or as the bearer of the New Being is the final revelation that judges every other revelation. In him, the reconciliation of essence and existence has been realized, constituting a new creation and a new life for all people who participate in him. Such participation is possible because if Jesus as the Christ is able to maintain essential unity with God, every human being is asked to take on the "form" of the Christ participating fully in the New Being present in an individual. Salvation, then, is transformation by the New Being and constitutes the purpose of preaching, which gives humanity faith, courage, and hope.

---

[21] Tillich, 11.

Contributors

RACHEL SOPHIA BAARD
Union Presbyterian Seminary
Rachel Sophia Baard is Assistant Professor of Theology and Ethics at Union Presbyterian Seminary in Richmond, Virginia and a Research Associate at the University of Stellenbosch in South Africa. Her first book, *Sexism and Sin-Talk: Feminist Conversations on the Human Condition*, was published by Westminster John Knox Press in 2019, and she is currently editing a volume titled *The Political Theology of Paul Tillich* for Lexington Press.

THOMAS G. BANDY
Consultant to Churches and Faith-Based NonProfits
Rev. Dr. Thomas Bandy is an international consultant for local and regional church bodies of all traditions, and for faith-based nonprofit agencies. He has written numerous books professionally and academically in theology of culture, contemporary spiritualities, church development, leadership, and organizational change. Today his focus is the impact of demographic and lifestyle research on ministry and social service. His most recent book is *Sideline Church: Bridging the Chasms between Churches and Culture* (Abingdon Press).

DANIEL BOSCALJON
Independent Scholar
Daniel Boscaljon has recently co-edited *Paul Ricoeur and the Hope of Higher Education* (2020) and *Teaching Religion and Literature* (2018) and completed a series on idolatry and film for *Religious Studies Review.* His website, www.danielboscaljon.com, also includes information on his work in agnosticism and his *Making Space for Yourself* program.

SHARON P. BURCH
University of Redlands Graduate School of Theology,
San Francisco Theological Seminary
The Rev. Sharon P. Burch, PhD is a retired professor, pastor, and pastoral counselor. She is an adjunct in the D. Min. program at San Francisco Theological Seminary in San Anselmo, CA, part of the University of Redlands Graduate School of Theology.

BENJAMIN J. CHICKA
Curry College
Benjamin J. Chicka is Lecturer of Philosophy and Religion at Curry College. He has expertise in philosophical theology (particularly process and ground-of-being approaches), religion and science, and American pragmatism. His current research is on theological ethics and video games, which has led to appearances on numerous podcasts as well as hosting the *TheoNerd Podcast*. His forthcoming book on the subject, *Playing God*, will be published by Baylor University Press.

PAMELA COOPER-WHITE
Union Theological Seminary
The Rev. Pamela Cooper-White, PhD, is Dean and Vice President for Academic Affairs, and Christiane Brooks Johnson Professor of Psychology and Religion, at Union Theological Seminary, New York. She has published nine books, including *Old and Dirty Gods: Religion, Antisemitism, and the Origins of Psychoanalysis* (Routledge, 2017).

CHRISTIAN DANZ
University of Vienna
Christian Danz is professor for systematic theology at the University of Vienna and President of the German Paul Tillich Society. His books include: *Religion als Freiheitsbewußtsein. Eine Studie zur Theologie als Theorie der Konstitutionsbedingungen individueller Subjektivität bei Paul Tillich* (Berlin/New York 2000); *Die Deutung der Religion in der Kultur. Aufgaben und Probleme der Theologie im Zeitalter des religiösen Pluralismus* (Neukirchen-Vluyn 2008); *Gottes Geist. Eine Pneumatologie* (Tübingen 2019); *Jesus von Nazareth zwischen Judentum und Christentum. Eine christologische und religionstheologische Skizze* (Tübingen 2020).

KIRK R. MACGREGOR
McPherson College
Kirk R. MacGregor (PhD, University of Iowa) is Associate Professor of Philosophy and Religion and Department Chair at McPherson College. He is the author of six books, including *Contemporary Theology: An Introduction*, and over thirty articles in forums such as the *Journal of the American Academy of Religion*.

BRADFORD MCCALL
PhD student in Process Philosophy at Claremont School of Theology
His dissertation is entitled "Contingency & Divine Activity: Toward a Contemporary Conception of Divine Involvement in an Evolutionary World." He has several books under contract for future publication, including *The God of Chance & Purpose: Divine Involvement in an Evolutionary World* and *Macroevolution, Contingency, & Uncontrolling, Amorepotent Love: How God Works in the (Late-)Modern World.*

ECHOL NIX
Claflin University
Echol Nix is Associate Professor of Philosophy and Religion and serves as Activity Director of the Visionary Leadership Institute at Claflin University. He is the author or editor of seven books, including *Ernest Troeltsch and Comparative Theology* (2010) and *Milestone Documents in African American History*, 2nd Edition (2017).

FREDERICK J. PARRELLA
Santa Clara University, Professor Emeritus
Frederick J. Parrella is Professor of Theology Emeritus in Religious Studies at Santa Clara University where he taught for forty-three years. He has edited and contributed to four books, three on Paul Tillich and one in Catholic Theology. His articles have appeared in the *Cambridge Companion to Tillich, Lumen Vitae*, *Communio*, *Jahrbuch für Tillich Studien*, *Spirituality Today*, *Proceedings of the Catholic Theological Society of America*, and *Dialog*. He served as President of the North American Paul Tillich Society and, from 1997 to 2020, as its Secretary Treasurer and editor of its *Bulletin*, as well as recipient of numerous awards for excellence in teaching.

ADAM PRYOR
Bethany College
Adam Pryor is Vice President for Academic and Student Affairs and Associate Professor of Religion at Bethany College in Lindsborg, KS. In addition to his scholarship on Tillich his work addresses topics in theology and science as with his most recent volume *Living with Tiny Aliens: The Image of God for the Anthropocene*.

WILLIAM G. RESSL
Independent Scholar/Co-Pastor in the United Church of Christ
Rev. William G. Ressl (PhD, Chicago Theological Seminary) has taught graduate courses in theology and social work with a primary focus on an integrative paradigm grounded in Tillich's theology and clinical social work. He is a co-founder of the Center to Awaken Kindness (www.CenterToAwaken-Kindness.com). He serves as a co-pastor in the United Church of Christ with his wife the Rev. Dr. Penny Taylor. His most recent publication is "A World in Need: Brokenness and Reconciliation Explored through Paul Tillich's Doing of Social Work" in *Tillich Jahrbuch/Yearbook* (Walter de Gruyter Press).

JARI RISTINIEMI
The University of Gävle
Jari Ristiniemi is a professor in Religious Studies at the University of Gävle, Sweden. His areas of interest include Philosophy of Religion and Didactics of Religion, with special reference to Paul Tillich. He is an author of several books, with one of his latest publications is in Ristiniemi, Skeie, and Sporre, *Challenging Life: Existential Questions as a Resource for Education* (Waxmann, 2018).

ZACHARY ROYAL
Graduate Student at Union Theological Seminary
Zachary W. Royal is a graduate student at Union Theological Seminary, New York. He is a systematic, philosophical, historical, and constructive theologian who interweaves classical and contemporary strands of theology, black theology, and liberation theology at the intersection of modernity, religion, and culture. He is the ardent pupil of Dr. Stephen G. Ray, President of Chicago Theological Seminary, and Dr. Dwight N. Hopkins, Alexander Campbell Professor of Systematic Theology at the University of Chicago.

BIN SONG
Washington College
Bin Song is an assistant professor of philosophy and religion. His teaching and research focus is Asian and Comparative philosophy, religion and theology, and particularly Confucianism (Ruism). His most recent publications include: "Robert C. Neville: A Systematic, Nonconformist, Comparative Philosopher of Religion," *American Journal of Theology and Philosophy* 40, no. 3 (September 2020); and "Comparative Metaphysics and Theology as a Scientific Endeavor: A Ruist (Confucian) Perspective," Socio-Historical Examination of Religion and Ministry 1, no. 2 (Fall 2019). See more in his personal website: www.binsong.live.

DEVAN STAHL
Baylor University
Devan Stahl is an Assistant Professor of Religion at Baylor University. She specializes in bioethics and disability ethics and works as a clinical ethicist consultant. Her last book, *Imaging and Imagining Illness: Becoming Whole in a Broken Body* is an edited volume examining the power of medical images on the experience of chronic illness and disability.

MARY ANN STENGER
University of Louisville, Professor Emerita
Mary Ann Stenger is currently working on a book exploring Tillich's understanding of justice in relation to contemporary cultural issues. She is the author of numerous articles and book chapters on Tillich's thought and served as the English-language editor for the *Tillich Jahrbuch* and Tillich Research Series. She is the co-author (with Ronald H. Stone) of *Dialogues of Paul Tillich.*

RONALD H. STONE
Pittsburgh Theological Seminary
Ron Stone is writing a book on political ethics for the Post-Trump era, and a new book, *The Ethics of Paul Tillich*, for Mercer University Press, to be published in Fall 2021. This last year he was appointed a Distinguished alum of Union Theological seminary in a ceremony in New York City.

MATTHEW LON WEAVER
Marshall School
Matthew Lon Weaver teaches Ethics and Religion at Marshall School, Duluth, MN. He translated Tillich's wartime radio broadcasts into Nazi Germany (*Against the Third Reich*, Westminster John Knox Press, 1998) and is the author of *Religious Internationalism: The Ethics of War and Peace in the Thought of Paul Tillich* (Mercer, 2010).

JEREMY D. YUNT
Independent Scholar and Author
Jeremy D. Yunt is an independent scholar with an interdisciplinary Master's degree in Ethics (Philosophy) and Depth Psychology from the GTU, Berkeley, CA. Among his published books are two on Paul Tillich: *Love, Gravity, and God: Paul Tillich and the Existential Depths of Reason and Religion* (2015) and *Faithful to Nature: Paul Tillich and the Spiritual Roots of Environmental Ethics* (2017). He has also published peer reviewed articles in publications such as *Philosophy Now*, the *Journal of Humanistic Psychology*, and the *Journal of Animal Ethics.*